ADMINISTRATIVE
THINKERS

ADMINISTRATIVE
THINKERS

edited by

D. Ravindra Prasad

V.S. Prasad

P. Satyanarayana

Y. Pardhasaradhi

STERLING PUBLISHERS (P) LTD.
Regd. Office: A1/256 Safdarjung Enclave,
New Delhi-110029. CIN: U22110DL1964PTC211907
Tel: 26387070, 26386209; Fax: 91-11-26383788
E-mail: mail@sterlingpublishers.com
www.sterlingpublishers.com

Administrative Thinkers
©2017, *D. Ravindra Prasad, V.S. Prasad,*
     P. Satyanarayana, Y. Pardhasaradhi
ISBN 978 81 207 5414 0
First Edition 1991
Sixteen Reprints
Second Revised and Enlarged Edition June 2010
Reprint 2011, 2012, 2013, 2014, 2015, 2016, 2017

PRINTED IN INDIA

Printed and Published by Sterling Publishers Pvt. Ltd.,
Plot No. 13, Ecotech-III, Greater Noida - 201306, Uttar Pradesh, India

Dedicated to

Our Teacher, Guide and Philosopher

Prof. G. Ram Reddy (1929-1995)
Social Scientist and Institution Builder

PREFACE

With the expansion of the discipline of Public Administration, the need for literature on administrative theory is being increasingly felt. There is not enough literature providing concisely various facets of administrative theory; particularly the contributions of thinkers to the development of the discipline. This book is an effort in the direction of filling this gap; albeit in part. The objective is to acquaint the scholars, teachers, students and practitioners of administration with the contributions of outstanding administrative theorists. The book provides an account of the ideas and contributions of twenty one thinkers to the discipline. It does not provide all the ideas of the thinker, but covers an outline of their life, writings, principal contributions to the administrative theory and a critical evaluation.

This volume is a cooperative academic effort. It is weaved together with the contributions of twenty-one teachers who have had vast experience in the study and teaching of public administration, political science, sociology and management. The result is a single source of reference on the theory of Public Administration; particularly the contribution of select thinkers. We thank the contributors profusely.

We express our profound sense of gratitude to Prof. G. Ram Reddy, an eminent social scientist, analyst of administrative process, above all a humanist and our teacher, for the enduring inspiration, encouragement and valuable support he gave to us in our academic endeavours. We respectfully dedicate this volume to his memory.

In this revised edition one chapter and two thinkers have been added. Otherwise the text remains as before except corrections where required and possible. In our modest effort we had the encouragement, help and assistance from a number of our colleagues, scholars and friends. In this revision we got help, support and assistance from many of our friends and colleagues. Ms. Eswari Alla, smilingly spared weekends and public holidays and helped us in the revision exercise, Mr. Murali Mohan, Ms. Vandana, Mr. Krishna, Mr. S. Chary, Ms. Vijayalakshmi, Mr. Safdar Ahmed and many others extended library, bibliographical and technical assistance. Prof. V.S. Chary helped us in more than one way and extended support. We thank them all.

We thank Mr. S.K. Ghai of Sterling Publishers who took a keen interest in the revision and extended technical support.

We owe a heavy debt of gratitude to our families for their encouragement, support and forbearance and meeting inchoate demands on work of this nature.

– Editors

CONTENTS

INTRODUCTION

Administration, though as old as society, began to attract attention as an activity and as an intellectual discipline only since the later part of the 19th century. The complex nature of the modern state resulted in an enormous expansion of the functions of government. Such expansion generated a compulsive need for an in-depth study and comprehensive research into various aspects of the administrative phenomenon. The seminal contributions of academics and practitioners to the development of various facets of administration and dissemination of knowledge pertaining to it, caused the germination of various theories and some particularly significant ones are permanently etched in the saga of administrative development.

Administrative theory is based on conceptualisation of experience of administrators or observation of the operational situations in administration; it may be derived or reinforced from the comparative studies or they may be ideas and opinions of intellectuals. Because of the integrated nature of the social sciences, developments in other disciplines help in the conceptualisation in administration as well. Thus, theoretical or practical development in other social sciences influence theoretical base of Public Administration and vice versa.[1]

The twenty one thinkers included in this volume have contributed substantially to the evolution of public administration as a discipline. There are many more whose contributions are substantial for expanding the frontiers of knowledge of public administration and stimulated research in the field. All of them could not be included in this short volume; space being one of the limitations.

Ancient Indian Wisdom on Statecraft

One of the outstanding contributions of ancient Indian wisdom to statecraft is Kautilya's *Arthashastra*. It ranks in importance with *Manusmriti* and *Kamashastra* and forms a triad in dealing with the three imperatives of the social philosophy of that time - *Dharma, Kama, and Artha*. Though it is titled as *Arthashastra* – science of economics – it actually deals with various aspects of political administration and management of state. It also deals with statecraft focusing on king, law and justice, foreign policy, war, espionage, financial and personnel administration, etc. The treatise is compared to Machiavelli's *The Prince* both in importance and contribution to the art and science of state administration and governance..

The *Arthashastra* is a textbook of practical politics and statecraft. It deals mainly with the science of polity, which according to Kautilya, is a combination of science of wealth, and science of government - *Vittashastra* (economics) and *Dandanithi* (statecraft). To Kautilya, finances provide the sinews of government and financial considerations are paramount in the government's activities. Thus, his treatise adopts the political economy approach to the understanding of the problems of governance. H.V.R. Iyengar described the *Arthashastra* "as an exceptionally able dissertation both on the aims of the state as well as on the practical means by which aims can be achieved". The *Arthashastra* is both an analytical and a perspective document revealing amazing perception and mastery of detail.

Kautilya's *Arthashastra* mainly discusses three aspects of the science of public administration, viz., the principles of public administration, machinery of government and the management of personnel. The principles of administration are not explicitly dealt with. They are detailed in the functions of the monarch, ministers, etc. The machinery of government, as described in the *Arthashastra*, mainly relate to the monarch, his relations with ministers, etc. The problems of the higher level personnel received greater attention than the lower level functionaries.

The Beginnings of the Study

Woodrow Wilson (1856-1924), who became the President of USA in his later years, was among the earliest to outline the concept of public administration as a separate discipline of study. Woodrow Wilson integrated history, philosophy and the concept of the good society in a way to make order for students of public administration. Wilson's seminal essay "The Study of Administration" published in the *Political Science Quarterly* in 1887, laid foundation for a systematic study of public administration. To many students, Wilson as an administrative theorist may sound illogical as he did not propound any concept or theory but it was he who delineated public administration as a distinct subject of study and emphasised the need for continued study and research. "The Study of Administration" stimulated interest among later scholars into this aspect of the functioning of the government. Wilson described administration as an art but emphasised that it be studied scientifically. He stressed the need to augment legal institutional analysis with the panoply of science and is required to manage complex organisations of men and machines.[2] The dichotomy between politics and administration was first mooted by Woodrow Wilson, and the cleavage acquired the name after him— 'the Wilsonian dichotomy'. His pioneering article stimulated quite a lot of interest in the study of administration not only from the standpoint of its relation with politics but also to examine administration and the way it works. Wilson articulated the need for developing methods of enquiry and emphasised the significance of comparative method in the study of public administration. The views expressed in "The Study of Administration" led to many controversies and varied interpretations. Wilson's theories may have been naive, as Peter Self observed, but they provided an 'ideological basis for reforms in administration in 19th century America'.[3]

Classical Perspectives

The classical organisational and administrative formulations are also variously termed as structural, mechanistic, formal, engineering, and empirical approaches. They are classical in the sense that they are in use for 'quite some time'.[4] They are labelled so very differently because the classicists attempted to propound simple principles of general application possessing characteristics of formality, symmetry and rigidity. The theories emphasise the importance of structure and subsume the amenability of humans to work to meet the administrative and organisational demands. The underlying assumption is that the patterns of behaviour and relationships can be deliberately planned for the members of an organisation. The concepts and principles formulated by Henri Fayol, Frederick Taylor, Max Weber and Gulick and Urwick come under this classical perspective.

Henri Fayol (1841-1925) is one of the earliest administrative theorists to propound universal principles of administration, based on his long personal experience. He perceived administration from manager's viewpoint and confined his analysis mostly to top managerial functions. He defined administration in terms of five elements, viz., planning, organising, command, coordination and control. These five elements provide a system of concepts, through which, managers may seek to clarify their perception of activities. He outlined fourteen additional principles of administration, to be regarded as fundamental tenets, applicable to both industrial and public administrations equally. Though Fayol was criticised for evolving principles solely based on his personal experience, he contributed significantly to the emergence of a general theory of administration. In the history of administrative theory Henri Fayol has an enduring place, as one of the earliest known theoretical analysts of managerial activity.

F.W.Taylor (1865-1915), a pioneer in management science, conducted studies during the early part of the twentieth century on humans, particularly at operating levels in industrial settings. The impact of his studies was so great that management, which was hitherto considered an art, was given the status of science. An engineer by profession and training, Taylor, with his varied work experience ranging from a labourer to that of a chief engineer, conducted many experiments in different industrial undertakings and introduced 'scientism' into management. To Taylor the primary object of management is to secure maximum prosperity to the employer and employee. He suggested four principles of scientific management viz., development of a true science of work; scientific selection and progressive development of the workman; bringing together of the science of work and the scientifically selected and trained men; and constant and intimate cooperation between management and worker. Application of these principles and the degree of their success, according to Taylor, depends on 'mental revolution'. He advocated an understanding and sharing of functions and responsibilities between the workers and management for achieving increase in production which logically results in more profits and more wages.

Through a series of experiments spread over a period of time, Taylor developed a number of tools and techniques to aid both the worker and manager. He insisted on high degree of specialisation to achieve better performance and propounded a theory of 'functional foremanship' to achieve this. A number of techniques like work study, work measurement, exception principle, etc., which are now being adopted in public and industrial organisations, were all initially developed by him. Urwick and Brech aptly observed that 'as our industrial civilisation develops, broadens and deepens, there will be an increasing recognition both of his originality and the fundamental value of the ideas which he initiated'.[5]

One of the inevitable consequences of the expansion in the functions of the state and the emergence of large organisations is *bureaucracy* - a term which raises ambivalent emotions. Though bureaucracy existed - both in private and public organisations - ever since the emergence of civilised life, it eludes a universally acceptable meaning and definition. Many analysed bureaucracy even before the 19th century, but systematic analysis and conceptualisation took place only at the hands of Max Weber. A German historian and sociologist, Max Weber (1864-1920) was essentially concerned with the analysis of authority in the 19th century European society. He categorised authority into three types: traditional, charismatic and legal-rational. He identified bureaucracy with the exercise of legal-rational authority and enunciated a few immutable characteristics of bureaucracy viz., hierarchy, merit based selection, specialisation, impersonality, etc. He assumed that any organisation possessing these characteristics can perform its functions most rationally and this results in maximum efficiency and effectiveness. Weber characterised his bureaucratic model as an ideal type. To the students of public administration Weberian model serves as the starting point for an analysis of the functioning of the government. Most present day research on bureaucracy endeavours to locate the degree of conformity with the Weberian model and where there are variations, examine the reasons and nature of such variations, and identify operational limitations and shortcomings.

Even to the critics, Weberian bureaucracy is the starting point for study and analysis. It is argued that the characteristics, which Weber advanced, lead to delays, dysfunctionality, etc. Few even went to the extent of calling it bureau-pathology. Few others argued that Weber's bureaucracy, which was essentially based on the European experience - particularly French and German, cannot be applied to the developing countries. Notwithstanding these criticisms, Weber's bureaucracy provides a very essential and basic framework for understanding the present day administrative organisations.

The classical theory, chronologically is the earliest and the credit for its systematisation goes to Luther Gulick (1892-1993) and Lyndall Urwick (1891-1983). Gulick as an administrator and academic and Urwick as management historian and consultant wrote extensively on administrative management. Keeping efficiency and economy as two basic values which the administration should attain, they tried to develop universal principles to achieve organisational goals. Gulick's acronym POSDCORB, a ' verbal artifact', is a word made up of the initial letters of the most distinct functions of administration. The four ' P' bases of departmental organisation, the concept of line and staff, the principles of organisation including span of control, unity of command, work division, coordination, etc., have all been emphasised by them based on their experience in the military, industrial and public organisations. These principles deal with, what Gross calls, ' the architectonics' of formal organisation.[6] Though their principles have many deficiencies, as is evident from the criticism by latter writers like Simon, POSDCORB still serves as a convenient starting point for innumerable writers interested in dealing with different aspects of administration and soon the term came into wide use to delineate the different administrative processes. Later writers on public administration took this as a cue and with additions, subtractions and amendments, adopted it according to their needs. Thus the 'universal principles' of Gulick and Urwick, despite varied criticisms, continue to be important and valid in administrative science.

The concepts, principles and theories propounded by the classical school were criticised for the neglect of human element and for viewing organisation "in a cold-blooded, detached spirit like the preparation of an engineering design"[7] ignoring mental attitudes which play an important role in administration. Another major attack on these formulations is their emphasis on universality. The criticisms, limitations, or development of new ideas, however, do not relegate the principles of these classicists to obsolescence. For, in the first place, these thinkers identified administration as a distinct area to be studied independently. Secondly, a clearer thinking was introduced concerning various aspects of organisation functioning like authority, delegation, etc.[8] Thirdly, these principles are not only widely used but are being ' staunchly supported'. As Koontz has observed that critics call these principles platitudes forgetting that a platitude is still a truism and truth does not become worthless because it is familiar.[9]

Beyond Classical Formulations

The inadequacy of classical administrative theoretical formulations to explain the totality of administrative phenomena led to more extensive researches into the working of human organisations. The principles and concepts developed by the classicists could not explain the behaviour of individual employees. The later researches, variously called human relations, behavioural, social, psychological, systems, etc., went beyond classical formulations and concentrated on human motivation and behaviour. These theories focus on understanding human behaviour at the work including motivations, conflicts, group dynamics, etc., which are critical for organisational and administrative analysis. They viewed employees as individuals, resources and assets and not as machines as classicists seem to have believed. While classical theorists emphasised the structural aspects of organisations, the behaviouralists and human relations theorists focused on the human factors. They also aimed, like classicists, at getting best of the employees and study social conditions of their work, work environment and individual and group relations. Mary Parker Follett, Elton Mayo, Chester Barnard, Herbert Simon, Abraham Maslow, Douglas McGregor, Chris Argyris, Herzberg, Rensis Likert, etc., come in this category of post classical theorists.

Mary Parker Follett (1868-1933), a political scientist turned management philosopher, made a study of the psychological aspects of administration and management. Her main field of interest was psychological foundations of human activity, and emotional factors that underlie the working of human beings. To her a human group is something more than the sum total of the individuals comprising it.[10]

To Follett, conflicts are inevitable in any organisation, as views, attitudes and emotions of individuals vary and assert that conflicts should be viewed constructively and not to be abhorred. To make constructive use of conflicts, she subscribes to integration, as opposed to domination and compromise, to be the best way. She felt that giving of orders to someone may affect the human dignity and may find resistance, and therefore, rejects the process of orders from individual to individual. She substitutes the process with what she calls the ' law of the situation', wherein orders flow from situation. She highlights the importance of depersonalising orders, to make a group cohesive, heralding 'with' concept, in place of 'under' concept. She applied the concepts of behaviouralism in her analysis of leadership, authority, responsibility, etc. She underpinned the importance of functional and integrative unity and to achieve this she developed four principles of coordination.

Follett can be considered as a link between the classical and behavioural theorists. It is said that chronologically she belonged to a scientific management era and philosophically to the social man era.[11] As a classicist, she developed certain principles and strongly believed in their universality. As a behaviouralist, she stressed the importance of human emotions. Thus, she was a precursor of behaviouralism and human relations movement.

Elton Mayo (1880-1949), an industrial sociologist, is widely recognised as the progenitor of the human relations movement and his work laid foundations for later management and organisational thinking. He tried to view the problems of workers from a different angle, to that of traditionalists. Through extensive research he proved the importance of 'human group', and its causal effect on the behaviour of individuals at work. In his studies, Mayo analysed the problems of fatigue, monotony, morale, work environment and their impact on the worker.

The famous Hawthorne experiments conducted under his leadership led to deeper insights into the phenomena of group behaviour and its significance to management. They also led to the modification of earlier notions in management and laid the basis for many subsequent studies. Mayo, through these studies found that the employees respond to non-physical variables like social organisation, perceived intentions of management, etc., more than to the physical variables. This meant that work gets affected through the worker attitudes and feelings and managements should lead, motivate and improve the morale of employees.[12] Another significant finding of these experiments is the 'discovery' of informal organisation and its pervasive influence in organisations. It was found, that the informal organisation provides an outlet to the aspirations of employees and the effectiveness of management depends on its capacity to use these informal relations, to achieve the organisational objectives. He also brought out the importance of the communication system to facilitate worker to motivate fellow worker. For Mayo, achieving the spontaneous cooperation between individuals in the organisation, is the main concern of management and administration. He sought to use social science insights to secure the commitment of individuals to achieve the ends of the organisation, through the realisation of ' human factor' in work situation.

Chester Barnard (1866-1961), a highly successful executive, is considered to be the spiritual father of the ' social system' school, which influenced many an organisational setting of administrative activity and institutionalised patterns of behaviour. He directed attention to the relationships of component parts in the administrative system. His *Functions of the Executive* published in 1937 is a classic in organisation and administrative theory.

Barnard begins his analysis on the basic premise that individuals have innate physical, social and biological limitations. To him the most effective method of overcoming these limitations is cooperative social action on which he builds his theory of organisation. He defines organisation 'as a system of consciously coordinated activities of two or more persons'. The organisation comes into being when there are persons able to communicate with each other and are willing to contribute action to accomplish a common purpose. Barnard disagrees with the concept of economic man and propounds a concept of 'contribution-satisfaction equilibrium'. The individual's contribution depends on the personal satisfaction he derives as a result of participation and the satisfaction in turn depends on the incentives or inducements. Barnard considers economic or material inducements as only one of the multiplicity of satisfactions, others being personal non-material like opportunities for distinction, prestige, personal power, desirable physical conditions of work, and ideal benefactions such as pride of workmanship, sense of adequacy, patriotism, etc. Organisation owes its existence to the maintenance of equilibrium between contributions and satisfactions.

Barnard considers informal organisation as very important and both formal and informal organisations as interdependent aspects of the same phenomena. To him maintenance of organisational communications, securing essential services from individuals, and formulation of purpose and objectives are the three important executive functions. His concepts on acceptance of authority and leadership as a process of fulfilling the purpose of organisation and management by consent have immense contemporary significance and they strengthen the democratic spirit in the modern 'administrative state'.

Studies on administrative science tend to cluster around two distinct points of view. The first concerns with the institutional arrangements of performance - job content, job structure and job relationships. This mechanistic approach subsumes the human participation in organisation, and thus relegates it to a secondary position in the order of importance, and in the analysis of administrative behaviour. The a priori assumptions on human elements are open to contest and in the process of disposing their fallacy, the second point of view emerges on the scene.

Herbert Simon (1916-2001) was very critical of the administrative studies of the scientific management era and called them superficial, oversimplified and lacked realism. He was particularly critical of the generalisations or universal principles enunciated by Fayol, Taylor, Gulick, etc., and criticised them as 'proverbs and myths' with many fundamental ambiguities. Simon's concern was to develop a general theory of administration based on the principles governing human behaviour. Only such a different grounding of administrative principles, Simon felt, would form the basis for administrative science and would insure correct decision-making as well as effective action. He built administrative theory around 'decision-making'. He described all administration as decision-making and explained various factors involved in the decisional process. To him decision-making is choosing between different available alternatives. In such a process the individual is conditioned by both value and factual premises. Though it is not easy to isolate value and factual premises, he emphasised that administration should be based on facts.

Rationality, according to Simon, is another important factor in decision-making. In the decisional process, the decision-maker is influenced by both rational and non-rational elements. A complete knowledge and better understanding of the latent non-rational elements is very essential, to make administration more and more rational. As the administrative behaviour is a complex totality of the behaviour of individuals, Simon emphasised on the need to understand the individual behaviour in an organisational context. In his later writings, Simon endeavored to apply his theory of decision-making to industrial administration using computers, cognitive science, simulation, operational research, etc. He was concerned with the use of modern science and technology to make decisions gradually programmed, thereby increasing rationality in administration. His concern, as is obvious, is to develop a value-free administrative science. Though his later research is concerned more with industrial administration, the thinning away of difference between public and private administration makes his research invaluable to public administration.

Abraham Maslow, Douglas McGregor, Chris Argyris, Rensis Likert and Frederick Herzberg attach great significance to the human behaviour in organisations and the psychological character of such grouping forms the foundations of their theories. Their stream of thought encompasses such diverse fields of study such as sociology, social psychology, industrial psychology, socio-metrics, economics, cybernetics, etc.

Abraham Maslow (1908-1970) developed his theory of human motivation in terms of need hierarchy. He identifies five important needs viz., physiological, security, social, self-esteem and self-actualisation. These needs can be arranged in a hierarchical order wherein physiological needs are at the bottom and self-actualisation needs on the top. If a need is not satisfied, the individual experiences dissatisfaction and is always motivated to satisfy his need. Once a need is fulfilled, he experiences satisfaction. A satisfied need, according to Maslow, ceases to be a motivator. Individuals first pay attention towards satisfying their physiological and security needs in the hierarchy. Once these basic needs are fulfilled reasonably well, the individual loses interest in them and diverts his attention towards satisfying next level needs in the hierarchy viz., belonging. When these needs are also met, the individual addresses to the fulfillment of next higher level needs.

Maslow's concept of need hierarchy has several implications to the organisations. The theory suggests that the organisations must provide opportunities and rewards to satisfy the needs of the members of the organisation which motivate them to make their contributions. As individuals grow in the organisation, the latter provides different rewards and opportunities to its members. As individuals move in the hierarchy, their needs and aspirations also move up in the hierarchy and the organisation should attempt to motivate them by fulfilling their needs so as to enable them to make their contributions. Maslow's theory was subjected to critical examination both on methodology and other grounds. Notwithstanding the criticisms, it has provided a base for understanding the basis for the contributions of individuals towards the organisation.

Douglas McGregor (1906-1964) treats the problem more confidently and optimistically. He starts with an explanation of causal factors of individual behaviour and investigates the phenomena of reluctance and enthusiasm encountered in organisations. He proceeds systematically from micro level of the individual, progressively to the macro level of organisational life, describing the ramifications of the multitudinous interactions at various levels and finally leads to a viable explanation. His explanation synthesise the tenets of clinical psychology with an underpinning of social dynamics. McGregor's theories ' X ' and ' Y ' are not straitjackets limiting the leader from delving further into the field of human endeavour. They are limits of a spectrum encompassing assumptions of classical school.

Chris Argyris (1923) focuses attention on individual dynamics, intermediate interaction between participating members based on a stimulus-response tandem. The concern is primarily with the process by which the individual and the organisation adapt to the needs of each other. Argyris suggests that the organisational objectives should reflect manifestations of individual goals. Such integration of goals could release the will on the part of the participants, to strive for the accomplishment of organisational goals. To bring this concept into reality, Argyris advocates a process of fusion of individual aspirations with organisational goals, individual skills with organisational position and individual conduct with organisational role. The emergent three-dimensional fusion is the basis for Argyris's fusion model. His comprehensive analysis lays emphasis on the behavioural aspect within an organisation, but the relationships in the field of forces, affecting the component element remain in a maze of confusion. His study is one of a descriptive character rather than prescriptive in nature.

Rensis Likert (1903-1981) makes the blurred field of application obtained from the studies of Argyris, as a point of departure. He analyses the blockades inhibiting effective fusion between an organisation and its members. His overview of leadership styles and interpersonal reactions in different organisations bring into fore the inadequacy of Newtonian mechanics to describe the organisational dynamics. His comparative analysis of organisational styles, explains the dysfunctionality of the authoritarian types of leadership. He advocates a switchover, albeit gradually, from authoritarian to cooperative and participatory styles. He also investigates the mechanics of institutional structuring to facilitate the switchover. The focus is on the systematic nature of enterprise and the motivational forces at work. The application of scientific procedures to relatively specific activities, such as selection and job-skill training are not included in his 'universe'. This preclusion is intentional. For, Likert recognises the role of psychiatrists in unravelling the mystery and leaves it to them.

During the 60s, behaviouralists began to examine the human problems facing management and searched for new techniques of human motivation. Frederick Herzberg (1923-2000), through his studies in Pittsburgh, developed a theory of motivation which has broad implications for human resource management. He concluded that workers have two different types of needs which are independent of each other but affect the human behaviour in many ways. His studies reveal that the events leading to satisfaction are different from those that lead to dissatisfaction. Five strong determinants of job satisfaction identified by Herzberg are: achievement, recognition, work, responsibility and advancement. Similarly, company policy and administration, supervision, pay, inter-personnel relations and working conditions were identified as important factors leading to job dissatisfaction. These factors are distinct and separate and are not opposite of one another. Instead, they are concerned with two different ranges of human needs. The satisfiers—when the people felt well about their job—are related to the work itself and the dissatisfiers are related to the work environment. Herzberg called the first set of factors *motivators* and the second set *hygiene or maintenance* factors. Before Herzberg, behavioural scientists emphasised on ' job enlargement' or ' job rotation' for worker motivation. But Herzberg suggested that what we really need is to enrich the job i.e., deliberate upgrading of the scope of the work as well as responsibility. Job enrichment calls for vertical job loading, introduction of new and more difficult tasks not previously undertaken, removal of controls, conferring additional authority, etc.

Wider Perspectives

During the post Second World War, problems of development in the newly independent countries and the problems of governance in the developed countries in the context of emerging complexities, the need for better understanding of statecraft became inevitable and urgent. Several streams of researches were undertaken focusing on developing models for administration, examining governance in the context of policy, and analysing public administration in the context of political processes and public management of state, economy and society. Though the contributions of theorists can be considered from the disciplinary perspectives of development, policy analysis, political administration and public management, we have put them in a broader rubric of *wider perspectives* as they have and continue to have immense influence and impact on theory and practice of public administration in all countries across the globe - developing and developed. Contributions of Fred Riggs, Dwight Waldo, Yehezkel Dror, and Peter Drucker come in this category.

After the Second World War many Afro-Asian countries attained independence and faced and continue to face challenging tasks of development. The western administrative models and practices were found wanting in many respects when they applied to these countries. It is in this context the need for developing entirely new concepts was felt and the result was the emergence of development and comparative public administration, which emphasise cross-cultural and cross-national administrative studies.

Fred W. Riggs (1917-2008), a pioneer in this field, developed many analytical models and approaches to study public administration in a comparative perspective. He used three important analytical approaches viz., ecological, structural-functional, and ideal models. He emphasised that the administration and its environment influence each other and therefore an understanding of the dynamics of this process is necessary to understand administration. This is termed as ecological approach. In analysing the administrative systems from the ecological point of view, Riggs mainly used structural-functional approach using a number of ideal models. Riggs is one of the most creative and ambitious model builders.[13] First, he constructed *agraria* and *industria* by classifying societies as agricultural and industrial. As this model proved to be too abstract to apply and failed to explain the transitional societies, he developed another set of models, fused, prismatic and diffracted. These models, Riggs says emphatically, are designed to be 'ideal' types not to be found in any actual society, but perhaps approximate to some, and useful for heuristic purposes and as an aid in the organisation of data.

Riggs made significant contribution to the field of comparative and development administration. He defined development as the increasing ability to make and carry out collective decision affecting the environment. He considered differentiation and integration as the two key elements in the process of development. The degree of differentiation and integration represent diffracted and prismatic conditions of the society. Riggs considers the prismatic society as less developed because of maladjustment of differentiation and integration. Riggs' ecological approach touches wider horizons than classical and behavioural theories, and provides an integrated approach of administrative system. This helps us in understanding the administrative process in developing countries. As Chapman observed that in spite of many limitations, Riggs models may deepen our insight into some of the underlying problems of administration in transitional societies.[14]

During the later part of the twentieth century public administration has come to emphasise 'public policy' concept of its scope and method. This, apart from having a substantial intellectual and practical interest, has had a significant impact on public administration as a discipline. [15] Yehezkel Dror (born in 1928) is a pioneer in attempting to carve out a separate field of policy science. He, in his wide ranging studies, identifies the inadequacy and weakness in public policy-making in the contemporary society and emphasises on the need for the development of supra discipline ' based on systematic knowledge, structured rationality and organised creativity'. His basic thesis is that there is a significant gap in the knowledge on how policies can best be made. The gap between available knowledge and practice of policy-making will get widened unless some radical changes are made in policy-making methods, organisations and qualifications of policy-makers. He particularly emphasised the need for integration of the existing knowledge for the enrichment of this new science. This is for two reasons - firstly, the inadequacy of the policy sciences to contribute to the growing demands of modernisation and challenges of development, and secondly, a more academic one, is the intellectual curiosity of the academics to apply the enormously increasing knowledge in various disciplines for qualitative improvement of the public policy-making.

Dror underpins the urgency and need for the development of policy science discipline identifies a number of problems blocking its evolution and explains the directions in which research is moving, and has to move. He critically surveys, in his various writings, the existing normative models of public policy-making, pinpoints their limitations and develops an optimum model which is a fusion of the merits of the normative models without their deficiencies. For improving public policy-making Dror identifies the major changes needed in the knowledge, personnel, structures, processes and environment viz., in the public opinion, culture, behaviour, etc. He attempts to find ways to integrate knowledge and power and makes a number of concrete propositions for improving public policy-making. He says that better policy-making is an essential precondition for development and modernisation and policy sciences aim to reassert the role of intellectualism and rationalism to guide human destiny.

Dwight Waldo (1913-2000), a 'defining figure' in the discipline of public administration, unequivocally abandoned politics-administration dichotomy. He contends that the separation is inadequate, either as a description of reality or as a prescription for administrative behaviour. He represents 'the administration as politics' approach and believed that there is much to learn from history. He was critical of anti-historical nature of public administration literature. He was critical of organisational paradigm of classical theory and identified three different stages of development of organisation theory viz., classical, neoclassical and modern organisation theory.

Discussing the trends in modern organisation theories, Waldo critically examined the nature of comparative and development administration. He played a significant role in New Public Administration Movement, whose goal was to establish new directions for the field and to reconcile public administrations' role in the context of social and political ferment of late

1960's and early 1970's. Waldo was more sympathetic to a 'professional' orientation in public administration despite being aware of limitations of public administration as a profession. Foreseeing the future world as turbulent and characterised by change, he examined the role of public administration in such turbulent times. He predicts that organisations of future will be more complex and less bureaucratic. The enterprise of public administration, according to Waldo, will be marked by philosophical, disciplinary and methodological pluralism as we attempt to survive, adopt and control change. Waldo's works are criticised for its essential ambivalence. Some of the areas of criticism relate to politics-administration relations, public and private administration differences and professional nature of public administration. Waldo may not have provided definitive answers to problems of public administration, but raised right questions and provided insights that better equip us to more informed choices between different alternatives.

Peter Drucker (1909-2005), the management guru and consultant, is a writer of uncommon verve and practicality and deals with management in the context of larger society. His vision can be uncovered from his voluminous writings over the last several decades and extrapolated to governmental administration. Drucker believed that the term management is generic and not related to business or any other profession. Tracing the historical developments in management studies, he laments that a feeling persists that management is business management. To him management is a specific tool, specific function and specific instrument to make institutions capable of producing results and ninety per cent of it is generic to all types of organisations. Describing management as a liberal art, Drucker says that it deals with fundamentals of knowledge, self-knowledge wisdom and leadership. It is an art because it deals with practice and application. He was the first to see management as a profession – a body of theoretical and practical knowledge about organisations, tasks and people. He believed that managers are made and not born and emphasised the importance of management education and training.

Drucker is very critical about the non-performance of public agencies and identified several 'sins' that contributed to non-performance. He argues that the government is a poor manager and is concerned with procedures and in the process becomes 'bureaucratic'. He advocated restructuring of government based on 'rethinking' and suggested continuous improvement and benchmarking in restructuring government. Aware of difficulties in 'rethinking' in government system, he pleads for 'a theory of what government can do' and maintains that government should 'abandon' functions that it cannot and should not do. The concept of Management by Objectives (MBO), as is understood today, was first conceptualised by Drucker. MBO refers to collective setting of organisation goals, targets and measurement. When it is considered that management exists to produce results, the MBO becomes an important tool for performance assessment and management by self-control. Drucker developed the concept of knowledge worker in organisations. He identified several factors that determine knowledge worker's productivity and argues that making them productive requires changes in the attitudes of individual workers as well as the entire organisation.

Despite phenomenal contributions by Drucker to the practice of management, there are many criticisms and they relate to journalistic nature of his work without much intellectual depth, failure to appreciate the different contexts of public administration, failure to recognise the limitations in application of market approaches in government, and failure to discern the actual tenor and texture of public management. Drucker through his writings on management, focused on relationships among human beings and they provide lessons on how organisations can bring out the best in people and how workers can find a sense of dignity in modern society. Many of his ideas formed the basis for New Public Management movement.

Marxian Perspective

Derived from the works of Karl Marx (1818-1883) and Friedrich Engels, Marxist theories focus on dialectical materialism and advocate proletarian revolution. These theories are the most powerful and are most debated. They inspired both dedicated exponents and bitter critics and are the basis for modern day communism. They envisage the emergence of classless society. Social and political institutions progressively change their nature as economic developments transform the material conditions. They believed that resistance to change necessitates overthrow of such institutions through class struggle than waiting for incremental changes and modifications. Marxism goes beyond the confines of any single discipline and encompasses anthropology, psychology, social theory, philosophy, economics, political science, public administration, etc.

It may look very unconventional to include Karl Marx among administrative thinkers. He is included consciously to provide a broader perspective on administrative theories. Though Marx did not particularly write about bureaucracy or administrative concepts, he dealt in sufficient detail on the nature of administration and role of bureaucracy in his various works on state and society. His ideas on bureaucracy can be mainly discerned from *The Eighteenth Brumaire of Louis Bonaparte, Critique of Hegel's Philosophy of Rights,* etc. Marx examined bureaucracy from the philosophical perspective of dialectical materialism. He considered bureaucracy as a part of the state's exploitative machinery and an instrument of the ruling class. In a class society bureaucracy is an inefficient and inhuman instrument because of its exploitative nature. He questioned the Hegelian assumptions about bureaucracy. The concept of alienation, which Marx explained in detail, is useful to understand the alienation of bureaucracy in the modern state. Marx visualised the transformation of the role of bureaucracy in a classless society from administration of persons to administration of things. It is very important to examine the views of Karl Marx on the bureaucracy in the context of experience of nature and role of administration in socialist countries.

Significant Works and Ideas of Thinkers

The *thinkers* included in this volume, through their studies and researches, have generated a large number of ideas, concepts and theories and wrote extensively on organisation, administration and management. As a pedagogic exercise, we have identified three important works and concepts/and ideas of each thinker which are useful to the scholars and students of Public Administration and included in table 1. This is a reflective exercise to further the knowledge in public administration.

– Editors

Table 1: Significant Works and Ideas of Thinkers

S.No.	Name	Three influential works	Three influential ideas/concepts
(1)	(2)	(3)	(4)
1.	Kautilya – 350-283 B.C Ancient Indian Philosopher Adviser to King Chandragupta Maurya.	1. Arthashastra 2. Neetishastra 3. Chanakya Neeti	1. Monarchy as the best form of government; Absolute powers to King. 2. Saptanga theory of elements of state. 3. Principles of public administration.
2.	Woodrow Wilson (1856-1924) Former President of America and Political Scientist	1. The Study of Administration, 1887. 2. Congressional Government, 1885. 3. The Constitutional Government in the United States, 1908.	1. Importance of study of administration as science. 2. Politics-administration dichotomy. 3. Public administration as 'Government in action'.
3.	Henri Fayol (1841-1925) French Mining Engineer and Administrative Theorist	1. General and Industrial Management, 1949. 2. The Theory of Administration of the State, 1923. 3. General Principles of Administrations (1908)	1. Principles of management. 2. General theory of management/management process school. 3. Gang plank/Level jumping.
4.	Frederick Winslow Taylor (1865-1915) Engineer, Inventor and Consultant	1. Shop Management, 1903. 2. The Principles of Scientific Management, 1911. 3. The Testimony Before the House Special Committee,1912	1. Principles of scientific management. 2. "One best way" of doing things. 3. Functional foremanship.
5.	Max Weber (1864-1920) German Sociologist and Political Scientist	1. The Theory of Social and Economic Organisation, 1947. 2. Economy and Society, 1909. 3. The Protestant Ethic and the Spirit of Capitalism, 1904.	1. Forms of authority. 2. Legal rational bureaucracy. 3. Protestant ethic.
6.	Luther Gulick (1892-1993) American Expert on Public Administration. Lyndall Urwick (1891-1983) British Management Consultant	1. The Papers on Science of Administration, 1937, (Edited by Gulick and Urwick). 2. Metropolitan Problems and American Ideas, 1962 (Gulick). 3. The Elements of Administration, 1947 (Urwick).	1. Structure based principles of organisation. 2. POSDCORB as functions of executive. 3. Bases of departmentalisation.

S.No.	Name	Three influential works	Three influential ideas/concepts
(1)	(2)	(3)	(4)
7.	**Mary Parker Follett** (1868-1933) American Political Scientist, Social Worker and Management Consultant	1. Dynamic Administration, 1924. 2. Creative Experience, 1924. 3. Freedom and Coordination, 1949.	1. Constructive conflict 2. Integration 3. Depersonalising orders
8.	**George Elton Mayo** (1880-1949) Australian Social Psychologist and Industrial Researcher	1. The Human Problems of Industrial Civilisation, 1933. 2. The Political Problems of Industrial Civilisation, 1974. 3. The Social Problems of Industrial Civilisation, 1975.	1. Human relations approach to organisations. 2. Hawthorne effect. 3. Role of informal organisations and groups in effecting the behaviour of individuals at work.
9.	**Chester, I. Barnard** (1886-1961) American Executive and Management Thinker	1. Functions of the Executive, 1938. 2. Organisation and Management, 1948. 3. Philosophy for Managers; Selected Papers of Chester I. Barnard, 1986.	1. Acceptance theory of authority and "Zone of Indifference" 2. Contribution-satisfaction equilibrium. 3. Functions of the executive.
10.	**Herbert A. Simon** (1916-2001) American Political Scientist and Economist	1. Administrative Behaviour, 1947. 2. Organisation, 1958. 3. The New Science of Management Decision, 1960.	1. Administration as decision-making. 2. Bounded rationality. 3. Zone of acceptance.
11.	**Abraham Maslow** (1908-1970) American Psychologist and Motivation Theorist	1. Motivation and Personality, 1954. 2. A Theory of Human Motivation, 1943. 3. Religion, Values and Peak Experiences, 1965.	1. Hierarchy of needs. 2. Self-actualisation. 3. Peak experiences.
12.	**Douglas McGregor** (1906-1964) American Social Psychologist and Management Consultant	1. The Human Side of Enterprise, 1960. 2. The Professional Manager, 1967. 3. Leadership and Motivation, 1969.	1. Theory "X" and Theory "Y". 2. Management education from cosmology to reality. 3. Transactional influence.
13.	**Chris Argyris** (July 16, 1923) American **Behavioural** Theorist and Management Writer	1. Personality and Organisation, 1957. 2. Integrating the Individual and the Organisation, 1964. 3. Organisational Learning, 1978.	1. Maturity-Immaturity theory. 2. T-Group Techniques; Single loop and Double loop learning. 3. Organisational learning.

S.No.	Name	Three influential works	Three influential ideas/concepts
(1)	(2)	(3)	(4)
14.	Frederick Herzberg (1923-2000) American Psychologist and Management Consultant	1. The Motivation to Work, 1959. 2. Work and the Nature of Man, 1966. 3. The Managerial Choice, 1982.	1. Hygiene - Motivation theory. 2. Job-enrichment. 3. Job loading.
15.	Rensis Likert (1903-1981) American Organisational Psychologist and Educator.	1. New Patterns of Management, 1961. 2. The Human Organisation, 1967. 3. New Ways of Managing Conflict, 1976.	1. Management system 1-4. 2. Linking pin model. 3. Interaction-influence system.
16.	Fred W. Riggs (1917-2008) Chinese born American Political Scientist and Administrative Model Builder	1. The Ecology of Public Administration, 1961. 2. Administration in Developing Countries, 1964. 3. Frontiers of Development Administration, 1970.	1. Prismatic society. 2. Sala model of administration. 3. Development as diffraction and integration.
17.	Yehezkel Dror (born in 1928) Israeli Political Scientist and Pioneer in Policy Studies	1. Public Policy-making Reexamined, 1968. 2. Design for Policy Sciences, 1971. 3. Ventures in Policy Sciences, 1971.	1. Societal direction system as a mega-knowledge system. 2. "Optimal model" of policy making. 3. Paradigms of policy sciences.
18.	Dwight Waldo (1913-2000) American Political Scientist and "Defining figure" in Public Administration.	1. The Administrative State, 1948. 2. The Study of Public Administration, 1955. 3. Public Administration in a Time of Turbulence, 1971.	1. Public administration as political approach. 2. Professional orientation to Public Administration. 3. New Public Administration.
19.	Peter Drucker (1909-2005) American Management Thinker, Professor and Consultant	1. The Practice of Management, 1954. 2. Management -'Tasks, Responsibilities, Practices, 1974. 3. Management Challenges for the 21st Century, 1992.	1. Management by objectives. 2. Restructuring Government/ New Public Management. 3. Knowledge society and knowledge workers.
20	Karl Marx (1818-1883) German Revolutionary Philosopher and Political Economist	1. Critique of Hegel's Philosophy of Right, 1844. 2. The Eighteenth Brumaire of Louis Bonaparte, 1850. 3. A Contribution to the Critic of Political Economy, 1859.	1. Bureaucracy as an exploitative class instrument. 2. Materialistic interpretation of history. 3. Alienation of bureaucracy.

References

1 See Chaturvedi, T.N., in Arora, Ramesh K., (Ed), *Administrative Theory*, New Delhi, Indian Institute of Public Administration, 1984, p.v.

2 Golembiewski, Robert T., *Public Administration as a Developing Discipline, Part I, Perspectives on Past and Present*, New York, Marcel Dekker, Inc., 1977, p. 5.

3 Peter Self, *Administrative Theories and Politics*, London, George Allen & Unwin Ltd., 1972, p. 20.

4 Baker, R. J.S., *Administrative Theory and Public Administration*, London, Hutchinson University Library, 1972, p.31.

5 Urwick, L., and Brech. E.F.L., *The Making of Scientific Management*, Vol. I. London, Sir Isaac Pitman & Sons, Ltd., Reprinted 1955, p.37.

6 Gross, Bertram M., *The Managing of Organisations: The Administrative Struggle*, Vol. I. New York, The Free Press, 1964, p. 145.

7 Ibid., p.145.

8 Baker, R. J.S.,op. cit., p. 23.

9 Koontz, Harold., " The Management Theory Jungle", in. Richards, Max D., and Nielander, William A., (Eds.), *Readings in Management*, Bombay, D.B .Taraporevala Sons & Co., P. Ltd., III Ed., 1969, p. 16.

10 Urwick, L., and Brech. E.F.L., op. cit., p. 51.

11 Wren, Daniel A., *The Evolution of Management Thought*, New York, The Ronald Press Company, 1972, p. 301.

12 Henderson, Keith M., *Emerging Synthesis in American Public Administration*, Bombay, Asia Publishing House, 1970, p. 17.

13 Caiden, Gerald E., *The Dynamics of Public Administration: Guidelines to Current Transformations in Theory and Practice*, New York, Holt, Rinehart and Winston, Inc., 1971, p. 260.

14 Chapman, Richard, A., " Prismatic Theory in Public Administration: A Review of the Theories of Fred W. Riggs", *Public Administration*, Vol. 44, Winter, 1966, p. 427.

15 Golembiewski, Robert T., op. cit., p. 4.

1

ADMINISTRATIVE THEORY

D. Ravindra Prasad
Y. Pardhasaradhi

Explosion of knowledge led to the emergence of disciplines over years resulting in growth of autonomous areas of specialisation each with distinct boundaries of its own. This is accompanied by the development of concepts and theories which form the basis of each discipline. An understanding of the discipline - specialised area of knowledge - presupposes an understanding of the related concepts and theories. What, then, is theory? What are its elements, functions and role? What constitutes a good theory? As the book is concerned with public administrative theory, it is necessary to understand what theory is and also the present status of public administration theory.

What is Theory?

The term theory is derived from the Greek word 'theoria'[1] which means 'looking at', 'viewing', 'contemplating', 'speculating'. Theories are ideas organised in a logical order to reinforce or demolish an existing conviction or to form the basis for a new conviction. It enables one to distinguish between real from the ideal and right from wrong. Theory represents a systematic explanation of causal factors and their fusion within a conceptual framework. Theory is based on logical reasoning and consists of a set of principles and generalisations which represent universal truths. These may initially constitute testable hypotheses, which in different situations may prove to be true or untrue when tested, others get incorporated into theory. Gradually a body of knowledge emerges containing a set of interrelated concepts, definitions, and propositions that provide a systemic view of the phenomenon by specifying relationships between variables with the objective of explaining and predicting phenomenon. Theory is systematic grouping of interdependent concepts and principles which give a framework to or tie together existing knowledge, explaining events or relationships and in the end predict what has not yet been observed.

Theory is a concise presentation of facts and logical set of assumptions. Kerlinger[2] defines theory as a 'set of interrelated constructs or concepts, definitions and propositions that presents a systematic view of phenomenon by specifying relations among the variables with the purpose of explaining and predicting the phenomenon'. Gibbs,[3] on the other hand, defines that 'a theory is a system of logically interrelated statements in the form of empirical assertions about properties, of infinite classes of events or things'. To Samuelson[4] theory is a set of axioms or postulates or hypotheses about observable reality.[5]

Elements of Theory

A theory has three important characteristics, viz., it consists of a set of propositions, these propositions are interrelated, and some of these propositions can be empirically tested. A proposition is a statement about the relationship between two or more concepts. The structure of the theory consists of certain elements that are built one upon the other, form a deductive system of reasoning. These elements are assumptions and they form a logical skeleton for the explanatory system and define the basic notions about the system. Such a conceptual abstract model is simpler than the real world and contains only the forces that the theory asserts to be important.

Classification of Theories

Theories are classified, according to their extent of application, as pure and practical. Pure theory builds conceptual model for explaining observable phenomena[6]. Practical theory generalises relations abstracted from observable phenomena and puts meaning and purpose into the logic of pure theory for the solution of practical problems. Henry Mehlberg,[7] a French philosopher, classified theories as independent and intradependent. The former are further classified into axiomatic, phenomenological and transcendent theories.

What Constitutes a Good Theory?

Theory should broadly conform to the criterion of objectivity, reliability, universality, coherence and comprehensiveness. Miner identifies seven criteria to examine whether a theory is good or not.[8] The criteria includes that a good theory should contribute to the goals of science, be explicit and helpful in focusing research, clearly delineate the domain of the discipline, be logically consistent both internally and externally, should be a testable reality, be a simple statement and most parsimonious. Miner adds that theories are not sacrosanct for all times and what was a good theory at one point of time may not be so good years later. The other criterion to which a good theory should conform include that it must be logically consistent and there should not be internal contradictions; must be interrelated; exhaustive and cover the full range of variations concerning the nature of the phenomena in question; there should be no repetition or duplication; and capable of being subjected to empirical scrutiny. Nan Lin[9] has identified three criteria viz., testability, clear and unambiguous language, and parsimony for evaluating theories and to decide which of them is superior.

Significance of Theory

Theory provides an organised and substantiated plan or reasoning about phenomenon and their interrelations. It provides a systematic method for conducting social research and leads to knowledge discovery. Henri Poincare, a French mathematician, provided excellent guide for understanding the role of theory in scientific research. He says that science is built with facts as house is built with stones, but a collection of facts is not science as much as a heap of stones do not make a house. Theory is an essential tool for the progress of civilisation and it enables people to communicate quickly and effectively. It is an intellectual shorthand, which saves each generation having to relearn all that has already been discovered or learnt.

Public Administration Theory

We shall now discuss the nature and status of theory in public administration for greater, deeper and proper understanding of the discipline. The governmental functions are on the increase, thereby increasing the role of public administration to achieve societal goals. Dynamic nature of society and complex nature of governmental activities makes it difficult for generalist administrator to function in an old fashioned way and yet realise the administrative goals. One of the reasons attributed for the failure of the administrator to realise the objectives is inadequate understanding of the administrative theory. The inflated sense of achievement and overrated sense of intellectual superiority of the generalist administrators have largely contributed to the failures in administration. One witnesses a general antipathy against theory, which is labelled as 'Ivory Tower Thinking', which the administrators feel is far removed from the reality they confront. Bureaucratic pretense of omniscience is another reason. The administrator believes that 'power is knowledge and his experience is greater than theory'. For this and many other reasons the administrators jealously guard their traditionalism abhorring and resisting change. But if the administrator has to fashion the administration to meet the societal requirements of change and manage the administrative system effectively one should have a broader and deeper understanding of the administrative theory.

In an 'administrative state', theory has an important role to play. Stephen Bailey[10] believes that "the objectives of public administration theory are to draw together the insights of the humanities and the validated prepositions of the social and behavioural sciences and to apply these insights and propositions to the task of improving the processes of government and aimed at achieving politically regimented goals by constitutionally mandated means". Bailey argues that we should select from the body of human knowledge whatever appears relevant and useful in explaining the nature of public administration, verifiable through observation or experiment and capable of predicting the behaviour of public organisations and the people who compose them and come into contact with them. Bailey further argues that theories should prescribe what conditions and relationships should exist in public administration. How should government be organised? How should public servants be selected? How should authority and responsibility be assigned to public agencies? What principles should govern public directions? etc.

Evolution of Public Administration

Public administration as a subject matter existed since the dawn of civilisation, though as an academic discipline it is of recent origin. Its origins can be traced to the organisation of King's household, which was divided into two different organs — one looking after King's personal services and the other looking after the administration of lands, finances, justice, armies, etc. In the past, public services were limited and confined to law and order, regulatory activities and select public works and communal welfare was limited and administrative methods unsophisticated and technologies simple. Mostly governmental functions were internally organised into specialised areas. Modern times are witnessing growth in legislation and consequently there has been a substantial increase in governmental administration.

Two important institutions that contributed significantly to the development of administrative theory and practice are the church and the military. The former is best exemplified by the Roman Catholic Church, which has endured for more than 2000 years with a five-level hierarchy i.e. Pope, Cardinals, Archbishops, Bishops and the Parish Priests.[11] Biblical references brilliantly explain the need to delegate authority in large organisations and to review exceptional cases that cannot be resolved by the subordinates. The latter contributed to the theory of administration substantially. The use of staff support, advise, uniform methods and discipline were practiced by the military. More recently, armed forces have attracted the attention of the scholars for studies on leadership, authority and conflict resolution. Another important influence on administrative theory building is industrial administration.

Streams in Administrative Theory

Modern state is characterised as an 'administrative state', signifying the preponderance of administration in governmental functions. Public administration is in constant flux as it is constantly expanding along with changing nature of state. Emergence of global society and new world order contributed to the expansion of the boundaries of public administration. Its growing pervasiveness in the daily lives of the community is evident in the proliferation of public laws expansion of public sector, growth in public capital and investment, growth of public employment, public provision of services, etc. This expansion made some people to believe that if the cycle is not soon reversed , it will become enslaved to a leviathan that will order all our affairs, while others hope that further extension will eliminate selfish, private interests that exploit the common man that bring good society nearer.

Administrative theory, though not explicitly, was in evidence during the ancient period as well. Kautilya's *Arthashastra* in India during the 4th century B.C and Sun Tzu's *The Art of War* in China during 6th century B.C have glimpses of administrative theory. The Chinese seem to have recognised the need for planning, organising, leading and controlling around 1000 BC. These are classic examples of the presence of administrative theory in this part of the globe even before Christ. Similarly, Egyptians practiced decentralisation and the use of staff advice almost 2000 years before Christ. The construction of pyramids is a reminder of the existence of systematic planning, organisation, leadership and control systems without which it would not have been possible to build them. This clearly indicates the effective practice of administrative principles.

If one were required to specifically pinpoint the time, when the modern administrative theory was born, the date would have to be the publication of F.W.Taylor's *'The Principles of Scientific Management'*. Taylor's efforts became known for his experiments on time and motion. In contrast to Taylor, Henri Fayol took a broader view and he can be described as the first administrative theorist i.e., those concerned with principles of organisation and the functions of administrator. Fayol's important contribution was the designation of administrative functions and recognition of the discipline. Taylor and Fayol were almost the first to discern certain postulates, which were later synthesised as 'principles' that form the basis and substance of classical approach to the study of organisations.

The classical theorists emphasised on the physiological and mechanistic aspects of public organisations. The next historical stream of administrative thought is described as a neo-classical or human relations approach. Starting with the human relations varied contributions from behavioural scientists have enriched administrative theory. The structuralist-mechanistic approach to public management was challenged by behaviouralist as the latter focused on the human and social elements. From the Hawthorne experiments of the 1920s, clinical investigations into human behaviour in organisational setting led to substantial modifications in the concepts and methodologies of public administration. The works of Follett, Barnard and Simon resulted in a significant change in the direction of administrative theory. Chester Barnard's social theory has broadened understanding of the relationship between public administration and society.

Although, much of public administration theory is culture-bound the study of comparative and development administration, a field virtually unknown before the Second World War, broke through cultural barriers and stimulated much original thinking. The ecological approach to the study of administration originated in the wake of emergence of Third World and increased realisation of relevance of most of the Western theories to the study of administration. F.W. Riggs and the comparative administration group of the American Society of Public Administration pioneered a new administrative vocabulary to describe different societal typologies, administrative cultures and systems. The result has been a questioning of the traditional framework of Public Administration and western egocentricity.

Dwight Waldo made substantial contribution to strengthen the administrative theory through his contributions to politics - administration dichotomy, organisation theory and launched the new public administration moment with the goal of finding new directions to the field of public administration which was in a ferment during the sixties and seventies. His contemporary Peter Drucker, a management thinker through his writings believed that management is generic and is equally applicable to government administration. He posited the view that the future organisations, both corporate and governmental, are going to be complex and knowledge-based and management becomes critical. He paved the way, in a way to the new public management moment which attracted the attention of scholars of public administration and began to work on administrative conceptive theories taking from management conceptive theories.

In recent years, public administration has come to emphasise public policy concept of its scope and method. This has a significant impact on public administration as a discipline. [12] The contributions of Dror are very significant in this area.

The contributions to the discipline of Public Administration have come mainly from the West and more so from the United States of America. The American Public Administration, rooted in American political and civic culture, is widely acknowledged as advanced capitalism blended with pluralism. The spirit of the discipline is naturally instrumentalist and management-oriented. This is a conventional and empirically oriented administrative theory. The marxist's concern for macro social structures and the historical transformation of the political economy needs to be related to organisational analyses and the study of Public Administration. A theory of Public Administration can be inferred from the large body of Marxist and non-Marxist literature on the nature of state and a radical Public Administration grounded in the Marxist perspective is yet to take definite shape. But the broad outline is steadily emerging with obvious attraction for the "Third World" scholars who are groping for a new paradigm to explain the socio-political reality of the third world.

This brief survey of administrative theories shows that traditional public administration assumptions are frequently shattered by contemporary happenings.[13] The actual configuration of public administration is in a constant state of flux. It is never the same from one period of time to another as perceptions change incessantly and with them the boundaries of public administration. The subject matter is exploding in all directions. Societal activities subject to political directions are expanding fast in response to contemporary needs. New types of public organisations are being created and new techniques and processes are being developed and service level benchmarks are being identified for improving the performance of public service delivery. As a result the administrative theory is in a constant flux.

Public Administration as an Academic Discipline

Public administration as a discipline evolved mostly in the West. Consequently administrative theorizing has been the work of practitioners and reformers in the United States of America and

Europe. A diversity of disciplines from social sciences, humanities and even physical sciences have made direct contribution to administrative theory. It is difficult to conceive of any area of academic study that is not or did not contribute to public administration. As such administrative theory is a product of diverse inputs.

Theory building in public administration is not an easy task, as there are various types of public organisations, administrative structures and processes. Therefore, public administration theorists have gone searching far and wide for new ideas, concepts and models that may have relevance to public organisations. Their search has carried them far beyond boundaries for administrative theory. This made Alberto Ramos[14] to observe that "Public administration may have lost a sense of its specific assignment and become a hodgepodge of theoretical ramblings, lacking both force and direction". More importantly it has lost its bearings to the mystification of both practitioners and students who can no longer relate theory to practice or vice-versa. As Martin Landau[15] commented administrative theory is marked by a plethora of competing schools, a polyglot of languages, and accordingly a confusion of logic. There is neither a common research tradition nor the necessary consensus for a common field of inquiry. Each of the competing schools questions the others. Consequently the whole field is confused, the core concepts need clarification. This makes many to argue that too little relevant public administration theory exists.

Many believe that public administration has yet to develop a systematic body of theory of its own as there are theories in public administration, but not theories of public administration. In fact the term public administration theory is rarely employed by the scholars in the literature of public administration. The disillusionment about the absence of theory of public administration persists from the days of Herbert Simon who questioned the bases of theory of public administration in his *Administrative Behaviour*. At about the same time Dwight Waldo in his *Administrative State* noted that the administrative theory as crude, presumptuous, incomplete, wrong in some of its conclusions, naive in its scientific methodology and parochial "in its outlook".

Theory Building in Public Administration

There are several reasons for the absence of proper and acceptable theory in public administration. Public administration, as a discipline has grown as part of either law or government. Formulation of theory, therefore, becomes difficult as it is an exercise in assimilation of knowledge drawing from different disciplines. Secondly, theory building in public administration becomes difficult, as the subject is mostly a practitioners domain. But the practitioners are not too interested to build theories. Most practitioners of public administration feel that theory is of no relevance to them. They believe that theirs is a practical world and their problems do not wait theoretical solutions. What is interesting is that the practitioners do employ theories, though unconsciously, and make assumptions, test concepts, verify hypotheses and evaluate ideas. Thirdly, theories in public administration should be based on social theory, but so far the letter has eluded everybody.

Theory building in public administration is inter-disciplinary and multi-disciplinary. As a result uni-disciplinary moorings cannot fathom the phenomena in all its ramifications. The nature of the state, social relations, political culture, etc., influences the working of all public organisations. Any theory that does not take into consideration these factors would analyse the phenomenon only partially. It is this aspect that is hindering the growth of theory in public administration. Another factor is the analysis by western scholars, or western oriented scholars who analyse the phenomenon without deep insights into the milieu within which the public organisations have to operate. Profession of public administration which considers it self omniscient and panacea for all social and political ills, harbinger of the peace and prosperity and policy formulator and implementer has systematically endangered the growth of the discipline with their touch-me-not attitude. The public administrators, coming as they do from different disciplines, could not integrate in them as to what is the administrative phenomenon, which they attempt to fathom. It is these factors that have hindered the growth of discipline.

Administrative studies in thirties began with a hopeful note on the possibility of building a science of administration. This is evident when Gulick asserted with confidence, that "we may expect in time, to construct a valid and accepted theory of administration".[16] Urwick was more emphatic when he said, that the principles can be studied as a technical question, irrespective of purpose of the enterprise, the personnel that compose it, or any constitutional, political or social theory underlying its creation.[17] There followed a number of studies, which led to the formulation of different theories in administration. However, the efforts to synthesise those theories did not bear fruit. The efforts of a few like Litchfield,[18] and Bertram Gross[19] have not been rewarding. As Caiden observed administrative theorists have shown no inclination to accept any framework [20]. Instead they continue to go in their respective ways and fly off at tangent, to the utter confusion of fellow theorists and newcomers to the administration theory. This failure made people like Waldo to remark that there is no reason to believe that agreement, unification, simplification and systematisation lying in the immediate future.[21]

What are the constraints that inhibit the theory building in administration? As Dimock noted, administration is concerned with all fields of knowledge and all matters which enter into carrying out of policies and programmes.[22] Therefore, it draws heavily from a variety of disciplines viz., political science, sociology, social-psychology, management, etc. It is unlikely that thinkers with different backgrounds, perceptions and expectations would tread a common path, with a common approach and with a common purpose. This, in part, appears to be the reason for the divergence in administrative theory. Another limitation, at integrating the several streams of administrative thought, is the impact of culture. No organisation can function beyond the pale of cultural constraints. For, culture of a society exerts immense influence on organisations and on those who work in them.[23] Therefore, administrative theory must take into account the cultural context. But mostly the efforts of theory building have taken place in America. Fifteen out of twenty one thinkers included in this volume are Americans and most of the "American writers concentrated on the local scene, with only incidental references to other systems" in understanding and analysing the administrative phenomena which Heady called parochial.[24] It is doubtful, then, to expect universal validity of such theories.

Administrative values have been changing through the passage of time. Gone are the days when administration is concerned with only such values as economy and efficiency, and gone are the days when administrator is concerned with only psychological and emotional factors involved in group behaviour. Today, societies all over the world are in a flux and social transformation is taking place at a faster rate, and administration is expected to meet and handle these challenges thrown up by the competitive global market. Social relevance of administration is being questioned.[25] There are new and varied demands from various sections of the society and the administrative structures are finding it difficult to address them in a rational and time-bound manner. The very efficiency of the administrative systems is being called into question necessitating the administration to learn new ways of transforming a society. As long as society continues to be dynamic and fast changing, the administration should also be dynamic and no static theory of administration will ever deliver the goods. The goal is to formulate theories and models that can help in better understanding the complex administrative phenomenon in different settings.

Viewed from a different perspective, administration qualifies itself to be labelled as science in the same sense as medicine and engineering are. The classical, behavioural, etc., approaches in the administrative studies are but segments of a unified and integrated field of administrative science. The bewilderment about administrative science is the consequence of a myopic view of science and its attributes of definiteness and universal validity. These attributes loose significance when applied in isolation. If they are to be meaningful and useful, they must aid in developing a body of knowledge that can further human welfare. Thus viewed, administration is definitely a science.

The perplexity about administrative science deepens when some consider the efforts of theory building a sterile exercise in the manipulation of abstract and empty concepts.[26] But the objective of theory building, as Mouzelis observed, is not to provide readymade solutions to the problems of social order or disorder, or the discovery of Newtonian-like Laws. But it only tries to elaborate conceptual tools which might help empirical investigation by suggesting useful ways of looking at realities. Such tools do not provide, according to Mouzelis, prefabricated answers to social problems; they simply prepare the ground for their adequate handling.[27] It is also to be emphasised that no conceptualisation will ever be final, definite and settled. It is' and must be, subject to continual alterations, elaborations, and refinements—all this being necessary in order to keep theory always at the service of empirical research.[28]

Administration as a separate intellectual discipline was the result of search for reforms in 1887. More than a century and a quarter later the administration continues to be in the same search for a theory of administration - an administration that can administer the complex societal transformations.

References

[1] See http://en.wikipedia.org/wiki/Theory

[2] Kerlinger, F.N., *Foundations of Behavioral Research* (4th ed.), Wadsworth, Belmont, CA, 2000, p.9.

[3] Gibbs, J. (Ed).,*Social Control: Views from the Social Sciences*, Sage Publications, Beverly Hills, CA, 1977, pp.83-114 .

[4] Samuelson, 'On Theory and Realism", *The American Economic Review*, Vol. 54, No. 5 ,Sep., 1964, pp. 733-735

[5] For other definitions see http://www.google.com/s e a r c h ? h l = e n & defl=en&q=define:theory&ei= ggxfS6OyB8-HkQXygYHlCw&sa=X&oi=glossary_ definition&ct=title&ved=0CAcQkAE.

[6] Allin, Bushrod W., "Theory: Definition and Purpose," *Journal of Farm Economics*, Vol. 31, August 1949, pp.410-16.

[7] Mehlberg, Henry, Cohen, Robert S., *Essay on the Causal Theory of Time*, New York, Springer-Verlag, 1980.

[8] Miner, John B., *Organisational Behavior: From Theory to Practice*, Volume 4, New York, M.E. Sharpe. Inc., 2007. Ch.1. See also Miner, John B., "The Validity and Usefulness of Theories in an Emerging Organizational Science," *The Academy of Management Review*, Vol. 9, No. 2 (April 1984), pp. 296-306.

[9] Lin, Nan, *Social Capital: A Theory of Social Structure and Action*, NY: Cambridge University Press, 2001.

[10] Bailey, Stephen. "Objective of the Theory of Public Administration," in Charlesworth, James C., (Ed.), *Theory and Practice of Public Administration : Scope Objectives, and Methods*, Philadelphia, American Academy of Political and Social Sciences, 1968. pp. 128-139.

[11] David Thenuwara Gamage & Nicholas Sunkeung Pang, *Leadership and Management in Educaton: Developing Essential Skills and Competencies*, Hong Kong, The Chinese University Press, 2003, p. 4.

[12] Henry, Nicholas, *Public Administration and Public Affairs*, Prentice Hall of India, New Delhi, 2007, p. 42.

[13] Lee, Eliza Wing-Yee, "Public Administration and the Rise of the American Administrative State," *Public Administration Review*, Vol. 55, 1995

14 Ramos, Albert Guerreiro, "Misplacement of Concepts and Administrative Theory", *Public Administration Review*, 38(6), 1978,pp. 550–557

15 Landau, Martin, "Redundancy, Rationality, and the Problem of Duplication and Overlap", *Public Administration Review*, 29(4), 1969, pp. 346–358

16 Gulick, Luther and Urwick, Lyndall, (Eds.), *The Papers on the Science of Administration*, New York, Institute of Public Administration, 1937, p. v.

17 Urwick, L., "Organization as a Technical Problem," in Luther Gulick and Lyndall Urwick, eds.,Ibid.p.49.

18 Litchfield, Edward H., "Notes on a General Theory of Administration", *Administrative Science Quarterly*, Vol.1No.1.June, 1956, pp.3-29.

19 Gross, Bertram, M., *Managing Organisations: The Administrative Struggle*, Vol.1., New York, The Free Press, 1964.

20 Caiden, Gerald, E., *Public Administration*, Palisades Publishers, California, 1982, p. 208.

21 Waldo, D., "Organisation Theory: An Elephantine Problem," *Public Administration Review*, Vol.11, 1961, p.20.

22 Quoted in Golembiewski, Robert T., op. cit., p.14.

23 Robson, William A., "The Managing of Organisation", *Public Administration*, Vol. 44, Autumn, 1966, p. 276.

24 Heady, Ferrel, *Public Administration: A Comparative Perspective*, Second Edition, New York, Marcel Dekker, Inc., 1979, p. 4.

25 See Marini, Frank, (Ed.), *Toward a New Public Administration: The Minnobrook Perspective*, New York, Chandler Publishing Company, 1971.

26 See Mouzelis, Nicos P., *Organisation and Bureaucracy: An Analysis of Modern Theories*, Rev. Ed., London, Routledge & Kegan Paul, 1975, p. 177.

27 Ibid., p. 177-178.

28 Ibid., p. 179

2
KAUTILYA

N.R. Inamdar

Introduction

The Mauryan era of ancient India gave the world a significant Sanskrit treatise, the *Arthashastra* of Kautilya.[1] It offers deep insights into political statecraft, particularly the principles of public administration, machinery of government, economic policy, military strategy, and personnel. Kautilya is known as the Indian Machiavelli because of his ruthless and shrewd tactics and policies reflecting an approach to statecraft including warfare. The *Arthashastra* counsels that no means are beyond the scope of the ruler to expand the territory, gain power and wealth.

The word *artha* denotes the substance of livelihood. The *Arthashastra* is thus a science which deals with the acquisition and protection of the means of livelihood. It shows how this activity should be carried out. It is also a means of ensuring the well-being of human being in general. Its objective is two-fold. The first, *palana*, refers to the administration and protection of state. The second, *labha*, is a conquest and acquisition of territory. *Artha* is

(c 4th Century B.C)

an all-embracing word with a variety of meanings. It is used in the sense of material well-being; livelihoods; economic and productive activity, particularly in agriculture, and in general as wealth. According to Kautilya, the *Arthashastra* deals with the perennial problem of "acquiring and maintaining the earth". Thus this *shastra*, writes *Kautilya*, "is composed as a guide to acquire and secure this world". It is the art of government in its widest sense. Therefore, the *Arthashastra* is a science that deals with statecraft in the internal as well as the external spheres.

Life and Works

Kautilya was a professor at Taxila University and later became the Prime Minister of the Mauryan Empire. It is being broadly felt that *Arthashastra* was compiled during the fourth century B.C. and some give the date as 350-283 B.C. But there is a dispute over the historical veracity of the treatise and disagreement over the authorship and the date of its composition. Kangle analysed several arguments exhaustively in his study.[2] Chandragupta Maurya ascended the throne around 321 B.C and various scholars concluded that the *Arthashastra* was compiled between 300 B.C and first century A.D[3]. Kautilya's authorship as well as the date of about 300 B.C. is supported by Shamasastry[4] and others.

A full text of the treatise was not available until a palm leaf in the *grantha* script along with a fragment of an old commentary by Bhattasvamin came into the hands of R. Shamasastry of Mysore in 1904.[5] He published not only the text in 1909 and an English translation in 1915 but also an index verborum in three volumes listing the occurrence of every word in the text.[6] In addition, there is a complete Sanskrit commentary by T. Ganapati Sastri, German translation with voluminous notes by J.J. Meyer, Russian translation as well as translations in many Indian languages.[7] R.P. Kangle of the University of Bombay devoted many years of painstaking scholarship comparing the various texts and translations.

Of the fifteen *adhikaranas* or books into which *Arthashastra* is divided,[8] the books relating to the pattern of public administration are four - first, second, fifth and sixth. Half of *Arthashastra* is devoted to strategies and tactics of foreign policy and defense. The second book entitled 'The Duties of Government Superintendents' deals with the departments. But a consideration of the machinery of government would be incomplete if portions in the first book regarding the relations of the king with the ministers, spies, envoys, and princes are not taken into account. Various aspects of personnel were dealt in *Arthashastra*, but higher personnel got more attention than the lower ones. The focus of attention was the King. Every member of the staff is considered not in isolation but as far as his behaviour affects the King and his domain. The qualitative aspect of the personnel is treated in minutest detail. This is obvious because in the absence of written and fixed rules relating to the various constituents of administrative machinery and personnel and prevalence of unstable political conditions, the character and the very existence of the government in Kautilya's times depended on the qualities of the King and the personnel assisting and supporting him.

Nature of State

The state of 'nature' is imagined to be one of total anarchy, in which 'might was right'. When people were oppressed by *matsyanyaya*, the law of the fish, according to which the bigger fish swallows the smaller ones; they selected Manu – son of Vivasvat – the king[9]. It was settled that the king should receive one-sixth of the grain, and one tenth of merchandise and gold, as his due[10]. It was the revenue which made it possible for the king to ensure the security and prosperity of his subjects. People agreed to pay taxes and be ruled by one person in order that they might be able to enjoy well-being and security. In Kautilya's *Arthashastra*, there is no explicit theory of social contract as laid down by the contractualists. Neither does Kautilya use the contract to make the king all powerful.

Since Manu was the son of Vivasvat, that is the Sun, the ruler was thought of as a descendent of God. Kautilya attaches an element of divinity to the king when he says: "Divine punishment also falls on those who treat kings with disrespect". A king, according to him, is able to grant favours like Indra and inflict punishment like Yama. Monarchy, rule by a single individual, is tacitly assumed to be the accepted norm. There is no reference to the election of a king. Kautilya also refers to some other forms of government, such as *Dvairajya*, which is a joint rule over the whole kingdom by the males of the same family and *Vairajya*, rule by a foreign ruler who seized the kingdom by force and ousted the legitimate ruler. Kautilya disapproves the latter form of government because a foreign ruler would have no genuine interest in the welfare of the conquered state and is likely to deplete it of its resources.

Nature of Duties

The *Arthashastra* brings out that an administrator must possess the knowledge of the science of Public Administration. According to Kautilya, an administrator can be an adept in the art of Public Administration only if he is conversant with the science of Public Administration. The proficiency in the science of Public Administration is enjoined on almost all the important dignitaries in the government such as the King, the crown-prince, the priest, the ministers, etc. Thus a prince is asked by Kautilya to study the sciences and to strictly observe their precepts under the authority of specialist teachers. The high priest, according to Kautilya, should be well versed in the science of government. About the ministers, Kautilya says that whoever is not well versed in science of government should be unfit to hear the council deliberations. An erring King, who is bent upon doing what is against the science, Kautilya insists, brings about destruction to himself and his kingdom by maladministration. Thus Kautilya exhorts a prince to study the science of *Artha* (economics) under government superintendents and the science of *Dandaniti* (the science of government) under theoretical and practical politicians. For the same purpose, he advises that when a prince possesses good and amiable qualities, he might be made the commander-in-chief or installed as heir apparent.

The crown prince is bestowed by some scholars with the membership of the inner cabinet of the King. With regard to the art of Public Administration two things are worth being noted. Kautilya does not say anything about proficiency in the art of Public Administration in the case of lower personnel below superintendents of departments. And secondly, knowledge of the art of Public Administration on the part of the King, according to *Arthashastra*, includes mastery of many more things, such as the system of espionage. The more the concentration of power, the more responsibility it entails. However, even a powerful king cannot run the state alone. The presence of certain elements is essential to make a state. These things are detailed in the well-known doctrine of *seven prakritis* or the *saptanga theory*. No ruler, however competent or powerful, can run the state alone. The *Arthashastra* says [11] "one wheel alone does not turn and keep the cart in motion".

Saptanga Theory

Kautilya enumerates seven *prakritis* or essential organs of the state[12]. They are *Swamin, Amatya, Janapada, Durga, Kosha, Danda* and *Mitra*.

The Swamin, or the Ruler

Kautilya gives extensive powers to the king and attaches an element of divinity. His foremost duty is protection of the subjects and their property. This is called as *rakshana* or *palana*. Protection is from both, natural calamities and anti-social elements. He is also to ensure their *Yogakshema*. *Yoga* refers to the successful accomplishment of an object while *kshema* refers to the peaceful employment of that object[13]. Yogakshema is a broad term implying the idea of welfare, well-being, prosperity and happiness. The text asserts[14]: "in the happiness of the subjects lie the happiness of king and in what is beneficial to the subjects, lies his own benefit". The king was expected to take an active part in war and the administration of justice. Appointments to the most important offices were made by him and he often laid down the broad lines of policy and issued codes of regulation, *dharmaniyama*, for the guidance of his officers and the people.

The Amatya, or the Minister

The Prime Minister and the High Priest are the most important ministers. With one or two additions they might form an inner cabinet. It is they who assist the King to examine the character of ministers appointed in government departments. The qualities of the High Priest are described thus: "He whose family and character are highly spoken of, who is well educated in the Vedas and the six Angas, is skillful in reading portents, providential or accidental, is well versed in the science of government, and who is obedient and who can prevent calamities, providential or human, by performing such expiatory rites as are prescribed in the *Arthashastra*, the King shall employ as high priest. As a student his teacher, a son his father, and a servant his master, the king shall follow him." Those whose character has been tested under all kinds of allurements are to be employed as prime ministers. In times of emergency, Kautilya asks the King to consult the members of wider council, wider than the body of ministers. This larger council is called Council of Ministers and body of ministers is known as Inner Cabinet. The important ministers in *Arthashastra* include the sacrificial priest, the teacher, the prime minister, the high priest, the commander of the Army, Chamberlain or Treasurer-General, and the Collector-General.

The Janapada or Population

In the analysis of Kautilya, citizens are not referred to directly. Their existence is to be understood by implication in the reference to the *janapada*. Kautilya says that the population should be prosperous enough to be able to pay taxes, should be loyal and should habitually follow the orders of the king. He goes on to say that the territory should have the best of natural resources [15] and neighbouring states should not be allowed to become very powerful.

The Durga or the Fortified Capital

The *durga* is as important as the *janapada* and is the symbol of the defensive and offensive capacity of the state. It should be fortified totally and must contain all facilities for the army. Kautilya describes four types of forts: *Audik* which is surrounded on all sides by water, *Parvat* which is in the centre of hills, *Dhanvan* which lies in a desert, and *Van Durga* which is situated in a forest[16].

The Kosha or the Treasury

The state treasury should be a permanent source of revenue for the state. The king is advised to take one-sixth part of the produced and there must be sufficient currency and valuable minerals like gold. The money in the treasury must be collected by just means and must be sufficient enough to let the state survive on it for a long time. It was not the personal treasury of the king. Each gift given to the king had to be entered in a record book.[17]

The Danda or the Army

The king should have at his command a strong military force. The army ought to be well-versed in military arts, be loyal and patriotic. A contented army, according to *Arthashastra*, is the key to the king's success.[18] Therefore, the king should cater to its needs properly. He considers the Kshatriyas as best suited for martial activities but, in case of emergencies, the *Shudras* and the *Vaishyas* could also be drawn. The head of defense department seem to be the *Senapati*. The *Senapati* is not the commander. Under him there are two branches, one in charge of actual defense forces controlling strategy and tactics on the field, and the other in charge of supplies. To the former branch belong the commander, the chief constable in charge of infantry, the chiefs of elephants, cavalry and chariots, charioteers, physicians of the army, and trainers of horses. The latter branch consists of the superintendents of infantry, cavalry, chariots and elephants, and guards of elephant forests.

The Mitra or Ally and Friend

Allies are valuable to the ruler in times of need. Allies should be made on a permanent basis and these should be chosen as friends with whom the possibilities of breaking off of relations are the lowest. The ally is, however, the ruler of another state and, therefore, does not form part of another state's internal organisation. All these are mentioned in connection with the foreign relations as explained in the *Arthashastra*. Transmission, maintenance of treaties, issue of ultimatum, gaining of friends, intrigue, sowing dissension among friends, fetching secret forces, breaking of treaties of peace, etc., are detailed in *Arthashastra* from the point of view of advancing the war-and-peace policy of the country rather than of advancing the economic interests.

Principles of Public Administration

The principles of public administration, that regulate the working of the machinery of government, can be grouped in two sets: firstly, principles of authority, obedience and discipline, of duty and interest, and of responsibility; and secondly, the principles of division of labour, of coordination, of separation, of speciality, of hierarchy, and of equity. The first set of principles embodies the essential attribute of the State, namely sovereignty. The second set of principles governs the actual methods of work of the administration. Both these sets of principles are found in *Arthashastra*. The former set is more explicitly stated than the latter.

The principles of authority,[19] obedience and discipline sum up the essence of the State according to the legalistic theory. The importance of these twin principles is expressed very graphically in *Arthashastra*. The passage runs as follows, "But when the law of punishment is kept in abeyance, it gives rise to such disorder as is implied in the proverb of fishes; for in the absence of magistrate, the strong will swallow the weak; but under his protection the weak resist the strong. Thus people consisting of four castes and four orders of religious life, when governed by the king with his scepter, will keep to their respective paths, ever devotedly adhering to their respective duties and occupations". From another passage, it would be clear that *Arthashastra* does not believe in the efficacy of the principles of authority and of obedience and discipline alone. Kautilya mellows these principles by laying stress on the principles of duty and interest and of responsibility. He abhors both severe and mild punishments. "But whoever imposes punishment as deserved becomes respectable. For, punishment[20] when awarded with due consideration, makes the people devoted to righteousness and to works productive of wealth and enjoyment, while punishments, when ill-rewarded under the influence of greed and anger or owing to ignorance," avers Kautilya," excites fury even among hermits and ascetics dwelling in forests, not to speak of householders."

Kautilya identifies five elements of administration[21] viz., the means of starting undertakings; the excellence of men and materials; appointment of place and time; provision against failure; and accomplishment of the work. The first concern of the King is his own personal safety, because on that depends thorough exercise of authority and the obedience of that authority on the part of the people. "Just as he attends to the personal safety of others through the agency of spies"[22], states Kautilya, "so a wise king shall also take care to secure his person from external dangers." And hence the wide prevalence of the system of espionage, not merely for the purpose of security of the King's person, but also for the purpose of maintaining security, integrity and stability of administration against the dangers of internal dissension and corruption and external aggression. No person including the highest government officer is immune from detection by spies. That the unity, stability, and independence of command are ensured in the kingdom is evident from many precautions prescribed in the *Arthashastra*. The unity of command [23] and direction is maintained because of the King's authority. All members of the bureaucracy derive their authority from the King, stand before the people as representatives of royal authority, and are ultimately responsible to the King. This is evident from the reference in *Arthashastra* to the enforcement, of orders, the sending of writs and the procedure of forming royal writes. As for the stability of command, Kautilya writes: "A royal father who is the prop for many (people) shall be favourably disposed towards his son. Except in dangers sovereignty may (sometimes) be the property of a clan; for the corporation of clans is invincible in its nature, and being free from the calamities of anarchy, can have a permanent existence on earth." On the King's demise, Kautilya does not favour usurpation of royal power by the minister, so he attaches much importance to the stability of royal command.

Fear, duty and interest, are among a number of motives behind the act of obedience for the orders of administration can be traced to *Arthashastra*. The motive of fear is expressed in the *Arthashastra* in the following words: "...the life of a man under the service of a king is aptly compared to life in fire; whereas, fire burns a part of the whole body, if at all, the King has power either to destroy or to advance the whole family, consisting of sons and wives of the servants." To emphasise the motive of duty Kautilya refers to the injunctions of the triple Vedas, which if observed by the world, would bring about progress. Kautilya brings out how, for carrying out orders of administration, cooperation of the people as well as of the bureaucracy is required. He points out many ways to make people and bureaucracy interested in carrying out orders of the administration.

The purpose of *danda*, the symbol of authority, is to make people devoted to righteousness and to works productive of wealth and enjoyments. This, the government of Kautilya's conception tries to achieve, by giving positive financial help to the needy and the distressed, as also by ensuring just treatment to the people in financial, economic, judicial, and other administrative matters by actively participating in or regulating activities in economic and other spheres. Government servants are to be enthused, according to Kautilya, to actively help the administration in carrying out orders by granting them promotion in salary, pension, financial and other kinds of help when needed, agricultural lands, and also by making them permanent in service. Authority is obeyed by the people on account of sanctions behind orders, position of the officer concerned who issues authority, and qualities possessed by the officer concerned. Kautilya prescribes a series of punishments for a number of offences committed both by people and the government servants. Qualities of the personnel are stressed at a number of places by

Kautilya. He lays down a series of qualities, differing in number and order, for officers holding different positions of responsibility. Kautilya mentions the principle of responsibility not only in the case of the king but also of the government officers.

The second set of principles is embodied in the machinery of the administration. The full import of this group of principles is not clear in *Arthashastra* in so far as some of the links between the different parts of government machinery are not joined. This is illustrated in a subsequent paragraph dealing with the machinery of government in the *Arthashastra*. The principle of division of labour is basic for the proper and efficient working of the machinery of the government. This is clearly brought out in the *Arthashastra* while elaborating the scheme of government. "Sovereignty is possible only with assistance. A single wheel can never move." Hence, tells Kautilya, "he shall employ ministers, and hear their opinion." The principle of coordination automatically evolves out of the principle of division of labour. Unless coordination is effected between the parts divided for the sake of efficiency and smooth working, division of labour would be futile. The application of these twin principles starts in the *Arthashastra* obviously at the level of the council of ministers. The principles of division of labour and coordination are affected at several levels of the hierarchy of government. The principle of hierarchy is followed to make coordination and execution possible. Authority would be frittered away if it is not channelised through hierarchical organisation and if it does not infiltrate down to the final stage of execution unimpaired and intact.

Machinery of Government

Some of the officers mentioned in the *Arthashastra* are directly under the King, while others are controlled by the King indirectly through higher officials. The King is the supreme executive of the land. The ministers are selected, not elected, by the King on the basis of their qualities. The ministers, in reality the highest officers directly under the King, are individually and collectively responsible to the King. The ministerial officer pertaining to a subject deals with administration of that subject, and as such is more competent than other ministerial officers, to contribute to the deliberations on his subject in the council of ministers. But Kautilya says[24], "These ministers shall have to consider all that concerns the parties of both the King and his enemy."

The *Arthashastra* catalogues a phalanx of officers, called superintendents, lower in importance than the ministerial officers and much below them, belonging to the sixth order, according to remuneration. They are not heads of departments. The superintendents might be regarded as chiefs of sections dealing with various economic and other activities of the government. Most of these sections are the modern business departments. A dual control is exercised over the superintendents. As far as control of the services of the personnel and collection of revenue are concerned, they are under the Collector-General. But in the matter of supply of produced and collected commodities and articles, they are responsible to the Treasurer-General. And there is the third control, that of the King, to which all offices are ultimately subject. The superintendents are helped by 'experts' in technical matters.

The division of departments is made according to the services required by the people and discharged by the government. Only in one case a separate section dealing with a class of persons seems to have been organised. The superintendent of prostitutes secures information from them regarding their earnings, inheritance, income and expenditure, collects fees from them, employs them in royal court, and regulates their relations with paramours and others.

Another instance where sections are organised on the basis of classes of animals is Superintendents and Chief of horses, chariots, and elephants. But these sections are organised on the basis of divisions of the army, and for efficient working of defense forces. The superintendent of cows, along with the officer in charge of rearing of animals, forms the department of animal husbandry and acts as an adjunct to the department of agriculture. The different functions of government seem to have been arranged horizontally. The department of revenue in the charge of the Collector-General and the City-Superintendent is a prominent example of vertical arrangement. Under the Collector-General are the commissioner, the district officer, and the circle officer-in-charge of a division, a district and a circle of villages, respectively. Under the City-Superintendent are the district officer in charge of a ward, one circle officer in charge of ward and the other in charge of a group of families. Whether the district officer and the circle officer are officers mainly representing the local government is not very clear. Kautilya does not mention them as representatives of the village and municipal governments. So the question whether *Arthashastra* prescribes territorial arrangement of functions is not very clear and cannot be answered definitely.

Important Officers of the State

Kautilya categorises the *amatyas, mantrins* and heads of departments into 18 *tirthas*. They are[25]:

1.	*Mantrin*	—	Minister/Counsellor
2.	*Purohita*	—	Priest
3.	*Senapati*	—	Commander of the Army
4.	*Yuvaraja*	—	Prince
5.	*Dauvarika*	—	Chief of Palace Attendants
6.	*Antarvamsika*	—	Chief of the King's Guards
7.	*Prasastr*	—	Magistrate
8.	*Samahartr*	—	Collector-General
9.	*Samnidhatr*	—	Chief Treasurer
10.	*Pradestr*	—	Commissioner
11.	*Nayak*	—	Town Guard
12.	*Paur*	—	Chief of the Town
13.	*Karmanta*	—	Superintendent of Mines
14.	*Mantrin-Parishad Adhyaksa*	—	Chief of the Council of Ministers
15.	*Dandpala*	—	Officer of the Army Department
16.	*Durgapal*	—	Guardian of the Forts
17.	*Antapala*	—	Office-in-charge, Boundaries
18.	*Ativahika*	—	Officer-in-charge, Forests

Financial Administration

The finance department consists of three officers[26] - the Collector-General of ministerial level in charge of revenue collection; the Treasurer - General of ministerial level in charge of treasury in the broad sense of the term consisting of treasurer-house, trading-house, storehouse of grains, storehouse of forest produce, armory and jail; and the Superintendent of Accounts much below ministerial level according to remuneration. These three departments are in a sense interdependent. But, as noted earlier, the Collector-General and the Treasurer-General are independent, the former controlling revenue collection and the latter controlling supplies of expenditure. Both exercise authority over superintendents of several sections. Kautilya's advice to the Treasurer-General is that he should attend to the business of revenue collection as it appears confusing. Revenue collection is looked after by the Collector-General. How is it that the same function is controlled by the two officers of the same level when already both of them are told to be in charge of separate functions? It seems Kautilya means 'Custody and Preservation of Revenue' when he uses the term 'revenue collection' with reference to the duty of the Treasure-General. The Superintendent of Accounts seems to be under the Collector-General. The examination of accounts is stated as one of the duties of the Collector-General and these accounts are receipts, expenditure and not balance. The district accountants who are asked to present themselves with sealed books, commodities and net revenues before the superintendent of accounts, seem to be district officers (or officers directly under district officers) under the Collector-General, or they might be separate accountants. The central accounts pertain not only to those submitted by district accounts, but they are also classified on the basis of works in hand, works accomplished and of work partly in hand. Both the accounts and audit are looked after by the superintendent of accounts, so there is no strict separation of audit from accounts although Kautilya lays down a separate audit procedure.

The King is asked to personally attend to the accounts of receipts and expenditure. He is expected to hear the narrative of the actual accounts pertaining to each department from the ministers in a council meeting. The Superintendents dealing in business activities are subject to the dual control of the Collector-General and the Treasurer-General and they include Superintendents of treasury, manufactories, mines, of metals, mint, ocean mines, salt, forest produce, gold, storehouse, and weaving. The superintendent of manufactories is given twelve times the remuneration secured by other superintendents. There are some other superintendents but they are treated under other departments. Of all the departments, the description in *Arthashastra* of the finance department consisting of three main officers is the most satisfactory.

The finance department, although a basic department, includes a number of business activities, according to *Arthashastra*. These business departments might be classified under the departments concerned with economic protection. The government of Kautilya's conception is engaged in a number of social welfare activities. It might be noted that in those days, when Kautilya wrote *Arthashastra*, social welfare was primarily the concern of religious corporations, villages and municipal communities, craft guilds and caste assemblies. Chapter I of Book II details many activities of social welfare in which the government ought to take interest. For example, Kautilya writes that those who do not head the claims of their slaves, hirelings, and relatives should be taught their duty, and the King should provide the orphans, aged, infirm, afflicted, and helpless with maintenance and should also provide subsistence to helpless pregnant women and also to the children they give birth to. In granting lands, exempting from duties, the government is exhorted by *Arthashastra* to look to social justice.

Home Department

The home department includes the Prime Minister, Doorkeeper, Superintendent of Harem, all of ministerial level, the Superintendent of Country Parts and that of boundaries, both belonging to the next order below the ministers mentioned above; and the Superintendent of Passports and that of pasture lands both of seventh order according to remuneration (getting 1,000 panas per annum). The Collector-General, like the District Collector under British regime and even today, also discharges magisterial function. The duty of a minister as specifically handling the home portfolio is not mentioned in the *Arthashastra*. Nor are his relations with other officers mentioned above related. The Doorkeeper and the Superintendent of Harem attend to the personal security, safety, and happiness of the King. They might be said to look after the King's personal establishment.

The Superintendents of Country and of Boundaries look after defense affairs. The Superintendents of Passes issues passes to those who want to leave or enter the country, as such he also controls the movement of aliens into and out of the country. The Superintendent of Pasturelands examines passes, protects forests, arrests thieves to secure safety of traffic, protects cows and also keeps roads in repair. The last duty does not strictly come under the home department. Besides the Superintendent of Laws, there seems to be a department of justice. The *Arthashastra* is silent as to whether the department of justice is under a minister.

Justice

The preponderance of administrative courts, consisting of three persons proficient in *dharmashastra* and three ministerial officers in the administration of law, is evident. There is a hierarchy of courts from the court of a group of ten villages rising up to the King's court. Whether the King personally or the Chief Judge presides over the Supreme Court is not clear in the *Arthashastra*. The regulation of liquor traffic is the function of the Superintendent of Liquor. Cases regarding slave traffic fall within the jurisdiction of courts of law. The spies are the most important field agency coming under the home department, in the special care of the King. The King is under an obligation to observe and carry out injunctions about social and economic justice in dharmashastras and customs among the people. The courts of law are, for example, to deal with cases of labourers, slaves and guilds. The departments in charge of the superintendents of a slaughter-house, prostitutes, liquor, and weaving are social welfare departments.

Wages and Salaries

According to the *Arthashastra* the more responsible the office is, the more numerous and the higher are the qualities required of that officer. According to remuneration, there are more than seven rungs of officers one below another, the highest officer, drawing 4800 panas per annum, and the lowest, less than 1,000 panas per annum. The *Arthashastra* is not clear about the relationships between different officers. The principle of equity also suffers from clarity on the same score. The machinery of administration in the *Arthashastra* also suffers from haziness in certain respects. The first characteristic of the machinery of government in the *Arthashastra* is worth noting is that we do not come across well-defined departments of administration as such. The division of the functions of government in different departments is a comparatively recent process.

Recruitment and Training

The *Arthashastra* prescribes certain tests before assigning critical responsibilities to the administrators. They relate to testing technical competence; intelligence, perseverance and dexterity; eloquence, boldness and presence of mind; ability to bear troubles during emergencies; uprightness, friendliness and firmness of devotion in dealing with others and strength of character.[27] According to the *Arthashastra*, recruitment of those getting 1,000 panas per annum and above seems to be made by the King, assisted by the higher priest and the prime minister. Superintendents are given the power to regulate the salaries, wages, transfer and appointments of the personnel under him getting 100 or 1,000 panas per annum. There is no reference in the *Arthashastra* to the training after recruitment except in the case of men in the army. There are no definite rules of promotion. But the *Arthashastra* suggests that the government servants who increase revenue and serve loyally should be made permanent, and that the King should increase the subsistence and wages of the servants in consideration of their learning and work. Transfer of personnel is suggested as a precaution and a remedy against misappropriation of government money.

Kautilya prescribes that there should be no transfer of officers employed in guarding royal buildings, forts and country parts. So it implies that transfers are made of other servants. No leave is allowed by Kautilya. If a government servant absents himself from work, his dependents that stand as sureties are asked to bear the loss to the government caused by absence. Every government servant is subject to punishment if he is found corrupt, slack or harassing the people. No rules about superannuation are given in the *Arthashastra*. Pensions to sons and wives of those servants, who die in harness, and so also to infants, aged and diseased persons related to diseased servants, are allowed. But no rule about pension to the servant after retirement is laid down by Kautilya. The king is requested to grant special presents to servants on funerals, sickness, and child birth. A code of conduct for government servants is specified in the *Arthashastra*.

Other Aspects of Public Administration

The reference to writs and letters in the Chapter on 'The Business of Council Meeting' (Book I, Chapter XV) brings out the development of 'written word' and its importance in public administration in Kautilya's times. A separate chapter (Book II, Chapter X) deals with the 'The Procedure of Forming Royal Writs'. The 'spoken word' retains its pre-eminence in the *Arthashastra*. Chapter VII of Book II on 'The Business of Keeping Up Accounts in the Office of Accountants' refers to 'shelves of accounts books', 'scaled books', – 'regulated form of writing accounts', and emphasis on documentation. The *Arthashastra* does not refer to a separate section of documents. The importance of statistics in administration was realised by Kautilya. The district officers and circle officers are asked to collect a variety of statistics regarding lands and other property, families, and persons. The collection and use of statistics in departments other than finance is not insisted upon, nor can he hit upon a central statistical organisation, because that is a very recent development.

In his description of business departments, Kautliya draws attention to the laws of supply and demand and to other business methods. Finance being a vital matter to Kautilya, it is proper that he pays adequate attention to the use of business methods in public administration. He decries decrease of expenditure on 'profitable works'. He advocates frequent meetings between the King and members of public as he is alive to the evils of bureaucratisation. Against corruption in administration he has devised punishments and checks. There are references to administrative architecture in the context of the construction of harem (Book I, Chapter XX), and of buildings in forts (Book II, Chapter IV). But from them we do not get a definite idea about the location and the architecture of administrative buildings. In Chapter VII of Book II, Kautilya writes that superintendents of accounts should have the accountants' office constructed with its door facing either the north or the east, with seats (clerks) kept apart and with shelves of account books well arranged. That shows that he realised the significance of administrative architecture in public administration.

Relationship between Organs of State

What are the relations between the administration on the one hand, and legislature, the judiciary, the executive, and the public, on the other, as envisaged in the *Arthashastra*? There was no legislature as such. The body remotely resembling the legislature is the Council of State. The ministers are included in that body. In an emergency, its meeting is to be called and decisions taken by the majority. The question whether the Council of State possesses the power to sit in judgment on the policies and actions of ministers was not discussed in the *Arthashastra*. The body of ministers is not a cabinet in the sense that it is elected by and responsible to the Council of State; their responsibility, collective and individual, is towards the King as the supreme executive. The judges are not independent of the executive. They are appointed by the King, controlled and removed from work if found unjust, slack, and corrupt, by the Collector-General. In the administration of justice they are not independent of the influence of the executive, because ministerial officers sit jointly with persons well-versed in *dharmashastra* as judges. The Government servants do not seem to come within the purview of courts of law if they violate rules in administration. For breach of law in their private conduct they can of course be tried by courts of law. The members of the administration have no rights as such against the executive, so the executive can treat them in any way it likes and remove them, if it thinks fit to do so.

An Evaluation

Kautilya's *Arthashastra* is a treatise concerned with political science and public administration as much as it is with statecraft, economy and diplomacy. It is written with the practical aim of showing how the government ought to be run. It is also a highly polemical discourse that has astonished scholars, particularly on the themes of violence, conspiracies, espionage, etc. From that point of view, it is highly embarrassing to put forth the *Arthashastra* as the symbol of Indian political thought together with what Greece has to offer by way of Plato's *Republic* and *Laws*, and Aristotle's *Politics*. However, the fact remains that Kautilya recommended such measures only against enemies and traitors in emergencies. His proposition was that politics and ethics do not mix easily. That does not mean that Kautilya disregarded ethics or morality. What he meant was that there is a difference between individual and public morality. Kautilya made no serious attempt at theory building. At best, he described and discussed empirical reality and was normative and prescriptive in his treatment. He was keen on efficiency and rationality aspects of administration. His maxims of administration include characteristics like hierarchy, defined competence of each office, selection by merit, promotion by seniority, compensation, training and discipline. The *Arthashastra* has many insights and lessons to offer even to the present-day students and practitioners of public administration.

In Brief

Kautilya's ideas on state and statecraft can be summarised as:

- Kautilya, author of ancient Indian classic *Arthashastra*, was an Adviser and Minister to the first Mauryan Emperor Chandraguta Maurya (C321-297 BCE). Though historical veracity of *Arthashastra* is disputed, it nevertheless offers deep insights into statecraft, particularly theories and principles governing a state. It is described as a manual on statecraft.
- In *Arthashastra* the focus was the king who was thought to be the descendent of God and Kautilya attaches an element of divinity to the king. Monarchy, rule by an individual, was considered as a desirable form of government. Kautilya justified absolute powers to the monarch.

- Kautilya enumerates seven prakritis or essential organs of the state, viz., Swamin (the ruler); Amartya (the minister); Janapada (people); Durga (fortified capital); Kosha (the treasury); Danda (the army); and Mitra (ally). He considered that no state is complete without these elements and described in detail the role and nature of each of these elements of state.

- Kautilya elaborated the principles of administration governing the activities of various elements of state and considered it necessary to everyone associated with state activities to possess the knowledge of science of public administration.

- Various aspects of personnel were dealt in the *Arthashastra*. Fear, duty and interest were considered as main motivators of employee behaviour. The *Arthashastra* prescribes regulations for the recruitment of officials and their salary. Loyalty to king is the important requirement in all the appointments. Realising the difficulty to detect the official's dishonesty, Kautilya elaborated on the methods of corruption and also prescribed an elaborate system of espionage and punishment.

- Kautilya elaborated on the organisation of government and categorised them into 18 Thirthas or units. The division of departments is made according to the services required by the people and discharged by the government. The organisation principles and functions of all the 18 Thirthas were discussed in detail.

- The *Arthashastra* provides philosophical foundations of monarchical form of government and the decisive role of the monarch in administration. The text asserts: "In the happiness of his subjects lies the happiness of king and in what is beneficial to the subjects lies his own benefit".

- Kautilya's approach of ends justifying means and absolute powers to the monarch were criticised as non-relevant ideas to modern democratic states. His views are compared by many to Machiavelli's *The Prince*.

- The paradox of Kautilya's philosophy is that some of his ideas are publicly criticised and privately practiced. Kautilya is alternatively condemned for his ruthlessness and trickery and praised for his timeless political wisdom and knowledge of human nature.

Notes and References

Parmar, A., *A Study of Kautilya's Arthashastra*, Delhi, Atma Ram & Sons, 1987.

Rangarajan, L.N.,

Rangaswami Aiyangar K.V., *Indian Cameralism*, Madras, The Adayar Library, 1949

Ray, B.N., *Tradition and Innovation in Indian Political Thought*, Delhi, Ajanta Books International, 1999.

Roger, Boesche, *The First Great Political Realist: Kautilya and His Arthashastra*, Lanham, Lexinton Books, 2003.

Sihag, B.S, "Kautilya on public goods and taxation", *History of Political Economy*, Vol. 37,No. 4, 2005, pp. 723-51.

Sihag, B.S, "Kautilya on institutions, governance, knowledge, ethical values and prosperity', *Humanomics*, Vol. 23 No. 1, 2007, p. 5.28.

Sihag, B.S, "Kautilya on economics as a separate science", *Humanomics*, Vol. 25 No. 1, 2009, pp. 8-36.

Sunil Sen Sarma, *Kautilya's Arthashastra: In the Light of Modern Science and Technology*, New Delhi, D.K.Print World , 2001.

[1] Kangle R.P., *Kautilya's Arthashastra*, New Delhi, Motilal Banarsidas, 1972.

[2] Ibid., Part-III, pp.61-98. See also http://www.newworldencyclopedia.org/entry/Arthashastra

[3] Bhashyam, A.L., *The Wonder that was India*, New York, 1954, p.79. See Trautmann, Thomas R., *The Structure and the Composition of the Kautilya's Arthashastra*, Ph.D., Thesis, University of Iowa, 1968 quoted in Rangarajan .L N., *Kautilya: The Arthashastra*, New Delhi, Penguin Books, 1992, p.19.

[4] Shamasastry, R., *Arthashastra of Kautilya*, Mysore, University of Mysore, Oriental Library Publications, 1908.

The identification of Kautilya with the Mauryan minister Chanakya would date the *Arthashastra* to the 4th century BC. Certain affinities with Smritis and references that would be anachronistic for the 4th century BC suggest assigning the *Arthashastra* to the 2nd through 4th centuries. Thomas R. Trautmann and I.W.Mabbett agree that *Arthashastra* is a composition from no earlier than 2nd century AD. Thomas Burrow goes even further and says that Chanakya and Kautilya are two different people. Seehttp://www.bhar atwiki.com/index. php?title=Arthashastra

[5] Rangarajan, L.N.,op.cit. p 21.

[6] Shamasastry, R., op.cit. Later references to *Arthashastra* are to this book.

[7] Rangarajan, L N., op.cit. p.21.

[8] The *Arthashastra* is mainly in prose in sutra form, with 380 *slokas*. The actual number of sutras and shlokas in Kangle's edition is 5,348. Rangarajan L N., op.cit. p.22.

[9] Beni Prasad, *Theory of Government in Ancient India*, Allahabad, Central Book Depot, 1968, p. 95 (Ph.D., Thesis approved by University of London in 1924).

[10] Ibid.,

[11] Book I, Chapter 7.

[12] Book VII, For details see Beni Prasad, op.cit., p.147

[13] Book I, Chapter 9.

[14] Ibid.,

[15] Book VII, Chapter 5.

[16] Ibid.

[17] Ibid..

[18] Ibid..

[19] Book I, Chapter 4

[20] Ibid.,

[21] Book I, Chapter 15

[22] Book I, Chapter 4 .

[23] Book I, Chapter 21

[24] Book I, Chapter 24

[25] Book V, Chapter 6.

[26] Book II, Chapter 19

[27] Book 1, Chapter 9

3

WOODROW WILSON

D. Ravindra Prasad
P. Satyanarayana

Introduction

The intellectual roots of 'Public Administration as a Discipline' are traced to the pioneering contributions made by Woodrow Wilson in the 1880's. Wilson, through his famous essay, 'The Study of Administration',[1] stimulated interest in and stressed the need for a scientific study of administration. His essay was epochal in delineating the conduct of government as a field for analytical study and generalisation,[2] and the beginning of public administration as a subject of enquiry. Woodrow Wilson provided the rationale for public administration to be an academic discipline and professional specialty.[3] Though Wilson asserted that the aim of his work was to produce a 'semi-popular introduction to administrative studies', the essay is regarded as the beginning of public administration as a specified study.[4] A significant feature of Wilson's contribution was that he wrote the essay when he had no personal experience of American administration and his article was regarded as a 'significant trail-blazing effort'. Wilson did not follow his early success in this field either with teaching or research though his later works contained elements of his administrative thought.[5]

(1856-1924)

Life and Works

Thomas Woodrow Wilson (1856-1924) was born in Stanton, Virginia, USA, and studied politics, government and law. He went to Davidson College for a year in 1873 and later transferred to Princeton from where he graduated in 1879. After graduation, he joined the law school of the University of Virginia for a brief period and later studied on his own and passed the Georgia Bar examination. Wilson started practicing law in 1882 in Atlanta. But after a year he joined Johns Hopkins University from where he obtained a Ph.D in 1886 in history and political science. An interesting feature of his academic career is that he published his first book *Congressional Government* in his twenty-eighth year when he was in his second year of graduation at Johns Hopkins University. This book was quite independent of his studies and was used only *ex post facto* for purposes of Ph.D.[6] The dissertation brought him fame and also teaching appointment at Bryn Mawr College for Women (1885-88). He later worked at Wesleyan University (1888-90). In 1890 he joined Princeton University as Professor of Jurisprudence and Political Economy and continued there for over a decade until 1902. He was President of Princeton University between 1902-1910 and his tenure saw sweeping reforms in curriculum and administration. He revolutionised teaching, established new faculties, and played a significant role in the development of the university as a great university in the twentieth century.[7] He was elected President of the American Political Science Association in 1911. Wilson was Governor of New Jersey (1911-1913) and President of USA (1913-1921). He wrote eight books [8] and published several papers. Wilson was a recipient of the Noble Peace Prize in 1919 for his peace efforts and contribution to the formation of League of Nations.

Wilson was an outstanding professor of political science, an administrative scholar, a historian, an educationist, a reformer and a statesman. Having been deeply influenced by contemporary events, he felt that the study of administration was a possible method for correcting the political abuses of the spoils system that were so apparent in those days. While Edmund Burke was more influential than any other person in shaping Wilson's political philosophy, Walter Bagehot turned his attention to administration and comparative government. [9] It was Professor Richard T. Ely of Johns Hopkins University, however, who influenced and stimulated Wilson's interest in administrative studies. His lectures were most significant to Wilson as they stimulated him to think about assimilation of European administrative systems into American democratic polity. As Ely wrote, "When I talked of the importance of administration, I felt that I struck a spark and kindled a fire in Wilson."[10]

The Study – Three Drafts

Wilson started serious work on comparative systems of administration soon after he started teaching at Bryn Mawr in 1885. Before his seminal essay was published in the *Political Science Quarterly in* 1887, Wilson prepared *three drafts* of the same topic. The first was entitled 'Notes on Administration'; it was changed to 'The Art of Government' and finally gave the title 'The Study of Administration'.[11] A look at these three drafts would clearly indicate that there was considerable change in Wilson's ideas from draft to draft. The paper, before it was published, was presented before the Historical and Political Science Association in Ithaca, New York at the invitation of its President, Charles K. Adams of Cornell University and a former teacher of Wilson. Although Wilson thought so light of it, as hardly to merit publication, it was considered one of the best he ever wrote. According to one authority, it immediately became famous among specialists on administration and has always been a mine of wisdom.[12] In his article, Wilson outlined the history of the study, how it was a comparatively new development in political science, very cogently presented the necessity and value of the study and indicated the methods by means of which it ought to be carried on.

Administration and Government

Wilson begins his essay by introducing the reader to the general field of administration. The study of administration developed, according to Wilson, as a consequence to the increasing complexities of society, growing functions of state and growth of governments on democratic lines. This ever-growing array of functions raised the question as to 'how' and in what 'directions' these functions should be performed. Wilson suggested that there was a need to reform the government and the reforms should be in the administrative field. To Wilson, the object of administrative study is to discover what government can properly and successfully do and how it can do these things with the utmost possible efficiency and the least possible cost either of money or of energy.[13] Another object is to rescue executive methods from confusion and costliness of empirical experiment and place them upon foundations, laid deep on stable principles.[14]

Wilson considered administration as the most obvious part of government and felt that it is government in action; it is the executive, the operative, the most visible side of the government.[15] But this 'government in action', did not provoke the students of politics, and therefore, no one wrote systematically about administration as an important branch of the science of government. Before the nineteenth century, political scientists were busy writing about the constitution, nature of state, essence and seat of sovereignty, popular power and king's prerogative and the purpose of government, etc. They were mostly concerned with the problems of democracy and monarchy. The question always was 'who' should make laws and what that law should be, and the question 'how' the law should be administered with equity, speed and without friction was put aside as practical detail which 'clerks' could look after.[16]

Wilson analysed the reasons for the neglect of the study of administration. Before the nineteenth century populations were small, and therefore, the functions of government and their administration were very simple. But by the 19th century, complexities of trade and commerce, emergence of giant corporations, problems of personnel management, etc., assumed ominous proportions and the once simple functions of government had, almost in all cases, became more complex, difficult and multiplying. The very idea of state and the consequent ideal of its duty had undergone phenomenal change. The problem, therefore, was 'how' these functions should be performed by the state.

Administrative Science

Wilson strongly believed that administration is eminently a science. This is clear when he said that the science of administration is the latest fruit of the study of the science of politics. Later in his essay he says that we are having now, what we never had before, a science of administration.[17] Wilson was critical that not much scientific method was to be discerned in American administrative practice. As a matter of fact, he felt, there were no clear concepts of what constitutes good administration. This was so because administrative science was first developed in Europe by French and German academics. Consequently, administration developed to meet the requirements of compact states and centralised forms of European government. The reasons for the growth of administration on European soil, according to Wilson, are two-fold: first, as governments in European countries were independent of popular assent, there was more government; and second, the desire to keep government a monopoly made the monopolists interested in discovering the least irritating means of governing. If one wants to use the concepts of European administrative science in other countries including America, one has to radically change its aims, thoughts and principles, Wilson argued.

The slow progress in the science of administration in America was attributed to the popular sovereignty. Wilson felt that it was difficult to organise administration in a democracy than in a monarchy. For, administration has to be continuously responsive to the 'multitudinous monarch called public opinion'. Wherever public opinion is a governing principle of government, administrative reforms will always be slow because of compromises. Wilson strongly believed that unless a nation stops tinkering with the constitution, it will be very difficult to concentrate on administration. This is because no constitution can last more than ten years without changes, and therefore, the governments would always be busy with these changes and alterations, leaving little time to concentrate on details of administration. Therefore, Wilson wanted that the debate on the constitutional principles should be set aside as they are of little practical consequence, and one should try to systematically analyse and understand the 'science of administration'. Wilson aptly observed that it is more difficult to run a constitution than to frame one. He was concerned with the implementation aspects and not just the principles enunciated in the constitution or other documents.

After discussing in detail the history of the study of administration and the difficulties in its study, Wilson discusses its subject matter and characteristics. To Wilson, public administration is a detailed and systematic execution of public law. Every particular application of a general law is an act of administration. Illustrating the point, he says that the broad plans of governmental action are not administrative though the detailed execution of such plans is. The distinction is between general plans and administrative means.[18] The study of administration, viewed philosophically, writes Wilson, is closely connected with the study of the proper distribution of constitutional authority.

Politics and Administration

Wilson examines the relationship between administration and politics. His views on the subject, however, do not appear to be very clear because at some places he explains the interdependence and intimate relationship between the two. This is clear when he says that "no lines of demarcation, setting apart administrative from non-administrative functions, can be run between this and that department of government without being run uphill and down dale over dizzy heights of distinction and through dense jungles of statutory enactment, hither and thither around 'ifs' and 'buts', 'whens' and 'howevers', until they become altogether lost to the common eye." [19] Later in 1891, Wilson wrote that "no topic in the study of government can stand by itself-least of all perhaps administration whose part it is to mirror the principles of government in operation.... Administration cannot be divorced from its connections with the other branches of Public Law without being distorted and robbed of its true significance. Its foundations are those deep and permanent principles of politics."[20] From these statements, it is evident that Wilson was aware of the interdependence between politics and administration, while trying to carve out the field of public administration.

Wilson argues, at other places, that administration and politics are separate. He felt that administration lies outside the sphere of politics. Administrative questions are not political questions.[21] He further says that politics is the special province of the statesman and administration that of the technical official. Later in his essay he says that "bureaucracy can exist only where the whole service of the state is removed from the common political life of the people, its chiefs as well as its rank and file. Its motives, its objectives, its policy, its standards must be bureaucratic."[22] Thus, Wilson tries to establish a distinction between administration and politics.

From the foregoing, it appears that Wilson vacillated between separability and inseparability of administration and politics. This made the later scholars to speculate differently about his ideas and intentions on the subject. For instance, Mosher stressed that Wilson made the most vigorous statement on the politics-administration dichotomy.[23] Riggs, on the other hand, thought differently. He says that for Wilson not only politics and administration are closely intertwined, but administrative actions are scarcely conceivable except as the implementation of general policies formulated by political means. Thus Wilson was under no illusion that administrative development could take place in a political vacuum.[24] Wilson attempted to outline a coherent idea about politics and public administration and how each should be separate, and yet work together. His idea was to improve efficiency of government operations by developing an administrative system free from political interference.

Administration and Business

There are also writers who argue that to Wilson 'the field of administration is a field of business' and 'is removed from the hurry and strife of politics.' 'Administration is business and like business it does not involve itself in questions of politics...administration being removed from politics is not subject to the vagaries and vicissitudes but it goes on uninterrupted continuing the promise of the system.'[25] Buechner argues that the "basic premise of Wilson's argument was that the affairs of public administration were synonymous with those of private administration." To him, the importance of Wilson's essay lies in his argument that the study of public administration should be akin to the central concerns of business administration, namely the values of economy, efficiency, and effectiveness.[26]

Administration and Public Opinion

The relations between public opinion and administration were also examined by Wilson. The question was what part public opinion should take in the conduct of administration. To this Wilson says that public opinion takes the place of an authoritative critic. But "the problem is to make public opinion efficient without suffering it to be meddlesome." Though public criticism in the details of administration is a clumsy nuisance, as a mechanism of superintending policy it is not only beneficial but also altogether indispensable. Therefore, Wilson felt that the administrative study should find the best means for giving public criticism this control and at the same time should shut it from all interference in administration.

The Civil Service

The indispensability of a technically schooled civil service was strongly advocated by Wilson. A civil service based on merit was necessary to organise democracy. Although, Wilson believed that administrators were in principle not involved in the political process, he was strongly opposed to the creation of bureaucratic elite not subject to democratic control.[27] He felt that the civil service reform, which was then in progress in America, was only a prelude to a fuller administrative reform; "a moral preparation for what is to follow". These reforms, which were intended to make the service unpartisan, opened the way for making administration businesslike. The reforms in the methods of appointment, he said, should be extended to executive functions and to methods of executive organisation and actions. He wanted the civil service to be "cultured and self-sufficient enough to act with sense and vigour, and yet so intimately connected with the popular thought, by means of elections and constant public counsel, as to find arbitrariness or class spirit out of the question." [28] Thus Wilson, as Nicholas Henry observed, facilitated the expansion of an ethical sense of public duty beyond the conceptual confines of the civil service and into the entire intellectual terrain of public administration.[29]

Comparative Method

Wilson, in the final section of the article, examined the methods best suited for the study of administration. He rejected the philosophical method and emphasised the historical and comparative methods. He says that nowhere else in the whole field of politics, can one use these methods more safely than in the province of administration.[30] Without comparative studies in government, Wilson asserted, we cannot rid ourselves of the misconception that administration stands on a different basis in democratic and other states. One can never learn the weaknesses or virtues or peculiarities of any system without comparing it with other systems. Allaying the fears that comparative method may lead to the import of foreign systems, he says; 'If I see a murderous fellow sharpening the knife cleverly, I can borrow his ways of sharpening knife without borrowing his probable intention to commit murder with it.'[31] Wilson felt that one can learn from European autocracies, their more efficient administrative methods without importing their autocratic spirit and ends; 'indeed that we must do so if democracy is to be able to meet the challenge of chaos from within and of force from without'.[32]

There are divergent interpretations of Wilson's thinking on the important aspect of export of administrative technology from one country to another. Riggs, for example, believes that "Wilson gave his highest loyalty to democratic government and he would never have approved export of administrative technology to non-democratic countries. He would have recommended first to concentrate on political development, in the sense of promoting democratic reforms as a prelude to administrative reorganisation." Thus Riggs felt that "Wilson was quite aware of the political context of administrative reform and of development administration.[33] But Heady thinks differently. He observes that Wilson's "essay seem to assume that there is no restriction on the availability of administrative technology for export, and his attention is given exclusively to the question of the circumstances under which it should be imported."[34]

The Government – New Meaning

Wilson, we have noted earlier, did not pursue his academic interest in public administration beyond "The Study". The publication of article "The New Meaning of Government"[35] a quarter century later in 1912 in a women's magazine in the month when he was elected as president of US, however, can be considered as a significant publication in which he again reflected on governance and administration. In this very short article, he reinforces some of the ideas and conceptions articulated in "The Study" and takes some of them further as he prepares to take the reins of administration and governance of the USA. An important aspect is that he focuses more on implementation aspects of administration. In "The Study" he talks of the 'consent of the governed' but in "The New Meaning of Government" he extends the consent to the 'participation in government of all classes and interests' and disentanglement of the government from all vested interests and 'free from every kind of private and narrow control' to become responsive to genuine public opinion and develop 'the vision of the nation'.[36] He reinforces the earlier argument that the government should be thoroughly 'efficient as a successful business organisation would be.'[37] He argues that 'the law(s) should be clear, explicit, founded upon fact, unmistakable in it's command and in it's penalties' and should be changed if they are bad. He emphasises on the implementation of the laws thoroughly, intelligently, fearlessly and without reference to 'persons or interests - financial or political.'[38] Wilson argues that the government must administer resources as a 'good trustee' and as an instrument of humanity for social betterment and identifies the priority functions as food security, conservation of natural resources including rivers and forests, maintenance of health and sanitation, development of agriculture, industries, education, women and cities and he calls this 'the new meaning of government'.

An Evaluation

The publication of Woodrow Wilson's famous essay marks the birth of public administration as a self-conscious inquiry.[39] Through this essay, Wilson sought to aid the establishment of public administration as a recognised field of study.[40] Doctrine after doctrine, which public administration has accepted as valid, was first clearly enunciated by Wilson in his essay.[41] The reader, after a study of Wilson's "The Study of Administration," however, remains uncertain about its actual substance. Wilson likens administration to business methods, instituting a civil service, fixing responsible to public for action or a problem of distributing constitutional authority, which is indeed exasperating to any careful reader.[42] Wilson observes that the object of administrative study is to discover what government can properly and successfully do in the very opening paragraph of the essay. But the essay is devoted largely to the argument on the separability of politics and administration, which according to Waldo, is a serious inconsistency.[43] This led the later scholars to interpret Wilson's views in differing ways.

"The Study of Administration", as Wilson himself noted, is too general, too broad and too vague.[44] Wilson was ambivalent on many issues and he raised more questions than providing answers. He failed to amplify what the study of administration actually entailed; what the proper relationship should be between administrative and political realms and whether or not administrative study could ever become a science akin to the natural sciences.[45] This makes one to wonder whether Wilson himself was clear as to what Public Administration really is. Some researchers, however, question the assumption that Wilson was the founder of the academic study of Public Administration. Van Riper, in particular, ascribes the initial version of American administrative study to the Founding Fathers of America and relieves Wilson and his essay of any responsibility.[46]

These limitations, however, do not undermine the significance of Wilson's contribution. Judged from the standpoint of the development of Public Administration in the 19th century, his essay can certainly be termed 'seminal'. As Waldo noted his essay is "the most important document in the development of public administration." [47] Louis Brownlow observed that Wilson through his essay 'laid down as a programme of study which I think everyone in the society, every one of us who is interested in either the art or science of public administration, would do well to read again and to heed.'[48] Through his 'most distinguished' essay, Wilson not only introduced the 'idea of administration',[49] but also launched Public Administration as a generic course.[50]

In Brief

Woodrow Wilson's contribution to the field of public administration may be summarised as:

- Wilson laid the intellectual roots for the emergence of public administration as a field/ subject of enquiry through his essay "The Study of Administration" in 1887;

- "The Study of Administration" traced the history of administration as a new development in Political Science, presented the value of the study and indicated the methods by means of which it ought to be carried;

- "The Study of Administration" was the result of Wilson's search to find answers to the political abuses of the spoil system and finding ways of assimilation of European administrative systems into American democratic politics;

- He emphasised the importance of study of administration in the context of increasing complexity in society, increasing role of state and democratic nature of governments;
- Wilson considered administration eminently a science and pleaded for the development of clear concepts of good administration;
- He examined the relationship between politics and administration and considered them as separate activities at one level and interdependent at another. This vagueness lead to different interpretations of his views on politics and administration relationships;
- He focused on the implementation aspects of government and advocated the need for technically competent civil service based on merit;
- Wilson emphasised the importance of comparative method, particularly learning from others about the ways of doing things without learning their motives and ends; and
- "The Study of Administration" was too general, too broad and too vague, as Wilson himself put it. It gave scope for different interpretations of Wilson's views and also assessment of his contribution to the study of public administration. Looking in a historical context when the political debate was mainly on "who" should make laws and "what" the laws should be, his focus on "how" laws should be 'administered' is a seminal contribution.

References

1 Woodrow Wilson, "The Study of Administration", *Political Science Quarterly*, Vol. 2, (June, 1887), pp. 197-222.

2 Stone, Alice B., and Stone, Donald C., "Early Development of Education in Public Administration", in Mosher, Frederic C., (Ed.), *American Public Administration: Past, Present, Future*, Alabama, The University of Alabama Press, 1975.

3 Shafritz, Jay M., and Hyde, Albert C., *Classics of Public Administration*, Fort Worth, Harcourt Brace Publishers, 1997, p.5.

4 Ibid., p.1.

5 Turner, Henry A., "Woodrow Wilson as Administrator", *Public Administration Review*, Vol. XVI, No. 4, 1956, p. 251.

6 Buchrig, Edward H., "Woodrow Wilson to 1902: A Review Essay", *The American Political Science Review*, Vol. 67, No. 2, June 1973, p. 590.

7 Link, Arthur S., http://etcweb.princeton.edu/ C a m p u s W W W / C o m p a n i o n / wilson_woodrow.html See also http:// e n . w i k i p e d i a . o r g / w i k i / Woodrow_Wilson#Early_life. Retrieved on 3rd January, 2010.

8 The eight books are: *Congressional Government* (1885); *The State : Elements of Institutional History and Administration* (1889); *Division and Reunion (1829-1889)* (1893); *An Old Master and Other Political Essays* (1893); *Mere Literature and Other Essays* (1896); *George Washington* (1896); *A History of the American People* (1902); and *Constitutional Government in the United States* (1908). For details of the studies on Woodrow Wilson see Robert Goehlert and Dawn Childress, Woodrow Wilson – A Bibliography of Books in English, Bloomington, Indiana University, 2006. http:// /www.indiana.edu/~global/resources/ guides/WilsonGuide.pdf Retrieved on 3rd January, 2010.

9 Turner, Henry A., "Woodrow Wilson as Administrator", *Public Administration Review*, Vol. XVI, No. 4, 1956, p. 249.

10 Ely, Richard T., *Ground under our feet*, New York, Macmillan Co., 1938, p. 114 cited in Turner, Henry A., op.cit, at footnote 5.

11 For the two early drafts see Link, Arthur S., *The Papers of Woodrow Wilson*, Vol. 5, Princeton, New Jersey, Princeton University Press, 1968, pp. 43-54.

12 Bragden, Henry W., *Woodrow Wilson: The Academic Years*, Cambridge, Massachusetts, Harvard University Press, 1967, p. 154.

13 Woodrow Wilson, op.cit., p.197.

14 Ibid.

15 Ibid.,p. 198.

16 Ibid.

17 Ibid., p. 200.

18 Ibid., p. 212.

19 Ibid., p. 211.

20 See, Link, Arthur S., *The Papers of Woodrow Wilson*, Vol. 7, op. cit., p. 115.

21 Woodrow Wilson, op.cit., p. 210.
22 Ibid., p. 217.
23 Mosher, Frederic C., *Democracy and Public Service*, New York, Oxford University Press, 1968, p. 68. Quoted in Stillman, II, Richard J., " Woodrow Wilson and the Study of Administration: A New Look at an Old Essay", *American Political Science Review*, Vol. 67, No. 2, June 1973, p. 582.
24 Riggs, Fred W., "Relearning an Old Lesson: The Political Context of Development Administration", *Public Administration Review*, Vol. XXV, No. 1, March, 1965, p. 71.
25 Woodrow Wilson, op.cit., p. 209.
26 Cited in Stillman, Richard J., op.cit., p. 582.
27 *International Encyclopedia of Social Sciences*, Vol. 16, p. 557.
28 Woodrow Wislson, op.cit., p.217.
29 Henry, Nicholas, *Public Administration and Public Affairs*, Englewood Cliffs, New Jersey, Prentice Hall Inc., 1975, p.190.
30 Woodrow Wilson, op.cit., p. 219.
31 Ibid., p. 220.
32 Waldo, Dwight, (Ed.), *Ideas and Issues in Public Administration*, New York, McGraw-Hill Book Company Inc.,1953.p. 406.
33 Riggs, Fred W., op.cit., p. 79.
34 Heady, Ferrel, "Bureaucracies in developing Countries", in Fred W. Riggs, (Ed.), *Frontiers of Development Administration*, Durham, North Carolina, Duke University Press, 1971, p. 474.
35 Woodrow Wilson,"The New Meaning of Government," *Public Administration Review*, May-June, 1984, pp. 193-5.
36 Ibid.
37 Ibid.
38 Ibid.
39 Waldo, Dwight, op.cit., p. 406.
40 Ibid., p. 64.
41 Ibid.
42 Stillman, Richard J., op.cit., p. 587.
43 Waldo, Dwight, op.cit., pp. 64-65.
44 The *Papers of Woodrow Wilson*, Vol. 5, 1886-1888, op.cit., pp. 518-521.
45 Stillman, Richard J., op.cit, p. 588.
46 See Van Riper, Paul P., "The Politics-Administration Dichotomy: Concept or Reality?" in Rabin, Jack and Bowman, James S., *Politics and Administration: Woodrow Wilson and American Public Administration*, New York, Marcel Dekker Inc., 1984, pp. 203-218. See also different articles in the volume for a critical analysis of Wilson's ideas and contribution to the discipline of public administration.
47 Waldo, Dwight, *The Enterprise of Public Administration*, Novato: Chandler and Sharp, 1980, p.46.
48 Brownlow, Louis, "Woodrow Wilson and Public Administration", *Public Administration Review*, Vol.XVI. No. 2, 1956, p.81.
49 White, Leonard D., *The Republican Era*, 1889-1901, New York, Macmillan Co., 1958, p. 46.
50 Schick, Allen, "The Trauma of Politics: Public Administration in the Sixties", in Mosher, Fredrick C., (Ed.) op.cit., p.166.

4

HENRI FAYOL

C.V. Raghavulu
B.P.C. Bose

Introduction

Scores of people have contributed to the evolution of western management thought. The credit for introducing the scientific method in many spheres, including management, goes to the Greeks.[1] Frederick Taylor and Henri Fayol, however, introduced refinements to the objective type of inquiry. Henri Fayol, French practitioner and theoretician, like Taylor, contributed significantly to the corpus of management concepts and is considered the founder of the 'Management Process School'. Although scientific management was for long considered an American invention and rooted in the writings of Taylor, Fayol's writings, in fact, precede those of Taylor. [2] It is no wonder that many historians of the European management thought consider Fayol as a pioneer of scientific management. It is a pity that, just as in the case of Weber, the importance of Fayol's ideas was discovered outside Europe only after the

(1841-1925)

translation of his works into English. Henri Fayol's *Administration Industrielle et Generale* was first published in France in 1916,[3] but it did not come to light in the English-speaking countries until its English translation published in 1949 under the title *General and Industrial Management*. His work is considered a classic and a foundation in classical management theory. The book offers a theory and principles of management.[4]

Life and Works

Henri Fayol was born in Constantinople, Istanbul, Turkey in 1841, where his father was working as an engineer. He was educated at the Lycee in Lyons (France) and thereafter at the

National School of Mines - Ecole National Superieur des Mines in Saint-Etienne from where he graduated in 1860. Nineteen-year-old Fayol started his career as an engineer at the mining company Compagnie de Commentry-Fourchambeau-Decazeville. He worked as junior executive during 1860-1872, was promoted as Manager in 1872 and Managing Director of the company in 1888; a post he held for about thirty years with distinction. Fayol retired as Managing Director in 1918, having spent his entire working life with the company, he remained Director of the company until his death in December 1925, at the age of eighty-four. Fayol's efforts as the Managing Director enabled the company to rise from a position of financial disaster to that of great financial success. As Urwick observed, the success with which Fayol carried out those duties as Managing Director is 'one of the romances of French industrial history'. [5] Fayol attributed his success not to his own personal attributes, but to the system of management, which he evolved and applied with great care and imagination. Fayol was influenced by Cartesian philosophy and Adam Smith's writings. His conception of functionalism could be traced to Adam Smith's ideas on division of labour. The bulk of his management concepts, however, grew out of his reflections as an executive. On retirement he devoted time to popularise his views on management and administration and development of theoretical studies. He founded the *Centre d'Etudes Administratives* [6] which has profound influence on business, army and navy in France. At the Centre he used to chair weekly meetings of prominent industrialists, writers, officials, academics, and members of the military. He also influenced the French government to pay attention to the principles of administration. He advised the government and investigated into the workings of the Posts and Telegraphs and the Tobacco industry.

Fayol was a prolific writer on technical and scientific matters as well as on management. Apart from ten publications on mining, engineering and geology, he published as many books/papers on management. The most outstanding of his writings is his book *General and Industrial Management* first published in 1916. [7]His reputation, to a large extent, rests on this single short publication, which is still being frequently reprinted. [8] A large number of his papers are concerned with the reform of the public services. His paper on *The Theory of Administration of the State* presented to the Second International Congress of Administrative Sciences in 1923, is considered a major contribution to the theory of public administration. [9]

Terminology - Administration and Management

There has been considerable disagreement and debate on the terminology used by translators of Fayol's works; particularly his *General and Industrial Management*. Fayol used the term administration in his classic *Administration and Industrielle et Generale*. But this was translated into management, creating confusion among scholars as well as disagreement. Lyndall Urwick and Brodie argued that the term should have been translated into English as 'administration'. Brodie says that if one has to go by Storrs translation, one cannot avoid the feeling that Fayol was mostly concerned with industrial management, which would be a mistake. The better and correct term would have been 'Business and General Administration'. For, Fayol nowhere distinguished business management and public administration.[10] Wren concluded that Storrs was inaccurate in adopting the word 'management' to define the activity which Fayol called 'administration'. He was critical that Storrs introduced the idea that management is a task that is restricted to 'working with people'. Urwick in his lengthy introduction to the Storrs translation expressed disappointment for use of the word 'management' instead of 'administration'. Similar confusion exists in case of other terms as well. [11]

Administrative Theory: Universal

A widespread tendency in the English-speaking countries was to draw a distinction between management as an activity confined to conducting industrial or commercial undertakings, and public administration as the art of conducting governmental activities. Fayol in his address to the Second International Congress of Administrative Sciences (1923) argued that such a distinction between management and public administration is false and misleading. He notes:

> The meaning which I have given to the word administration and which has been generally adopted broadens considerably the field of administrative science. It embraces not only the public service but also enterprises of every size and description, of every form and every purpose. All undertakings require planning, organisation, command, coordination and control, and in order to function properly, all must observe the same general principles. We are no longer confronted with several administrative sciences, but with one, which can be applied equally well to public and to private affairs.[12]

To Fayol, the attempt to sub-divide the study of *Management or Administration* in accordance with the purpose of the activity is untenable. It is sometimes argued that this could simply mean that Fayol is concerned only with industrial management, whereas his claim to universality is categorical when he says that the "Management plays a very important part in the government undertakings, large or small, industrial, commercial, political, religious or other".[13] Indeed, in his later years he studied the problems of state public services and lectured at the *Ecole Superieure de la guerre*. It can be presumed that his intention was to initiate a theoretical analysis appropriate to a wide range of organisations.

Fayol's ideas about managerial activity are presented in the context of his writings on industrial undertakings.[14] The totality of activities of an industrial undertaking is divided into six groups viz.:

1. *Technical activities* - production, manufacture, adaptation: These are sometimes more conducive to the progress and goal attainment than other activities.
2. *Commercial activities* - buying, selling, and exchange: Knowledge of commercial activity is just as important as knowledge of efficient production. Commercial activity includes, together with acumen and decisions, a through knowledge of the market and of the strengths of the competitors, long-term foresight, the use of contracts and price regulation.
3. *Financial activities* - search for and optimum use of capital: Capital is a prerequisite for personnel, plant, raw material, expansion of the plant or machinery, reserves, etc. Proper financial management is necessary to obtain capital, to make optimum use of available funds for the success of the undertaking.
4. *Security activities* - protection of property and persons: It is necessary to safeguard the property and person's theft, fire and flood and all social disturbances including strikes.
5. *Accounting activities* - stock-taking, balance sheets, costs, and statistics: An efficient accounting system, providing an accurate idea of the organisation's financial condition, is a powerful managerial instrument.
6. *Managerial activities* - Fayol describes management as a function, a kind of activity. He is quite indifferent whether those exercising this activity are described as 'Managing Directors', or 'Supervisors', or 'Clerks'. He is connected with the function, not with the status of those who exercise it. However, he is sensitive to the fact that those holding

positions at higher level in the hierarchy would devote a larger proportion of their time to this function than employees at lower levels. Fayol classifies this key function into five main elements viz., planning, organisation, command, coordination and control.

Fayol says that irrespective of the nature of organisation – big or small, simple or complex, non-industrial or non-profit making - the six activities are always present though the importance and significance of the first five activities may vary.[15] He laments that management was not being taught and was not part of the curriculum. This was not because its importance was not recognised, but because of the absence of theory. He felt that without theory no teaching is possible.[16] His "General and Industrial Management" is an attempt to fill this gap.

Elements of Management

Fayol identified, as we have seen earlier, five elements of management viz., planning, organisation, command, coordination and control which are discussed below.

Planning

Fayol used the French term *Prevoyance* which in French means to 'foresee', to 'anticipate' and to 'make plans'. The administration's chief manifestation and most effective instrument, to Fayol, is the plan of action. Planning enables the separation of the short-run events from the long-range considerations. It endows forethought to the operations of an organisation. Fayol considers that experience is an asset in drawing a realistic plan. To him, unity, continuity, flexibility and precision are the broad features of a good plan of action.[17]

Organisation

To organise an industrial firm or a government agency is to provide it with everything required for its functioning: raw materials, tools, capitals, personnel, etc. Fayol classifies these activities into two categories: the material organisation, and the human organisation. The latter includes personnel, leadership and organisation structure. Every organisation has to perform the following managerial functions[18]:

1. Ensure that the plan is judiciously prepared and strictly carried out;
2. See that the human and material organisation is consistent with the objectives, resources and requirements of the concern;
3. Set up a single, competent, energetic guiding authority;
4. Harmonise activities and coordinate efforts;
5. Formulate clear, distinct, precise decisions;
6. Arrange for efficient selection and appropriate placement of the employees;
7. Define duties clearly;
8. Motivate employees to show initiative and demonstrate responsibility;
9. Reward employees in a fair manner for services rendered;
10. Make use of sanctions against irregular and unethical conduct;
11. Provide for the maintenance of discipline;
12. Ensure that individual interests are subordinate to the general interest;
13. Pay special attention to unit of command;
14. Supervise both material and human organisations;
15. Provide for appropriate controls; and
16. Prevent excess of regulations, red tape and paper controls.

Command

The art of command, according to Fayol, rests on certain personal qualities and knowledge of the general principles of management. Its degree of proficiency differs from unit to unit. Fayol claims that the manager who has to command should:

1. Have a thorough knowledge of his personnel;
2. Eliminate the incompetent;
3. Be well-versed in the arrangement binding the business and its employees;
4. Set a good example;
5. Conduct periodic audit of the organisation and use summary charts;
6. Bring together his chief assistants by means of conferences, at which unit of direction and focusing of effort are provided;
7. Not become engrossed in detail; and
8. Aim at making unity, energy, initiative and loyalty prevail among the personnel.[19]

Coordination

It consists of working together and 'harmonizing' all activities and efforts so as to facilitate the functioning of the organisation. Essentially, the objective of coordination is to ensure that one department's efforts are coincident with the efforts of other departments, and keeping all activities in perspective with regard to the overall aims of the organisation.[20]

Control

Its objective is to obtain conformity with the plan adopted, the instructions issued and principles established. In the process, weakness and errors have to be rectified and their recurrence prevented. For control to be effective it must be done within a reasonable time and be followed up by sanctions. He uses the term control in the wider French sense of watch, monitor, check, audit and obtains feedback.

Attributes of Manager

Fayol suggests that Managers should have the following attributes[21]:

1. *Physical* : Health, vigour and appearance.
2. *Mental* : Ability to understand and learn, judgment, mental vigour and adaptability.
3. *Moral* : Firmness and willingness to accept responsibility.
4. *General Education* : General acquaintance with matters not belonging exclusively to functions performed
5. *Special Knowledge* : Special knowledge of the functions being handled - be it technical, commercial, financial or managerial,
6. *Experience* : Knowledge arising from the work proper.

Principles of Administration

Henry Fayol states that the principles of administration/management are not rigid. On the contrary, they must be capable of adaptation to various enterprises and settings. Fayol derives fourteen principles viz.:

1. *Division of work:* Specialisation of labour produces more and better work with the same effort.

2. *Authority and responsibility*: Authority should be commensurate with responsibility. In other words, the occupant of each position should be given enough authority to carry out all the responsibilities assigned to him.

3. *Discipline*: Obedience should be observed in accordance with the standing agreements between the firm and its employees.

4. *Unity of command*: For any action, an employee should have only one boss.

5. *Unity of direction*: One head and one plan for each activity.

6. *Subordination of individual interest to general interest*: The interest of one employee or group should not prevail over that of the total organisation.

7. *Remuneration of personnel*: The remuneration paid for services rendered should be fair and afford satisfaction to both personnel and the firm.

8. *Centralisation*: The degree of initiative left to managers varies depending upon top managers, subordinates and business conditions.

9. *Scalar chain (Hierarchy)*: The line of authority of superiors ranging from the ultimate authority to the lowest ranks.

10. *Order (Placement)*: Once the basic job structure has been devised and the personnel to fill the various slots have been selected, each employee occupies that job wherein he or she can render the most effective service.

11. *Equity*: For the personnel to be encouraged to fulfill their duties with devotion and loyalty there must be equity based on kindness and justice in employer-employee relations.

12. *Stability of tenure of personnel*: Suitable conditions should be created to minimise turnover of employees.

13. *Initiative:* The ability to think afresh would act as a powerful motivator of human behaviour.

14. *Esprit de corps*: Harmony, union among the personnel of an organisation is a source of great strength in the organisation.[22]

Need for Administrative Training

Fayol is a pioneer in suggesting the need for systematic training in administration. He criticises civil engineering colleges in France for excluding administration from their syllabi. Fayol stresses on administrative training in the following words:

Everyone needs some concepts of administration; in the home, in affairs of State, the need for administrative ability is in proportion to the importance of the undertaking and for individual people the need is everywhere greater in accordance with the position occupied. Hence, there should be some generalised teaching of administration: elementary in the primary schools, somewhat wider in the post primary schools, and quite advanced in higher social educational establishments.

Fayol suggests that training is a continuous process, starting from the school and covering in-service training of the employees within an organisation. He considers every superior officer in an organisation as a teacher to his immediate subordinates.

Gangplank

The Gangplank refers to the need for 'level jumping' in a hierarchical organisation. Although Fayol places emphasis on formal organisation, he is alive to the dangers of conformity to hierarchy and formalism. 'It is an error to depart needlessly from the line of authority, but it is even greater one to keep it when detrimental to the business', asserts Fayol. He illustrates the problem with reference to the figure given below. If 'F' follows the principles of proper channel of communication, he has to send his message or file to 'P' through 'E', 'D' and so on, covering nine levels. It is, however, possible for 'F' to use 'gangplank' and avoid going through 'A' and all the other intervening layers as intermediaries. Recourse to 'gangplank' is possible only when the immediate superiors (in the case, 'E' and 'O') authorise such a relationship. Whenever a disagreement develops between 'F' and 'P', they must turn the matter to their superiors. While suggesting 'gangplank,' Fayol is rather cautious. He feels that it may be less relevant to Government agencies in which the lines of authority are less clear than in private organisations.

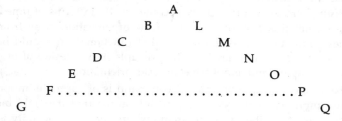

Fayol and Taylor: A Comparison

Fayol and Taylor can be considered as the pioneers of scientific management. Both were trained as engineers before they became managers. They attempted to build management theory on the basis of observation of the practical issues. The stable European pattern of life led Fayol to assume a relatively stable industrial organisation, whereas Taylor had to respond to a rapidly changing capitalist industrial organisation, in the USA. Taylor developed specific management principles to be applied directly in the field of production but Fayol dealt with a general theory of administration to be applied at the top-management level. Management was not viewed by Fayol from the perspective of workshop management as in Taylor's case, but as a universal set of principles applicable to any kind of functional and organisational setting. Despite these dissimilarities, the writings of Fayol and Taylor are essentially complementary. [23] Their ideas on management indicate the need to arrange processes, material resources and people into a structural hierarchy that is more or less permanent. This structure, in turn, provides a starting point for accomplishing organisational objectives. While their approach is fairly mechanistic, it remains a useful approach for studying organisations and their operations.[24] Consequently, contemporary thought on organisational design does not disregard the work of Fayol and Taylor. Instead, it builds on their concepts with findings from the behavioural sciences.

Criticism

'Fayolism' has been criticised on several grounds. Some argued that while devoting considerable attention to functional classification Fayol neglected the structural aspect and his treatment of the organisation was considered defective.[25] Peter Drucker, a major critic of Fayolism, observes that some of the worst mistakes of organisation-building have been committed by imposing a mechanistic model of an 'ideal' or 'universal' organisation on a living business.[26] Moreover, the fourteen principles, which Fayol lists, have a great deal of overlapping.

Functional organisation was designed by Fayol in the early years of the twentieth century. Although functionalism is empirically expedient, it is found to be deficient in design and logic. It takes a single dimension of management to determine all facets of the organisation structure around it.[27] Besides, the empirical base used by Fayol for generating a full-fledged theory of management is too narrow. Fayol proceeded to theorise functionalism on the basis of functions undertaken in a manufacturing company. It would be unrealistic to expect that the insights and derivations from the mining organisation would be equally applicable to the needs and challenges of other organisations. Mining was a fairly large business at the turn of the century, but it would be considered a small business today. Contemporary organisations are definitely larger in size and much more complex. Peter Drucker, therefore, argues that anything more complex, more dynamic, or more entrepreneurial than a typical mining firm of Fayol's time demands performance capacities which the functional principles do not possess.[28] If used beyond the limits of Fayol's model, functional structure rapidly becomes costly in terms of time and effort, and runs a high risk of misdirecting the energies of the organisation away from performance. Considering these limitations, it is imperative that functionalism should be used only as one of the several principles and never as the principle in the design of organisations that are large in size, complex and innovative in goal orientation.

To Henri Fayol the principle of unity of command is of supreme importance and 'can be violated with impunity'. Critics of the principle argue that it would be dysfunctional to the organisation to strengthen this hierarchy, where the sense of unity is less, personal contact is limited and real differences of outlook are desirable.[29] It is further suggested that the application of the principle would overwhelm the chief executive with problems of coordination.

Fayol's ideas have been criticised by critics of the classical administrative theory for their value judgments involving 'should' or 'ought' statements, for lack of a sufficient experimental basis and for their internal contradictions. Elaborating their criticisms, Barnard and Simon argue that a managerial organisation cannot be explained purely in terms of a set of principles about formal organisation structure.[30] They suggest that the actual behaviour of organisational participants departs in many ways from the behaviour that is planned. Writers of the human relations school feel that Fayol (and Taylor) have mostly ignored the social-psychological or emotional needs of the employees.

An Evaluation

Devoid of Max Weber's sweep for social science generalisations or Frederick Taylor's passion for empiricism, Henri Fayol tries to generate a theory of management that has rudiments of both. His predilection for macro-level theory building has a Weberian flavour. Indeed among the early writers on management Fayol has the unique distinction of attempting to build a universal science of management applicable to 'commerce, industry, politics, religion, war or philanthropy'.[31] Unlike other contemporary writers, Fayol wrote extensively on problems of public administration. Fayol shares Taylor's pragmatic approach in suggesting that the success of an enterprise depends upon the presentation and application of simple methods in a logical and coherent manner.[32] As Brech noted that Fayol made a systematic analysis of the process of management and administration and advocated that management can and should be taught.[33]

Fayol tried to design a rational system of organisation in which the fulfillment of the primary goal of the enterprise constitutes the basic objective. To him the enterprise justifies its existence only by meeting the primary goal of providing value in the form of goods or services to consumers. Attaining the objective permits the organisation to reward employees, managers, etc., for their contributions.[34] Fayol was a pioneer of the concept of viewing management as being made up of functions. He provided a broad and inclusive perspective of the management and developed a framework, which stimulated subsequent writers on management theory. One of the most important and interesting part of his conceptualisation is that at the higher levels the proportion of technical knowledge diminishes, but administrative skill and knowledge are of great importance.

The principles Fayol developed are widely used today in planning and developing company organisation structure.[35] Among the most widely used are 'unity of direction' (one head and one plan for each activity) and 'unity of command' (each person should have only one boss). Another principle with a high frequency of utilisation is that responsibility should be equal to authority or authority should be commensurate with responsibility. In other words, the incumbent of each position should be given sufficient authority to carry out the responsibilities assigned to him. Even Peter Drucker, a severe critic of Fayol's theory of functionalism, acknowledges that the latter's model is still unsurpassed in some respects. Fayol's functional organisation is still the best way to structure a small business; especially a small manufacturing business.[36] Max Weber considered the chain of command to be an extremely important element of the formal organisation. Fayol referred to this hierarchical structure of authority as the scalar concept and discussed its role in improving communication and decision-making.

Critics of Fayol seem to overstress the point that Fayol was oblivious of the human factor in his writings. As Albers asserts Fayol was not ignorant of the importance of the human factor.[37] He is credited to have followed a human relations approach in his dealings with employees of the French mining firm in which he was the chief executive. The following statement of Fayol indicates his awareness of the issue even at a theoretical level:

There is no limit to the number of principles of administration. Every administrative rule or device which strengthens the human part of an organisation or facilitates its working takes its place among the principles for so long as experience proves it to be worthy of this important position.[38]

Fayol's ideas concerning human relations have a broader conception than Taylor's. As Bertram Gross points out, to Fayol personnel is the essence of organisation.[39] Fayol was also careful to state that his principles should not be considered as rigid rules. This is clear when he observes:

There is nothing ...absolute in management affairs. Seldom do we have to apply the same principle twice as in identical conditions; allowance must be made for different changing circumstances.[40]

It was in this spirit, Fayol was prepared to revise his earlier views about the place of unity of command within his theory of functionalism. He was able to appreciate the criticism that functionalism posed great difficulties for the maintenance of unified control and command. Fayol clearly admitted that his own formulations could be improved upon, and that these did not represent 'one best way', which could be applied without modifications to varying organisational situations.

In Brief

Henri Fayol's contribution to the theory of public administration is as follows:

- Henri Fayol, a successful executive of a mining company in France, made significant contributions to the management concepts and is considered as the founder of "Management Process School".

- He considered management as a science which can be developed, studied and applied equally well to public and private affairs.

- He emphasised the universality of management processes and made a distinction between management and public administration.

- He identified five key elements of organisation *viz.*, planning, organisation, command, coordination and control.

- Fayol derived fourteen principles of administration which are capable of adaptation to various enterprises and settings. He emphasised the importance of training in administration.

- Although Fayol places great emphasis on formal organisation, he is alive to the limitations of hierarchy and formalism. Therefore, he suggested Gangplank – "level jumping" - in a hierarchical organisation.

- A comparison of contributions of Henri Fayol, a French manager and F.W. Taylor, an American engineer is useful to understand the complementarity of their contributions and the differences in their approach and focus. Taylor focused mainly on the management principles to be applied directly to the field of production and Fayol mainly focused on the development of general theory of administration to be applied at the top-management level.

- Fayol's theory of functionalism is criticised for its narrow focus, mechanical approach and neglect of complex factors affecting human behaviour in organisations.

- Fayol's framework of systematic analysis of administrative processes stimulated subsequent writers on administration and management. His principles of administration, in variant forms, are applied in the working of modern organisations.

Notes and References

[1] See Gager, Curtis H., "Management throughout History," in Mayward, H. B., (Ed), *Top Management Handbook*, New York, McGraw-Hill Book Company, 1960.

[2] It is important to note that while Taylor's book on *Principles of Scientific Management* was published in 1913, Fayol's major work was ready for the press in 1914, but was prolonged in its publication until 1916. A major paper by Fayol on General Principles of Administration was published as early as 1908.

[3] About 15,000 copies of the book seem to have been published by 1925 signifying the attention it attracted. See Wren, Daniel A., "The Influence of Henri Fayol on Management Theory and Education in North America", *ENTRPRISE ET HISTOIRE* ,Vol.34. No. 3,2003. p.98.

[4] Charles de Freminville published a brief but comprehensive summary of Fayols' scientific studies and an overview of his administrative ideas in Taylor Society Bulletin in 1927. This was followed by JA Coubrough's translation *Industrial and General Administration* in 1930 on the initiative of Urwick. Finally, it was Constance Storrs translation of the book under the title *General and Industrial Management* in 1949 that brought the book to the English speaking audiences and had a major impact on management education in USA. See for details Daniel A. Wren, op.cit. pp. 98-107. Storrs translated Fayol's term *administer* as *manage* in contrast to Coubrough's to administer. Urwick disagreed with the Storrs translation of administration as management but conceded that in the absence of French equivalent, the Storrs

translation was accurate and convenient. Daniel A. Wren, op.cit. p.102.

5 Urwick, Lyndall, in his 26 page foreword to the English translation of Henri Fayol's *General and Industrial Management*, London, Isaac Pitman, 1949, p. vii.

6 Breeze, John D.,"Henri Fayol's Centre for Administrative Studies," *Journal of Management History*, Vol. 1, No. 3, 1995, pp.37-62.

7 '*Administration Industrille et Generale* 'This article consists of first two of four section of what Fayol wishes to publish on administration. These two sections were later published by Dunod as a volume in 1918 in a two volume set on administration. It is this work that forms the basis of many English translations of Fayol's works. See Wood, John D. and Wood Michael D. *Henri Fayol: Critical Evaluations in Business and Management*, Vol. 2, London, Rutledge, 2002, p.18.

8 Pugh, D. S., Hickson , D. J., and Hinings, C. R., *Writers on Organisation*, Ontario, Penguin, 1976, p. 60; *The Administration Industrielle et Generale* was translated into English, Spanish, Italian, Portuguese, German, Swedish, Polish, Hebrew, Greek and other languages. Daniel Wren, op.cit. p.107.

9 For details of life, work and a critical analysis of his contribution see different articles in Wood, John D. and Wood Michael D. op.cit.

10 For details see Cuthbert, Norman, "Fayol and the Principles of Organisation" in Wood, John D. and Wood Michael D. op.cit.,pp.3-25.

11 For details see Breeze, John D., "A Discussion of the Translation of Some of Fayol's Important Concepts", in Wood, John D. & Wood Michael D., op.cit., pp.79-101.

12 Henri Fayol, "The Administrative Theory in the State," in Gulick Luther, and Urwick, L., (Eds.), *Papers in the Science of Administration*, New York, Columbia University Press, 1937.

13 Quoted in Pugh, D. S., Hickson , D. J., and Hinings, C. R., op.cit., p. 60.

14 Henri Fayol, op.cit., pp. 3-6.

15 See Sheldrake, John, *Management Theory*, London, Thomson Learning, 2003. p.46.

16 Henri Fayol, op.cit, p.14

17 Ibid., pp. 43-45.

18 Ibid., pp. 53-54.

19 Ibid., pp. 97-98.

20 Ibid., p. 103.

21 Ibid., p. 7.

22 Ibid., pp. 19-41.

23 Urwick, Lyndall, in his foreword to the English translation of Henri Fayol's *General and Industrial Management*, op.cit., p. ix.

24 Trewatha, Robert L., and Port, Gene M., Management: *Functions and Behaviour*, Business Publications Inc., Dallas, 1976, pp. 53-54.

25 Urwick, L., and. Brech, E. F. L, *The Making of Scientific Management*, Vol.I, London, Isaac Pitman, 1955, p. 43.

26 Drucker, Peter F., *Management: Tasks, Responsibilities, Practices*, London, Heineman, 1974, p. 559.

27 Ibid., pp. 551-52.

28 Ibid., p.563.

29 Albers, Henry H., *Principles of Organisation and Management*, New York, John Wiley, 1961, p. 110.

30 Barnard, Chester I., *The Functions of the Executive*, Cambridge, Mass, Harvard University Press, 1938, p. 163 and Herbert A. Simon, *Administrative Behaviour*, New York, The Free Press, 1957, Chapter II.

31 Henri Fayol, op.cit., p. 41.

32 Urwick, L., and Brech, E. F. L., op.cit.., p. 40.

33 See Brech, E. F. L., (Ed.), *The Principles and Practice of Management*, London, Longman, 1953, p.86.

34 George, Jr. C.S., *The History of Management Thought*, New Delhi, Prentice Hall, 1972, p. 114.

35 For a detailed statement see Dale, Earnest, *Readings in Management: Land Marks and New Frontiers*, New York, McGraw-Hill Book Company, 1970, pp. 146-47.

36 Drucker, Peter F., op. cit. pp. 551-52.

37 Albers, Henry H., op. cit., p. 36.

38 Henri Fayol, op. cit., p. 19.

39 Ibid.

40 Ibid.

5

FREDERICK TAYLOR

V. Bhaskara Rao

Introduction

At the turn of the twentieth century, the first ever-serious effort was made by Frederick Taylor to make researches in management of industry in the USA. He is one of the most influential persons who made very significant impact on the management science and thought. A mechanical engineer, he sought to improve industrial efficiency. He is regarded as the father of scientific management and was one of the first management consultants. Though a controversial figure in management history, he was considered as one of the intellectual leaders of efficiency movement and his ideas were highly influential. A pioneer of modern management approaches and techniques, Taylor believed that the "best management is a true science," applicable to all kinds of human activities. He believed that his principles of management are 'applicable with equal force to all social activities; to the management of homes, farms, churches, philanthropic institutions, universities, and government departments'.[1] A study of Taylor's ideas, therefore, is indispensable for everyone concerned with administration and management.[2]

(1856-1915)

Life and Works

Frederick Winslow Taylor was born in Germantown, Pennsylvania on March 20, 1856. He studied for two years in France and Germany and in 1872 entered Philips Exeter Academy at Exter, New Hampshire. Although he passed the entrance examination for Harvard Law School, he could not continue his academic pursuits because of impaired eyesight owing to too much study under kerosene light. In 1873, at the age of 18 he joined the Enterprise Hydraulic Works of Philadelphia and served as apprentice for four years without wages. In 1878, he went to work at the Midvale Steel Company as a labourer and over years was promoted as Gang-boss, Foreman, Research Director, and finally became Chief Engineer in 1884. Taylor received a master's degree in Mechanical Engineering from Stevens Institute of Technology of Hoboken, New Jersey through night study and correspondence courses which was most unusual at that time. In 1890, he became General Manager of the Manufacturing Investment Company in Philadelphia. In 1893, he started a consulting agency in Philadelphia. In 1898, Taylor joined Bethlehem Steel, where he developed high speed steel with his colleagues for which he received a gold medal at a Paris exhibition in 1900 and was awarded Elliott Cresson Gold Medal by the Franklin Institute, Philadelphia. In 1906, he was awarded the honorary Doctorate of Science by the University of Pennsylvania. He also worked as a professor at the Tuck School of Business at Dartmouth College. [3] Taylor published a large number of papers based on his studies and research and made presentations before professional bodies. [4] He invented a cutting tool, a steel hammer, hydraulic power loading machine, tool feeding mechanism and a boring and turning mill. From 1901, he devoted his time for research for improving the techniques of scientific management till his death on March 28, 1915. He became president of the American Society of Mechanical Engineers in 1906. Taylor is important and interesting not only because of his work, but also because of his personality. His passion for efficiency was boundless and his capacity for work phenomenal. His incredibly active life illustrates a remarkable character.[5]

Soldiering

Taylor believed that industrial management during his times was amateurish and felt that best results could be achieved through partnership between trained staff, qualified management and cooperative workers. He noticed a phenomenon of workers purposely operating below their capacity and called the phenomenon as 'soldiering' or 'skiving'. He attributed three reasons for this, viz.

- workers deliberately do as little as one can safely do due to the belief that if they become more productive, some of them would become surplus and would be eliminated;
- non-incentive wage systems encourage low productivity, employees take care never to work at a high pace for the fear that higher pace may become the standard as a result of which, the employees fear that their wages may come down; and
- workers waste their time and effort by relying on rule-of-thumb and unscientific methods and practices than those scientifically determined.

To counter the practice of soldiering and to improve efficiency,[6] Taylor undertook experiments to determine the best level of performance for jobs - the process of present day benchmarking - and what was necessary to achieve this level of performance. They were characterised by the use of stop-watches to time a worker's sequence of motions with the objective of determining the 'one best way to perform a job'. Taylor attracted public attention in 1880s when he reduced the number of workers shovelling coal at Bethlehem Steelworks from 500 to 140 without any loss of production.

The term 'scientific management', which is associated with Taylor, was not coined by him. It was Louis Brandies, who later became a judge of the Supreme Court, who coined the term during his arguments before the Interstate Commerce Commission in 1910. Brandies argued that the railroads could save 'a million dollars a day' by applying scientific management methods. Taylor was initially opposed to the phrase, thinking that it sounded too academic, [7] but later used it as the title of his monograph *The Principles of Scientific Management* in 1911.

Development of Scientific Management

During the latter part of the 19th century a new industrial climate began to descend upon American business giving rise to the growth of managerial class. The practices of management began to change from a day-to-day problem-solving approach to a more all-inclusive, comprehensive, long-term approach to grapple with the emerging managerial problems, which were not faced previously. Prominent leaders like Henry R. Towne and Henry Metcalf tried to develop a unified system of management and Towne called this new philosophy-science of management. Towne in 1886 presented a paper entitled "The Engineer as an Economist" to the American Society of Mechanical Engineers (ASME). Taylor, who joined the society in the same year, was inspired by Towne's ideas and directed his efforts to understand all facets of a firm and to develop scientific management. Taylor's contribution to the development of scientific management was recorded in his papers *A Piece-Rate System* (1895); *Shop Management* (1903); *The Art of Cutting Metals* (1906) and *The Principles of Scientific Management* (1911). [8]

Taylor's first paper, *A Piece-Rate System* was considered as an outstanding contribution to the principles of wage administration. He proposed a new system consisting of three parts: (a) observation and analysis of work through time study to set the 'rate' or standard, (b) a 'differential rate' system of piece work, and (c) 'paying men and not positions'. In his second paper on *Shop Management* he discussed at length workshop organisation and management. He focused attention on this paper on his philosophy of management. [9] To him the objective of management should be to pay high wages and have low unit production cost to achieve the increased industrial efficiency. The other objectives of his philosophy include:

- application of scientific methods of research and experiments to the management problems;
- standardisation of working conditions and place the workers on the basis of scientific criteria;
- giving formal training to workers and specific instructions to perform the prescribed motions with standardised tools and materials; and
- ensuring friendly cooperation between workers and the management.

Taylor wanted to develop a new and total concept of management. He advocated that the traditional managers, instead of being authoritarian, should develop a new approach and change to a more comprehensive and broader view of their jobs incorporating the elements of planning, organising and controlling. While at Midvale Steel Company, after serious observation and study of operations of factories, he identified many defects in the management. They include:

- management had no clear understanding of worker-management responsibilities;
- lack of effective standards of work;
- restricted output because of "natural soldering" and "systemic soldering" of work by the workers;
- failure of management to design jobs properly and to offer the proper incentives to workers to overcome soldering;
- most decisions of the management were unscientific as they were based on hunch, intuition, past experience, and rule-of-thumb;
- lack of proper studies about the division of work among departments; and
- placement of workers without consideration of their ability, aptitude and interests.

Taylor experienced bitter labour-management conflicts, particularly between foreman and workers, over the quantity of output. He failed to resolve the problems by persuasion and even force. Realising that the new industrial scheme was essential to prevent encounters, he began searching for a science of work. In the process he conducted a series of experiments for more than two decades. He experimented with machine tools, speed, metals, materials, etc. His experiments at the Midvale and Bethlehem Steel Company led to the discovery of high-speed steel that revolutionised the art of cutting metals. His paper on *The Art of Cutting Metals*, presented to American Society of Mechanical Engineers as presidential address in 1906, was considered as the most remarkable ever presented to a learned society. The paper was based on the longest and most exhaustive series of 30,000 to 50,000 recorded experiments with experimental tools, in addition to many unrecorded, conducted over a period of 26 years, at a cost of about $2,00,000. The experiments were designed to find answers to recurring questions like what tools to be used? What should be the cutting speed? What feed should be used? etc.[10] The achievements of metal cutting experiments were considered more important than Taylor's other contributions, because they initiated a major breakthrough in the development of the American industry.

In the development of the shop system, Taylor wished to know, that under controlled conditions, how long a man or a machine would or should take to perform a given task, in a specified process, using specified materials and methods. He used scientific fact-finding methods to determine empirically instead of traditionally the right ways to perform tasks with the help of a stopwatch. Taylor recognised the need for scientific method of selection of the right men for the right jobs considering their initial qualifications and potential for further learning. He wanted the effective supervision of a worker and his working conditions after placing the worker in the right place. Taylor wanted to lay down the foundation for sound personnel management i.e. to match the worker's abilities to the job.

In other experiments on motion and time study he analysed how the workers handled materials, machines and tools and developed a coordinated system of shop management. Taylor set out to determine scientifically the ability of workers in dealing with equipment and materials and this approach led to the true beginning of scientific management.

Taylor's Concept of Management

The principle object of management, according to Taylor, is to secure the maximum prosperity for the employer, coupled with the maximum prosperity for each employee. His philosophy of scientific management is that there is no inherent conflict in the interest of the employers, workers and consumers. The primary concern of Taylor was that the results of higher productivity should equally benefit all people i.e., workers, employers, and consumers in the shape of higher wages to the workers, greater profits to the management and payment of lower prices for the products by the consumers. Taylor observed that management neglected its functions and shifted its burden to the labour while keeping for itself minor responsibility. He advised that management should take the responsibility for determining standards, planning work, organising, controlling and devising incentive schemes.

Principles of Scientific Management

Taylor emphasised, in the interest of societal prosperity, close collaboration and deliberate cooperation between the workmen and the management for the application of scientific methods. His philosophy of management was based on four basic principles of scientific management:

* development of a true science;

- scientific selection of the workers;
- scientific education and development of workers; and
- intimate and friendly cooperation between the management and the men.[11]

Development of a True Science of Work

When science is viewed as 'organised knowledge', every act of a workman can be reduced to science. In the interest of the worker and management, it is necessary to know as to what constitutes a fair day's work. It saves the worker from the unnecessary criticism of the boss and enables the management to get the maximum work from the worker. This needs a scientific investigation of a 'large daily task' to be done by qualified workers under optimum conditions. This can be done by gathering traditional knowledge of the workers, which are their lifelong fixed capital and a most valuable property. The results of investigation have to be classified, tabulated, and reduced into rules and laws to find out the ideal working methods or what is called 'one best way of doing a job'. Such development of science of work enables the organisation to produce more; enables the worker to receive higher wages and a much larger profit to the company.

Scientific Selection and Progressive Development of the Workman

There is a need to select the worker scientifically possessing physical and intellectual qualities to ensure the effective performance of the scientifically developed work. This needs a deliberate study of the aptitude, nature and performance of the worker and finding out what possibilities and limitations one has for future development. Taylor believed that every worker has the potential for development. He insisted that every worker must be systematically trained. Taylor felt that it is the responsibility of the management to develop the worker offering him opportunities for advancement to do the job to the fullest realisation of his natural capacities. It is necessary to ensure that the employees accept the new methods, tools and conditions willingly and enthusiastically.[12]

Bringing together Science of Work and Scientifically Selected and Trained Men

To enable the worker to do his job and to ensure that he may not slip back to the earlier methods of doing work, there must be somebody to inspire the workers. This, Taylor felt, is the exclusive responsibility of the management. He believed that workers are always willing to cooperate with the management, but there is more opposition from the side of the management. Taylor maintained that this process of bringing together causes the mental revolution.

Division of Work and Responsibility between Management and Workers

In the traditional management theory, the worker was entirely responsible for the work and the management had lesser responsibilities. But Taylor's scientific management assumes equal responsibility between management and the worker. This division of work creates between them an understanding and mutual dependence. There will also be constant and intimate cooperation between them. This results in elimination of conflicts and strikes.

None of the above principles, however, could be isolated and called scientific management. It is a combination of all the elements that constitutes scientific management. The philosophy of these principles may be summarised as:[13]

- science, not rule-of-thumb;
- harmony, not discord;

- cooperation, not individualism;
- maximum output, in place of restricted output; and
- development of each man to his greatest efficiency and prosperity.

Functional Foremanship

Taylor doubted the efficacy of the 'linear' system or military type of organisation in which each worker is subordinate to only one boss. He replaced this system with what is called functional foremanship in which the worker receives orders from eight specialised supervisors. Thus, he divided work not only among workers, but also at the supervisory level. Of the eight functional bosses, four are responsible for planning and the remaining four for execution. The order of work and route clerk, the instruction card clerk, time and cost clerk and shop disciplinarian are the four planning bosses. The gang-boss, repair-boss, speed-boss and the inspector are the four execution functional bosses. Taylor believed that in this functional type of organisation, the foreman can be trained quickly and specialisation becomes very easy. This concept of division of work between planning and execution was subsequently incorporated in the staff specialist in line and staff concept.[14] Taylor specified nine qualities viz., education, technical knowledge, manual dexterity and strength, tact, energy, grit, honesty, judgment and good health [15] which will make a good 'foreman'.

Apart from functional foremanship, Taylor also developed mechanisms to operate his principles of scientific management. They include:

- time study, with the implements and methods for properly making it;
- standardisation of all tools and implements;
- acts or movements of workmen for each class of work;
- the desirability of a planning room or department;
- the 'exception principle' in management;
- use of slide-rules and similar time saving implements;
- instruction cards for the workman;
- the task idea in management, accompanied by a large bonus for the successful performance of the task;
- the 'differential rate' system;
- mnemonic systems for classifying manufactured products as well as implements used in manufacturing;
- a routing system;
- modern cost system, etc.[16]

Taylor observed that scientific management is not an efficiency device. To him it is not a new scheme of paying men; not a new system of figuring costs; not a time study or motion study; and it is not divided foremanship or functional foremanship.[17] Taylor believed in all these efficiency devices but emphasised that in whole or in part they are not scientific management; they are useful adjuncts to scientific management as they are also useful adjuncts of other systems of management.

Mental Revolution

Scientific management, according to Taylor, primarily involves a complete mental revolution on the part of the workers and the management as to their duties, towards their work, towards their fellow workers, and towards all of their daily problems. It demands the realisation of the fact that their mutual interests are not antagonistic and mutual prosperity is possible only through mutual cooperation. Without this great mental revolution on both sides, Taylor said, scientific management does not exist.[18]

Taylor was of the view that the great revolution that takes place in the mental attitude of the two sides under scientific management is that both parties take their eyes off the division of the surplus as the all important matter and together turn their attention towards increasing the size of the surplus until the surplus becomes so large that it becomes unnecessary to quarrel over how it should be divided.[19] Then, both the sides stop pulling against one another, and instead both turn and push shoulder to shoulder in the same direction till the size of the surplus created by their joint effort is truly astounding. Both the sides realise that friendly cooperation and mutual helpfulness make the surplus so enormously greater than it was in the past and there is ample room for a large increase in wages for the workers and equally great increase in profits for the manufacturer. "It is along this line of complete change in the mental attitude of both sides, of the substitution of peace for war; the substitution of hearty brotherly cooperation for contention and strife; of both pulling hard in the same direction instead of pulling apart or replacing suspicious watchfulness with mutual confidence; or becoming friends instead of enemies." Taylor said that along this line scientific management must be developed.

Criticism

Although scientific management became something of a 'movement' and offered the hope of resolving industrial problems, organised labour and managers as well were antagonistic to it. The trade unions were against the methods of increasing output by introduction of the premium bonus system. The labour leaders considered Taylorism as not only destroying trade unionism but also destroying the principle of collective bargaining. They thought that the system was a menace to the community at large as it causes continuous increase in unemployment. The trade unions felt that Taylor was more interested in the mechanical aspects of work and not much concerned about the total work situation.

Scientific management, though had enormous impact on industry and improved productivity, it increased monotony and resulted in the absence of skill variety. The use of stop-watches was protested and led to strikes where Taylorism was under implementation. There were complaints that Taylorism was 'dehumanising'. A number of agitations by the labour organisations and their representations to the American Congress led a Special Committee of the House of Representatives to investigate into Taylorism in 1912. Although the report of the Committee neither clearly favoured the labour nor Taylor, the trade unions in 1915 succeeded in getting an amendment to the Army Appropriation Act, forbidding the use of stopwatches or the payment of premiums or bonuses in Army arsenals. It was only in 1949 that these restrictions were lifted.

The trade union's opposition to Taylorism also led to an investigation conducted by Professor Robert Hoxie for the United States Commission on Industrial Relations. In his report, Hoxie criticised scientific management and Taylor's approaches, as they were concerned only with mechanical aspects and not with human aspects of production. The report also stated that the basic ideals of scientific management and labour unionism were incompatible.

Taylorism was also often attacked by managers. Those who wanted quick promotions to the high managerial positions without any merit based on higher education opposed Taylor's stand, which advocated training by experts. The managers did not appreciate his scornful comments on rule-of-thumb methods. Those who had fought their way to higher managerial positions without the benefit of higher education were sensitive to Taylor's stand that unless assisted by highly trained experts they were unqualified to manage.[20] It is very interesting to note that Taylor had to resign from both Midvale Steel Works and Bethlehem Steel, because of the friction with the company managers.[21]

Oliver Sheldon, a British management expert, Mary Parker Follett, an American business philosopher, Elton Mayo, Peter Drucker and others criticised Taylor's ideas. They charged that Taylor's scientific management was impersonal and underemphasised the human factor. The classic, 'Hawthorne experiments' of Elton Mayo and other studies on human relations and group dynamics in industry rejected Taylorism. Elton Mayo, through his classic "Hawthorne investigations", conclusively proved that it is not the structural arrangements of the organisation, which are important for increasing productivity and efficiency. But it is the emotional attitude of the worker towards his work and his colleagues. Taylor's philosophy that men were generally lazy and try to avoid work has also been disputed. It is evident from Brown's analysis that "work is an essential part of man's life, since it is that aspect of life which gives him status and binds him to the society. When they do not like it, the fault lies in the psychological and social conditions of the job, rather than the worker."[22]

The behaviouralists charged that Taylor's methods of scientific management sacrifice the initiative of the worker, his individual freedom and the use of his intelligence and responsibility. Simon and March described the scientific management as the 'physiological organisation theory'.[23] There are also criticisms that Taylorism dehumanised the industry and made workers automatons and assumed that the workers are satisfied with money alone. His specification of what should be done and in what time leaves no scope for the worker to think.

Another criticism of Taylor is that he did not properly understand the anatomy of the work. Taylor's emphasis on the minute division of work and specialisation was severely criticised on several grounds. Firstly, the work gets depersonalised, the worker becomes a mere cog in the machine, and the relations between the worker and executives become remote as a result of which the worker lacks the sense of participation in the work. More than anything, the worker finds no outlet to exhibit his abilities and potential. Secondly, it may even lead to automation of the workers, which may have physiological and neurological consequences. As aptly put by Peter Drucker, the organisation becomes a piece of poor engineering judged by the standards of human relations, as well as by those of productive efficiency and output.[24] Thirdly, Taylor's division of work into planning and executive divisions has severely been criticised. It is argued that in such situations it is difficult to develop proper team spirit, and if planning is totally diversed from the execution it is difficult to secure the participation of the workers in the progress of the firm. It has also been argued that Taylor overlooked the fact that the principle of division and sub-division of work into minutest parts is subject to the law of diminishing returns.[25] Taylor's philosophy was summarised in the following words: "First, he confuses the principle of analysis with the principle of action.... Second, planning and doing are separate parts of the same job; they cannot be totally divorced." [26]

There are studies, however, which counter some of these criticisms. For example, it is significant to note that Taylor himself recognised the potential for abuse of his methods. This is clear when he said that "it may be used more or less as a club to drive workmen into doing a larger day's work for approximately the same pay that they received in the past."[27] Some argue that the current literature presents a partial view of Taylor's work. But in fact Taylor anticipated several key motivational strategies generally associated with human relations movement. He created a sense of mission, increased two way communication, understood that higher needs are also important as against economic man approach, used esteem as a motivator and gave workers a chance at self-actualisation, etc. It is also argued that Taylor's writings show that he used managers to realise that technical success requires enhanced human relations and to get an accurate sense of Taylor's message one has to read his own account.[28]

An Evaluation

Despite the limitations - limitations concerning an adequate understanding of human psychology, sociology and the anatomy of work - Taylor's work remains important. By all accounts Taylor must be regarded as a pioneer in the study of human beings at work.[29] He was the first to apply quantitative techniques to the study of industrial management. Modern scientific management - operations research, method study, time study, system analysis, management by exceptions, etc., - are all part of Taylor's heritage. His concepts of work design, measurement, production control, etc., changed the nature of industry and began to establish departments of work study, quality control, etc. Taylor's scientific management became something of a movement. In an age of growing achievement in physical sciences it offered the hope of resolving industrial problems through the use of objective principles. For young and imaginative engineers, it provided an ethos and a mission. After the initial period of resistance, it conquered the citadels of old fashioned industrial management in the United States and had a tremendous effect on industrial practice.[30] It even spread to Germany, England, France, USSR, and other European countries. Scientific management was supported in Russia and Taylor's principles were included in the curriculum of the education and training of the engineers. Taylor in brief, combined theory and practice, thought and experiment and doing and teaching all in one life. His scientific management had a major influence on the growing reform and economy movements in public administration.[31] The impact can be seen in several disciplines including accounting, education, library science, architecture, health, military, gender and public administration. [32]

In Brief

Frederick Taylor's contribution to management and administration can be summarised as:

*   Frederick Winslow Taylor, a mechanical engineer by training, was regarded as the "Father of Scientific Management" for his pioneering work in the study of human beings at work;

*   Based on extensive studies of industrial work situation, Taylor identified defects in management and proposed a philosophy of management for industrial efficiency, which was subsequently labelled as "Scientific Management" by Louis Brandies;

*   Taylor's philosophy of scientific management is that there is no inherent conflict in the interests of employees, workers and consumers. Based on this philosophy he developed four principles of scientific management viz., (a) development of a true science of work; (b) scientific selection of workers; (c) scientific education and development of workers, and (d) intimate and friendly cooperation between the management and the men;

*   Taylor developed many management techniques like functional foremanship; time and motion study; piece-rate system; standardisation of tools; the exception principle; the differential rate system, etc., as application tools of scientific management. The tools, Taylor felt, will help in identifying "one best way of doing things";

- The essence of scientific management, according to Taylor, is mental revolution i.e. change of attitude on the part of workers and management towards their work and their relationships;

- Both trade unions and managers of the day were very critical of scientific management, though for different reasons. The trade unions considered the scientific management as anti-labour and anti-trade union, focusing on mechanical aspects of work ignoring the human aspects. The labour organisations protested the "dehumanising" aspects of Taylorism;

- The managers did not appreciate the criticism of rule-of-thumb methods and prescription of technical training to managers to increase efficiency and effectiveness in organisations;

- Taylor's principles and prescriptions were criticised by latter writers for their failure to understand the anatomy of work. Simon and March characterised scientific management as the "physiological organisation theory"; and

- Taylor's work, in spite of limitations and criticisms, greatly influenced the study and practices of industrial administration in the modern world. Taylor's heritage is visible in many modern management techniques like operation research, method study, time study, etc. Taylor should be given due credit for laying foundations for the systematic study of work and worker.

References

[1] Taylor, Frederick W., *Principles of Scientific Management*, New York, Harper Brothers, 1947, See Introduction. http://www.eldritchpress.org/fwt/ti.html

[2] For details of Taylor's life, career, contribution and impact on society, economy, polity, administration and management see different articles in Wood, John C., and Wood, Michael C., *F.W. Taylor: Critical Evaluations in Business and Management*, New York, Rutledge, 2005.

[3] http://en.wikipedia.org/wiki/Frederick Winslow Taylor.

[4] Taylor's main works include *Shop Management* (1903), *The Principles of Scientific Management* (1911) and *The Testimony before the Special House Committee* (1912). For a detailed bibliography of his publications as well as studies on Taylor's work and contribution see Roberta A. Cowan, "Annotated Bibliography – Frederick Winslow Taylor (1856-1915)", in Wood, John C., and Wood, Michael C., (Eds), op.cit. pp.15-67.

[5] Sapre, S. A., *F. W. Taylor: His Philosophy of Scientific Management*, Bombay, Government Central Press, 1970, p. 1.

[6] The concept of efficiency articulated by Taylor continues to be the starting point in any discussion of efficiency in the New Public Management era. For a discussion see Schachter, Hindy Lauer, "Does Frederick Taylor's Ghost Still Haunt the Halls of Government? A Look at the Concept of Governmental Efficiency in Or Time", *Public Administration Review*, Sep. - Oct., 2007, Vol.67, No.5, 2007, pp.800-810.

[7] Shafritz, Jay M., and Hyde, Albert C., *Classics of Public Administration*, Fort Worth, Harcourt Brace College publishers, 1997, p.3.

[8] *Shop Management, The Principles of Scientific Management* and F. W. Taylor's *Testimony before a Special Committee of the House of Representatives in* 1912, were later published in one volume under the title *Principles of Scientific Management*, op.cit.

[9] See Claude S. George, Jr. *The History of Management Thought*, New Delhi, Prentice-Hall of India Private Limited, 1972, p. 92.

[10] See Hayward, Elizabeth Gardner, Classified Guide to the Frederick Winslow Taylor Collection, http://www.stevens.edu/ses/about soe/history/frederick winslow taylor.html Retrieved on 3rd January, 2010

[11] Taylor, Frederick W., op. cit., pp. 36-37.

[12] Sapre, S. A., op. cit., p. 14.

[13] Taylor, Frederick W., op. cit., p. 140.

[14] Ibid., pp. 99-107.

[15] Ibid., p.96.

[16] Ibid., pp. 129-30.

[17] "Hearing before Special Committee of the House of Representatives to Investigate the Taylor and other Systems of Shop Management under Authority of House Resolution 90," Washington, D. C. U. S.

Government Printing Office, 1912. Quoted in Wren, Daniel A., *The Evolution of Management Thought*, New York, The Ronald Press Company, 1972, pp. 142-143.

18 Ibid.

19 Ibid., p. 143.

20 Gross, Bertram M., *The Managing of Organisation: The Administrative Struggle*, Vol. I, New York, The Free Press, 1964, p. 125.

21 Ibid.

22 Brown, J. A. C., *The Social Psychology of Industry*, Pelican, 1954.

23 March, James G. and Simon, Herbert A., *Organisations*, New York, John Wiley & Sons, 1958, pp. 12-22.

24 Quoted in Sapre, S.A., op. cit.,p.25.

25 Ibid, pp. 25-26.

26 Ibid.

27 Taylor, Frederick W., op. cit., pp.133-34

28 For details of this perspective see, Hindy, Lauer Schachter, "Frederick Winslow Taylor and the idea of Worker Participation: A Brief Against Easy Administrative Dichotomies", *Administration and Society*, Vol.21, NO.1, May 1989, pp.20-30.

29 Sapre, S. A., op. cit., p. 29.

30 Gross, Bertram M., op. cit., p. 127.

31 Ibid., p. 128.

32 For details see different articles in Wood, John C., and Wood, Michael C., op.cit., pp.9-10.

6

MAX WEBER

C. Lakshmanna
A.V. Satyanarayana Rao

Introduction

In administrative sciences, bureaucracy occupies a significant place. Max Weber's name is synonymous with bureaucracy and he enjoys a unique place in the galaxy of social scientists who have attempted to explain the concept of bureaucracy. Weber's analyses encompassing such diverse fields ranging from history to comparative social sciences, have earned him immortality. Weber's influence on the thinkers on administration is obvious from the fact that a majority of propositions and models on bureaucracy spanning about a century are considered either as different versions of Weberian model or attempts at controlling it, thus making the Weber's conceptualisations an important point of beginning. Similarly, Weber's theories on legitimacy and domination formed the basis for a number of further studies.

(1864-1920)

Life and Works

Maximilian Carl Emil Weber (1864-1920) was born in a wealthy and political family in Erfurt, Thuringia, then part of Prussia and now in Germany. In 1882, Weber went to the University of Heidelberg to study Law. Breaking his studies in 1884 he spent a year in Strasbourg as a conscripted Junior Officer in the German Army. Weber completed his university studies in 1886 and spent the next three years in Berlin working in a minor legal position while preparing his doctoral dissertation on the History of Medieval Trading Companies. He received Ph.D in 1889. He joined the University of Berlin as an instructor in law and completed his second work called *Roman Agrarian History and its significance for Public and Private Law* in 1891. He wrote a number of papers on law focusing on the social, political and economic factors prevalent at that time. In 1894, Weber became a Professor of Political Economy at Fidelburg University and in 1897 returned to the University of Heidelberg as a Professor of Economics. The death of his father in 1897 left a serious crisis in his life affecting his physical and mental health. He resigned his professorship, travelled throughout Europe and the USA and avoided teaching for about twenty years. During this period he shifted his academic interests from law and economics to sociology. In 1918, he returned to teaching initially in Vienna and later at Munich. He died at the height of his intellectual power and a bulk of his writings were incomplete. His academic interests are very wide spanning economics, history, religion, politics and sociology. [1]

There are some factors in Weber's life, which need to be considered before attempting to analyse his writings. First, Weber's urge for analysis and systematised study began at the age of thirteen. Second, he always preferred knowledge obtained through practical experience than library research. Third, he was progressive in outlook and yet conservative at heart. Fourth, his writings reflect social conditions of Germany of his times. He saw the decline of liberalism and the threat to the individual in the bureaucratisation of society.

Authority, Organisation and Legitimacy

Among Weber's works on administration, his theories on domination, leadership and legitimacy merit special mention. He propounded these theories with a broad perspective, keeping in view religion and society and the way they mould the patterns of leadership. Weber differentiated authority, power and control. To him, a person could be said to possess power, if in a social relationship, his will could be enforced despite resistance. And such exercise of power becomes controlled. Structuring of human groups owe their existence to a special instance of vested authority. It manifests when a 'command of definite content elicits obedience on the part of specific individuals'[2]. To Weber, 'authority' was identical with the 'authoritarian power of command'.[3] Weber identified five essential components of authority:

1. An individual or a body of individuals who rule;
2. An individual or a body of individuals who are ruled;
3. The will of the rulers to influence the conduct of the ruled and an expression of that will or command;
4. Evidence of the influence of the rulers in terms of the objective degree of command; and
5. Direct or indirect evidence of that influence in terms of the subjective acceptance with which the ruled obey the command.

An authority exists as long as it is accepted as legitimate by the ruled. An organisation thus can rule or administer only when it has legitimacy. Explaining the authority of different kinds, in various organisations, Weber concluded that "all administration means domination".[4] He categorised the persons in organisations as those who:

1. are accustomed to obey commands;
2. are personally interested in seeing the existing domination continue because they derive benefits;
3. participate in that domination in the sense that the exercise of functions is divided among them; and
4. hold themselves in readiness for the exercise of these functions.

Weber defined administration as domination or exercise of authority while most other administrative scientists defined it as service or performance of duty. He identified three forms of legitimacy each with a different type of 'apparatus' to justify the power of command. They are traditional, charismatic, and legal authority.

Traditional Authority

Traditional authority derives its legitimacy from the acceptance of its hoary past. The persons exercising authority generally are called 'Masters,' who enjoy personal authority by virtue of their inherited status. Their commands carry legitimacy because of the custom but they can also give orders based on their personal decision. Thus conformity with customs and personal arbitrariness are two characteristics of traditional authority. The persons who obey the orders are called 'Followers'. They carry out the commands of the master out of sheer personal loyalty and a pious regard for his time-honoured status. In this patrimonial regime, the persons who carry out the orders are personal retainers, household officials, relatives, favourites of the master, etc. In a feudal society they are the loyal allies of the master. Under this type of authority, according to Weber, the administration becomes irrational as development of rational regulations is impeded as there would be no staff with formal and technical training. [5] Thus, in the system of traditional authority, the officials carrying out the orders look like the 'household staff' of the master and their spheres of activity change according to the master's whims and fancies. However, all the actions are legitimised in the name of tradition and customs.

Charismatic Authority

The power exercised by a leader - may be a prophet, a hero or a demagogue – substantiating the claim by virtue of his magical powers or heroism or other extraordinary gift or qualities. Charisma and its acceptance form the basis for legitimacy. Weber defines charisma as the quality of an individual personality by virtue of which he is set apart from ordinary men and treated as endowed with supernatural, superhuman or at least specifically exceptional powers or qualities.[6] The persons who receive the commands obey the leader because they believe in his extraordinary abilities rather than the stipulated rules or the dignity of a position. The charismatic leader selects his disciples or the followers as his officials based purely on their personal devotion to him rather than on their special qualification or status. These 'disciple officials' constitute the organisation and their sphere of activity and power of command depends upon the likes and dislikes of the leader.

Legal Authority

Manifestations of legal authority are found in organisations where rules are applied judicially and in accordance with ascertainable principles valid for all members in the organisation. The members who exercise the power are the superiors who are appointed or elected by legal procedures to maintain the legal order. The subject persons to the commands are legal equals who obey 'the law'. The 'apparatus' that implements the system of legal authority is also subject to the same principles. Thus, organisation is continuous and its members are subject to rules, which limit their authority with necessary controls in its exercise.

Weber believed that all the three types of authority claim legitimacy as long as the 'ruled' accept them. The authority ceases to carry legitimacy when the rulers do illegal things, ignore the traditions and lose charisma. Weber discusses in detail the three types of authority as also the kinds of leadership. He states that, 'pure type' of authority are always found in combination rather than separated from each other. But Weber insists that there is a need to analyse them separately to find out the composition of legal, traditional and charismatic elements present in a combination. It is always possible that with the passage of time one type of authority tends to acquire the characteristics of the other resulting in modifications in the institutional structure. Of the three types of authority, Weber preferred the legal type of authority or domination because of the inherent rationalities in it. He maintains that legal authority or domination alone is suitable for the modern governments and Weber designed his model of bureaucracy keeping the 'legal-rationality' in mind. In what follows, an attempt is made to elucidate the various characteristics of Weberian model of bureaucracy - an institutional mechanism for the exercise of legal-rational authority.

Bureaucracy

The bureau or public offices, in some form or the other, were always adjuncts of organised governments all over the world. For instance, in China, even in 186 B.C., public offices were in existence and persons for those offices used to be recruited through competitive examinations. History is replete with instances to show that individuals appointed to government offices acquire special characteristics some of which were even universal.

It was Mr. de Gourney, French economist, who used the word 'bureaucracy' for the first time, during the first half of the 18th century. Several French writers, after de Gourney, popularised the word while the British social scientists started using the word only in the 19th century. J. S. Mill, an eminent political economist, included bureaucracy in his analysis. Mosca and Michels are two other important sociologists who wrote extensively on bureaucracy.[7] Yet, one is reminded of Max Weber whenever there is a discussion on bureaucracy. For, Weber was the first social scientist who made a systematic study of bureaucracy and its characteristics. The Weberian model of bureaucracy is a source of inspiration to many because it largely reflects the spirit of modern bureaucracy. That is the reason why Weberian model is being used as a reference base for other models on bureaucracy.

Weber never defined bureaucracy; he only described its characteristics. To him bureaucracy is "an administrative body of appointed officials". In bureaucracy he included explicitly appointed officials only leaving out the elected ones. As in the case of authority, Weber categorised bureaucracy into (i) patrimonial bureaucracy found in traditional and charismatic types of authorities and (ii) legal-rational bureaucracy found only in legal type of authority. The characteristics of legal-rational bureaucracy, popularly known as Weberian model, are analysed further. Weber believed that legitimacy was basic to nearly all systems of authority and legitimacy of authority depends on the following five important beliefs that:

1. a legal code can be established which can claim obedience from members of an organisation;
2. law is a system of abstract rules which are applied to specific cases, and that administration looks after the interests of the organisation within the limits of law;
3. the individual exercising authority also obeys this impersonal order;
4. only qua member does the member obey the law; and
5. obedience is not to the person who holds authority but to the impersonal order which grants him the position.

These five elements substantiate the view that Weber laid greater stress on the relationship between legitimacy and impersonal order. Four factors seem to have influenced Weber in his discussion on bureaucracy. They are: (1) the historical, technical and administrative reasons that form the process of bureaucratisation particularly in western civilisation; (2) the impact of the rule of law upon the functioning of bureaucratic organisation; (3) the occupational position and typical personal orientation of bureaucratic officials as an elite group; and (4) the most important attributes and the consequences of bureaucracy in the modern world, particularly of governmental bureaucracy.

Model of Bureaucracy

The model of legal-rational bureaucracy designed by Weber has the following characteristics:[8]

1. Official business is conducted on a continuous basis;
2. An administrative agency functions in accordance with stipulated rules and is characterised by three inter-related attributes: (a) the powers and functions of each official is delimited in terms of impersonal criteria; (b) the official is given matching authority to carry out his responsibility; and (c) the means of compulsion at his disposal are strictly limited and the conditions under which their employment is legitimate are clearly defined;
3. Every official and every office is part of a hierarchy of authority. Higher officials or offices supervise while lower offices and officials have the right of appeal;
4. Officials do not own the resources necessary for rendering the duties, but they are accountable for use of official resources. Official business and private affairs, official revenue and private incomes are strictly separated;
5. Offices cannot be filled by the incumbents as private property which can be sold and inherited; and
6. Administration is conducted on the basis of written documents.

Weber also discussed in detail the characteristics of the official. The official:

1. is personally free (and not a servant to anybody personally) and appointed to an official position on the basis of a contract;
2. exercises the authority delegated to him in accordance with impersonal rules, and his loyalty is expressed through faithful execution of his duties;
3. appointment and job placement depends on his technical (administrative) qualification;
4. administrative work is his full-time occupation; and
5. work is rewarded by a regular salary and by prospects of regular advancement in a lifetime career.

Weber thought that this legal-rational bureaucracy is technically superior to all other administrative systems. Further he stressed that the people once ruled by bureaucracy can never think of any other alternative. Hence, it is permanent and indispensable. In Weberian model of bureaucracy the main elements are impersonal order; rules; sphere of competence; hierarchy; personal and public ends; written documents; and monocratic type. These elements are discussed in detail.

The Impersonal Order

In Weber's 'ideal type' construct of bureaucracy the most striking and thought-provoking idea is his belief that 'impersonal order' should orient the actions of the bureaucracy both in the issuance of the commands to subordinates and their obedience to them.[9] In the words of Merton, "authority, the power of control, which derives from an acknowledged status, inheres in the office and not in the particular person who performs the official role." The stress on depersonalisation of relationships also plays its part in the bureaucrat's trained incapacity.[10]

Rules

The fundamental characteristics of Weberian rational legal authority is the attribute of continuous organisation of official functions bound by rules.[11] The rules which regulate the conduct of an office may be technical rules or norms. Their rational application, however, requires specialised training.[12] As has been rightly said by Merton, adherence to the rules, originally conceived as a means, becomes an end in itself; there occurs the familiar process of displacement of goals whereby "an instrumental value becomes a terminal value."[13] Rules become more important than the 'game'. This apart, rules cause procedural delays as they create complications in administration.

Sphere of Competence

To Weber a specified sphere of competence involves (a) a sphere of obligation to perform functions which have been marked off as a part of a systematic division of labour; (b) the provision of the incumbent with the necessary authority to carry out these functions; and (c) the clearly defined means of compulsion subject to definite conditions in their uses.[14]

Hierarchy

Weber argued that "the organisation of offices follows the principle of hierarchy, that is, each lower office is under the control and supervision of a higher one.[15] He also states that, "the whole administrative staff under the supreme authority...is organised in a clearly defined hierarchy of offices."[16] Weber attaches greater importance to the principle of hierarchy in the organisation of offices and also in regard to administrative staff who man them.

Personal and Public Ends

There is a great amount of utility and relevance in Weber's ideal type as far as it pleads for the separation of administrative staff from the ownership of the means of production or administration. It also pleads for the complete absence of appropriation of official position by the incumbent.[17] These are necessary checks on the bureaucrats to prevent them from misusing their positions.

Written Documents

The last principle of Weberian bureaucracy is that "the administrative acts, decisions and rules are formulated and recorded in writing even in cases where oral discussion is the rule or is even mandatory."[18] Documents make the administration accountable to people and provide a ready reference for future action.

The most commendable part of the Weberian model is its insistence on the selection of technically qualified people. The other criteria for the official are the 'fixed salaries paid in money', the full-time occupation in the office, the prospects for further promotion in the career, and the strict and systematic discipline and control. Weber asserted that the monocratic bureaucratic organisation, from a purely technical point of view, could be capable of attaining the highest degree of efficiency.[19]

Critics of Weber

Weber's model of bureaucracy attracted criticism mainly on three points viz., the rationality in his model; suitability of the model to the administrative requirements of different places and changing times; and whether the model can attain maximum efficiency as visualised by Weber?[20] Robert Merton and other sociologists have questioned the rationality of the legal-rational model of Weber as it produces certain dysfunctional consequences. To Merton, the structures - especially its hierarchy and rules, which is rational in Weber's sense, can easily generate consequences which are unexpected and detrimental to the attainment of objectives of an organisation. In stressing this point Merton is only providing a more sophisticated vindication of the view that bureaucracy means inefficiency.[21] Philip Selznick, pointing to the division of functions in an organisation, shows how sub-units set up goals of their own which may conflict with the purpose of the organisation as a whole. Merton and Selznick have shown that the formal specification of organisational structure outlined by Weber is insufficient as a description of how bureaucrats will in fact behave, because the officials have their own characteristics as social beings beyond those which the administrative code specifies. These criticisms reflect the major insights on the behavioural side of the industrial sociology.

Talcott Parsons, who translated Weber's famous book *Wirtschaft and Gesellschaft*, questions the internal consistency of Weber's ideal type of bureaucracy. Parsons draws attention to the fact that Weber expects the administrative staff to be technically superior as well as possess the right to give orders. But this itself gives rise to conflicts within bureaucracy since it is not always possible to ensure that high position in the hierarchy of authority will be matched by equivalent professional skill. In such case the individuals working in an organisation will face the problem of whom to obey, the person with the right to command or the man with the greater expertise.[22]

Using Parson's criticism as starting point, Alvin Gouldner distinguishes two major types of bureaucracy. Firstly, punishment-centered bureaucracies, where members of the organisation conform reluctantly to rules which they consider are imposed on them by an alien group. Secondly, representative bureaucracy, where the members regard rules as necessary on technical grounds and in their own interest.[23] Gouldner and others have raised the problems of compliance with rules by the members of an organisation not so much because of the informal processes arising within an administrative structure but to conditions outside the organisation which orient the behaviour of the members *vis-à-vis* the rules. The critics feel that the Weberian model does not include the orientation of members in relation to the rules in an organisation. A number of other writers also emphasised on the significant influence of environmental factors on the behaviour of organisations and pointed to these shortcomings in Weberian model. Rudolf complained that Weber's model carries a misconception that administration was a rational machine and officials were mere technical functionaries. Reinhard Bendix, one of the famous intellectual biographers of Weber, argues against the belief that it is possible to adhere to a rule without intrusion of general social and political values. All rules have to be applied to particular cases and it is here that the attitude of the officials plays a dominant role in making decisions.

A number of critics like Peter Blau believed that Weberian model of bureaucracy cannot be applied to administration of different places and times. Blau felt that a fresh look has to be taken at the concept of rational administration. In a changing environment "the attainment of organisational objectives depends on perpetual change in the bureaucratic structure.' That is why efficiency cannot be guaranteed by tethering the official to a set of rigid rules. According to Blau, the efficient administration is possible only when an individual is allowed to identify with the purpose of the organisation and to adopt his behaviour to his perception of changing circumstances.

Robert Presthus considers that Weber's concept of bureaucracy makes implicit assumptions about human motivations, which are not necessarily valid in non-western environments. William Delaney considers that patrimonial bureaucracy may well be more conducive to economic growth in underdeveloped societies than rational bureaucracy of the Weberian type. Joseph La Palombara believes that developing societies may find Russian or Chinese methods of administration more effective than western bureaucracy.

H.C. Creel and A.B. Spitzer took objection to Weber's claim that rational bureaucracy is a modern phenomenon. Creel, for instance, asserted that almost all the characteristics of Weberian model existed in China by 200 B.C. Spitzer considers that the functions of the Prefect in the 19th century France are far more comprehensive than those attributed to Weber's bureaucrat. According to Frederick Burin, Weber's thesis ignores the important changes brought about in the operation of the bureaucracy by the rise of the doctrines of public liability and accountability and their enforcement by the council of the states. All these criticisms, are directed to prove that Weberian model does not fit in changing circumstances and requirements of administration particularly in non-western countries. They also proved, with necessary empirical proof, that Weberian model of bureaucracy cannot attain maximum efficiency. In fact Barnard and Simon argued that administrative efficiency would fall if we follow Weber's structural approach and efficiency in the organisation would increase through informal relations and unofficial practices.[24]

Weber defined his ideal type as internally consistent [25] and only due to this reason he might have thought that it attains maximum efficiency. But Gouldner, who tested Weber's ideal type empirically, found that it has internal contradictions such as the tensions between the 'claims of expertise' and the 'claims of obedience' based on discipline. La Palombara points out that, "a bureaucracy heavily encumbered by Weberian norms may be less efficacious instrument of economic change". While giving Indian example, he adds that "in a place like India, public administration steeped in the tradition of the Indian Civil Services may be less useful as development entrepreneurs than those who are not so rigidly tied to motions of bureaucratic status, hierarchy, and impartiality,"[26] William Delaney, who has tried to utilise Weberian ideal types for creating a development construct concludes that unless further ideal types are created, the existing Weberian work seem to have little applicability outside western Europe and certain commonwealth countries and the United States.[27]

Simon and March included Weber in the company of classical thinkers like Gulick and Urwick as he too did not pay any attention to the human behaviour in organisations.[28] Weberian ideal type would not attain maximum efficiency as it emphasises more on the structure of the bureaucracy than on the human beings who personify it. Philip Selznick and others criticised Weber for his neglect of the power that a bureaucrat assumes whereby he is 'increasingly preoccupied with his own social position and in the end subverts the professed goals of the organisation only on his own power position'. No impersonal order can stop bureaucrats becoming power mongers and may even encourage clandestine motives in them. In a democratic setting it is also very difficult to a bureaucrat to be neutral and impersonal in the face of hectic political activity around him.

It is doubtful whether the specified sphere of competence stands as good as Weber thought it to be in relation to development administration. Development administration throws multifarious new challenges and the administrator can only justify his services by meeting them rather wait to get the clarification from superiors whether a particular new situation falls under his competence or not. Strict adherence to this Weberian principle leads to delays and inefficiency in administration by providing an excuse for the officers to shirk responsibility.

Rigid adherence to the principle of hierarchy was also criticised; it does not contribute to repose of mutual-trust, either in the inter-organisational or inter-personal relation in the administration. This only embodies 'mutual suspicion' as its prime tenet in the relationship patterns of organisation and their staff. These apart, there are some dangers inherent in this principle, which are disastrous to the modern administration. The first danger is authoritarianism of the superiors, which is detrimental to the organisational necessity to work with a team spirit. This is a division tool, which will impede the forming of bureaucracy into a cohesive team.

Documents, which Weber insisted as important in his rational bureaucracy, also have negative effects; particularly in the context of welfare bureaucracies committing to development. Firstly, the expert drowned in the files becomes a 'glorified clerk' and secondly, Weber's insistence that every oral discussion should be recorded would result in too much formalism. Both are deleterious for efficiency and effectiveness of the bureaucratic organisation.

Succinctly, these criticisms point out to three main defects in the Weberian model, viz., (1) the rationality of the model is disputed both because of factors omitted from it, and because of internal inconsistency; (2) the degree of rationality bureaucracy can have, is held to depend on the cultural context in which it is located. Accepting that there is rational bureaucracy everywhere in the world, the critics hold that it must have different features from those, which Weber listed, and (3) finally, the very basis on which Weber constructed the ideal type is held to be invalid. Carl Friedrich explained as to how the words 'ideal' and 'type' cancel each other.

An Evaluation

The critics of Weber argued that the Weberian bureaucracy lacks empirical validity, particularly when it is related to modern administration. But Weber constructed his ideal type keeping the conditions of Germany of his times. To say that it does not suit the modern conditions is not appropriate because at the start of the nineteenth century, nobody including Weber, could ever visualise the changes that have come about in the last five or six decades which altered the very nature of the society. If Weber has said that his ideal type is superior and permanent it is only because he compared his legal rational model with the traditional and charismatic types of organisations.

As observed by Martin Albrow, Weber in his German writings would have used the words 'rationality' and efficiency in different contexts. Moreover, Weber might not have visualised all the meanings attached to the English word 'efficiency'. If Weber has said that his model would attain maximum efficiency, it was because of his love for legal rationality. He thought that his model is permanent simply because he expected that the advancement in civilisation in its train would also increase the adherence to rationality. Can there be any dispute with Weber when he says that legal rational model with skilled officials would attain maximum efficiency when compared to the non-skilled and servantile bureaucracies found in traditional and charismatic types of organisations?

The other criticism is on his stress on formalism. As noted by Albrow the formal rationality has increased manifold in the present day administration, thanks to advancement of management techniques. The researchers on decision-making, operation research and other management techniques would contribute to the scientific content of administration, which in turn enhances formalism in administration. Today, we see in practice in all societies of the world, Weber being proved correct when he said that the societies, which are once governed by bureaucracy, can never get rid of it. The Afro-Asian countries starting from India could get rid of the alien rule, but not the bureaucratic practices established by the colonial rulers.

Weberian model, no doubt includes both positive and negative elements. Elements such as selection through merit and technical qualifications, complete absence of appropriation of official positions by the incumbents come under positive category. Elements such as impersonal order, rules, spheres of competence, hierarchy, technical rules, and written documents form the negative category. As the negative elements are given greater weightage in the model, the positive elements get gulfed and enfeebled by the huge stream of negativism.

Those who criticise Weberian model are not criticising Weber but the present day bureaucracies, which more or less reflect his model. The talk of de-bureaucratisation or less bureaucracy appears to be idealistic; for, we are not able to avoid bureaucracy even in our welfare and development organisations because of the weakness inherent in the individuals and the organisations. Social scientists in large numbers now are engaged in finding out ways and means to reduce the bureaucratic influences in development and welfare sectors of public administration. Writers like Presthus have even constructed models of bureaucracy that would suit the welfare requirements. But even those theorists who argue for de-bureaucratisation cannot proceed further without understanding the Weberian analysis. Weber appears to be the source of inspiration for the students of bureaucracy at present. And there is no wonder if he inspires the future scholars as well.

From students of administration to research teams greater focus is being laid on the influences of bureaucracy on administration today. Administrators are considered as the change-agents and bureaucracy as a catalyst of modernisation and development. As long as this consideration dominates the administrative studies, bureaucracy attracts wider interest and the analysis and discussion on Weberian bureaucracy goes on and on.

In Brief

Weber's contribution to the study of bureaucracy can be summarised as:

- Max Weber, a broad-based scholar with academic interests spanning economics, history, politics, religion and sociology made a significant contribution to the analysis and understanding of bureaucracy. Today, there cannot be any study or discussion on bureaucracy without reference to Max Weber.

- Weber defined administration as exercise of authority and identified different forms of legitimacy viz., traditional, charismatic and legal and analysed the nature of exercise of authority in ideal-type authority.

- Weber considered legal authority as rational and called it legal-rational. He considered bureaucracy, the institutional form of legal-rational authority, as the most appropriate to modern governments.

- He described in detail the characteristics of legal rational bureaucracy which is popularly known as Weberian model of bureaucracy.

- Weber laid stress on legitimacy of legal-rational authority which is based on impersonal orders, rules, sphere of competence, hierarchy, written documents, technically qualified people and separation of personal and public ends.

- Weberian model of bureaucracy attracted criticism mainly on three grounds i.e., rationality, suitability of model to different places and changing times, and its ability to attain maximum efficiency.

- The core of criticism is on its' emphasis on structure and neglect of human behaviour. The model is described by some as a structural approach to organisations.

- The Weberian model has both positive and negative features. In assessing Weberian ideal type, the historical context of Germany of his times should be kept in mind.

- The Weberian model continues to be the framework for the analysis, criticisms and for improvements in bureaucracy. That is the immortality of the model.

Notes and References

1. Sheldrake, John, *Management Theory: From Taylorism to Japanisation*, London, International Thompson Business Press, 1966, p.57.

2. Albrow, Martin, *Bureaucracy*, London, Macmillan, 1970, p. 39.

3. According to Bendix, Weber did not use 'authority as a separate technical term but appeared to think of it as a synonym for domination.' For details see Bendix, Reinhard, *Max Weber: An Intellectual Portrait*, London, Heinnmann, 1960, p. 296. As distinct from this several others used the term authority. In this paper the latter term is used.

4. Ibid., p. 295.

5. Max Weber, *The Theory of Social and Economic Organisation*, (Translated by AM Henderson and Talcott Parsons), New York, Oxford University Press, 1947, p.343.

6. Ibid., p.358.

7. Martin Albrow, op. cit., pp. 16-37.

8. See Max Weber, op.cit.

9. This stands good even for political offices.

10. Merton, Robert K., et. al., (Ed.), *Reader in Bureaucracy*, Glencoe, Free Press, 1952, p. 361.

11. A young and energetic fresh graduate enters bureaucracy with a lot of zeal and enthusiasm. But we find him becoming 'Bureaucratic': that is passive, indifferent, rule-minded, delaying, and either irresponsible or too cautious as the time passes off, may be, as said by Merton, this is 'trained incapacity'. Bureaucracy socialises its incumbents to the 'incapable' and unmindful of the change. It provides a training ground for 'incapacity'.

12. Max Weber, op.cit. p. 330.

13. Ibid., p. 331.

14. Merton, Robert K., op. cit., p. 365.

15. Max Weber, op.cit. p.331.

16. Ibid., p. 333.

17. Ibid., p.332.

18. Ibid.

19. Ibid., p. 337.

20. In writing this section the authors drew from Albrow, Martin, op. cit., pp 54-61.

21. Ibid., p. 55

22. Parsons, Talcott, *Structure and Process Modern Societies*, Glencoe, Free Press.

23. Gouldner, Alvin, *Patterns of Industrial Bureaucracy*, Glencoe, Free Press, 1954.

24. Blau, Peter M., *Bureaucracy in Modern Society*, Random House, New York, 1962, p. 36.

25. Max Weber, *The Methodology of the Social Sciences*, (Translated and edited by Edward A. Shils and Henry A. Finch), The Free Press, New York, 1969, p.90.

26. Palombara, Joseph La,"Bureaucracy and Political Development", in his edited *Bureaucracy and Political Development*, Princeton, N. J. Princeton University Press, 1963, p. 12.

27. Quoted in Diamont, Alfred, "Political Development: Approaches to Theory and Strategy", in Montgomery, John D., and Siffins, William J., (Eds.), *Approaches to Development: Politics, Administration and Change*, New York, McGraw-Hill Book Company, 1966, p. 29.

28. March, J.C., and Simon, H. A., *Organisation*, John Wiley & Sons Inc. New York, 1963, p. 36.

7

LUTHER GULICK AND LYNDALL URWICK

S.P. Ranga Rao

Introduction

With the coming of the industrial revolution in the 19th century many attempts were made to develop the principles of organisation to meet the requirements of the emerging industry. Among such attempts mention should be made of the works of F. W. Taylor, an American engineer and Henry Fayol, a French manager, who developed what today is known as the classical organisation or management theory. There are also many others who contributed to the conceptualisation of the theory. They developed theories of keeping organisational efficiency and increased productivity as their goal. Subsequently, American and British theorists synthesised the organisational or management theories as applicable to public organisations. Among such writers Gulick and Urwick merit prominently. Their edited volume *The Papers on the Science of Administration* (1937) is considered to be an important landmark in the development of the science of administration. They synthesised and integrated the ideas, writings and researches of earlier theorists on organisations, structures and executive functions.

(1892-1993)

Life and Works

Luther Halsey Gulick III (1892-1993), an acknowledged founder of administrative thought, a pioneer and a legend, was born in Yumamoto, Japan where he spent his initial twelve years before returning to the USA. He graduated from Oberlin in 1914 majoring in political science with high honours and obtained Ph.D in 1920 from the Columbia University. He secured Litt.D in 1939 and was conferred LL.D. in 1954. He was Director, Institute of Public

(1891-1983)

Administration from 1921 to 1961 and later chairman of the Board of Trustees of the Institute for another 21 years. Gulick served on the National Defence Council during the First World War, Administrator of New York City (1954-56) and was Eaton Professor of Municipal Science and Administration at Columbia University (1931-1942). He undertook several consultancy assignments on administration in US Administration and in several other countries including one at Calcutta, India concerning water supply under the aegis of World Bank. He was a member of the President's Committee on Administrative Management in 1936. He authored more than 20 books and research studies, over 160 articles and over 250 unpublished papers, studies, reports, etc. Nctable among his publications include *Administrative Reflections from World War II, Metropolitan Problems and American Ideas, Modern Management for the City of New York* and *The Papers on the Science of Administration.* He promoted the establishment of notable institutions like Brookings Institution, International City Managers Association, American Society for Public Administration, etc. He was president of both American Political Science Association and American Society of Public Administration; a distinction he shared with LD White.[1]

Lyndall Fownes Urwick (1891-1983), an avid advocate of scientific management, an outstanding management consultant, thinker and prolific writer, was born at Malvern, Worcestershire, UK. After graduation from New College, Oxford in 1913, he joined the family business and during the First World War he joined the army rising to the rank of Major. In 1922, he joined Rountree at York and later worked as Director of International Institute of Management (1928-33). During 1934-61 he was associated with Urwick, Orr and Partners Limited in the capacities of president, managing director, and chairman. During the Second World War (1940-42), he worked as advisor to the Treasury. He chaired the Urwick Committee appointed by the Ministry of Education to investigate what educational facilities are required to ensure adequate training facilities for its managers. He was actively involved in spreading management education and undertook several consultancies across the globe including the USA and India. He was a key figure in the establishment of Administrative Staff College at Henley-on-Thames (now called Henley Management College). He was recipient of several international awards and gold medals including Taylor Key, Gantt Memorial Medal (1959) and in 1958 was elected as a Fellow of International Academy of Management. He published several books including *Management of Tomorrow; The Making of Scientific Management* (3 Vols.); *The Elements of Administration; The Patterns of Management and Leadership in the XXth Century Organisations, Dynamic Administration, Freedom and Coordination.* He, along with Gulick, edited *The Papers on the Science of Administration,*[2] and founded the *Administrative Science Quarterly.*[3]

Gulick and Urwick had rich experience in the working of the civil service, military and industrial organisations. It is because of this, that one finds continued references to discipline and efficiency in their writings. They borrowed concepts like line and staff from the military organisation. They influenced by the machine model of man developed by Taylor. The studies in industrial management conducted by Henry Fayol also influenced their thinking.[4] Deriving inspiration mainly from their works, the two thinkers synthesised the classical theory of organisation, which is also known as the Administrative Management theory. They believed that it is possible to develop a science of administration based on principles. They pointed out to the fact that even an engineer at one time, was considered to be a craftsman who developed his skills at the bench only. It was only, through empirical observations, analyses and systematised findings committed to recording and documentation over a considerable period, a science of engineering became possible. In the same way if the experiences of administrators are processed it could be possible to develop a science of administration. Administration hitherto remained an art and there is no reason why it cannot be developed into a science; they believed.

Structure of Administration

One notable feature in the writings of these thinkers is the importance they attached to the structure of administration while almost neglecting the role of men in the organisation. Urwick remarks that 'it is impossible for humanity to advance its knowledge of organisation unless the factor on structure is isolated from other considerations, however artificial such isolation may appear".[5] He traces a large proportion of friction and confusion in society, with its major consequences, to the faulty structural arrangements in organisations. He defined organisation as determining activities that are necessary for a purpose (or plan) and arranging them in groups, which may be assigned to individuals.[6] Thus while the identification of the tasks and their grouping is given top priority, the individuals to whom the functions are entrusted come later. Urwick is aware of the fact that to begin with one may not have a clean slate but he suggests that one may assume to have a clean slate and design an ideal structure of organisation. Any alterations, if required, may be made later.

While conceiving an organisation chiefly as a designing process, Urwick felt that lack of design is illogical, cruel, wasteful and inefficient. Illogical because it is inconceivable to appoint a person and pay him wages without an idea of the position he is likely to occupy. Cruel when an organisational member does not know the qualifications required for the job and the duties assigned to him in the job situation. Wasteful because if jobs are not arranged properly, functional specialisation is not possible and training people to occupy jobs falling vacant due to death or retirement becomes difficult. Inefficient because the supervisors have nothing to fall back except on personalities in the event of conflict and confusion.[7]

Principles

Having stressed the importance of the structure as a designing process Gulick and Urwick devoted their attention to the discovery of principles based on which the structure may be designed. Gulick enumerates ten principles of organisation.[8] In working out these principles, Gulick was influenced by Henry Fayol's fourteen basic elements of administration. The principles are:

- Division of work or specialisation;
- Bases of departmental organisation;
- Coordination through hierarchy;
- Deliberate coordination;
- Coordination through committees;
- Decentralisation;
- Unity of command;
- Staff and line;
- Delegation; and
- Span of control.

Among the ten principles of administration, Gulick lays special emphasis on division of work. He feels that the division of work is the basis for organisation; indeed the reason for organisation.[9] The other classical administrative theorists also made the division of labour as the central tenet. Work division implies that the job to be performed is broken into its component functions and again each of the component functions be broken down into simple repetitive activities. At each stage the sub-division of work is followed by the inter-relating of the divided parts. The focus of attention shifts from grouping the various activities into sub-units, collecting the sub-units together to form units and inter-relating the units to create the overhead organisation. Thus, Gulick says that division of work and integration are the bootstraps by which mankind lifts itself in the process of civilisation.[10] However, Gulick was conscious of the limitations beyond which the division of work cannot go. He cites volume of work, technology, custom and physical and organic limitations.[11]

Urwick identified eight principles of organisation, viz., (1) the 'principle of objectives', - organisation should be an expression of a purpose; (2) the 'principle of correspondence' - authority and responsibility must be co-equal; (3) the 'principle of responsibility,' - responsibility of superiors for the work of subordinates is absolute; (4) the 'scalar principle'; (5) the 'principle of the span of control' - a superior cannot supervise directly the work of more than five or six subordinates whose works interlock; (6) the 'principle of specialisation' - limiting one's work to a single function; (7) 'principle of coordination' and (8) the 'principle of definition'- a clear prescription of every duty.[12]

Later by integrating Fayol's fourteen principles, Mooney and Reiley's principles of process and effect, Taylor's principles of management and the ideas of Follett and Graicunas, Urwick derived twenty-nine principles and a host of sub-principles. They are: (1) investigation, (2) forecasting, (3) planning, (4) appropriateness, (5) organisation, (6) coordination, (7) order, (8) command, (9) control, (10) the coordinative principle, (11) authority, (12) scalar process, (13) assignment of functions, (14) leadership, (15) delegation, (16) functional definition, (17) determinative, (18) applicative, (19) interpretative, (20) the general interest, (21) centralisation, (22) staffing, (23) spirit, (24) selection and placement, (25) rewards and sanctions, (26) initiative, (27) equity, (28) discipline and (29) stability.[13]

Urwick felt that the administrative organisation is still an unexplored field and there are many unknown factors for a fuller understanding. He, therefore, suggests that his principles are a framework of thought and an arrangement of ideas which would help others to synthesise out of their own experience.[14]

Executive Functions

Gulick identified the executive functions and coined the acronym POSDCORB incorporating the first letter of the functions identified.[15] Each letter in the acronym represents one important function of the manager. The first letter 'P' stands for planning. Planning is concerned with the identification of the various activities required to reach the goal and arranging them in terms of priorities and sequence so that the objectives of the organisation may be reached in a systematic and efficient manner. In other words, it is the function of planning to estimate the human and material resources available to the organisation and discover ways and means of reaching the goals of organisation through appropriate means while aiming at economy and efficiency.

'O' stands for organisation. After planning the activities of administration one should think of the structure of administration, viz., organisation through which the activities are operationalised and objectives achieved.

'S' stands for staffing and it is concerned with all aspects of personnel administration. Recruitment, appointment, promotion, discipline, retirement, etc., are functions which must receive due attention of the executive. As the efficiency of the organisation largely depends upon its personnel, most of the time of the executive usually is devoted to this function.

'D' stands for directing and relates to the orders issued by the managers to the subordinates directing the activities of the administration.

'Co' stands for coordination and relates not only to the evidence of conflicts and duplication in organisations but to secure cooperation and teamwork between the various units and employees.

'R' stands for reporting and it symbolises upward flow of information to the executive. It is the responsibility of the executive to keep himself posted with the progress of activities in the organisation. A good communication system is imperative through which such progress is reported to the executive. It is through reporting that the executive becomes aware of the problems in the organisation for which he may initiate corrective measures by issuing necessary directions.

Finally, the word 'B' stands for budgeting covering the entire field of financial administration. As finance is indispensable for any administration, the executive has to pay adequate attention to budgeting, financial procedures, accounting, etc.

Theory of Departmentalisation

The theory of departmentalisation addresses the problem of bases on which work may be divided and departments created. Luther Gulick identifies four bases viz., purpose (function), process, persons (clientele), and place, which are popularly known as the '4Ps'. He discussed at length the merits and demerits of each one of these bases of departmentalisation.[16] The main proposition of the discussion is that the advantages of each of the bases prove to be less costly in terms of the others.

In the first place, the work may be divided on the basis of major purpose or function. One has to identify the major functions and goals of organisation and create departments for each one of such functions. Gulick emphasises on the self-containment of the organisation and low coordination costs involved as advantages of this base. Secondly, process or skill specialisation is suggested as an alternative to purpose. If this basis is accepted then all work based on similar process or skill should be grouped together since it involves use of the same knowledge, skills and processes.

Gulick discusses at length the merits and demerits of the two bases. For instance, he lists out advantages of the purpose as bases. He says it makes more certain, the accomplishment of a given purpose or project by bringing the whole job under a single director with immediate control of all the experts, agencies and services which are required in the performance of the work with minimum outside interference. He can devote all his energies to get on with the job. After listing out the other advantages of the base, he also comments on its demerits. For instance, he says that there is a danger that an organisation created on the basis of purpose will fail to make use of the most up-to-date technical devices and specialists because there may not be enough work of a given technical nature to permit efficient sub-division and utility. Likewise the virtues of the process basis are mentioned by Gulick thus: "...bringing together in a single office a large amount of each kind of work (technically measured) makes it possible in each case to make use of the most effective division of work and specialisation. Second, it makes possible also the economies of the maximum use of labour saving machinery and mass production. These economies arise not from the total mass of the work to be performed, but from the fact that the work is performed with the same machine, with the same technique, with the same motions."

Specialisation of work according to the clientele served is the third bases. Gulick. observes that the members of the department develop specialised skills in serving a particular group. But this principle is not only inadequate for universal application but coordination between such organisations becomes difficult on account of overlapping and duplication. Territory or place is another bases. In this all functions performed in a given area are clubbed together and departments created. This base may be fruitfully used for the intensive development of any area. The members of such departments also become area specialists.

The theories of departmentalisation are based on such common sense terms that the basic truths underlying division of work cannot be denied. Even today, whenever work is to be divided and sub-units are to be created, the merits and demerits of the bases have to be weighed before taking a decision. But Gulick did not consider other important factors, which influence work division. For instance, of the four bases the type of specialisation may be determined by the culture in which the organisation is situated, by the environment and by the availability of personnel and political factors.

Single Executive

Gulick and Urwick did not favour organisations headed by plural bodies like committees but insisted on single top executive. Urwick, for instance, felt that the committees encourage irresponsibility. They are used to shield mistakes and to avoid responsibility. To him committee is like a corporation without 'a soul to be damned or a body to be kicked'. [17] To substantiate his point he quotes from the *Report of the US President's Committee on Administrative Management*, of which Gulick was a member. The Committee says, 'for purposes of management, boards and commissions have turned out to be failures. Their mechanism is inevitably slow, cumbersome, wasteful and ineffective and does not lend itself readily to cooperation with other agencies.... The conspicuously well-managed administrative units in the government are almost without exceptions headed by single administrators'.[18] They also felt that a subordinate should receive orders only from one superior. At the same time they were aware of the fact that this principle of unity of command is not capable of universal application. It is a known fact that Taylor proved that the functional supervision would help increase efficiency. But Gulick argues that we may prefer the advantages that are likely to accrue when we follow the principle rather than the confusion, inefficiency and irresponsibility that may follow its violation.[19]

Staff Principle

The principle of staff is born out of the principle of unity of leadership. When all authority rests with the leader, he requires assistance in running the organisation. The staff renders such assistance - both special and general. Gulick and Urwick feel that the special staff units do not exercise any direct authority and that their job is to render technical advice and provide timely and adequate information. The objective of staff agencies is to discharge knowing, thinking and planning functions and they must get the things done by 'authority of ideas'. The general staff is also necessary to assist the executive in the tasks of command, control and coordination. They must draw up and transmit orders, follow up operations and help coordinate the work of staff specialists without themselves taking on any specialised functions.[20] As a member of the President's Committee on Administrative Management Gulick applied his idea to the civil organisation and paved the way for the creation of present staff agencies under the American President.

Delegation

The delegation of authority is another important principle mentioned by these classicists. They stressed the need for the administrators to keep the requisite authority with them and delegate the rest to their subordinates. In the absence of delegation, the subordinates cannot discharge their responsibilities and administer the functions entrusted to them. They also discussed as to how and when to delegate authority. Urwick says that organisations do not function efficiently, if executives do not have the enterprise to delegate and also do not know how to delegate.[21] He emphasised the need to delegate responsibility of executives in whom authority is vested that they should be 'absolute' and that they should be personally accountable for the actions of their subordinates.[22] He maintains that authority and responsibility must be coterminous, co-equal and defined. These authors emphasised the principle of 'correspondence of responsibility and authority'. [23]

Span of Control

The principle of span of control postulates that an official cannot effectively control simultaneously more than a certain umber of subordinates, at a time. Urwick says that 'no superior can effectively supervise directly the work of more than five or, at the most, six subordinates whose work interlocks'. He observes that if the number of subordinates increases in arithmetic progression, there is a simultaneous geometrical growth in the permutations and combinations of the relationships requiring the superior's attention.[24] Urwick, however, was not dogmatic about the number and says that the span of control is not a rigid rule to be applied woodenly in all situations. But it is a very useful general principle and a diagnostic instrument in cases where organisational weakness exists.[25] However, Gulick unlike Urwick was less categorical in fixing the maximum number of subordinates an executive can effectively manage. Instead, he discussed some of the factors that determine the span of control. Three factors that would determine the span were identified by him.[26] In the first place, the span depends on each individual supervisor. A person with superior knowledge - intellect and personality - may effectively be able to control more number of subordinates. It is also a matter of time and energy of the executive. Secondly, the span depends upon the kind of work - work transacted by the subordinates. Where the work is routine, repetitive, measurable and homogenous it will be possible to effectively supervise many of them. On the other hand, where work is diversified, qualitative and workers are scattered executive can supervise only a few. Thirdly, element of time span will be more in stable organisations, which are in existence for a long time. The procedures, methods and techniques of administration in such organisations could have been consolidated and consequently there could be less necessity for the intervention by the superiors. On the other hand, in new and changing organisations the superiors have to keep a constant watch for good precedents to be established and proper procedures adopted for the administration. Gulick wanted further research on the subject. [27]

Human Factor and Time in Public Administration

Gulick in his later writings noted that much has happened to affect the field of Public Administration and his analysis of its nature since he edited *The Papers on the Science of Administration* seventy years ago. Based on fifty years of analysis, he notes that 'after all, governments are constituted of human beings, are run by human beings and have as their main job helping, controlling and serving human beings'.[28] He considers human beings as the major and essential variables for understanding the nature of Public Administration today and guiding the field into the future. On this foundation, he identifies as to how human beings constitute the dynamic factors that are intrinsic in the study of administration. Gulick emphasises that the main functions of the state should be human welfare, survival and improvement to meet the challenges of the ever changing environment and not war.[29] But unfortunately, the structure of the modern state is specifically designed for war and is distinctly military. It is authoritative, with all authority concentrated at the top and all the work, but not the authority, assigned to subordinate echelons and field commanders. In public administration our very vocabulary is military in origin. We talk about "line and staff", "field commanders", and "material and manpower", and when we make cost-benefit analyses we manipulate hard statistics, not human values and human welfare.[30]

Gulick emphasises the needs to introduce greater decentralisation in place of the present centralised, hierarchical, military structure. He suggests that public administration should forget the non-existent economic man, deal realistically with the non-existent free market and include human welfare and compassion in its embrace.[31] Gulick also emphasises that time is the crucial factor in every event. Without it there is no change, no growth, no cause and effect and no responsibility for management. He notes that all public policy innovations are rooted in timing and in democracy timing is the hallmark of the statecraft.[32]

Gulick identifies five different aspects of time, namely, time as an input, time as an output, time as the flow of events, time as a gap between two or more significant events or processes and finally, timing as a management policy.[33] He emphasises that time has practical and significant implications for public administration. It means that the principles of management and administration should be eternally tied to the culture in which they work, and that the culture must evolve appropriately well before major changes in human organisation can be successfully undertaken. Timing is essential for any organisation as it is not a machine but an organism.[34] He emphasises that time must become a central strategic and moral concern in public management. Therefore, government must plan and work with this flow in time and for time.[35] But he laments that time has been a neglected factor.

A Critical Evaluation

The principles of organisation of Gulick and Urwick were subjected to severe criticism. While writing so much about principles they have not made it clear as to what they meant by them. Normally principles are universal truths subject to verification. However, such universal validity appears to be absent as far as principles of administration are concerned. They appear more in the nature of postulates of experienced men who have closely observed organisations at work. At best they may be action recommendations but not scientific principles. L. D. White says that the terms line, staff and auxiliary agencies, hierarchy, authority, centralisation, were useful terms for describing or classifying administrative situations; they are no more. They are not rules. They suggest only working rules of conduct which wide experience validated.[36]

Herbert Simon stands high among those who attacked the 'principles'. Bertram Gross noted that 'Simon will long be reread with pleasure for his free-swinging attacks on Gulick and Urwick principles as homely proverbs, myths, slogans, inanites'. [37] Simon says that "it is a fatal defect of the current principles of administration that, like proverbs, they occur in pairs. For almost every principle one can find an equally plausible and acceptable contradictory principle.

Although the two principles of the pair will lead to exactly opposite organisational recommendations, there is nothing in the theory to indicate which the proper one to apply". [38] For instance one of the 'proverbs' says that administrative efficiency increases by specialisation. But it is not made clear whether area specialisation is good or functional specialisation. The principle of specialisation does not help in choosing between the two alternatives. It appears to be simple; a simplicity that conceals fundamental ambiguities. [39] Likewise, there is contradiction between the principle of specialisation and the principle of unity of command. The unity of command of Gulick's specification never existed in any administrative organisation. The specialists working in organisations are always subject to the duel control of the superiors in administration and in technical matters. The evidence of 'actual administration practices would seem to indicate that the need for specialisation is to a very large degree given priority over the need for unity of command".

Another contradictory situation relates to the principle of span of control. One principle asserts that administrative efficiency increases by keeping the levels of organisation to the minimum. This is supposed to help the simplification of the procedures. But when levels are thus reduced, the span of control increases resulting in the violation of another important principle. Moreover, the specification of the ideal number of subordinates as between 5 and 11 has no scientific validity at all. [40] Simon also pointed out to the contradictions involved in choosing between the principles of departmentalisation. Simon felt that "the principles of administration are at best criteria for describing and diagnosing administrative situations." All the stated principles are to be considered in the design of an efficient administrative organisation. [41] None of them should be considered superior or inferior *inter se*. Keeping the overall efficiency in view, the relative advantages and disadvantages of the various principles have to be comparatively weighed and the relevant one should be selected for the occasion. Perhaps the most critical failure of the classical administrative science is its incapacity to "confront theory with evidence". The principles tend to dissolve when put to test; partly this is because of the consequence of difficulties in operation. It is not possible to conduct controlled experiments to test the theories time and again.

The bases of departmental organisation are criticised on the basis that they are incompatible with each other. There is an overlap between them and they are said to be vague. Further, it is pointed out that the principles are prescriptive rather than descriptive and they state how work should be divided rather than how work is actually divided. Organisations grow according to the dictates of the situation and in consonance with the requirements of efficiency and goal achievement. Thus, one may see that all the four bases of departmental organisation are being adopted though not deliberately, in a single organisation. For instance, the Defense Department based on purpose may have geographical subdivisions as the basis of its working. They may have clientele sub-unit which looks after the welfare of the war-widows. Again, there may be an accounts division in the department based on skill specialisation.

The classical administrative theory is criticised for its neglect of the human element in an organisation. In the writings of classical thinkers, there are certain trends, which are considered by humans as insignificant in administrative processes. In the first place, there is a tendency to treat the human being as an instrument incapable of individual contribution based on personal qualification. It is this critical failure that gave rise to the human relations movement and behavioural studies. The new developments compensated the failure of the classical theorists by viewing organisations essentially as human associations. Being living entities, the humans have both psychological and physiological processes involved in their behaviour. Hence, human element cannot be taken for granted. Mere assignment of duties and functions does not ensure the optimum contribution of effort by the employees. Moreover, personnel are not static factor but a variable in the system. We may not get persons to suit organisational requirements. At best there could be only an adjustment of personnel who approximately suit the requirements of the jobs. Hence, the vagary of human resources is an important limitation to the mechanistic approach to organisations. It is a fact that humans have to be constantly motivated to contribute their efforts towards the attainment of their goals. These motivational assumptions in classical theories are incomplete and hence, inaccurate. Several writers have subsequently devoted considerable attention on aspects of motivation, morale, etc.[42]

There is no doubt, that some evidence has been found in the writings of the classical theorists that they were aware of the human element in organisations. For instance, Gulick says social experiments must be made by men on men. This greatly restrict the process of verification of hypothesis not only because of the value and dignity of human life but also because, human beings continually interfere with experiments involving themselves.[43] He also pointed out that in dealing with human beings we encounter a rare dynamic element which is compounded in proportions of predictable and unpredictable or rational or emotional conduct. Secondly, we are not able, except in the rarest circumstances, to set up controlled experiments and test the theories over and over at will.[44] From these observations, it is evident that the classical theorists were aware of the human element in an organisation. However, they took into consideration, only the rational behaviour of the humans. It was left to thinkers like Simon, to point out to the several limitations to rationality in human behaviour. It is a matter of common knowledge today, that rationality in decision-making as well as behaviour is subject to a particular frame of reference compounded by the knowledge of employee, his perception of goals of organisation as well as the consequences of his decisions and actions. But the subjective character of rationality did not receive the due attention of the classical theorists.

There are arguments that Gulick and Urwick have shown concern only for the formal organisation to the total neglect of the informal organisational process. It is a matter of common knowledge that organisations do not conform to the formal model all the time. The humans behave in a way that suits their instincts and wants. Hence, the actual behaviour always differs from the intended behaviour. Neglect of this vital truth is very unrealistic as far as the administrative processes are concerned.

The dynamic nature of administration and the ever changing setting in which it functions is not given adequate attention by the classical theorists. As Alfred Diamant[45] says, most of the conceptual constraints in organisations have a 'steady' bias. The organisations and organisational goals undergo a constant change as a result of the economic, social or political stimuli and hence, any study of administration must take into consideration this element of change. No doubt, Gulick to some extent was aware of the role of change when he observed that the principles "appropriate at one stage may not be appropriate at all during succeeding stages'. But the fact is that the change as such has not received adequate attention of the classical theorists.

Simon and March point out important limitations to the classical administrative science. The first relates to the improper motivational assumptions. Secondly, there is little appreciation of the role of intra-organisational conflict of interests in defining limits or organisational behaviour. Thirdly, the constraints placed on the human being by his limitations as a complex information processing system. Fourthly, little attention was given to the role of cognition in task identification and classification. Lastly, the phenomenon of programme evaluation receives little attention.[46] The last of these limitations is in fact very significant. It is wrong to assume that the administration is not concerned with the specification, elaboration and redefinition of goals of the organisation. Failure to identify the administrative functions may be said to be a vital lapse on the part of the classical theorists.

V. Subramaniam points out two important limitations of the classical theories. In the first place, there is lack of sophistication in the theories. They appear to be commonplace general knowledge propositions, which do not appeal to the intellectual curiosity of the academicians and practitioners of administration. Secondly, all the classical theorists exhibited a pro-management bias in their theories. The theorists only dealt with the problems of management in the organisation and not the other operational problems that involve the other levels of management.[47]

In spite of the varied criticisms, Gulick and Urwick's ideas and conceptualisations stand out prominently in the literature of public administration. No textbook on Public Administration is complete without a discussion of the principles. The simple truths underlying the propositions stated as principles by the classical thinkers cannot be denied. But these propositions are misleading as they, at best, represent only half-truths. While calling them proverbs, Simon devoted considerable space to these principles in his writings. Even he could not discard them. The inescapable conclusion is that they do not represent all aspects of administration. However, there is a common element between the classical theorists and the works of several contemporary writers on administration. The commonness of approach relates to an interest in the structure, economy and efficiency, settlement of conflict, delegation of authority, decentralisation, etc.

Gulick captured the development of the field of public administration and pointed to the importance of public administration as a managerial, political, moral and ethical concern. As Denhardt has noted that we now recognise that administrative action is permeated by moral choices and whether we like it or not administrators are model of not only technical and professional but also moral behaviour. [48]

In Brief

The contribution of Gulick and Urwick to the administrative theory are summarised below:

- Luther Gulick, an acknowledged founder of administrative thought, and Lyndall Urwick, an outstanding management consultant with their rich experience in civil and military administration made significant contribution to the synthesis of classical administrative theory;

- *The Papers on the Science of Administration,* edited by them, is considered a landmark in the development of the science of administration. In their view the process of development of engineering science, which is based on empirical observations and analysis, is equally applicable to the development of science of administration;

- Gulick and Urwick emphasised the importance of structure in administration. They considered structure as a designing process and devoted their attention to the discovery of principles based on which the structure may be designed. They considered principles as a framework of thought and arrangement of ideas to help in the development of science of administration;

- Gulick discussed in detail the executive functions and coined POSDCORB by incorporating the first letters of all the functions of the executive. The acronym, though not comprehensive, helps in understanding and analysing the functions of the executive;

- Gulick considered division of work as the basis of organisation. His theory of departmentalisation addresses the basis of division of work for the creation of departments. The four basis of departmentalisation *viz*, purpose, process, persons and place, popularly known as the "4Ps", are extensively used in the creation of departments/

units in organisations. Gulick and Urwick in their writings discussed in detail the application of many other principles like single executive, staff principle, delegation, span of control, etc.

- Gulick, in his later writings focused on human factors in administration. Based on his fifty years of analysis, Gulick observes: "after all governments are constituted of human beings, are run by human beings and have as their main job, helping, contributing and serving human beings". He considered the human being as the dynamic factor intrinsic in the study of administration;

- Gulick also emphasised time as the crucial factor in organisations. He identified five aspects of time, viz., time as input, time as an output, time as the flow of events and time as a gap between two or more significant events or processes and finally timing as a management policy. He considers time factor as critical in public administration;

- The principles of organisation of Gulick and Urwick were criticised for their contradictions and inadequacy to answer practical organisational questions and also for their neglect of role of human element in organisational processes. In his later writings Gulick emphasised the role of human beings in organisations; and

- There cannot be any serious study of the science of administration without reference to the principles of organisation. Understanding and theorising the dynamic nature of application of these principles in different administrative situations is the major challenge of administrative studies today.

References

[1] See for details, Fitch, Lyle C., "Luther Gulick", *Public Administration Review*, Vol. 50.No.6, 1990, pp.604- 08; Paul P. Van Riper, "The Literary Gulick: A Bibliographical Appreciation", *Public Administration Review*, Vol. 50.No.6,1990, pp.609-14. http://www.bartleby.com/65/gu/GulickL92.html

[2] See for details A Schedule of the Lyndall Fowness Urwick Archive, http://www.cardiff.ac.uk/carbs/icon/boyns/schedule.pdf. Retrieved on 26th May, 2009. See also Sheldrake, John., *Management Theory*, London, Thomson Learning, 2003, p.93.

[3] See http://en.wikipedia.org/wiki/Lyndall Urwick retrieved on 26th May, 2009

[4] For details of ideas of Taylor and Fayol see the companion articles in this volume.

[5] Urwick, L., "The Functions of Administration with special reference to the work of Henry Fayol", in Gulick, Luther, and Urwick, L., (Eds.), *The Papers on the Science of Administration*, New York, Institute of Public Administration, 1937, p. 122.

[6] Urwick, L., *The Elements of Administration*, London, Sir Issac Pitman and Sons Ltd., 1947 (2nd Ed.), p. 36.

[7] Ibid., pp. 38-39

[8] Gulick, Luther, "Notes on the Theory of Organisation," in Luther Gulick and L. Urwick, (Eds.), op. cit

[9] Ibid. p. 3.

[10] Ibid. p. 4.

[11] Ibid. pp. 4-5.

[12] Quoted in Wren, Daniel A., *The Evolution of Management Thought*, New York, The Ronald Press Company, 1972, pp. 357-58.

[13] See, Urwick, L., *The Elements of Administration*, op. cit.pp.118-23.

[14] Ibid., p. 118.

[15] Gulick, Luther, "Notes on Theory of Organisation," op. cit. p. 13.

[16] Ibid.

[17] Urwick, L., *The Elements of Administration*, op. cit. p. 72.

[18] Ibid.

[19] Gulick, Luther, "Notes on Theory of Organisation," op. cit. p.9.

[20] D. Gvishiani, *Organisation and Management*, Moscow, Progress Publishers, 1972, p. 198.

[21] Urwick, L., *The Elements of Administration*, op. cit. p. 51.

[22] Ibid., p. 125.

[23] Ibid., pp. 45-46.

[24] Ibid., pp. 52-53.

[25] Urwick, Lyndall F., "The Manager's Span of Control", *Harvard Business Review*, Vol. 34, No, 3, May-June 1956, p. 41

[26] Gulick, Luther," Notes on Theory of Organisation," op. cit. pp. 7-9.

[27] See Meier, Kenneth J., and Bohte, John, "Span of Control and Public Organisation: Implementing Luther Gulick's Research Design", *Public Administration Review*, Vol.63,No.1, January-February, 2003, pp.61-70

[28] Luther Gulick,"The Dynamics of Public Administration Today as Guidelines for the Future",
Public Administration Review, No. 3, May-June, 1983, p. 193.

[29] Ibid., 196.

[30] Ibid.

[31] Ibid., 198.

[32] Gulick, Luther,"Time and Public Administration", *Public Administration Review*, No., 1, Jan-Feb., 1987, pp. 115-116.

[33] Ibid., p. 116.

[34] Ibid., p. 118.

[35] Ibid., p. 119.

[36] White, L. D., *An Introduction to the Study of Administration*, New York, Macmillan Company, (III Ed.), 1948, p. 37.

[37] Gross, Bertram M., *The Managing of Organisations: The Administrative Struggle*, London, The Free Press of Glencoe, 1964, p. 182.

[38] Simon, Herbert A., *Administrative Behaviour: A Study of Decision-Making Process in Administrative Organisation*, New York, The Free Press, 1965, p. 20.

[39] Ibid., p. 21.

[40] Ibid., p. 21.

[41] Ibid., pp. 35-38.

[42] For details of the ideas of Elton Mayo, Chris Argyris, McGregor, Rensis Likert, etc., see the relevant articles in this volume.

[43] Gulick, Luther, "Science, Values and Public Administration," in Gulick, Luther, and. Urwick, L., (Eds.), op. cit., p. 194.

[44] Ibid., p193.

[45] See, Diamont, Alfred, "The Temporal Dimensions in Models of Administration and Organisation/" in Waldo, Dwight, (Ed.), *Temporal Dimensions of Development Administration*, Durham, North Carolina, Duke University Press, 1970.

[46] See March, J. G., and Simon, H., *Organisation*, New York, John Wiley, 1959.

[47] Subramaniam, V., "The Classical Organisation Theory and its Critics," *Public Administration Review*, Vol. 44, Winter, 1966, pp. 435-42.

[48] Denhardt, Robert B., quoted in Paul P. Van Riper, op.cit. p. 613.

8

MARY PARKER FOLLETT

D. Ravindra Prasad

Introduction

Mary Parker Follett occupies a prominent place among the contributors to administrative thought, though she is less known to the public and even to some writers and teachers on administration.[1] She carved out a prominent place in what was then largely a man's world. But unfortunately, her works have been undeservedly forgotten.[2] It goes to her credit for initiating studies on industrial groups which had seldom been subject matter of study by political or social scientists. She turned her attention from the traditional subjects of study - the state or the community - to concentrate on the study of industry. She evolved principles of human association and organisation specifically in terms of industry and convinced businessmen of the practicability of these principles in dealing with current problems.[3] Follett blended theory, fact and ideal admirably. She demonstrated

(1868-1933)

her beliefs by drawing illustrations almost from every walk of life - from the affairs of government, industry and business, home, war and peace, international institutions, etc.[4] She was a gifted writer with a rare capacity for presenting original ideas with great simplicity and lucidity. Her writings are replete with practical wisdom, deep flashes of intuition, undepartmentalised thinking and an all-pervading spirit of democratic dynamism.[5] Most prominent among those associated with the 'classic' or scientific management schools like Ordway Tead, Henry Fayol, Oliver Sheldon and Lyndall Urwick were influenced by her philosophy. Peter Drucker, the management theoretician, called her 'the prophet of management' and his 'Guru'.[6] A better understanding of some of the present trends in administrative thought, therefore, requires a study of her works.[7]

Life and Works

Follett (1868-1933) was born in Quincy, Massachusetts, USA and had her early education at Thayer Academy in Braintree, Boston. She was influenced by her teachers from whom she got stimulation of intellect and learnt simplicity of life. She joined Redcliff College, the Women's Branch of Harvard in 1892, and went to Newnham College, England for studies but returned to graduate *summa cum laude* in economics, law, philosophy and government in 1898. She went to Paris for a year for post-graduate studies. An interesting part of her career is that while she was still a college student, she published *The Speaker of the House of Representatives* in 1896. As a student, she was keenly interested in philosophy, history and political science, which she pursued with enthusiasm. After her studies, she developed interest in social administration and social work. From 1900 to 1908 she devoted her time to social work in the Roxbury Neighbourhood, Boston. In 1908, she became Chairperson of the Committee on Extended Use of School Buildings of the Women's Municipal League, Boston. In 1911, she opened East Boston High School Social Centre and was instrumental in the formation of such centers throughout Boston which helped her to transform her views on democracy. She did social work for women, children and slum dwellers. In 1912, she took to vocational guidance and became a member of the Placement Bureau Committee, Boston. In this capacity, she came in contact with industry and contributed to the management thought. She also served on the Massachusetts Minimum Wage Board and in 1917 became Vice-president of the National Community Centers Association. During 1915-33, she presented papers on industrial organisation at the annual conferences of business executives. Thus Follett, a political scientist turned her attention to social administration and the solutions to social problems and thence smoothly to the realm of business management and administration. She published *The Speaker of the House of Representatives* (1896), *The New State* (1918), *Creative Experience* (1924), *Dynamic Administration* (1941) posthumously edited by Metcalf and Urwick and *Freedom and Coordination: Lectures in Business Organisation* (1949) edited by Urwick.

Follett's ideas and conceptions provide a fascinating perspective on critical management and administrative themes like conflict, power, authority and responsibility, leadership, control, role of individual in group, participation, place of business in society, labour-management relations, etc., and they have continued relevance even today. Her ideas are characterised by cohesiveness of thought, subtlety of language, breadth of understanding, and wisdom of insights. It is very difficult, almost impossible, to summarise her administrative ideas and concepts. We shall examine some of them, which have been particularly influential.

Constructive Conflict

Follett accords a very high importance to the problems of conflict in organisations. She presented her celebrated paper 'Constructive Conflict' before the Bureau of Personnel Administration in 1925. She advances the idea of "constructive conflict" recognising thereby that conflicts should be regarded as a normal process in any activity of an organisation by which socially valuable differences register themselves for the enrichment of all concerned.[8] To Follett, conflict is neither good nor bad and has to be considered without passion or ethical prejudgements. Conflict is not warfare, but is only an appearance of difference - difference of opinions, of interests not only between the employer and the employee but also between managers, between directors or wherever differences appear.[9] Conflict is not a wasteful outbreak of incompatibilities, but a normal process by which socially valuable differences register themselves for the enrichment of all concerned.[10] Because of individual differences, conflict is unavoidable in human organisations. Since conflict is unavoidable, instead of criticising it as something bad, one should try to capitalise on it and make use of it to do something good. To Follett, conflict is a moment in the interaction of desires. Just as there are destructive ways of dealing with such moments, there are also constructive ways. Conflict, as the moment of appearing and focussing of differences, may be a sign of health and a prophecy of progress. Drawing analogies from the universe she says: "All polishing is done by friction. We get the music from the violin by friction and we left the sewage state when we discovered fire through friction." [11]

The question is how to make conflict work constructively. Follett says that there are three ways of resolving a conflict: domination, compromise and integration.[12] Domination is a victory of one side over the other and this is the easiest way of resolving conflicts. Though it is the easiest for the moment, it is not successful in the long run. The problem with domination is that, in addition to the discomfort caused to the 'dominated', the repressed tendencies are always there to rebel against the dominator whenever possible. Since each party retains the action tendencies that led to the confrontation in the first place, as soon as it is possible and at the earliest the confrontation will surface again. This is evident from what has happened after the First World War. Compromise is generally the way people settle most of their conflicts. In this, each side gives up a little and settles the conflict so that the activity, which has been interrupted by the conflict, may go on. In this, each side involved in the conflict gives up a part of its 'desire' to settle the issue. Though compromise is a widely accepted method of resolving conflicts, rarely people want to compromise, as this involves giving up something.

Integration is the third method of resolving conflicts. In this, two desires are integrated and neither side needs to sacrifice its desires. Follett considers integration as a method of dealing with conflict, as it has some advantages compared to compromise. She says that compromise does not create but only deals with the existing, whereas integration creates something new, leads to invention and to the emergence of new values.[13] It leads to the use of better techniques and also saves time and resources. Another advantage is that integration goes to the root of the problem and puts an end to the conflict permanently. If we deal with conflicts through compromise, they may come up again in some other form, as people are not always happy with the fulfillment of only a part of their desire but want to fulfill the 'whole' desire. She illustrates this point from the industrial and international controversies where this often occurs. But integration stabilises and conflicts are settled permanently.

While pointing out the advantages of integration as a method of settling conflicts, Follett is not unaware of the difficulties involved in achieving it. Follett does not think that it is always possible to achieve integration. She says when two men want to marry the same woman; there can be no integration. There may be many such cases of conflict where integration is difficult; almost impossible. Follett says that it is often difficult to say whether a decision reflects true integration or something of a compromise. However, she asserts that the desire of the people to solve their problems through integration in itself is encouraging. If we are conscious of its advantages, we can try integration instead of compromise or domination.

Bases of Integration

Follett discusses the bases of achieving integration. The first step towards achieving integration, according to her, is to bring the differences into the open instead of suppressing them. "We cannot hope to integrate," she asserts, "our differences unless we know what they are." [14] What is needed, therefore, is to uncover, identify and understand the real issues involved in a conflict. This involves finding out the significant, rather than the dramatic, features involved in a conflict. This is more so the case with conflicts involving complex situations and numerous and overlapping activities. This is necessary because there is a tendency among managers to deal with the dramatic moments forgetting that they are not always the significant moments and that leads to the uncovering of the real conflict.

The second step is breaking up of the whole i.e., to consider the demands of both sides involved in conflict and to break them into their constituent parts. This involves examination of symbols, use of which is unavoidable in organisational work. This in turn involves a careful scrutinizing of the language used to see what it really means. To Follett, all language used is symbolic, and therefore, one should be on guard to know as to what is being symbolised. Integration not only involves breaking up of the whole but sometimes one has to do the opposite. It is important to articulate the whole demand, the real demand which is being obscured by miscellaneous minor claims or by ineffective presentation.[15]

Anticipation of conflict is the third step. Anticipation does not mean avoidance of conflict but responding to it differently. To illustrate this, Follett gives the example of a man who liked motoring, while his wife liked walking. He anticipated what her response might be to a suggestion that they motor on a Sunday afternoon by tiring her out playing tennis in the morning. To Follett, integration is like a game of chess. Anticipation of response is by itself not enough; there is need for preparation for response as well. This involves building up of certain attitudes in the people. Response is of two types - circular and linear. A good example of circular response is the game of tennis. This concept of circular response and behaviour throws much light on conflict. In fact, circular behaviour as the basis of integration, Follett says, is the key to constructive conflict.

Obstacles to Integration

Integration requires high intelligence, keen perception, discrimination, and a brilliant inventiveness. It is always easier to fight than to suggest better ways of resolving conflicts. As long as intelligence and inventiveness are not there, resolving conflicts through integration would be difficult. Another obstacle is the people's habit of enjoying domination. To many, integration is a tame affair; it does not give them the thrill of conquest or satisfaction of victory. Follett says that people with such habit patterns always prefer domination to integration. Theorising the problem instead of taking them as proposed activities or practical issues needing immediate solutions is the third obstacle to integration. Quite often, people, forgetting that disagreements will disappear if they stop theorising, go on theorising the problem. Follett says that intellectual agreement alone does not solve conflicts and bring integration. Language used is the fourth obstacle. Language used, Follett says, must be favourable for reconciliation and should not arouse antagonism and perpetuate the conflict. Sometimes language used creates new disputes, which were not there earlier. A fifth obstacle to integration is the undue influence of leaders. Finally, the most important of all obstacles to integration is lack of training. Follett says that in most cases there is a tendency to 'push through' or to 'force through' the plans previously arrived at, based on preconceived notions. Therefore, she pleads that there should be courses to teach the art of cooperative thinking, to master the technique of integration, both for workers and managers.

Giving Orders

Follett examines at length the question of giving orders and the principles underlying the different ways of giving orders. To Follett there are four important steps in giving orders viz.:

- a conscious attitude - realise the principles through which it is possible to act on in any matter;
- a responsible attitude - to decide which of the principles one should act on;
- an experimental attitude - try experiments and watch results; and
- pooling the results.[16]

Follett says that most people, without even knowing the different principles that underlie giving orders, give orders every day. To her, to know the principles that underlie any given activity is to take a conscious attitude. After recognising the different principles, one must think of what principles one should act on and then give orders in accordance with those principles. To give orders based on principles is a responsible attitude. Trying experiments, noting whether they succeed or fail and analysing as to why they are successful or failures is taking an experimental attitude. Finally, one should pool the experiences of all and see to what extent and in what manner the methods of giving orders can be changed if the existing methods are found inadequate.

Many think that giving orders is very simple and expect that they would be obeyed without question. But in practice, issuing orders is very difficult. Past life, training, experience, emotions, beliefs, prejudices, etc., form certain habits of mind, which the psychologists call 'habit-patterns', 'action-patterns' and 'motor-sets'. Unless these habit-patterns and mental attitudes are changed, one cannot really change people. Sometimes orders are not obeyed because the employees cannot go contrary to lifelong habits. For instance, Follett says, the farmer has a general disposition to manage the lands alone, and this is being changed by the cooperatives. To bring about such a change, Follett suggests three steps viz., (1) building up of certain attitudes; (2) providing for their release; and (3) augmenting the released response, as it is being carried out.[17] Follett gives the example of a salesman who creates in us an attitude that we want his article; then at just the psychological moment, he produces his contract form which we may sign and release the attitude; then if we are preparing to sign, someone comes in to tell us, how pleased he is with his purchase of this article and that augments the response being released.[18]

Before giving orders, the employer should consider the ways and means of forming the 'habits' among the employees to ensure acceptance of the orders. This involves four important steps: first, the officials should be made to see the desirability of a new method; second, the rules of the office should be so changed to make it possible for the officials to adopt the new method; third, a few people should be convinced in advance to adopt the new method to set an example. The last step is intensifying the attitude to be released. This will prepare the way for the acceptance of orders.[19]

Follett then turns her attention to the environment of giving orders and says that the response to the orders depends upon the place and the circumstances under which orders are given. She says that the 'strength of favourable response to an order is in inverse ratio to the distance the order travels'. [20]To Follett, both giving and receiving orders is a matter of integration through circular behaviour. There are two dissociated paths in the individual. Therefore, before integration can be made between order giver and order receiver, there is need for integration within the individual. An order should seek to unite and integrate the dissociated path.[21]

The manner of giving orders is equally important. Alleged harassing, tyrannical and overbearing conduct of officials is an important reason for many a controversy. Treating men without regard to their feelings and self-respect would result in strikes and strained industrial relations. The language used often arouses wrong behavioural patterns. The more one is bossed, the more one develops opposition to bossing.

Depersonalising Orders

From the foregoing it is evident that giving orders is a complex process. Therefore, either people stop giving orders or become 'authoritarian' to ensure compliance to their orders. To avoid too much of bossism in giving orders or giving no orders at all, Follett suggests depersonalising the orders. This involves a study of the problems to discover the *'law of the situation'* and obeying it by all concerned. One should not give orders to another, but both should agree to take orders from the situation. If orders are a part of the situation, the question of someone giving and someone receiving does not arise and both take orders from the situation. Follett says that two heads of departments do not give orders to each other. Each studies the situation and decisions are made as the situation demands. Depersonalising orders, however, does not mean that one should not exercise authority. It only means exercising the authority of the situation. She gives the example of a boy who says no and then gets a pail of water to his mother. In this case, he resents the command, but recognises the demand of the situation.

Follett also observes that the situation is never static; it always develops and evolves. Therefore, the orders too should never be static; but should always keep pace with situations. The external orders can never keep pace with the situations and only those drawn fresh from the situation can do so. Therefore, Follett says, that orders must always be integral to the situation. Another factor to be kept in mind in giving orders is that people resent a feeling of being 'under' someone or subordinate to somebody. People would like to work 'with' someone, not because it connotes functional unity, but the study of the situation involves 'with' proposition. 'With proposition heightens self-respect and increases efficiency.'

Giving orders is a complex process and it is fraught with many a problem. The first is how much and what kind of supervision is necessary or advisable in order to see that the orders are carried out. Many people do not like and object to being watched. Supervision is necessary, but it is resented. How to make integration here? Another problem is when and how to point out the mistakes and misconduct. Follett suggests that supervision should not be for the sake of supervision, but to accomplish something. The subordinates should always be told in that form, at the time, under those circumstances, which provide a real education to them.[22]

Power, Authority and Control

Follett gives special attention to the problems of power, control and authority. She reveals profound, penetrating and strikingly original insight in her analysis of power. She defines power as "the ability to make things happen, to be a causal agent, to initiate change".[23] Power is the capacity to produce intended effects. It is an instinctive urge inherent in all human beings. She makes a distinction between 'power-over' and 'power-with'.[24] The former may tend to be 'coercive-power' while the latter is a jointly developed 'coactive-power'. Power-with is superior to power-over as it is a self-developing entity, which promotes better understanding, reduces friction and conflict, encourages cooperative action and promotes participative decision-making. Follett does not think it possible to get rid of power-over, but thinks that one should try to reduce it. This can be accomplished by integrating the desires, obeying the law of situation and through functional unity. In a functional unity, each has functions and one should also have the authority and responsibility, which goes on with that function.[25] Follett believes that power can never be delegated or handed out or wrenched from someone as it is the result of knowledge and ability. But, she feels, we can create conditions for the development of power.[26]

Follett defines authority as vested power - the right to develop and exercise power. Authority in terms of status and the subordination of one another offends human dignity and may cause undesirable reaction and friction. Therefore, it cannot be the basis of organisation. To her authority stems from the task being performed and from the situation, and suggests that function is the true basis from which authority is derived. Therefore, she says that central authority i.e., derivation of authority from the chief executive should be replaced by authority of function in which each individual has the final authority within the allotted functions. She feels that the authority can be conferred on others and such conferment is not delegation. She expresses in clear terms that 'delegation of authority' should be an 'obsolete expression'.[27] Like authority, responsibility also flows from the function and situation. Therefore, one should ask, "for what is he responsible?" than "to whom is he responsible?" Follett believed in pluralistic concept of responsibility or cumulative responsibility and rejects ultimate responsibility as an illusion.

Control, like authority and responsibility, is an important aspect to achieve organisational goals. Unlike classical thinkers, Follett believes in fact-control rather than man-control and in correlated-control than superimposed control.[28] Since facts vary from situation to situation, control should depend upon the facts of each situation instead of superiors controlling subordinates. Similarly, situations are too complex for central control to be meaningful and effective. Follett suggests, therefore, control mechanisms should be correlated at many places in the organisational structure. If organisations are to be well integrated, unified and coordinated, control should be designed and developed as part of the unifying process as a unified organisation is self-regulating and self-directing, organism. In all such organisations, Follett feels, control tends to be self-control.

Planning and Coordination

To Follett, planning is a scheme of self-adjustment and self-coordination of various and varying interests. The process of self-adjustment is possible only through coordination. Follett postulates four principles of organisaton: [29]

1. *Coordination as the reciprocal relating of all factors in a situation*: All factors in a situation have to be related to one another and these inter-relationships themselves must be taken into account.

2. *Coordination by direct control*: Responsible people in the organisation must be in direct contact with one another irrespective of their position in the hierarchy. She believes that horizontal communication is as important as vertical chain of command.

3. *Coordination in the early stages*: All people concerned should be involved at the stage of policy formulation than being involved only at the implementation stage. Such participation at the early stages will benefit the organisation through increased motivation and morale.

4. *Coordination as a continuing process*: Follett emphasises the need for a permanent machinery to achieve coordination from planning to activity and from activity to further planning. The advantages of such machinery, Follett feels, would be immense. Similarly, she emphasises the importance of information based on continuous research. The information itself would be a form of control. For, there would be a tendency to act in accordance with the information given, if it were accepted as accurate.

Leadership

Follett discusses at length the process of leadership. She believes that the old ideas of leadership are changing because of the changes in the concept of human relations and developments in management.[30] To Follett, a leader is not the president of the organisation or head of the department, but one "who can see all around a situation, who sees it as related to certain purposes and policies, who sees it evolving into the next situation, who understands how to pass from one situation to another". [31] According to her, leader is "the man who can energise his group, who knows how to encourage initiative, how to draw from all what each has to give".[32] He is "the man who can show that the order is integral to the situation".[33] Leadership goes to the person who can grasp the essentials of an experience and "can see it as a whole" and "to whom the total inter-relatedness is most clear".[34] Leader is the expression of a harmonious and effective unity, which he has helped to form, and which he was able to make a going concern.[35] Such people, Follett feels, are found not just at the apex but throughout the organisation. According to Follett, coordination, definition of purpose and anticipation are the three critical functions of a leader.[36] A leader has also to organise experience of the group and transform it into power.[37] Follett stresses that leaders are not only born but can be made through education and training in organisation and management.

Follett distinguishes between three different types of leadership - of position, of personality and function. In the first, the leader holds a position of formal authority and in the second, one becomes a leader because of one's forceful personality. One who holds both position and personality can 'lead' much more easily. But in modern organisations, it is not the persons of formal authority or of personality who 'lead' but those who possess expert knowledge. They exercise leadership because others are influenced by their judgements. "The man possessing the knowledge demanded by a certain situation tends in the best managed business, and other things being equal, becomes the leader of that movement."[38] Thus leadership goes to the person with the knowledge of the situation, who understands its total significance and who can see it through. The experts can give orders even to those of higher rank. For example, Follett says the dispatch clerk can give orders to the superintendent and the stores clerk can tell the purchasing in-charge when to act. Thus, the leadership of function is inherent in the job. Though personality plays a large part in leadership, Follett also believes that leadership of function is becoming more important than leadership of personality.[39] Follett believes that the success of any organisation depends on its being "sufficiently flexible to allow the leadership of function to operate fully - to allow the men with the knowledge and the technique to control the situation".[40] Thus, Follett called attention to the emergence,in American life of "leadership by functions", long before the term "situational approach" came into use.[41]

An Evaluation

Follett was called by some writers on organisation a 'classical' thinker; while others criticised her stating that 'there is nothing classical in her ideas'. Follett herself criticised the classical theory for its one-sidedness, mechanistic approach and for ignoring psychological aspects.[42] But her own ideas on various aspects of administration and management were not free from criticism. She was criticised for ignoring the social nature or the processes involved in the management of organisation. Her ideas on integration were criticised as being illusory. She was also criticised for not interpreting social content of organisation scientifically.[43] Baker observes that Follett was never a systematic writer, she threw out interesting ideas more or less randomly and, therefore, the thread of consistency was hard to find and harder to follow.[44] Not all her readers would see where her thoughts would lead them.[45] Therefore, her valuable ideas and useful recommendations do not conform to a theoretically well founded and integrated system; few observe.

Two reasons were attributed for Follett's failure to gain stature as an administrative and management theoretician. First, she never had the institutional base to facilitate a secure position. Secondly, as Drucker and Kanter have argued, ideology of cooperation, negotiation, conflict resolution and consensus were not in sync with a world during her professional life - before, during or post-war period.[46] Some also attributed that her ideas were neglected as she was a woman, though Drucker did not agree.

Notwithstanding these criticisms, Follett's contribution to administrative theory is "seminal and indeed prophetic".[47] Her ideas in the realm of conflict, integration, coordination, control, authority, leadership, etc., convince everyone about the validity and justification of the multi-dimensional focus of her universalistic approach. A pioneer and a fundamental theorist, her theories are often invoked and have been consistently lauded through generations of scholarship.[48] As Metcalf and Urwick have observed, 'her conceptions were in advance of her time. They are still in advance of current thinking. But they are a gold mine of suggestions for anyone who is interested in the problems of establishing and maintaining human cooperation in the conduct of an enterprise.'[49]

In Brief

Follett's contribution to the theory of administration and organisation can be summarised as:

- Mary Parker Follett, whom Peter Drucker called "The Prophet of Management", is a political scientist of repute and is known for her work in social administration and business management. Her work is characterised by "practical wisdom, deep flashes of intuition, undepartmentalised thinking and all pervading spirit of democratic dynamism".

- She accorded high importance to the problems of conflict in organisations. Considering that conflicts are unavoidable, she advanced the idea of "constructive conflict" – a way of looking at conflict as a constructive activity in organisations. Follett says that there are three ways of resolving a conflict *viz*, domination, compromise and integration.

- Follett considered integration as the best way of conflict resolution and discusses the basis of achieving integration. Realising the difficulties in achieving integration, she discusses the methods to overcome the obstacles to integration.

- Giving orders is an important management activity in organisations. She analysed the nature, principles and context of giving orders and suggested depersonalisation of orders and preferred orders emanating from situations than from persons. This phenomenon is called as "law of situation".

- Follett gives special attention to the problems of power, authority and control. Defining power "as the ability to make things happen", she makes a distinction between "power over" and "power with". Defining authority as vested power, she prefers function and situation as the basis of authority and questions the effectiveness of person-based authority in organisations. Follett also believed in pluralistic concept of responsibility or cumulative responsibility and rejects ultimate responsibility as an illusion. Similarly, she believed in "fact control" rather than "person control".

- She discussed various principles of planning and coordination and preferred self-adjusting and self-coordination of various and varying interests.

- Follett took a broad and functional view of leader's role and identified coordination, definition of purpose and anticipation as three leadership functions. She distinguished between three types of leadership i.e., leadership of position, personality and function and considered "leadership by function" most effective.

- Follett's views are criticised mainly for ignoring the social context of organisations and the complex social processes involved in the management of organisations. Some are critical of Follett's ideas for lack of rigour and being illusory.

- Follett laid foundations for the application of democratic concepts and practices to organisations. Better understanding of the present trends in administrative thought and practices requires a study of Follett's ideas and works.

References

1 Gross, Bertram M., *The Managing of Organisation*, Vol. I, New York, Free Press, 1964, p. 151.

2 See for details Drucker, Peter F., "Introduction: Mary Parker Follett: Prophet of Management" in Graham, Pauline, (Ed.) *Mary Parker Follett: Prophet of Management - A Celebration of Writings from the 1920s*, Cambridge, MA: Harvard Business School Press, 1995, pp.1-10.

3 Urwick, L.*The Golden Book of Management*, London, Newman Limited, 1956, pp. 132-133.

4 Urwick, L., and Brech, E. F. L., *The Making of Scientific Management*, Vol. I. London, Sir Isaac Pitman & Sons. Ltd., 1955, pp. 54-55.

5 Gross, Bertram M., op. cit, p. 152.

6 Graham, Pauline, op.cit., p.12.

7 Waldo, Dwight, *The Administrative State*, New York, The Ronald Press Company, 1948, p. 210.

8. Metcalf, Henry, C., and Urwick, Lyndall, *Dynamic Administration: The Collected Papers of Mary Parker Follett*, New York, Harper and Row, 1940, p.30.

9 Ibid., p. 30.

10 Follett, M. P., *Creative Experience*, London, Longmans Green, 1924, p. 200.

11 Metcalf, Henry C., and Urwick, Lyndall, op. cit., pp. 30-31.

12 There is also fourth form which Follett calls manipulation. It's main technique is an emotional appeal designed to obscure differences that may exist. For details see Fox, Elliot M., "Mary Parker Follett: The Enduring Contribution", *Public Administration Review*, Vol. XXVIII, No. 6, Nov.-Dec. 1968, p. 526.

13 Metcalf, Henry, C., and Urwick, Lyndall, op. cit., p. 36.

14 Ibid., pp. 30-31.

15 Ibid., p. 42.

16 Ibid., p. 51.

17 Ibid., pp. 51-52.

18 Ibid., p. 52.

19 Ibid., pp. 52-53.

20 Ibid., p. 54.

21 Ibid., p. 56.

22 Ibid., p. 67.

23 Ibid., p. 99.

24 Ibid., p. 101.

25 Ibid., pp. 106-107.

26 Ibid., pp. 112-113.

27 Follett, M. P., *Freedom and Coordination—Lectures in Business Organisation*, London, Management Publications Trust Ltd., 1949, p. 4.

28 Follett, Mary Parker, "The Process of Control", in L.Gulick and L. Urwick (Eds.), *Papers on the Science of Administration*, Columbia University, 1937, p. 161.

29 Ibid., pp. 161-166

30 Metcalf, Henry, C., and Urwick, Lyndall, op. cit., p. 247

31 Ibid., p.266.

32 Ibid., p.247.

33 Ibid., p.275

34 Ibid., p.279.

35 Sapre, S. A., *Mary Parker Follett: Her Dynamic Philosophy of Management*, Bombay, Government Central Press, 1975, p. 38.

36 Metcalf, Henry, C., and Urwick, Lyndall, op. cit., pp.260-266.

37 Ibid., p.258.

38 Ibid., p.277.

39 Ibid.

40 Ibid., p.278.

41 Negro, Felix A., and Nigro, Lloyd G., *Modern Public Administration*, (3 Ed.), New York, Harper & Row, Publishers, 1973, p. 238.

42 Gvishiani, D,.*Organisation and Management, A Sociological Analysis of Western Theories*, Moscow, Progress Publishers, 1972, p. 218.

43 Ibid.

44 Fox, Elliot M., op. cit., p. 521.

45 Baker, R. J. S., *Administrative Theory and Public Administration*, London, Hutchinson University Library, 1972, p. 44.

46 See the Preface and Introduction chapters by Rosabeth Moss Kanter and Peter Drucker respectively in Graham, Pauline, op. cit.

47 Ibid.

48 Monin, Nanette, *The manager who lost his mojo: Mary Parker Follett's nowhere man*, See http://www.le.ac.uk/ulsm/research/conf jan08/pdf/monin ab.pdf. Retrived on 1st June 2009

49 Metcalf, Henry, C., and Urwick, Lyndall, op. cit., p. 9.

9

ELTON MAYO

M. Kistaiah

Introduction

Few researchers and very few research studies have the distinction of exercising influence for more than half a century as was exercised by Elton Mayo and his Hawthorne studies. His studies on Industrial Psychology are profound and he is considered as one of the pioneers of human relations approach. He was one of the most influential social scientists of his times. He is widely recognised as the progenitor of human relations movement and his work laid foundations for later works highlighting the importance of communications between the workers and management. Though Mayo's findings were contrary to the theories of his contemporaries that the worker is motivated by self-interest, his work on motivation revolutionised the theory and practice of management.

(1880-1949)

Life and Works

George Elton Mayo (1880-1949) born at Adelaide, Australia, had a chequered schooling and aborted medical education.[1] He was educated at Queen's School and the Collegiate School of St. Peter. In 1897, he joined the University of Adelaide to study medicine but soon left the university and went to UK to study at medical schools in Edinburgh and London. Bored with medical education, he went to West Africa in 1903 but returned soon and spent time as a journalist and by teaching English at the Working Men's College. At Edinburgh, he was associated in a study of psychopathology, which helped him in later years as an industrial researcher. Returning to Adelaide in 1905, he joined a partnership printing firm. In 1907, he reentered the University of Adelaide to study philosophy and psychology and graduated with honours in 1910. In 1911, he joined as a lecturer in mental and moral philosophy at the University of Queensland. Mayo successfully organised psychiatric treatment to the soldiers who suffered from shell shock during the First World War in recognition of which he was appointed the first Chairman of Philosophy Department in 1919. At the University he taught Logic and Ethics in addition to Philosophy.

He migrated to the US in 1922 with a Rockefeller Fellowship and joined the Wharton School, University of Pennsylvania as a research associate. In 1926, he joined as Associate Professor of Industrial Research and Director of the Department of Industrial Research and in 1929 as Professor of Industrial Research at the Harvard School of Business Administration where he undertook path-breaking Hawthorne experiments. He concentrated on private industrial establishments and was supported by Rockefeller and Carnegie Foundation grants. After retirement in 1947, he moved to Surrey, UK where he died. In tribute to his contributions Elton Mayo School of Management was established in Adelaide.

The influence of the world famous psychologists Pierre Janet and Sigmund Freud was profound on Mayo. In all his research programmes Mayo focused attention on the behaviour of the workers and their production capacity keeping in view the physiological, psychological and economic aspects. He called this a clinical method. Mayo published a few books [2] and contributed a number of scholarly articles to journals.

Early Experiments

Elton Mayo in his studies concentrated on fatigue, accidents, production levels, rest periods, working conditions, etc., of industrial workers in factories. In 1923 while at Pennsylvania, he was involved in research for which he subsequently became world famous. He started research in the spinning department of a textile mill near Philadelphia. The mill provided all facilities to the workers, was well organised and considered to be a model organisation. The employers were highly enlightened and humane but the president and director of personnel faced problems in the mule-spinning departments of the textile mill. The labour turnover in all the departments was estimated to be approximately 5-6 per cent per annum while in the multi-spinning department the turnover was estimated at nearly 250 per cent. It meant that about 100 industrial workers were required every year to keep about 40 working. Since it was a crucial department for the smooth functioning of the mill, the management introduced a number of schemes by way of incentives but to their surprise all attractions failed to retain the workers. Efficiency engineers were consulted and several financial incentives were introduced on their suggestion, but they yielded no appreciable results. Despite setbacks, the president of the mill refused to accept the situation to be beyond remedy.

Mayo studied the problems of the multi-spinning department intensely from various angles i.e., physical, social and psychological. After a long participant observation, he found that almost every piecer working in the mule-spinning department, suffered from foot trouble for which they had no immediate remedy. This trouble developed since every piecer had to walk up and down a long alley, a distance of 30 yards or more, on either side of which the machine head was operating for spinning the frames with cotton thread. While these frames moved back and forth, the worker was expected to watch the working of the machine closely to weave the ends together whenever there was a broken thread. Since there were 10 to 14 such machines in the care of a single worker he felt miserable attending to the job.

Mayo also found that although there were two or three piecers in the section they were located far apart and communication between them was almost difficult due to the noise of the machine. Added to this, some of the workers were young - in their twenties - and others were in their fifties. All of them confessed that they were too fatigued to enjoy social evenings after work. But the workers would never protest, as most of them worked under the company President, who was a Colonel in the US Army in France both before and during the First World War. Mayo found these details with the help of a nurse to whom the workers confided the problems on the promise of maintaining secrecy.

On the basis of the information collected by the nurse and his own findings, Mayo with the permission of the management started experimenting with rest periods. He introduced two rest periods of ten minutes each in the morning and again in the afternoon with every team of piecers. From the beginning the results were encouraging. Gradually, the rest period scheme was adapted by all the workers to eliminate the problem of physical fatigue. The workers evinced interest in the scheme and were pleased with the results. The symptoms of melancholy disappeared; the labour turnover almost came to an end, production increased and the morale improved.

In addition to the elimination of physical fatigue, Mayo suggested a new formula to earn bonus, which the mule-spinning department never had. Under this scheme, if the workers were to produce more than a certain percentage, they would earn bonus in proportion to the extra production. With rest periods and new bonus formula, the workers were happy. But the new schemes were not, however, without problems. The immediate supervisors never liked the sight of workers lying asleep on the sacks while they did not enjoy the same privilege. They suggested that the workers should 'earn' their rest periods. That is to say, if a task was finished in a given time, the men were allowed to rest. Under the new scheme the workers earned three to four 'rests' everyday.

The situation continued for sometime but in view of a heavy demand for goods, the supervisors had done away with the new system. Within a week the production fell and the workers were unhappy and the old symptoms started reappearing. At this point the president of the company, "The Colonel" took charge of the problem. After prolonged discussions with Mayo and his research team, the president ordered that the spinning department should be shut down for ten minutes, four times a day and that all hands from the supervisors down to the workers should avail the opportunity to rest. With this pessimism disappeared, production picked up and the workers started earning bonus.

Mayo in his first research study was able to probe into the problem and suggest remedies. In his endeavour, he found the Colonel a sincere president who had immense faith in his workers, evinced interest in their welfare and, true to his military background, neither wavered in his decisions nor forgot his men and their problems. In addition, the president also introduced another change. He placed the control of rest periods squarely in the hands of workers which led to consultations among workers. Social interaction was set in motion. A new awakening began whereby the assumptions of 'rabble hypothesis' which assumes 'mankind as a horde of unorganised individuals actuated by self-interest', was questioned. Mayo summarised the findings of his experiments as follows:

- Spinning produces postural fatigue and induces pessimistic reverie;
- Rest pauses relieve these conditions and increase productivity by restoring normal circulation, relieving postural fatigue, and interrupting pessimistic reverie;
- Rest pauses are more effective when they are regular and the workers have received instruction in the techniques of relaxation; and
- The life of the worker outside the mill has improved as workers become more interested in their families and become more sober. [3]

Mayo believed that the turnover was not the result of working conditions but the result of emotional response of workers to the work performed. He also believed that the monotony *per se* was not the problem but repetitive work done under conditions of isolation lead to abnormal preoccupations. [4]

Hawthorne Studies

Mayo's major involvement was with the now popular Hawthorne Studies at the Western Electricity Company, Chicago employing 25,000 workers and was conducted in different phases.[5] At that time it was felt that there was a clear-cut cause and effect relationship between the physical work, environment, the well-being and productivity of the worker. The management assumed that given proper ventilation, temperature, lighting and other physical working conditions and wage incentives, the worker could produce more. The problems, which blocked efficiency, were believed to be improper job design, fatigue and other conditions of work. Illumination of the work place was also believed to be an important aspect since it affected the quality, quantity and safety. Therefore, the National Research Council of the National Academy of Science decided to examine the precise relationship between illumination and the efficiency of the worker with a research programme at the Hawthorne Plant of Western Electricity Company. The research began in 1924.

The Great Illumination (1924-27)

Two groups of female workers, each consisting of six, were selected and located in two separate rooms, each group performing the same task. The rooms were equally illuminated and this was mainly designed to examine the level of production on the basis of varying levels of illumination. In the beginning, the physical environ in which the girls were working was stabilised to acclimatize them to room temperature, humidity, etc. Slowly the conditions of work were changed to mark the effect of this change on the output. The researchers observed the groups and kept accurate record of production. This research spread over a period of one-and-a half years, established that regardless of the level of illumination, production in both the control and experimental groups increased. The researchers were surprised to note this and abandoned the illumination theory and began manipulating wage payments, rest periods, duration of working hours, etc. Subsequently, instead of group incentive plan, an individual piece rate plan was introduced. All these changes led to a continued rise in production. Reduction in working hours and total work time in a week, provision of refreshments like coffee, soup, etc., yielded a further rise in output.

Surprised by the results, the research team decided to abolish all the newly introduced privileges and return to the conditions prevailing at the beginning of the experiments i.e., the original conditions of work with the exception of individual piece rate arrangement. For a while the output fell a little but soon it rose to a point higher than at any other time. The rise in production, in spite of the withdrawal of incentives, puzzled the research team. The illumination hypothesis was rejected as the relationship between incentive schemes, rest periods, etc., had no apparent relevance to the productivity *per se*. It was surmised that it might be due to the interest shown by the research team in the workers or to the incentive wage plan that was retained while several other privileges were withdrawn.

During the winter of 1927, George Pennock happened to attend a lecture programme of Mayo at the Harvard Club in New York. Pennock told Mayo of the rest room experiments and invited him to the Hawthorne Plant to unravel the problems confronted by the research team. In these studies, Mayo had the benefit of knowledge of the company officials like Pennock, William J. Dickson, and Harold A. Wright. From the academic side T. North Whitehead, W. Lloyd, E. Warner and L. J. Henderson joined the research group. In this study Mayo collaborated with F.J. Roethlisberger, who later became a leading exponent of the philosophy of human relations. The results of the National Research Council experiments were so intriguing that

Mayo felt that there was a remarkable change in the mental attitude of the group and this was perhaps responsible in the behaviour of the workers at the Hawthorne Plant. Mayo elaborated that the test room girls became a social unit and because of the increased attention of the research team, the unit developed a sense of participation in the project. Thus, Mayo opened the door to research into social man. The Harvard group then picked up the loose threads of the National Research Council studies and found far more valuable insights into industrial man than earlier studies. They proposed five hypotheses to explain the failure of the original illumination project. [6] They are:

Firstly, improved material conditions and methods of work were present in the test room, leading to greater output. It was rejected because the level of illumination had been purposely reduced and yet the output had increased.

Secondly, the rest periods and shorter working days had provided relief from fatigue. It did not explain the results since output still increased despite the withdrawal of all the privileges.

Thirdly, relating relief from monotony to increased production was not conclusive because monotony had nothing to do with the physical environment as it was a matter pertaining to the state of mind.

Fourthly, the individual wage payment incentive had stimulated increase in the output.

Lastly, changes in supervisory techniques had improved the attitudes and output.

The last two hypotheses were examined and tested through supplementary experiments. Two groups of five girls each were identified for the study. These girls were placed on an individual incentive plan on a piecework basis. In the beginning total output went up and then remained constant at the level. In the case of second group, although they were placed on individual incentive system, they were subject to variations in rest periods and duration of work and change in the output were recorded. In this group over a period of 14 months there was an average rise in production. Therefore, the research team explained that the fourth hypothesis was also rejected since it was not wages but something else that led to greater output in both the groups. This conclusion, led to test of the last hypothesis. Since the research team consisted of a different set of managers, there was a perceptible change and the atmosphere was more relaxed and congenial. The girls were allowed to talk freely and supervisors also took personal interest. A better social situation developed within the group and the experiment-oriented supervisor was not regarded as the boss. The second important factor was the modified managerial practices. Workers were consulted and advised about changes and their views were considered. This process allowed the workers to feel free to air their problems and they established new interpersonal contacts with their fellow workers and supervisor.

Mayo and his team re-discovered Robert Owen, who earlier, advocated more attention to the workers as against the machines by the mill owners. Mayo felt that work satisfaction depends to a large extent on the informal social pattern of the group. He thought that the supervisor could be trained to play a different role, which would help him to take a personal interest in the subordinates and discharge his duties better than earlier. He also noted that the workers should be made to come out openly with their needs, interact freely and without fear with company officials. Improving morale is to be closely associated with the style of supervision. This link between supervision, morale and productivity became the foundation stone of the human relation movement. These experiments were hailed as the Great Illumination because it had thrown light on the new areas of industrial relations.

Human Attitudes and Sentiments (1928-31)

In 1928, the Harvard study team started in the same plant, a special study of human attitudes and sentiments. The workers were asked to express freely and frankly their likes and dislikes on the programmes and policies of the management, working conditions, how they were treated by their boss, etc. In the beginning the interview schedule was tight but as there was no direct relation between the subject matter and the views of workers, the interview technique was changed. The interviewer played a minor role. After a brief initial explanation of the topic, he displayed real interest in everything the workers spoke. This change caught the imagination of the employees and each one of them took more time than they did earlier in answering the schedule. After a few days there was a change in the attitude of the workers. Although no reforms were introduced, the workers thought in view of their complaints that the working conditions were changed. They also felt that the wages were better although the wage scale remained at the same level. It appeared that there was an opportunity to 'let off steam' which made the workers feel better even though there was no material change in the environment.

After interviewing 21,126 workers, the complaints were analysed and it was found that there was no correlation between the nature of complaints and the facts. The research team concluded that there were two types of complaints: the manifest material complaints and latent psychological complaint. The Harvard team felt that the pre-occupation of the worker with personal problems like family tragedies, sickness etc., which Mayo labelled as 'pessimistic reveries' in his early research, inhibited the performance in the industry. The study succeeded in identifying the following three aspects:

First, the workers appreciated the method of collecting the information on the problems of the company from them. They thought they had valuable comments to offer and felt elated with the feeling that they had an equal status with management. They realised that they were allowed to express freely and felt satisfied with it. They entertained a feeling that the conditions in the environment were changed to the better although no such change took place.

Second, there was a change in the attitude of the supervisors because they realised that their method of supervision was closely observed by the research team and the subordinates were allowed to comment freely about their supervisor.

Third, the research team realised that they had acquired new skills in understanding and dealing with their fellow beings. It was felt that in the absence of proper appreciation of the feelings and sentiments of the workers it was difficult to understand their real problems, personal feelings and sentiments derived from both an employee's personal history and his social situation at work.

Social Organisation (1931-32)

The final phase of the research programme at Western Electric was to observe a group of workers performing a task in a natural setting. Observation method was adopted to analyse the group behaviour. A number of employees consisting of three groups of workmen whose work was inter-related were chosen. Their job was to solder, fix the terminals and finish the wiring. It was known as 'the Bank Wiring Experiment'. Wages were paid on the basis of a group incentive plan and each member got his share on the basis of total output of the group. It was found that the workers had a clear-cut standard of output, which was lower than management target. The group, according to its standard plan, did not allow its members to increase or decrease the output. Although they were capable of producing more, the output was held down to maintain a uniform rate of output. They were highly integrated with their social structure and informal pressure was used to set right the erring members. The following code of conduct was maintained for group solidarity:

- One should not turn out too much work. If one does, he is a 'rate buster'.
- One should not turn out too little work. If one does, he is a 'chesler'.
- One should not tell a supervisor anything detrimental to an associate. If one does, he is a 'squealer'.
- One should not attempt to maintain social distance or act officious. If one is an inspector, for example, he should not act like one.[7]

Mayo and his Harvard team found out that the behaviour of the team had nothing to do with management of general economic conditions of the plant. The workers viewed the interference of the extra departmental personnel, such as 'efficiency men' and other 'technologists' as disturbance. They thought that the experts follow the logic of efficiency with a constraint on their group activity. Further, the supervisors were considered as a separate category representing authority to discipline the workers. The logic of efficiency did not go well with the logic of sentiments, which had become the cornerstone of 'social system'.

Mayo and his colleagues concluded that one should not miss the human aspects of organisation while emphasising technical and economic aspects. The Hawthorne experience suggested a new mix of managerial skills. In addition to the technical skills, the management should handle human situations, motivate, lead and communicate with the workers. Mayo also felt that overemphasis on the technical progress and material life at the expense of social and human life was not good and laid the blame at the feet of David Ricardo and his 'rabble hypotheses'. Mayo suggested that the concept of authority should be based on social skills in securing cooperation rather than expertise.

Absenteeism in Industries

During the Second World War, Mayo came across a typical problem faced by the foundry shops in three industrial undertakings manufacturing important components for aircrafts. In view of the war situation, there was all-round dislocation in several walks of life, including the industrial establishments. People migrated from industry to armed forces or joined other speculative activities, which resulted in an uncertain situation. The turnover of labour in the two industries was more than 70 per cent and absenteeism was chronic while the situation in the remaining industry was, however, better. Alarmed at this state of affairs, the managements requested Mayo to study the problem of heavy turnover and unjustified absenteeism and suggest remedial measures. The research began in 1943.

On the basis of Hawthorne experience, Mayo and his research team found a few distinctive characteristics in the three plants. In the industry in which turnover was minimum and absenteeism was negligible, the management was found to have introduced group wage scheme and made it clear that workers would earn group wage without any shortfall in any shift in a day. In the event of any shortfall in any shift, the cut in wages was uniformly applied. Therefore, all the workers became alert and formed into a group under a natural leader who devoted time and energy in consolidating the group solidarity. Now it was the turn of the employees to ensure smooth functioning of the wheels of the industry. Mayo found out how an informal group demonstrated its strength and capacity in raising the level of production by cooperating with the management. In the present case, the positive response was possible because the supervisors and his assistants were too busy otherwise and rarely paid any visit to the department. All the work was under the charge of a man who had no official standing and this person emerged as a natural leader of the team. In the case of other two factories there were neither informal groups nor natural leaders to knit the workers into a team. They were unable to form a team because of certain personal eccentricities, as they were not given an opportunity to form an informal team. Hence, there was a heavy turnover and labour absenteeism in the production centres. Mayo prescribed that to the extent possible the management should encourage formation of informal groups and treat the problems of the worker with humane understanding. He suggested that the workers should be treated as human beings but not as cogs in the machine. The labour should not develop a feeling that they were subject to exploitation by the management.[8] Mayo thought the managements should take the initiative in the development of human relations in the industry and encourage a conducive situation among the industrial workers.

The significance of the Hawthorne studies was in discovering the informal organisation. Mayo was also interested in discovering as to how spontaneous cooperation could be encouraged in organisations, so that organisational objectives may be achieved without breakdowns. His studies led to a realisation and understanding of the human factor in work situations, importance of an adequate communication system, particularly upwards from workers to management.[9]

Criticism

Mayo and his research findings were subjected to bitter criticism. Firstly, they were criticised on the ground that the theory tried to substitute human relations-oriented-supervisors for union representation. He was criticised for not understanding the role of unions in a free society.[10] It was argued that Mayo never tried to integrate unions into his thinking and was criticised as anti-union and pro-management. In fact, in 1949, United Auto Workers lashed out at Mayoism with bitter criticism and branded the Hawthorne researchers as 'cow sociologists'. Secondly, sweeping conclusions were drawn from a relatively few studies which, some critics pointed out, were full of pitfalls.

Critics like Carey pointed out that the Hawthorne group selected in their first experiment 'cooperative' girls who were willing to participate in the research programme and this type of research was 'worthless', since a sample of five or six cannot be taken as a reliable sample to make generalisations. Carey also observed that the evidence obtained from the experiments does not support any of the conclusions derived by the Hawthorne investigators. There exists a vast discrepancy between the evidence and the conclusions. On the other hand, the data only supports, according to Carey, the old view of monetary incentives, leadership and discipline as motivating factors for better performance. He also criticised Hawthorne's investigations for their lack of scientific base.[11]

Peter Drucker criticised human relationists for their lack of awareness of economic dimension. He felt that the Harvard group neglected the nature of work and instead focused on interpersonal relations.[12] Mayo was criticised for his sentimental concentration on the members of an organisation to the neglect of its work and purposes, and a general softness and lack of direction.[13] He was criticised as encouraging a paternalistic domination of the private lives and even the private thoughts of individuals by their employers.[14] The critics argue that there was no place in Mayo's philosophy for conflict, and he sought to achieve organisational harmony through the subordination of individual and the group interests by the administrative elite.[15]

Bendix and Fisher argued that Mayo as a social scientist failed to define sharply the ethical pre-suppositions of his scientific work. Without making pre-suppositions clear, the knowledge and skill, which Mayo finds so undervalued in democratic societies, deserve no higher rating than they get.[16] Daniel Sell was one of the bitter critics of the human relations theory propounded by Mayo and his colleagues. He said the methodology adopted by the Harvard group was defective. Others pointed out that to think that a conflict-free state and worker contentment would lead to success of the company was not tenable because some tensions and conflicts were inevitable in every human situation. The goal should be to provide healthy outlets instead of indulging in utopian ideals of conflict-free society. Therefore, the critics argued that the team displayed a total lack of awareness of larger social and technological systems.[17]

An Evaluation

The contribution of Mayo to administrative organisation theory is innovative and substantial. For the first time, he made an attempt to understand the problems of the industrial labour from an angle different from the traditional approach of scientific management era. In addition to human relations in organisations, Mayo critically examined the employee-employer relations, stability of the labour, supervision, etc., of the industrial workers. Although the detailed analysis of his work was conducted by his associates in the Hawthorne Plant and elsewhere, he was the moving spirit behind all these attempts at various stages. The Hawthorne studies soon became historic and a landmark in administrative thought.[18] The studies, as Drucker has put it, "are still the best, the most advanced and the most complete works in the field of human relations. Indeed, it is debatable, whether the many refinements added since by the labour of countless people in the industry, labour unions and academic life have clarified or observed the original insight".[19] The contributions of Mayo are immensely useful not only to the industrial sector but also in the administrative system of a state, particularly in the case of bureaucracy. His work also paved the way for adequate communication system between the lower rungs of the organisation and the higher levels. His main emphasis was on the individual well-being with the help of social skills in organisations. The total contribution of Mayo is such a phenomenon that he is regarded as one of the founding fathers of human relations concept in the administrative thought. He was a behavioural scientist long before the term became popular.[20] Taken as a whole, the significance of Hawthorne investigations by Mayo was in 'discovering' the informal organisation, which it is now realised, exists in all organisations. The importance of group affecting the behaviour of workers at work was brilliantly analysed through these experiments.

In Brief

Elton Mayo's contribution to organisation theory can be summarised as:

- Elton Mayo is well-known for his Hawthorne experiments and considered as one of the pioneers of human relations approach to organisation.
- Mayo's early experiments were concentrated on fatigue, accidents, rest periods, production levels, etc., of the industrial workers in the factories. His studies resulted in new awakening

questioning the 'rabble hypothesis', which assumes mankind as a horde of unorganised individuals actuated by self-interest.

- The Great Illumination experiments at Hawthorne Plant of Western Electrical Company, popularly known as Hawthorne studies, mainly focused on understanding the cause and effect relationship between the physical work, environment, well-being and the productivity of the worker. The later study known as 'bank wiring' equipment focused on group behaviour in a work situation.

- Mayo, based on extensive studies, concluded that the workers' productivity is not the result of working conditions but the result of emotional response of the workers to the work performed.

- Mayo's studies at Hawthorne found that there is a continuous increase in the productivity of workers under observation in spite of positive and negative changes in the working conditions. This phenomenon, called 'Hawthorne Effect', is a form of reaction whereby subjects improve their behaviour being experimentally measured in response to the fact that they are being observed, not in response to any particular experimental manipulation.

- Mayo and his colleagues concluded that one should not miss the human aspects of organisations. They emphasised that the group behaviour and dynamics in industrial organisations greatly influence the productivity of the worker.

- The studies recognised the importance of informal groups in organisations. The effect of informal groups was closely observed in the experiments. The experiments show the positive effects of treating the worker with human understanding and conclude that they affect the productivity.

- The studies were criticised for drawing generalisations based on limited sample and discrepancies between the evidence and the conclusions. Mayo's studies were also criticised for their failure to take into account the impact of larger economic, social and technological factors on the productivity of worker in organisations.

- Mayo and his colleagues should be credited with significant contribution to the realisation of importance of human relations in work situations. The experiments led to a better appreciation of the role of informal organisations and internal group dynamics in the functioning organisations.

References

[1] For details of Mayo's life and work see Wood, John D. and Wood, Michael D., (Eds.), *Gorge Elton Mayo: Critical Evaluations in Business and Management*, London, Rutledge, 2004. Also see, Fry, Brain R., *Mastering Public Administration: From Max Weber to Dwight Waldo*, Chatham, NJ, Chatham House Publishers, 1989, pp.123-125. http:// adbonline.anu/biogs/A100454b.htm;

[2] Important books of Mayo include: *The Human Problems of Industrial Civilization*, Boston, Harvard Business School, 1946, 2nd ed. ; *The Social Problems of Industrial Civilization*, London, Routledge & Kegan Paul, 1975; *The Political Problems of Industrial Civilization*, Boston, Harvard Business School, 1974. For

details of his studies, bibliography of his works and a critical evaluation of his contribution see the various articles in Wood, John D. and Wood, Michael D., (Eds.), op.cit.

[3] Mayo, Elton, "Revery and Industrial Fatigue," Personnel Journal, Vol.3, No. 8, December 1924, p. 280, quoted in Fry, Brain R., op.cit., p. 135.

[4] Ibid.

[5] For details of the Hawthorne's experiments see, Roethlisberger, Fritz J., and Dickson, William J., *Management and the Worker*, Cambridge, Mass, Harvard University Press, 1939, See also Mayo, Elton, *The Human Problems of Industrial Civilization*, op. cit., L. Urwick and E. F. L. Brech, *The Making of Scientific*

Management, London, Sir Isaac Pitman & Sons, Ltd., 1955, Vol. III.

[6] Roethlisberger, Fritz J., and Dickson, William J., op. cit., pp. 86-89.

[7] Ibid., p. 522.

[8] Gross, Bertram M., The Managing of Organisations: The Administrative Struggle, Vol. I, New York, Free Press, 1964, p. 166.

[9] Pugh, D. S., et al., Writers on Organisations, Penguin Books, 1971, pp. 129-130.

[10] Sheppard, Harold L., "The Treatment of Unionism in Managerial Sociology", American Sociological Review, Vol. 14, No. 2, April 1949, pp. 310-313.

[11] See Carey, Alex, "The Hawthorne Studies: A Radical Criticism", American Sociological Review, Vol. 32, No. 3, June 1967, pp. 403-416. See also Miller, Delbert and Form, William, Industrial Sociology, New York, Harper 1951, pp. 74-83.

[12] Drucker, Peter F., The Practice of Management, London, Mercury Books, 1961, pp. 272-273.

[13] Baker, R. J. S., Administrative Theory and Public Administration, London, Hutchinson University Library, 1972, p. 44.

[14] Whyte, William H., The Organisation Man, Penguin, 1960, pp. 36-40, and 45-46.

[15] International Encyclopedia of the Social Sciences, Vol. 10, p. 83.

[16] Bendix, Reinhard and Fisher, Lloyd H., "The Perspective of Elton Mayo" The Review of Economic and Statistics, Vol. 31. No. 4 November 1949, p. 319.

[17] For details of criticisms see Wren, Daniel A., The Evolution of Management Thought, New York, The Ronald Press Company, 1972, pp. 370-381. See also Knowles, William H., "Human Relations in Industry: Research and Concepts", in Huneryager, S. G., and Heckmann, I. L., (Ed.), Human Relations in Management, Bombay, D. B. Taraporewala Sons & Co. P. Ltd. 1972, pp. 31-58.

[18] Gross, Bertram M., op. cit., p. 160.

[19] Drucker, Peter F., op. cit. pp. 268-269.

[20] Pugh, D.S., et al., op. cit., p. 129.

10

CHESTER BARNARD

P.A. James
A. Amruta Rao

Introduction

Chester Barnard, a business executive, public administrator and author of management and organisation theories, is one of the very few administrative theorists who propounded management and organisational theories and principles based on personal experience. He is considered the spiritual father of the 'social system' school, which influenced many organisational thinkers of the last century.[1] His classic *'The Functions of the Executive'*, was based on a series of lectures he gave on administration at the Lowell Institute at Boston and is a compulsory reading in all public administration, management and organisation studies across the globe. As Bertram Gross noted, Barnard is one of the few theorists in modern administrative thought who was highly successful as a man of affairs and also as a theoretician.[2]

(1886-1961)

Life and Works

Chester Irving Barnard (1886-1961), born at Malden, Massachusetts, USA in a family of modest means, had to work very hard for his livelihood. He joined as an apprentice to a piano tuner and while working he prepared for the pre-school and joined the prestigious Mount Herman School. In 1906, he joined Harvard and majored in economics and government. Though he successfully completed his studies by 1909, he failed to obtain a degree on technical grounds - because of lack of training in science and his inability to master chemistry.[3] To support his studies financially he undertook diverse tasks like typing, conducting dance orchestra, etc. In 1909, he joined as a statistician with the Bell Telephone Company and was promoted as a Commercial Manager in 1915. In 1922, he became Assistant Vice-president and General Manager of the Bell Telephone Company at Pennsylvania and was promoted as Vice-president of the company after four years. In 1928, he became President of the Bell Telephone Company of New Jersey at the age of forty-one and continued until 1948. After retirement from the Bell Company, he worked as President of the Rockefeller Foundation (1948-52)[4] and Chairman, National Science Foundation (1952-54). During his long career with the Telephone Company, he was also associated with voluntary public service. He worked with the New Jersey Emergency Relief Fund and New Jersey Reformatory. During the Second World War he was the president of the United Services Organisation (1942-45), Director of the National War Fund and member of the Naval Manpower Survey Committee. He also served as Assistant to the Secretary of Treasury, Consultant Federal Office of Science Research and Development, Member Atomic Energy Committee, Director, National Bureau of Economic Research and member on the Boards of several companies. Thus he occupied many positions both in government and private administrations. His experiences in various capacities and in different organisations afforded him an opportunity to understand administrative processes in the government. Despite his not earning a 'degree', he was awarded several honorary degrees by prestigious universities like Princeton, Pennsylvania, Brown and Rutgers. During his long career he authored his most influential and best known classic *The Functions of the Executive* and published 37 papers [5] and earned a distinct place in the history of administrative thought.

Barnard spent considerable time in understanding and analysing management. Oliver Sheldon, Elton Mayo, M.P. Follett, etc., inspired his thinking. While being an active manager, he taught in various universities in United States and published_books on management.[6] His *The Functions of the Executive* brought him fame and continues to be the most thought-provoking book on organisation and management ever written by a practicing executive. It is the direct outcome of Barnard's failure to find an adequate explanation of his own executive experience in classic organisations or economic theory.[7] *The Functions* reflects Barnard's wide readings in psychology, sociology, social psychology, economics, anthropology, law, political theory and philosophy of science.[8] The reasons for the endurance of Barnard's thought, according to Andrews, is his stamina in abstract thought, his capacity to apply reason for professional experiences, and his probable sensitivity and expertness in practice.[9] The impact of Barnard's thought is considerable both on theory and practice of management and has inspired a number of outstanding thinkers like Simon. As Mahoney noted, Barnard combines two cultures – the science of organisation and the art of organising and his book was written for posterity.[10]

Organisation as a System of Human Cooperation

Barnard viewed the organisations as systems of cooperation of human activity. But the individual human being possesses a limited power of choice and is constrained by factors of the total situation for cooperation. The most important limiting factors in the situation of each individual are his own biological limitations, others being physical and social. The most effective method of overcoming these limitations, according to Barnard, is cooperative social action. This requires that he adopts a group or non-personal purpose and takes into consideration the process of interaction. With the basic premise that individuals must cooperate, Barnard builds his theory of organisation.

Rejecting the old definitions of organisation as emphasising membership, Barnard defines organisation as a system of consciously coordinated activities or forces of two or more persons.[11] In this definition, he emphasises the system of interactions. It is a system composed of the activities of human beings, a system in which the whole is always greater than the sum of its parts and each part is related to every other part in some significant way. As a system, it is held together by some common purpose by the willingness of certain people to contribute to the operation of the organisation, and by the ability of such people to communicate with each other.[12]

Raising the question as to why an individual should contribute his activities to the operations of any organisation, Barnard strongly disapproves the concept of economic man [13] and propounds the theory of contribution-satisfaction equilibrium. Contributions, which may be regarded in terms of organisation as activities, are possible only when it is advantageous to individuals in terms of personal satisfaction. Barnard says that if each person gets back only what he puts in, there is no incentive, that is, no net satisfaction for him in cooperation. What he gets back must give him advantage in terms of satisfaction; which almost always means return in a different form from what he contributes.[14] The satisfaction which an individual receives in exchange for his contribution may be regarded from the view of organisation as inducement or incentive. Barnard, while rejecting the viewpoint that man is mainly motivated by economic incentives, analyses the multiplicity of satisfactions and identifies four specific inducements. They are: [15]

- material inducements such as money, things or physical conditions;
- personal non-material opportunities for distinction, prestige and personal power;
- desirable physical conditions of work; and
- ideal benefactions, such as the pride of workmanship, sense of adequacy, altruistic service for family or others, loyalty to organisation in patriotism.

Barnard also mentions four types of 'general incentives'. They are:

- associational attractiveness based upon compatibility with associates;
- adoption of working conditions to habitual methods and attitudes;
- opportunity for the feeling of enlarged participation in the course of events; and
- conditions of communicating with others, a condition based on personal comfort in social relations and the opportunity for comradeship and for mutual support in personal attitudes.[16]

In discussing the relationship between the specific inducements, Barnard maintains that economic rewards are ineffective beyond the subsistence level. He also says that the inducements cannot be applied mechanically, and their proportion depends on particular situations, time and individuals. The arrangement of inducements is a dynamic process, requiring experiences and imagination. Barnard feels that the primary function of the executive is to handle the economy of incentives within an organisation.

Formal and Informal Organisations

Barnard defines formal organisations, as we have seen earlier, as a system of consciously coordinated activities or forces of two or more persons. Organisation comes into existence only when (1) there are persons able to communicate with each other, (2) who are willing to contribute action, (3) to accomplish a common purpose. Thus communications, willingness to serve and common purpose are the three elements in a formal organisation. There can be no organisation without persons. More than the persons their services or acts should be treated as constituting an organisation. Willingness can be expressed in terms of loyalty, solidarity and strength of organisation. It implies, surrender of personal conduct and depersonalisation of personal action.

Barnard maintains that in a modern society "the contributors to an organisation always are only a small minority actually having positive willingness," and a majority is negative in their commitment. More importantly, the commitment of individuals always fluctuates, thereby creating unstable conditions in organisations. Willingness, positive or negative, is the expression of the net satisfaction or dissatisfaction experienced by each individual. From the viewpoint of the individual, willingness may be the joint effect of personal desires and reluctance and from the point of organisation, it is the joint effect of the objective inducements offered and the burdens imposed.

For cooperation, there must always be an objective or 'purpose'. The necessity to have a purpose is axiomatic, implicit in the words "system, coordination, and cooperation". The purpose need not always be specific; sometimes it can be inferred. Unless a purpose is accepted by all those whose efforts constitute the organisation, it will not stimulate cooperative action. It may be useful to distinguish between the cooperative and the subjective aspects of purpose. A purpose can serve as an element of a cooperative system as long as the participants note that there is no serious divergence of their understanding of that purpose as the object of cooperation. To Barnard, an objective purpose that can serve as the basis for a cooperative system is the one that is believed by the contributors to be the determined purpose of the organisation.[17] Again, a distinction has to be made between organisational purpose and individual motive. Individual motive is internal, personal and subjective. Common purpose is impersonal, external and objective. The one exception to the general rule is that the accomplishment of an organisation purpose becomes itself a source of personal satisfaction and a motive for many individuals in many organisations.[18]

In organisations, the accomplishment of a common purpose through the persons contributing towards it can be achieved only through 'communication'. This is a dynamic process, which translates purpose into action. The methods of communication may be verbal, or written or observational. The absence of suitable techniques of communication eliminates adopting some purpose as the basis for organisation.

The formal organisations as systems are part of a wider social system with interdependencies with dynamic changes and the organisations are more than the sum of its constituent parts. [19] Barnard identifies four characteristics of formal organisations viz., systems, depersonalisation, specialisation and informal organisations.[20] In organisations the efforts of the individuals are 'depersonalised' in that they are determined by the organisations than the individual. Specialisation is another characteristic and in this Barnard's analysis is more or less on the lines of Gulick's analysis of four bases of purpose, process, personnel and place. [21] And lastly, Barnard argues that in all complex orgnisations there exists an informal organisation.

Informal Organisations

Individuals in the organisation continuously interact based on their personal relationships rather than the organisational purpose. Such interaction may be due to the gregarious instinct or fulfillment of some personal desire. Because of the continuous nature of interactions, relations become systematised and they result into what are called 'informal organisations'. Barnard describes informal organisations as the aggregate of personal contacts and interactions and the associated grouping of people. Such organisations are indefinite, structureless and are a shapeless mass of varied densities. Such informal organisations will have a serious impact on the members of the formal organisations, thereby bringing a continuous interaction between formal and informal organisations. An informal organisation, to be effective, must always establish formal organisations within it. In turn, formal organisation creates informal organisations as a means of communication and to protect the individuals from the domination of the formal organisation. In Barnard's word, "they are interdependent aspects of the same phenomenon

- a society is structured by formal organisations, formal organisations are vitalised and conditioned by informal organisations".[22] What is asserted is that there cannot be one without the other. If one organisation fails, the other will necessarily disintegrate.

Though the relations between formal and informal organisations appear to be a contradiction in the very nature of their definitions, it is a fact of vital importance. It is only when the individuals have the discretion to exercise their personal choice unimpaired by the purposes of the formal organisations, one can safeguard the personality and contribute to the formal organisation to realise its purpose. Many executives with experience either deny or neglect the existence of the informal organisation within their own formal organisation. This may be due to their pre-occupation with the problems of the formal organisation or reluctance to accept the existence of what is difficult to define or describe. It may be noted that the organisations are quite unaware of the widespread influences, attitudes and agitation within their own organisations. This is equally true of political organisations, governments, army, churches and universities. Barnard says that one cannot understand an organisation from the organisation chart or its rules and regulations or not even by watching its personnel. It is important to learn the organisation ropes - "in organisation - that is chiefly learning who's who, what's what and why's why of its informal society".[23] Barnard considers communication, maintenance of cohesiveness through regulating the willingness to learn and the ability of the objective authority, and maintenance of the feeling of personal integrity, self-respect and independent choice are the functions of informal organisations.[24] Barnard feels that informal organisations should not be viewed as avoidable evil and asserts that where they do not exist, they need to be created as they perform a number of functions to sustain the formal organisations.

Theory of Authority

Barnard's conceptualisation of authority is most significant. He did not agree with the traditional concept of authority and introduces 'acceptance' as the basis of authority. He defines authority as "the character of a communication (order) in a formal organisation by virtue of which it is accepted by a contributor to, or 'member' of, the organisation as governing the action he contributes; that is as determining what he does or is not to do so far as the organisation is concerned".[25] This definition has both subjective and objective aspects. The former implies acceptance of a communication as authority. The latter is concerned with the character in the communication by virtue of which it is accepted. The individuals in the organisation accept authority only when the following four conditions obtain simultaneously: [26]

1. *When the communication is understood:* Unless the communications are intelligible, they cannot be understood and in consequence have no authority. Orders issued in general terms encounter problems of interpretation, and implementation. As most communications in organisations are general and unintelligible, Barnard says, most of the time is spent in interpretation and reinterpretation of orders to concrete situations.

2. *Consistency with the organisational purpose:* Any communication, not compatible with the purpose of the organisation, is unlikely to be accepted. Because of the cross purposes, it may result in frustrated action. An intelligent person will deny authority if he understands that it is a contradiction with the purposes of the organisation. Any apparent conflict has to be explained, otherwise, orders are not likely to be executed.

3. *Compatibility with personal interests:* If the communications are detrimental to the personal interests of the individuals, they have little chance of being accepted. Similarly, the orders should also provide positive inducements to the individual to motivate them. Or else the

orders would be disobeyed or evaded as inconsistent with personal interest. The case of voluntary resignations from organisations can be explained on this basis.

4. *Physical and mental ability to comply*: In cases where a person is unable to comply with an order, it will generally be disobeyed or disregarded. Therefore, orders should not be beyond the mental and physical capacity of the individuals.

From the foregoing, it is evident that the determination of authority lies with the subordinate. Then question is how to ensure enduring cooperation of an individual in an organisation. According to Barnard, it is possible under three conditions: (a) when the orders issued in organisations are in accordance with the four conditions discussed above; (b) when the orders fall within the 'zone of indifference'; and (c) when the group influences the individual resulting in the stability of the zone of indifference. The principle of good executive conduct is that the orders that cannot be obeyed should not be issued. When the issue of orders, which are initially or apparently unacceptable, becomes necessary, then a preliminary education or persuasive efforts or offering of inducements should be made so that the issue is not raised, resulting in the acceptance of authority.

Zone of Indifference

The acceptance of authority in organisations, as noted, depends on the zone of indifference. If the orders are arranged in order of their acceptability to the person affected, they fall into three different categories, viz., (1) those which will clearly be unacceptable and not obeyed, (2) those which are on neutral line i.e., either just acceptable or just unacceptable, and (3) those which are unquestionably acceptable. Orders, which fall under the last category, come within the 'zone of indifference'.[27] As long as the orders fall within this 'zone', they will be accepted by the individuals unmindful of the nature of authority. The zone of indifference will vary depending upon the inducements offered and the burdens and sacrifices made by the individuals in the organisation. It is clear that when the inducements are not adequate, the range of orders that will be accepted will be limited. The executives in the organisation should be conscious of the 'zone' and issue only those orders, which fall within the 'zone'. To do otherwise would be to open themselves to the charge that they do not know how to use authority or are abusing it.[28] Acceptance of the authority is also based on the realisation that denying the authority of an organisation communication is a threat to the interests of all individuals who derive a net advantage from their connection with the organisation.

The Fiction of Authority

The efficiency of an organisation depends on the degree to which the individuals accept the orders. Normally, the authority of a communication will not be denied, as they know it is a threat to all individuals who receive a net benefit from the organisation. Therefore, at any time, the contributors have an active personal interest in the orders, which to them are within the zone of indifference. This interest is maintained largely because of the informal organisation. It may also be due to public or organisational opinion, feeling in the ranks or group attitude.[29] The fiction of authority establishes the presumption that individual accepts orders from superiors because they want to avoid making issue of such orders and avoid incurring personal subservience or loss of personal status with their colleagues. The contributors accept the authority of communication, as care is taken to see only acceptable communications are issued; most of them fall within the zone of personal indifference and the communal sense influences the motives of the contributors.

The fiction of superior authority appears to be necessary for two reasons. Firstly, it enables the individual to delegate upward or to the organisation, responsibility for what is an organisation decision. Most persons obey authority because they dislike the personal responsibility when they are not in a position to accept it. The difficulties in the operation of the organisation lie in the reluctance of the individuals to take the responsibility for their own actions in organisation, and not in the excessive desire of individuals to assume responsibility for organisational action. Secondly, the fiction drives home the point that what is at stake is the good of the organisation. Disobeying authority for arbitrary reasons and twisting organisational requirements for personal advantage must be construed as deliberate attack on the organisation itself. According to Barnard, "to fail in an obligation intentionally is an act of hostility". No organisation will permit it and it will respond with punitive action.

Barnard holds the view that a superior is not an authority and, strictly speaking he may not have any authority. A communication may not be authoritative unless it is an effort or an action of the organisation. In fact, assent of those to whom the communications are sent determines the character of the authority. Authoritative official communications are only related to organisational action. They have no meaning to those whose actions do not fall within the cooperative system. For instance, the laws of one country have no authority for citizens of another.

Authority is imputed to communications from superiors if they are consistent and are credited to the positions. This authority is independent of the personal ability of the incumbent. Sometimes even if the incumbent has limited personal ability, his advice may be superior by reason of the advantage of the position he occupies. This may be called the authority of position. But some men have superior ability and they command respect, irrespective of their position because of their knowledge and understanding. Authority is imputed to what they say in an organisation for this reason. This may be called the authority of leadership.

The determination of the authority finally remains with the individuals. A leader can have authority as long as he is adequately informed. Authority depends, however, upon the cooperative personal attitudes of the individuals and upon the system of communication in the organisation. If a system results in inadequate, contradictory and inept orders, many adherents of an organisation will quit, because they cannot understand who is who and what is what and are deprived of the sense of effective coordination. The following factors control the character of the communication system as a system of objective authority: [30]

- The channels of communication should be definite;
- Objective authority requires a definite formal channel of communication to every member of an organisation;
- The line of communication should be as direct and as short as possible;
- The complete line of communication should usually be used;
- The competence of the persons serving as communication centres, that is, officers and supervisory heads should be adequate;
- The line of communication should not be interrupted during the time when the organisation is functioning; and
- Every communication should be authenticated.

Responsibility

Barnard examines responsibility in greater detail, along with authority. To him, responsibility is the most important function of the executive. He examines responsibility from the point of view of morality and defines it as the power of a particular private code of morals to control the conduct of the individuals in the presence of strong contrary desires or impulses.[31] Responsibility is not determined by any one single moral code but by a complex set of moral, legal, technical, professional, and institutional codes. Therefore, these codes always regulate the working of organisations. In this process of regulation, the internal moral sanction of individuals is more effective than the external sanctions. Since individual conduct or behaviour is governed by a complex of codes, it may result in conflicts. This is particularly so with codes having substantially equal validity. Such conflicts may result in[32]:

- the paralysis of action accompanied by emotional tension, and ending in a sense of frustration, blockade, uncertainty, or in loss of decisiveness and lack of confidence; or
- there is conformity to one code and violation of the other resulting in a sense of guilt, discomfort, dissatisfaction, or a loss of respect; or
- find some substitute action which satisfies immediate desire or impulse or interest, or the dictates of one code, and yet conforms to all other codes.

Barnard argues that executive actions are always conditioned by the concepts of morality. But business is totally unaffected by the higher concepts of morality. Therefore, he argues, that more and more research needs to be undertaken on this important aspect of the relations between executive behaviour and principles of morality. He feels that large organisations cannot be operated unless responsibility is delegated. [33] But he laments that one of the great weakness of *The Functions of the Executive* is that it did not adequately address the question of responsibility and its delegation and emphasis is too much on authority.[34]

Decision-Making

Organisations take decisions to achieve the purposes for which they come into being. Barnard defines decisions as acts of individuals which are the result of deliberation, calculation and thought involving the ordering of means to ends. [35] There are two types of decisions - personal and organisational. The former relates to the participation or otherwise in the organisational process and are taken outside the organisation based on incentives the organisations offer and they need not necessarily be logical. The latter relate to the organisational purpose, information-based, logical and can be delegated. They are the result of discrimination, analysis and choice. Decision-making in organisations, according to Barnard, is a specialised process. He emphasises that organisational decisions need not always be positive. This is clear when he says that the 'fine art of executive decision consists in not deciding questions that are not pertinent, in not deciding prematurely, in not making decisions that cannot be made effective and in not making decisions that others should make'. [36] Based on his long years of experience, Barnard says that decision-making in orgnisations is a burdensome task. For fear of criticism, the executives avoid taking decisions and there is also a tendency not to delegate decisional powers resulting in the executives being overwhelmed with the burdens of decision-making.

The Executive Functions

In organisations, executives perform various functions necessary to ensure coordination of the cooperative system. They also act as channels of communication. However, all the work undertaken by them, according to Barnard, is not executive work. Quite often, the executive may undertake certain functions like the Vice-Chancellor giving classroom lectures or a manager selling the products, which cannot be called executive work. To Barnard, executive work involves a specialised work of maintaining the organisation in operation. The executive functions are like those of the nervous system, including the brain in relation to the rest of the body. Barnard classified the functions of the executive under three heads viz.,

- formulation of purpose and objectives;
- maintenance of organisation communication; and
- securing essential services from the individuals.[37]

Formulation of Purpose and Objectives

The first function of the executive is to formulate and define purpose, objectives and ends of the organisation. The purpose of the organisation must be accepted by all the contributors to the system. Purpose must be subdivided into fragments and specific objectives must reflect the detailed purposes and actions. The purpose can be geographic, social and functional, and a single executive can accomplish and can do only that part of it which relates to his position.

Assumption of responsibility and delegation of authority are crucial aspects of the functions of the executive. At every level below, purpose, objectives and direction get redefined with reference to that level, the time and the results to be accomplished. All this may involve up and down communications, reporting obstacles, difficulties, impossibilities, accomplishments, redefining and modifying purposes, level after level.

Purpose is defined in terms of specification of the work to be done and specifications are made when and where work is being done. The purpose becomes more and more general as units of organisation become larger and more and more remote. Responsibility for long run decisions is delegated up the line and responsibility for action remains at the base. The formulation and definition of purpose is a widely distributed function and only the general part of which is executive. The formulation and redefining of purpose requires sensitive systems of communication, imagination, experience and interpretation. The functions of the executive are elements in an organic whole and their combination makes an organisation. The combination involves two inducements to action: (a) executive functions are partly determined by the environment of the organisation, and (b) it depends on the maintenance of vitality of action, that is, the will to effort. In short, the executive role is mainly related to the synthesis of physical, biological and social factors.

Maintenance of Organisation Communication

This function has three important phases. The first is defining the 'scheme of organisation' or defining the organisational positions; second is maintaining a personnel system and the third is securing an informal organisation. The scheme of organisation deals with the organisational charts, specification of duties and division of labour. It represents securing the coordination of work by dividing the purpose into subsidiary purposes, specialisation and tasks. It is also related to the kind and quality of services of the personnel that can be brought under a cooperative system. The inducements that are to be offered are also relevant. But defining the scheme of organisation or organisational positions is of little consequence unless there are people to fill the positions. The process includes, to Barnard, the selection of men and offering of incentives, techniques of control permitting effectiveness in promoting, demoting and dismissing men.

The personnel recruited for organisational positions should be loyal and possess specific personal abilities. These abilities are of two kinds: general abilities involving alertness, comprehensiveness of interest, flexibility, faculty of adjustment, poise and courage; and specialised abilities based on aptitudes and acquired techniques. The first two phases are both complementary and are dependent on each other. Since, according to Barnard, men are neither good nor bad but become good or bad in particular positions, there is a need to restructure the organisations, taking into consideration the available manpower.

The informal organisations promote the means of organisational communication. With good informal organisations, the need for formal decisions gets reduced except in emergencies. Even a formal order implies the informal agreement. The executives must always try to avoid orders, which are clearly unacceptable and should deal with such situations through informal means. The informal organisations perform the following functions:

* communicate unintelligible facts, opinions, suggestions and suspicions which cannot easily pass through formal channels;
* minimise excessive clicks of political influence;
* promote self-discipline of the group; and
* make possible the development of important personal influences in the organisation.

Securing the Essential Services from Individuals

The task of securing essential services from individuals has two main aspects, viz., bringing of persons into cooperative relationship with the organisation, and eliciting of services after they have been brought into that relationship. These are achieved by maintaining morale and by providing incentives, deterrents, supervision, control, education and training. Every organisation, in order to survive, must deliberately attend to the maintenance and growth of its authority, to do things necessary for coordination, effectiveness and efficiency. Barnard uses 'efficiency' in the specialised sense of an organisation's capacity to offer effective inducements in sufficient quantity to maintain the equilibrium of the system.

Leadership

Barnard attaches significance to leadership in organisations as it is critical to achieve 'cooperation'. To him the cooperation is the creative process and the leadership is the 'indispensable fulminator' of its forces.[38] One of the functions of the leader is to create an environment that will facilitate commitment of the members to the organisation. Barnard argues that a leader should be a realist and should recognise the need for action even when outcomes cannot be foreseen. He should also be an idealist to pursue the goals which may not be achieved in the immediate future.[39] Barnard lists out five essential qualities of a leader viz., vitality and endurance, decisiveness, persuasiveness, responsibility and intellectual capacity.

Organisational Science

Barnard believed that it is possible to develop a science of organisation. He argued for the integration of two cultures of management - its science and art. To develop a science of organisation requires understanding of social anthropology, sociology, social psychology, institutional economics, management, etc. It also requires higher order intellect.[40] Intellect by itself is not enough; it is also necessary to inculcate a sense of unity and create common ideals.

An Evaluation

Kenneth Andrews, who wrote a highly complementary introduction to *The Functions of the Executive*, provides some of the criticisms on Barnard's work. They include abstractness of the presentation, the paucity and pedestrian quality of examples and the difficult style as the main weaknesses of the book.[41] Baker considers the absence of practical examples from experience as unfortunate. [42] Barnard who is conscious of these limitations feels that theorising, and when it is being addressed to so many groups of widely different attitudes and experience, a certain amount of abstractness is inevitable. Barnard acknowledges these deficiencies.[43]

Even though Barnard considers purpose as central to the cooperative effort, Andrews felt that he has not given full descriptive or prescriptive attention to the process of its formulation. Barnard's definition of authority, according to Andrews, understates the role of objective authority and appears to assign individuals the choice of acceptance or rejection rather than participation in the active integration of conflicting alternatives and interpretations. He further says that leadership is effectively but abstractly examined; its problems are not analysed.[44]

Barnard argues that the individuals make utilitarian decisions based on available incentives. Matthew Ensor, on the other hand argues, that the psychological perspective sees the key to cooperation as the avoidance of regressive behaviour and it is the function of the executive to provide an environment where the individuals in the organisation can examine themselves and the context of their work from a collective perspective. [45] This perspective also challenges the executive to take a more holistic role in enabling ongoing organisational change. Barnard also did not attempt to resolve the apparent paradoxes in the relations between man and organisation is another criticism. Instead, Fry observes, Barnard accepts the inevitable tensions in the relationship while seeking a balance between the needs of the individual and the organisation.[46]

Notwithstanding the criticisms, cooperation as a basic necessity of human life and as the cause of human development is profoundly elucidated by Chester Barnard. The physical, biological and social factors affecting cooperative action and the functions of the executive to facilitate the cooperative effort are brilliantly analysed with practical wisdom. A number of his remarks, conclusions and evaluations demonstrate an unusually profound understanding of the complexity of organisation processes. The point he makes about the constant need to consider strategic factors in taking managerial decisions is worthy of attention, so is his formulation of the zone of indifference. His acceptance concept of authority, leadership as a process of fulfilling the purposes of organisation and management by consent have an immense contemporary value and strengthen the democratic spirit in the modern world.

Barnard dismantles the outdated concept of 'economic man' and effectively applies the ideas of Mayo and other human relations thinkers to middle and top levels of management. In an age of organisations, his analysis of formal and informal organisations and their mutual interaction has practical utility and scientific value to everyone interested in understanding social problems. His theories, though abstract, are of practical importance to modern executives interested in the effective and efficient functioning of the organisation or in maintaining the organisation in operation. The views of Barnard still hold relevance because they are the combination of intellect and experience and are the outcome of rational analysis of the reality, viewing the situation as a whole. The impact of his ideas is indisputable and *The Functions* is one of the most widely cited in the literature on organisations and continue to have substantial influence. [47] Barnard's contribution was a conscious effort towards a 'science of organisation' [48] and he combines the science of organisation with the art of organising.

In Brief

Chester Barnard's contribution to organisation and management can be summed up as:

- Chester Barnard, an American business executive, is considered as the spiritual father of "social system" school. His classic *"The Functions of the Executive"* is the most influential work in administrative and management theory.

- Barnard viewed the organisations as systems of cooperation of human activity and proposed the theory of "contribution-satisfaction-equilibrium" as the basis for individual contribution to organisations. Barnard rejected the theory of economic man and analysed multiplicity of satisfactions and inducements as the basis for actions in organisations.

- He examined the role of informal organisations and considers them as essential and complementary to formal organisations.

- Barnard's conceptualisation of authority is most significant. Introducing "acceptance" as the basis of authority, he explains the conditions of acceptance and proposes the concept of "Zone of Indifference" as the basis for acceptance of orders. Elaborating on the nature of exercise of authority, Barnard describes the features of communication system forming the basis of objective authority.

- Barnard examines responsibility from the point of view of morality and considers internal moral sanctions as more effective than external sanctions in controlling individual behaviour in organisations.

- Elaborating the functions of executive, Barnard classified them under three heads viz., formulation of purpose and objectives; maintenance of organisation communication; and securing essential services from the individual.

- Barnard believed that it is possible to develop a science of organisation. He argued for the integration of two cultures of management i.e., science and art.

- The criticisms of Barnard's work include abstractness of ideas and the paucity and pedestrian nature of examples. Barnard's views on authority are criticised for understating the role of objective authority and for giving an impression that individuals will have an option to accept or reject authority in organisations.

- The impact of Barnard's ideas is very extensive both on theory and practice of management and administration. His theory of authority, role of informal organisations and functions of executive are of practical relevance to modern organisation and practitioners.

Notes and References

[1] Gvishiani, D., *Organisation and Management: A Sociological Analysis of Western Theories*, Moscow, Progress Publishers, 1972, p. 38.

[2] Gross, Bertram M., *The Managing of Organisations: The Administrative Struggle*, Vol. 1, New York, The Free Press of Glencoe, 1964, p. 171

[3] Fry, Brain R., *Mastering Public Administration: From Max Weber to Dwight Waldo*, Chatham,N.J, Chatham House Publishers, 1989, p.158. For biographical details see Wolf, William B., *The Basic Barnard: An Introduction to Chester I. Barnard and His Theories of Organisation and Management*, Ithaca, N.Y. New York State School of Industrial and Labor Relations, Cornell University,1974.

[4] See also Sheldrake, John, *Management Theory: From Taylorism to Japanisation*, London, International Thompson Business Press, 1966, pp.117-119.

[5] Fry, Brain R., op.cit. p.159. For a detailed list of Barnard's articles, lectures, and manuscripts of Barnard see Wolf, William B. , *The Basic Barnard*, op.cit., Appendix 1.

[6] Two of his most important books are: Barnard, Chester I., *The Functions of the Executive*, Cambridge, Massachusetts, Harvard University Press, 1938; *Organisation and Management*, Cambridge, Massachusetts, Harvard University Press, 1948. His last published writing is Elementary Conditions of Business Morals based on a lecture given in 1958. Barnard, Chester I., *The Functions of the Executive*, Cambridge, Massachusetts, Harvard University Press, 1938, p. x.

[7] Barnard, Chester I., *The Functions of the Executive*, op.cit., p. x.

[8] Mahoney, Joseph T., "The Relevance of Chester I. Barnard's Teachings to Contemporary Management Education: Communicating the Aesthetics of Management", *International*

Journal of Organisation Theory & Behaviour, Vol.5, No. 1&2, 2002, p.162.

[9] Kenneth R. Andrews in Chester I. Barnard, *The Functions of the Executive*, op. cit., p. xii.

[10] Mahoney, Joseph T., op.cit., p.160.

[11] Barnard, Chester I., *The Functions of the Executive*, op.cit., p. 72-73.

[12] Ibid., pp. 82-91.

[13] Barnard, Chester I., *Organisation and Management*, op. cit., p.15.

[14] Ibid., p. 58.

[15] Barnard, Chester I., *The Functions of the Executive*, op. cit. pp. 142-146.

[16] Ibid., pp.146-149.

[17] Ibid., p. 87.

[18] Ibid., p. 89.

[19] Ibid., p. 79.

[20] Fry, Brain R., op. cit. pp 162-64

[21] Ibid.

[22] Barnard, Chester I., *The Functions of the Executive*, op. cit. p. 120.

[23] Ibid., pp. 121

[24] Ibid., pp.122.

[25] Ibid., p. 163.

[26] Ibid., pp. 165-166.

[27] Ibid., pp. 168-69.

[28] Ibid., p. 168.

[29] Ibid., p.169.

[30] Ibid., pp. 175-181. See also Gross, Bertram M., op. cit., pp. 178-179.

[31] Barnard, Chester I., *The Functions of the Executive*, op. cit., p. 263.

[32] Ibid., 264.

[33] See, Wolf, William, B., *Conversations with Chester I. Barnard*, School of Industrial Labor Relations: Cornell University, ILR Paperback Number 12, Ithaca, NY, 1973, p. 35.

[34] Ibid., p.15

[35] Barnard, Chester I., *The Functions of the Executive*, op. cit., p. 185.

[36] Ibid., 194.

[37] Ibid., pp.175-181.

[38] Ibid, p.259

[39] Barnard, Chester I., *Organisation and Management* , op.cit., pp.109-110

[40] Barnard, Chester I., *The Functions of the Executive*, op. cit., p.293.

[41] Ibid, p. xii.

[42] Baker, R. J. S., *Administrative Theory and Public Administration*, London, Hutchinson University Library, 1972, p. 48.

[43] Andrews, Kenneth R., op. cit., p. xii; and Chester Barnard's preface, p. xxxiii.

[44] Andrews, Kenneth R., op. cit., p. xiv.

[45] Ensor, Matthew, A *Psychoanalytical Critique of Chester I. Barnard's "The Functions of the Executive"*, September, 2002 See http://homepages. paradise.net.nz/ensor/papers/barnard.pdf Retrieved on 13th January, 2010

[46] Fry, Brain R., op.cit., p.178.

[47] Andrews, Kenneth R., op.cit., p.vii.

[48] Mahoney, Joseph T., op. cit., pp. 159-172.

11

HERBERT SIMON

N. Umapathy

Introduction

Administrative studies in the 1930s and the 40s reflect a significant amount of empiricism, which led to a substantial modification in the previously held views about man in an organisation. These studies have built theoretical constructs of social systems and some essential notions of human behaviour. These behavioural studies deal with human behaviour through interdisciplinary approach drawing from the knowledge available in anthropology, sociology and psychology and have become a part of the vital development that is generally labelled as behavioural science. In the field of administrative behaviour, major studies pertain to bureaucracy, human relations, motivation and decision-making. A polymathic intellectual, Herbert Simon's contribution has been particularly significant in the field of decision-making. He is considered a founding figure in the field of artificial intelligence, a creator of thinking machine and a central figure in the cognitive revolution in psychology in

(1916-2001)

the 1960s when computer models began to be used to study the thought processes of humans. His pioneering studies on decision-making led him to develop a theory of bounded rationality.

Life and Works

Herbert Alexander Simon (1916-2001), born in Milwaukee, Wisconsin, entered the University of Chicago in 1933 and studied social sciences and mathematics. He obtained B.A. (1936) and Ph.D (1943) in political science with a major field in public administration from the University of Chicago. Simon started his professional career in 1936 with the International City Manager's Association as an assistant to Clarence E. Ridley, moved to Administrative Measurement Studies at the Bureau of Public Administration, University of California as its Director in 1939. In 1942, he joined as Associate Professor of Political Science at the Illinois Institute of Technology where he was chairman of the Department of Political and Social Sciences during 1946-49. He became Professor of Administration and Psychology at the Carnegie Mellon University in 1949 and later became Professor of Computer Science and Psychology at the Richard King Mellon University and remained there until his death. His irrevocable and indelible influence could be seen in several schools and departments of the university including philosophy, Social and Design Sciences, Graduate School of Industrial Administration, the Heinz School of Public Policy, School of Computer Science, etc. He was also a member of the Board of Trustees of the University. Simon was associated with several public organisations including Bureau of Budget, Census Bureau, Economic Cooperation Administration, President's Science Advisory Committee, American Social Science Research Council, etc. He was associated with several professional bodies of political science, economics, psychology, sociology, computer science, management, philosophy, etc., signifying that he was a true social scientist.

Simon did not remain a political scientist for long. In 1940's he began work in econometrics, in mid 50's he started researching in psychology of problem solving which earned him American Psychology Association's Life Time Achievement Award and in mid 50's wrote his first computer programme which brought him the AM Turing Award (1975). For his pioneering research on decision-making process within economic organisations Simon received the Noble Prize in Economics (1978). Simon received the Distinguished Scientific Contribution Award of the American Psychological Association (1969), National Medal of Science (1986), American Psychological Association's Award for Outstanding Lifetime Contribution (1993), inducted into the Chinese Academy of Sciences (1994), Research Excellence Award of the International Joint Conference on Artificial Intelligence (1995), membership of National Academy of Science, and awards from several professional organisations including American Society of Public Administration.

Simon was influenced by Follett's idea on group dynamics in organisations and the human relations approach pioneered by Elton Mayo and others. Barnard's *Functions of the Executive* had a positive influence on Simon's thinking about administration. Simon is one of the most influential social scientists and his role in shaping the 20th century social sciences was unparalleled.[1] He was an indefatigable advocate of social sciences and an exemplar[2] of a modern scientist. He was called a scientist's scientist and received major awards from different science communities.[3] He authored over 1,000 highly cited publications, many of which were translated into various languages including Turkish, Persian and Chinese. His publications, if need to be classified into disciplines, include public administration, political science, operation research, management, system's theory, organisation theory, decision theory, economics and econometrics, sociology, social psychology, cognitive psychology, socio-biology, mathematics, philosophy, linguistics and computer science.[4] Human decision-making and problem solving processes and the implications of these processes to social institutions provide the thread of continuity in all his studies. Simon started his research work in the 30's on city management that culminated into a book titled *Measuring Municipal Activities* in 1938.[5] Simon published his doctoral dissertation as *Administrative Behaviour* [6] in 1947 and it is one of the twentieth century's ten top most influential works in political science, public administration and management. This, along with his later work *Organisation (1958),* became a staple in courses on business education, public administration and organisational sociology.[7] His other principal publications include *Public Administration* (1950), *Fundamental Research in Administration* (1953), *The New Science of Management Decision (1960), Shape of Automation (1960), Science of the Artificial* (1969) and *Human Problem Solving* (1972). [8] Simon received honorary degrees from over two dozen universities from around the world including Harvard, Columbia, Yale and Chicago (United States), Lund (Sweden), McGill (Canada), and the Netherland School of Economics. [9]

Administrative Science

Simon sought to develop a science of administration and unlike classicists made human decision-making as the central theme of his studies all through his life. He considered the decision-making as a process of drawing conclusions from premises and therefore the premise than the whole decision serves as the unit of analysis.[10] He equated 'administration' with decision-making and laid emphasis on how decisions are made and how they be made more effectively. In addition to the major emphasis on decision-making as the alternative to the 'principles approach' of the traditionalists, Simon recommended an empirical approach to the study of administration. He offers a series of hypothetical propositions of empirical relevance. He considered the concepts of 'efficiency' and 'economy' as serviceable criteria of administrative effectiveness in the context of theoretically demonstrable 'means-ends chain constructs'.[11]

Based on theories and methodology of logical positivism, Simon proposed a new concept of administration with focus on decision-making. He argued that decision-making is the core of administrative action. The shift in emphasis from the 'doer' to decision-making in administration is not novel. The exponents of 'classical' school had earlier separated 'technology from operation' in their administrative theories. But this does not mean that Simon's contribution is less significant as his writings aided in the fuller understanding of the administrative phenomena. Another reason for the acceptance and popularity of Simon's theory was due to its apparent subsuming of several administrative functions such as Fayol's POCC and Gulick's POSDCORB into a single all embracing concept of decision-making.

Simon disapproved policy-administration dichotomy both on descriptive and normative grounds and in its place proposed, based on his decision-making schema, fact-value dichotomy, which he believed provides a better basis for a science of administration. To Simon, a science of administration should be based on factual premises of administrative decisions. This is important for the development of a science of administration.[12] This should be based on systematic, empirical investigation and analysis, inductive and descriptive methods. He talks of two kinds of administrative sciences - pure and practical - and observes that the latter assists the administration in decision-making. Simon believed that the science of administration is applicable to both private and public organisations as they have more similarities than differences.[13] He argued that the first task to develop an administrative theory is to develop concepts that permit the description of administrative situations, [14] which provide the basis for prescription. To Simon 'until administrative description reaches a higher level of sophistication, there is little reason to hope that rapid progress will be made toward the identification and verification of valid administrative principles'. [15]

Classical Theory: An Indictment

Simon passes a critical indictment on the narrowness and sterility of the traditional approach and the 'principles' of administration and calls them as proverbs and myths.[16] In this attack, as Bertram Gross noted, Simon gave expression to the widespread disenchantment of many people, both academics and practitioners, who were disturbed by the yawning gulf between the principles and effective practice.[17] Simon says that when research has been done, when a basic vocabulary to the satisfaction of many scholars has been developed, when decision-making as well as the 'doing' have been analysed, when the limits to rationality imposed by restricting abilities, habits, values, and knowledge have been explored fully - then and only then - it may be possible to have valid principles of administration and know-how to apply them.[18] The principles of work division, unity of command and span of control were attacked as being ambiguous and as mere proverbs, each paired with a contradictory proverb. The reason for such an ambiguity, according to Simon, is the 'inadequate' diagnosis of situations and definition of terms and lack of detailed research into real situations.[19] He says that these principles are more like a series of orderly cubicles contrived according to an abstract architectural logic than of a house designed to be inhabited by the human being. He finds no compatibility between the perfection of administrative processes as conceived in the POSDCORB formula, and their utility in the attainment of objectives. Through these attacks, Simon points to the gap between the principles and practice. The missing factor, according to him, is correct decision-making, by which he meant the optimum rational choice between alternative courses of action. Thus begins his search for rational decision-making models from which guides to real world decision-making might be derived.

Decision-Making

An organisation is viewed by Simon as a structure of decision-makers. To him decisions are made at all levels of the organisation, some of them affecting many members, while others are relatively less important decisions about detail. Each decision is based on a number of premises and Simon focuses his attention on how these premises are determined. Some of these premises pertain to the decision-maker's preferences; some to his social conditioning, and others to the communications he receives from component units of the organisation. Simon asserts that the top management cannot dictate to every member of the organisation what each decision must be, but it can influence some, perhaps the most important premises on which the decisions are based. It can also create a structure which will permit and stimulate the transmission of necessary information. [20]

Decision-making process, according to Simon, involves three phases viz., intelligence activity - finding occasions for decision-making, design activity - finding possible courses of action, and choice activity - choosing among courses of action.[21] The first stage involves finding occasions calling for decision. The executive tries to understand the organisational environment and identifies conditions which need fresh action. The second stage involves identifying, developing and analysing all possible alternative courses of action involving more time and energy than the first stage. Finally, the executive selects one of the alternative courses of action available to him. Simon says that though these three stages appear to be simple and one preceding the other, in practice the sequence is more complex. Each stage may involve all the three stages in itself.

Fact and Value in Decision-Making

Simon maintains that to be scientific one must exclude value judgments and concentrate on facts, adopt precise definition of terms, apply rigorous analysis, and test factual statements or postulates about administration. 'An administration science, like any science, is concerned purely with factual statements. There is no place for ethical (value) statements in the study of science.' Simon explains that decision-making basically involves choice between alternative plans of action, and choice in turn, involves facts and values. To him, every decision consists of a logical combination of fact and value propositions. A fact is a statement of reality indicating the existing deed, act or state of things. A factual premise can be proved by observable and measurable means. A value is an expression of preference. A value premise can only be subjectively asserted to be valid. Simon, however, is aware that most premises have both factual and value elements and his purpose of stressing this distinction is only to clarify the different criteria of correctness that may be applied in analysing the ethical and factual elements present in a 'decision'. He asserts that the rules of scientific analysis, most particularly the rule of observation, preclude ethical judgements although both values and facts are inextricably joined. Most value premises involve intermediate facts and they are open to segregation only for purposes of illustrative analyses. To bring out the difference between fact and value, the means-ends distinction is sometimes used. Simon considers this phenomenon as significant because of the amenability of facts to rational decision as against values, whose base, he traces out to non-rational cause such as faith.

Mixed issues of fact and value impinge on administration complicating the decision process. The relevance of this impingement on administration is to be seen in the purposive character of organisation, which develops groups of individuals to achieve goals ordinarily beyond their individual reach. The continuum of purposiveness includes the concept of a 'hierarchy of decisions'. Simon concludes that behaviour in an organisation - a complex network of decision process - is, therefore, intendedly rational in character, adjusted to the goals that have been erected. Speaking of the complex network of decision process, Simon says that 'each decision involves the selection of a goal and a behaviour relevant to it; this goal may in turn be mediate to a somewhat more distant goal; and so on, until a relatively final aim is reached'.[22] The ambiguous synonym between means-ends and fact-value, is clarified through a definition that in so far as decisions lead to the selection of final goals, they may be treated as 'value judgments' - i.e., the value component predominates, and in so far as the decisions relate to implementation of such goals, they may be treated as 'factual judgments' - i.e., the factual component predominates.[23] The relationship of a decision to a set of ends remains a factual proposition. Simon does not refer to 'value decisions' and 'factual decisions'. For, there are only value or factual premises and components and in administration both value and factual premises are intertwined.

Rationality in Decision-Making

After establishing fact-value continuum of decision-making, Simon delves into the dynamics of decision on a different plane - the plane of rationality. He expounds the necessity of being rational in making a choice. He defines rationality as one concerned with the selection of preferred behaviour alternatives in terms of some system of values whereby the consequences of behaviour can be evaluated.[24] To him it requires a total knowledge and anticipation of the consequences that will follow on each choice. It also requires a choice from among all possible alternative behaviours.[25] He explains rationality in terms of means-ends construct. The term 'ends'- ultimate purpose – refers to any state or situation, which is later in a purpose chain or set of chains. The same state or situation may always be a means from one point of view and an ultimate objective from another. If appropriate means are chosen to reach desired ends, the decision is rational. However, there are many complications to this simple test of rationality.

For, it is difficult to separate means from ends because an apparent end may only be a means for some future end. This is commonly referred to as the means-ends chain hierarchy. Simon points out that "the means-end hierarchy is seldom an integrated and connected chain. Often the connection between organisation activities and ultimate objectives is obscure, or they are incompletely formulated or there are internal conflicts and contradictions among the ultimate objectives, or among the means selected to attain them." [26] Besides, seemingly rational decisions based on inaccurate conclusions, may produce undesirable, sometimes, even unanticipated results. Finally, the inherent problems of means-ends analysis are summed up by Simon as follows:

"First, the ends to be attained by the choice of particular behaviour alternative are often incompletely or incorrectly stated through failure to consider the alternative ends that could be reached by selection of another behaviour...."

"Second, in actual situations a complete separation of means from ends is usually impossible...."

"Third, the means-end terminology tends to obscure the role of the time element in decision-making...." [27]

Simon differentiates between different types of rationality. A decision is:

1. objectively rational where it is correct behaviour for maximising given values in a given situation;
2. subjectively rational if the decision maximises attainment relative to knowledge of the subject;
3. consciously rational where adjustment of means to ends is a conscious process;
4. deliberately rational to the degree that the adjustment of means to ends has been deliberately brought about;
5. organisationally rational if it is oriented to the organisation's goals; and
6. personally rational if the decision is directed to the individual's goals.[28]

Simon disputes the concept of total rationality in administrative behaviour and observes that human behaviour is neither totally rational nor totally non-rational. It involves, what he calls, 'bounded rationality'. The bounded rationality was Simon's building block in everything from public administration to economics to artificial intelligence. Though it was a simple concept, it has revolutionary implications.[29] He discounts the possibility of optimizing decisions, which flows from the concept of total rationality. These concepts are based on the assumption that the decision-makers know all the alternatives; they know the utilities (values) of all alternatives; and they have an ordered preference among all alternatives.[30] As Simon finds these assumptions to be 'fundamentally wrong', he rejects the theory of total rationality. In the place of optimising decisions, which was based on total rationality, he advances the idea of 'satisficing'- a word derived from satisfaction and sufficing. Satisficing involves the choice of a course of action, which is satisfactory or at least good enough.

Models of Decision-Making Behaviour

Simon attempts at describing various models of decision-making in vogue and builds a model incorporating his concepts. There are many models of decision-making behaviour and these models attempt to determine the extent of rationality of the decision-makers. The models range from complete rationality to complete irrationality of the economic man and the social man respectively. Simon develops the model of 'administrative man' who stands next to the economic man.

As the administrative man cannot perceive all possible alternatives nor can predict all possible consequences, he instead of attempting to arrive at 'optimal solutions', is satisfied with 'good enough' or 'some-how muddling through'. Again as the administrative man recognises that the world he perceives is the simplified version of the real world, he makes his choices using a simple picture of the situation that takes into account just a few factors he regards as most relevant and crucial.[31] Thus the administrative man makes his choice without 'examining all possible alternatives', 'with relatively simple rule-of-thumb that do not make impossible demands upon his capacity for thought'. In a sense Simon's administrative man tries to rationalise man, but he does not have the ability to maximise and satisfice. However, the difference between maximising and satisficing is relative. Under certain conditions satisficing and maximising are far apart. The construct of a model depicting the administrative man is followed by attempts at understanding the impediments and obstacles that come in the way of maximisation. To Simon resistance to change, desire for *status quo*, or dysfunctional conflicts caused by specialisation, etc., may impede maximisation.

Programmed and Non-programmed Decisions

The process of decision-making in organisations was examined by Simon in greater detail. He makes a distinction between two types of decisions – programmed and non-programmed. Decisions are programmed to the extent that they are repetitive and routine in nature. In such cases definite procedures can be worked out and each decision need not be dealt with separately. Decisions are made based on established practices. Non-programmed decisions are those which are novel, unstructured and have to be tackled independently as no cut-and-dried methods are available for handling them. In all such cases the executives have to work out new decisions in each case. Simon identifies characteristics common to both kinds of decisions. They include definition of the situation, analysis of means and ends to link actions to the organisational objectives, division of problems into independent parts, choosing the alternatives based on 'satisficing' than 'optimising' criteria, uncertainty absorption and routinisation of the process.[32] The major difference between these two types is that in case of the former the organisation provides the alternatives through routines or strategy and in case of the latter the organisation only provides the parameters for the search procedures. [33]

The techniques to deal with programmed decisions are habit, clerical routines, knowledge and skills, and informal channels. Rule-of-thumb, selection and training of executives, higher skills, judgment, innovative ability, etc., are the techniques to deal with non-programmed decisions. Simon suggests that it is possible to construct mathematical models to make a rational choice. The application of mathematical tools, operations research, electronic data processing, systems analysis, computer simulation, etc., can profitably be used to make decisions. Use of such techniques will reduce the dependency on the middle managerial personnel and lead to centralisation in decision-making. Simon argues that the use of computers and the new decision-making techniques will lead to recentralisation.[34] He points out that the use of new techniques of decision-making will radically change the concept of delegating responsibility and decentralising decision-making, making it possible for more rational and coordinated communication of decisions than is otherwise possible.[35] With the increased use of computers and simulation models more and more decisions can be programmed, which in turn increases rationality in decision-making. Therefore, he thinks it most desirable to computerise as much of the decision-making process as possible. Such automation and rationalisation of decision-making will alter the climate of organisations in many important ways. It will also make the executive's work easier and satisfying.[36]

Modes of Organisational Influence

The behaviour of organisation man is subject to two types of influences - internal and external. The former involves establishing in the employee, attitudes and habits, which lead him to reach the desired decisions. This is achieved through organisation loyalty, concern with efficiency and training. The latter involves imposing on the employee decisions reached elsewhere in the organisation. This is achieved through authority and advisory and informational services. The individuals accept these influences as the organisation objectives also indirectly become personal objectives of the individuals and acceptance of influences satisfying personal motives. These influences are, however, neither exhaustive nor mutually exclusive.[37]

Authority

Authority is one of the means through which organisation man is made to conform to the organisational demands. However, the general impression that authority flows from above is not correct. For, the exercise of authority, in the ultimate analysis, depends upon the willingness of those who accept it. It should also be noted that authority might operate at various levels and not necessarily downwards. Organisations develop both formal and informal relations and authority is largely used to settle the disputes in the organisation. Simon says that the operative employee is said to accept authority whenever he permits his behaviour to be guided by the decision of the superior. Following Barnard's 'zone of indifference', Simon discusses about the 'zone of acceptance', and says that if exercise of authority is attempted beyond this zone, the subordinate disobeys it. The magnitude of this zone of acceptance depends upon the sanctions available to enforce the authority. [38]

Organisational Loyalties

It is generally observed that members in an organisation identify themselves with it. Such type of loyalty is fundamental for an organisation. Organisation loyalty fulfils a most important function of making individuals in the organisation confine themselves to their tasks instead of probing into the basics of the problems. However, narrow loyalties lead to friction and over competition for the resources. Nevertheless organisation loyalty renders group effort possible. Internal influences are equally important.

Advice and Information

Continuous flow of information downwards, upwards and sideways is essential for effective functioning of an organisation. However, the nature of information and advice to be tendered may change from situation to situation. Therefore, collecting dependable information and proper utilisation of it ensures greater effectiveness in the decision-making and provides adequate lines of communication and persuasion.

Training

Training is a vital device through which administrative man is equipped to face challenges. An efficient training programme would facilitate greater discretion to the individual in decision-making. Training is applicable to the process of decision whenever the same elements are involved in a number of decisions. Further, training supplies facts, provides frame of reference and indoctrinate desirable values. Thus, it can be used for developing effective decision-making.

Administrative Efficiency

The administrator, according to Simon, must be guided by the criterion of efficiency of the complicated nature of its application in governmental organisations, which are not commercial in nature. The criterion of efficiency 'dictates' that choice of alternative, which produces the largest results for the given application of resources.[39] It demands, of the two alternatives having the same cost, the one that leads to the greater attainment of the organisation objective to be chosen; and of the two alternatives leading to the same degree of attainment that one which entails lesser cost should be chosen.[40] The criterion of efficiency is closely related to both organisation and conservation of objectives. It is related to the organisation objectives in so far as it is concerned with the maximisation of output. It relates to the conservation of objectives in so far as it is concerned with the maintenance of a positive balance of output over input.[41] Where resources, costs and objectives are variable, decisions cannot be taken purely on the basis of efficiency criteria. However, when these are given, efficiency becomes the controlling factor of administrative choice.[42] Simon in his later writings, however, downgrades the efficiency criteria. He applies it only to the lower level decisions, as higher-level decisions do not lend themselves to measurement and comparability.[43] While authority and organisational loyalty influence the value premise of the individual, the criterion of efficiency influences his capacity to handle the facts. Efficiency implies adoption of shortest path and cheapest means in achieving the desired goals. "Be efficient" is one of the major influences on organisational man. This leads to rational behaviour.

An Evaluation

Simon focused on the dynamics of decision-making processes and its role in organisations through his penetrating study and analysis. His studies provide deep insights into administrative behaviour and the interaction between decision-making processes and administrative behaviour found in organisations. But while concentrating on the processes and the role of decision-making, Simon relegates social, political, economic and cultural factors into the background although their role is no less significant in the analysis of administrative decision-making and behaviour. Similarly exclusion of value premises, which are integral and essential components of policy-making, would steer the study of public administration to mechanical, routine and less important aspects. Simon's idea of fact-based administrative theory, it is argued, is more relevant to business administration than public administration.

In 1945, Simon decided to revise his thesis for publication and sent 200 mimeographed copies to friends for comments. The comments received on the manuscript contained both positive aspects as well as criticisms. On the positive side there was agreement on his argument that decision-making is the heart of administration. [44] But some found it to be too abstract, too formalistic and too functionalistic arguing that it did not take into account personal motivations and emotions.[45] James Mc Camy felt that individual disappeared into organisation and that emotion had vanished in a puff of reason.[46] The most significant critique was Chester Barnard. While appreciating that it was the first good book on administration, he commented that Simon was trying to produce physics and at the same time trying to solve the riddle of the universe. Barnard's criticism on Simon's manuscript boils down to four aspects viz., it was inconsistent in its use of the terms rational and efficient; did not take into account the enormous amount of uncertainty involved in most decisions; did not pay sufficient attention to the processes of communication within organisations and did not take a politically neutral stance.[47]

Simon's critics mainly contend that although the decision-making process is an important aspect in the organisational situation, it alone is not adequate to explain the totality. To them decision-making is a process involving the other dimensions - emotional or expressive as well as rational or instrumental. Simon's study of decision-making incorporates and makes use of the logical positivists' distinction between fact and value. This approach has been attacked as reviving in a new guise the discredited politics-administration dichotomy.[48]

Simon's efforts to construct a value-free science of administration was criticised by Norton E. Long on the ground that it may lead to the unintended and logically unwarranted result of reviving the policy-administration dichotomy in new verbiage and may also lead to empirically untenable and ethically unwarranted view of administration as largely instrumental. Long further observes that bureaucracy is not, and cannot be, a neutral instrument solely devoted to the unmotivated presentation of facts to, and the docile execution of orders from, political superiors.[49] Selznick argues that radical separation of fact and value too often identified with the logical distinctions between fact statement and preference statements encourages the divorce of means and ends.[50]

Simon's analysis assumes that administration plays a similar role in all societies. But it is observed from experience that administrative systems in developing countries do not have similar role orientation as their counterparts in developed countries. Therefore, developing a theory purely on the basis of administration in developed countries, more particularly on the basis of American experience, cannot be universally valid as the factors affecting decisional process and behaviour vary.

Simon's concept of efficiency was subjected to frequent criticism. Some criticised the term equating it with economy and others objected to the use of the term on the ground that it leads to a mechanical concept of administration and to an inconsistent relationship between means and ends. Efficiency is not, and cannot be, the only goal of administration because there is a whole range of other major categories of organisational purposes, such as, satisfaction of various interests, production of goods and services, mobilizing resources, conforming with certain organised codes and using the most rational techniques. Anyone of these objectives may, under certain circumstances, be more important than efficiency. Further, the goal of efficiency may often decline in importance. Efficiency is relevant only to the extent of scarcity of resources and its perception by members of the organisation. It is measurable in precise terms only when it is possible to quantify both inputs and outputs. This is the reason for Simon's later conclusion that efficiency criteria are applicable largely to lower level decisions.[51]

The study of decision-making encounters many difficulties. For one, executives believe that it is often unwise to reveal the reasons for a decision or the procedure followed. For another, by the time the facts are released via the 'memoirs' route, the matter is no longer important. Nevertheless, it is good for men aspiring to be executives to learn how decisions are made.[52]

Simon's theory of decision-making is criticised as being extremely general. Though it provides a framework, it does not provide details to guide the organisation planners. His concept of rationality is also criticised. For example, Argyris opines that Simon, by insisting on rationality, has not recognised the role of intuition, tradition and faith in decision-making. Simon's theory focuses on *status quo ante*. It uses satisficing to rationalise incompetence.[53]

The utility of Simon's study in the decision-making process in terms of search and comparison and its criteria of maximising or satisfying, despite the criticisms, are unquestionable. Indifference to the effective use of fact-value distinction by many decision-makers is no argument against its effective use by academics as a tool in the analysis of decision-making phenomena.[54] Simon's contribution is undoubtedly a major breakthrough in the evolution of administrative theory despite criticisms on several of his propositions. It is unfortunate that after his major work on *Administrative Behaviour,* Simon did not concentrate much on public administrative system but diverted his attention to economic and business systems. It is equally unfortunate that the subsequent administrative theories do not adequately deal with decision-making in public organisations.

In Brief

Simon's contribution to public administration theory, particularly the decision-making process and behaviour, can be summarised as:

- Herbert Simon is one of the most influential social scientists and received Nobel Prize in Economics in 1978 for his pioneering work in decision-making process in organisations.

- Based on theories and methodology of logical positivism, Simon sought to develop science of administration with a focus on decision-making. He viewed organisation as a structure of decision-makers and identified three phases in decision process viz., intelligence activity, design activity and choice activity.

- He makes a distinction between facts and values in decision-making and analyses fact and value continuum.

- Simon considered rationality as an important basis in decision making and explains it in terms of means - ends construct. To him, choice of appropriate means to reach the desired end is rational. Realising the impossibility of total rationality in administrative behaviour, Simon proposed the concept of 'bounded rationality'. Instead of 'optimising' he suggests 'satisfying' as the basis of decisions.

- Simon describes various models of decision-making in vogue and builds a model incorporating his concepts. He develops a model of 'administrative man' whose decisions are based on bounded rationality in contrast to the model of 'economic man' based on complete rationality and 'social man' based on complete irrationality.

- Simon distinguishes between programmed and non-programmed decisions. He discusses the techniques of two types of decisions and suggests the application of mathematical tools, operations research, computer simulation, etc., in making rational decisions. Simon was the founder of the field of artificial intelligence which may be used as a tool in decision-making.

- Discussing the modes of organisational influences, Simon proposes 'zone of acceptance' as the basis of exercise of authority in organisations. Simon considers efficiency – the adoption of shortest path and cheapest means in achieving the desired goals – as one of the major influences on organisational man.

- Simon's efforts to construct a value-free science of administration were criticised as unrealistic. His theory of decision-making is criticised as inadequate to explain the totality of organisation. His other concepts like fact-value distinctions, rationality are also subjected to criticism.

- Simon's studies provide deep insight into administrative behaviour in organisations; particularly in the field of decision-making.

References

1. Augier, Mie, and March, James G., "Herbert A. Simon, Scientist", in Mie Augier and James G. March, *Models of Man : Essays in Memory of Herbert A. Simon* , MIT Press, 2004, p.3

2. Ibid, p.4

3. Ibid, p.3

4. Hunter, Crowther-Heyek, *Herbert A. Simon: The Bounds of Reason in Modern America,* Baltimore, The Johns Hopkins University Press, 2005, p.3

5. Ibid, p.8

6. Simon, Herbert A., *Administrative Behaviour: A Study of Decision-Making Processes in Administrative Organisation,* New York, The Free Press, 1957, 2nd Ed.

7. Hunter, Crowther-Heyek, op.cit., p.2

8. For details of his life, works and impact on social science disciplines see the different articles in Wood, John D. and Wood, Michael D., (Eds.), *Herbert Simon: Critical Evaluations in Business and Management,* 3 Vols., London, Rutledge, 2007.

9. See also Brain R. Fry, *Mastering Public Administration : From Max Weber to Dwight Waldo,* Chatham, NJ, Chatham House Publishers, 1989.

10. Simon, Herbert A., *Administrative Behaviour,* op.cit., p. xii.

11. Hoselitz , Bert F., (Ed.), *A Reader's Guide to the Social Sciences,* New York, The Free Press, 1970, pp. 156-157.

12. Fry, Brain R., op.cit., pp.186-188.

13. Ibid.

14. Simon, Herbert A., *Administrative Behaviour,* op.cit., p.37.

15. Ibid., p.38

16. For details of Simon's indictment of principles see Simon, Herbert A., 'The Proverbs of Public Administration,' *Public Administration Review,* Vol.6, No. 1, Winter 1946, pp.53-67; Simon, Herbert A., *Administrative Behaviour,* op. cit., Ch. II; March, James G., and Simon, Herbert A., *Organisations,* New York, John Wiley & Sons, Inc, 1958, Ch. II.

17. Gross, Bertram M., *The Managing of Organisations: The Administrative Struggle,* London, The Free Press of Glencoe, 1964, p. 182.

18. Henderson, Keith M., *Emerging Synthesis in American Public Administration,* Bombay, Asia Publishing House, 1970, pp. 19-20.

19. Baker, R. J. S., *Administrative Theory and Public Administration,* London, Hutchinson University Library, 1972, p. 51.

20. Haynes, Warren W., and Massie, Joseph L., *Management: Analysis, Concepts and Cases,* Englewood Cliffs, N. J. Prentice-Hall, Inc, 1961, p. 86.

21. Simon, Herbert A., *The New Science of Management Decision,* New York, Harper & Row Publishers, Inc., 1960, pp. 1-4.

22. Simon, Herbert A., *Administrative Behaviour,* op. cit., p. 4.

23. Ibid., pp. 4-5.

24. Ibid., p. 75.

25. Ibid., p. 81.

26. Simon, Herbert A., *Administrative Behaviour,* op. cit., p.64.

27. Ibid., p. 65.

28. Ibid., pp. 76-77.

29. Hunter, Crowther-Heyek, op.cit., p.9

30. *International Encyclopedia of Social Sciences,* Vol. IV, p. 56.

31. Herbert A. Simon, *Administrative Behaviour,* op. cit., p. XXIX.

32. Fry, Brain R., op.cit., pp. 202-03.

33. Ibid., p 206

34. Simon, Herbert A., *The New Science of Management Decision,* op. cit., pp. 44-45.

35. Ibid.

36. Ibid., p.50.

37. Simon, Herbert A., *Administrative Behaviour,* op. cit., pp. 11-16.

38. Ibid., p.12.

39. Ibid., p. 179.

40. Ibid., p. 122.

41. Ibid., p. 173.

42. Ibid., p. 122.

43. Gross, Bertram M., op.cit. p. 185.

44. Hunter, Crowther-Heyek, op.cit., p.131

45. Ibid.

46. Quoted in Ibid, p.131

47. Ibid, p.132

48. Subramaniam, V., "Fact and Value in Decision-Making", *Public Administration Review,* Vol. XXIII, No. 4, December 1963, p. 232.

49. Quoted in Subramaniam, V., Ibid., p. 233.

50. Phillip Selznich, *Leadership and Administration,* Row, Peterson & Sons, 1957, pp. 79-82.

51. Gross, Bertram M., *Organisations and Their Managing,* New York, The Free Press, 1968, pp. 104-105.

52. Charlesworth, James, *Contemporary Political Analysis,* New York, The Free Press, 1967, p. 5.

53. Ibid.

54. Subramaniam, V., "The Fact-Value Distinction as an Analytical Tool", *The Indian Journal of Public Administration,* Vol. XVII, No. 1, Jan.-March 1971, pp. 1-2.

12

ABRAHAM MASLOW

D. Ravindra Prasad

Introduction

The most widely known need hierarchy theory was developed by Abraham Maslow as part of his theory of human motivation during the 1940's.[1] Maslow's interest in research in understanding human behaviour was the result of his early career as a psychologist. He tried to understand human behaviour through psychoanalysis. His clinical experiences as a psychologist enabled him to develop his five level theory of need hierarchy. Based on his studies, Maslow started writing a book during the 30's and it was 'intended to be a systematic psychology of the older type'.[2] His efforts were 'to synthesise the holistic, the dynamic and the cultural emphasis which, each one, excited so many young psychologists of the time'.[3] Maslow published his studies at periodic intervals during the 40's and 50's and his writings generated interest among clinical and personality psychologists. Managers and administrators, however, began to read Maslow only after McGregor popularised his ideas.

(1908-1970)

Life and Works

Abraham Harold Maslow (1908 - 1970) born in Brooklyn, USA was an American sociologist and is known for his conceptualisation of the 'hierarchy of human needs' and considered as the father of humanistic psychology. Maslow studied law at the City College, New York and later went to the University of Wisconsin to study psychology and pursued original research on primate dominance behaviour and sexuality. He received BA in 1930, MA in 1931 and Ph.D in 1934 - all from the University of Wisconsin. Later, he moved to Columbia University where he continued his research in psychology. Between 1937-1951, Maslow was on the faculty of Brooklyn College and from 1951-1969 was professor and chair of the Psychology Department at Brandies University and then became Roosevelt Fellow at the Laughlin Institute in California. He wrote extensively on psychology that emerged in the 1950s and 1960s which was later referred as the third force. He compiled his early publications and brought out his popular book

Motivation and Personality in 1954. Later, he wrote several books and articles. His publications include *A Theory of Human Motivation* (1943), *Religion, Values and Peak Experiences* (1965), *Eupsychian Management* (1965), *The Psychology of Science* (1966), and *Towards Psychology of Being* (1971).[4]

Human behaviour is a reflection of their conscious and unconscious goals. It can be analysed from their actions and the motives behind them. These assumptions about human motivation have been familiar since the days of Sigmund Freud. Analysing human behaviour through human needs and motives is a new path in social psychology. Among the many contributors to the motivation theory, Maslow's contribution in the form of his need hierarchy is significant in organisational research. It provides the framework to study and analyse human motivation. As Maslow's theory is not synonymous with behaviour theory, the motivations are only one class of determinants of behaviour. While behaviour is almost motivated, it is also almost always biologically, culturally and situationally determined as well. [5] Maslow's contribution to motivation theory lies in his simple and straightforward analysis of human motivation by taking human needs as the basis of behaviour. Maslow felt that most motivation theories mainly focused on physiological needs and omitted other important needs relating to personal growth. He addressed these aspects in his theory.

Need Hierarchy

Human being is an organism, which drives into action to fulfill its needs and several drives play a critical role in motivation. Physiological drives cannot become a central point in explaining the motivation theory. A sound theory of motivation depends on the ultimate goals of human beings. Human behaviour at a time is a reflection of more than one motive. All human actions are outcomes of several unfulfilled needs and motives. Human needs operate in an order of hierarchy of prepotency. A satisfied need gives place to another unsatisfied need and this process goes in a continuum because human is a perpetually wanting animal. The motivation theory is a part of the behaviour theory and motives are part of the behaviour.

Maslow's theory is based on the idea of prepotency of needs. Accordingly, he developed a scale on which at one end is lower order needs like physiological and security needs and at the other end higher order needs like self-actualisation. In between there are middle order needs, viz., social and self-esteem needs. Once the physiological needs are satisfied, then the need for other needs arise in a step-by-step manner, each

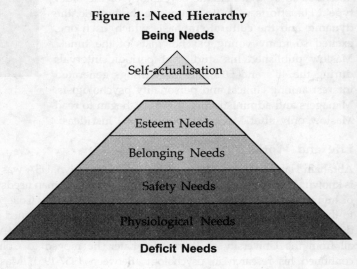

Figure 1: Need Hierarchy

lower order need once satisfied, gives way to an unfulfilled higher order need. A satisfied need no longer motivate a person. Maslow propounded his theory on the basis of several assumptions and conclusions.[6] Maslow arranged human needs in a hierarchy as shown in

Figure 1. The fulfillment of a lower order need is a precondition for a higher order need to surface. Unless the lower order needs are fulfilled, the middle or higher order needs would not surface. In what follows the meaning and connotation of each of the five needs in the hierarchy, viz., physiological, security, social, esteem and self-actualisation are further discussed.[7]

The Physiological Needs

Physiological needs are synonymous with the biological needs of the human beings like hunger, thirst, sex, etc. The grip of these needs on the human beings is so strong that unless these needs are satisfied there is no room for other needs. To a hungry person the utopia is a world full of food and he thinks not only of food but also of comfort to body and mind, which can be fulfilled by eating food. For a person who has missed most of the basic needs in his life, physiological needs are the main motivating forces. For people whose world is just fulfillment of physiological needs, all other things like freedom, love, community life, etc., are unimportant. Those who have not faced food problem any time in their lives, it is appetite need, which is the physiological need. Such people have their need in a particular food, which is to be fulfilled. Once a physiological need is satisfied, the human organism looks for social needs. If hunger is satisfied, it becomes unimportant in the current dynamics of the individual. People who have always satisfied a need are capable of tolerating its deprivation in future.

The Security Needs

Human being searches for security and safety from natural calamities, dangers and deprivations. Human organism is a safety-seeking organism. For a person whose physiological needs are satisfied, his next goal is safety, security, stability, and protection. For him everything looks less important than safety. The need for safety can be better observed in infants and children among whom we can clearly see the reactions to bodily illness and injury. A child, who is sick, has a need of reassurance from parents that the sickness will be cured and will never repeat. Another feature of the security need, very clearly seen in children, is their preference for a rhythm and routine in daily life. Even adults, for that matter, are normally against any disturbing changes in life. In an orderly, peaceful and civilised society, the safety and security is taken care of, to a great extent, by the government. In such societies safety need is no longer a motivator. We can see the expression of safety needs in people's preference for a job with tenure and protection, the desire for a saving bank account, insurance, etc. In Indian society, the need to have a male child in a family is an expression of security need.

The Belongingness and Love Needs

Human being is described as a social animal. Once physiological and safety needs are fulfilled, he/she seeks affection, love and belongingness from other human beings and the society around. A person with social needs severely feels the absence of friends, family, spouse and children. He/she craves for affectionate relationships and a place of belongingness with his/her people. Children who are products of broken homes or those who are neglected by their parents in their childhood develop a strong desire for love and affection. These desires motivate their behaviour consciously and unconsciously. The need for love is not synonymous with sex which may be studied as a mere physiological need.

The Esteem Needs

People have a desire for respect and recognition from society, work place, family and friendship circles. People normally have a high estimate of themselves. They have a need for self-respect and self esteem. They desire to work according to their own norms and beliefs. Self-esteem needs can be broadly divided into two groups, viz., achievement needs and recognition needs. Achievement needs are expressed in the form of desire to be with self-confidence, desire to possess strength and assertiveness and a desire to be free from depending on others. Recognition needs are expressed in the form of aspiring respect from others, recognition in society, attracting attention and the desire to become an important person. Satisfaction of esteem needs makes a person confident, adequate and useful. Non-fulfillment of these needs makes one feel inferior, weak and helpless. This need plays an important role in moulding the personality of a human being.

Maslow calls all the four needs as deficit needs or 'D' needs. Deficiency motivation occurs when we lack something and attempt to meet that deficiency. If one doesn't have enough of something i.e., there is deficit, then one feels the need. If one gets all that is needed, they cease to be motivating. Maslow also talks about these levels in terms of 'homeostatis' – a principle on which furnace thermostat works. When it gets too cold, it switches the heat on and when it gets too hot, it switches the heat off. Maslow extends this homeostatis principle to human needs. He also calls these needs as 'survival needs'. They are needed for maintenance of health and they are built into the human beings genetically like instinct and he calls them *instinctoid* - instinct like needs.

The Self-actualisation Needs

Self-actualisation, a term that was first coined by Kurt Goldstein, is considered to be the highest need in the hierarchy of needs and as such is directed towards searching the meaning and purpose in life. Even if all other needs are satisfied, a human being feels restless and tries to achieve excellence in fields dearer to him. The desire for self-fulfillment, actualisation and living a meaningful life is reflected in this need. The specific form this need takes varies from person to person. For example, one may desire to become an ideal mother, another may desire to become an ideal teacher and so on. At the same time, these needs need not necessarily be a need for creativity.

Maslow used a variety of terms to refer to this level - growth motivation in contrast to deficit motivation, being needs or 'B' needs in contrast to 'D' needs and self-actualisation. These do not involve homeostatis; they continue to be felt and may even become stronger as they get fulfilled. But a prerequisite of self-actualisatioon is satisfaction of physiological, safety, love and esteem needs; at least partially. Only a small fraction of people are predominantly self-actualising; not more than two percent. What is self-actualisation? Maslow says that "a musician must make music, an artist must paint, a poet must write, if he is to be ultimately at peace with himself. What a man can be, he must be. This need, we may call self-actualisation." It is a basic force that drives a person forward and onward. Maslow adopted biographical method to study the lives of famous people like Abraham Lincoln, Eleanor Roosevelt, Gandhi, Thomas Jefferson, Albert Einstein, etc., He looked at their writings, works, etc., and developed a list of qualities. He found several similarities in their lives and called those features as 'self-actualising tendency'. Self-actualisers are:

- reality centered – could differentiate real from fake and genuine from dishonest;
- problem centered – treated difficulties as problems demanding solutions;

- need privacy – comfortable being alone;
- are independent of culture and environment – relied on their own experience and judgment;
- resist enculturalism - not susceptible to social pressures; in a way non-conformists;
- have democratic values - open to ethnic and individual variety;
- have unhostile sense of humor - prefer jokes at their own expense.
- have freshness of appreciation - have ability to see even ordinary things with wonder;
- have spontaneity and simplicity - prefer to be themselves than being pretentious;
- have a quality called *Gemeinshaftsgefuhl* (social interest compassion and humanity), freshness of appreciation and ability to be creative.

Self-actualisers, Maslow did not think, are perfect. They suffer anxiety and guilt, absentmindedness and have unexpected moments of ruthlessness. The emergence of this need depends on the fulfillment of all other lower order needs. However, in any society, satisfied people will always be very few and as such how many people have this need for self- actualisation is a question for further research. Despite this fact, we have examples of people who have reached heights of excellence in different fields in life. Maslow felt that this need is a challenging problem in research. Self- actualisation is presumably the highest desire of any normal individual. Who, then, is a self- actualised person? What features characterise such a person? Maslow undertook several studies to get answers to these questions and based on these studies provided an exhaustive list of characteristics of a self-actualised person.[8] They:

- lack overriding guilt, crippling shame and anxiety;
- like solitude and privacy and at the same time retain their dignity even in undignified surrounding and situations;
- like autonomy and freedom to pursue their endeavours in life and work;
- derive ecstasy, inspiration and strength from the basic experience of life;
- have mystic experience and a deep feeling of identification, sympathy and affection for mankind;
- maintain interpersonal relations with a few people;
- democratic and they can differentiate between ends and means and right and wrong; and
- have a sense of humour and possess creativeness and originality.

A self-actualised person possesses an unusual ability to detect the spurious, the fake, and the dishonest and in general, to judge people correctly and efficiently.

How a Self-actualised Person is Motivated?

In case of needs other than self- actualisation, it is possible to predict behaviour and as such the accuracy of the prediction will be higher when one goes lower and lower on the hierarchy. In case of a self-actualised person, if the lower order needs are gratified and his behaviour is only influenced by self-actualisation need one might be able to predict what such people do, but such a prediction is not possible on the basis of motivation theory. It is even questionable whether self-actualised persons are motivated or not. As Maslow emphasised that "they work, they try and they are ambitious even though in an unusual sense. For them, motivation is just character growth, character expression, motivation, and development is a word self-actualisation."[9] Maslow also talks of the special and driving needs of the self-actualisers. They include truth, goodness, uniqueness, perfection, justice, self-sufficiency, meaningfulness, etc. When self-actualisers don't get these needs fulfilled, they respond with metapathologies and develop depression, despair, disgust, alienation and cynicism.[10]

The Basic Needs: Some Further Characteristics

Maslow, after discussing in detail the basic needs of humans and their hierarchical order, discusses a few characteristics of these basic needs.[11] Firstly, the hierarchy is not as rigid as it is implied theoretically and there is no fixity in the hierarchy of needs. There is scope for deviations. For example, some people have a strong preference for self-esteem than to a social need. This is a deviation from the hierarchy of needs. But, such behaviour is due to the notion that a self-confident person attracts love and affection. Presumably, people who lack love and affection try to seek it by putting a brave face. Some people may have a very low level of aspiration. Among such people the less prepotent goals may disappear forever and they get satisfied with very low levels of need fulfillment. Psychopathic personalities, for example, suffer permanent loss of low needs. When a need has been satisfied for a long time, it loses its power to influence a person. People who never experienced hunger, consider food as basic and important. Again a person may sacrifice a lower order need for a certain period of time to satisfy his higher need and vice-versa.

Secondly, the hierarchy of needs is not watertight compartments. Satisfaction is a relative term. Emergence of a particular need, after satisfaction of a lower order need, is not sudden; but a gradual phenomenon. Thirdly, in an average person, need areas are more often unconscious than conscious. Fourthly, the basic needs and desires are the same irrespective of the societies and cultures they live in. Fifthly, human behaviour is multi-motivated and as such it is not influenced by a single variable like a need. All behaviours cannot be determined by the basic needs. And finally, a satisfied need is not a motivator.

Peak Experiences

Maslow expounded the concept of peak experiences.[12] The term represents Maslow's attempt to naturalise those experiences which were generally identified with religious experiences. He describes peak experiences as exciting moments in life involving feelings of happiness, well- being and an awareness of transcendental knowledge of higher truth. He describes them as a state of witnessing or cognitive blissfulness, achievement of which requires long and hard effort and also self-actualisation. These experiences come suddenly and are the result of meditation, exposure to art, music and nature. Maslow describes how peak experiences tends to be uplifting, releases creative energies, gives a sense of purpose, and feeling of integration and leaves a permanent mark on the individual. Peak experiences can be therapeutic increasing individual's creativity, determination, and empathy. The highest peak, Maslow says, refers to feelings of limitless horizons opening up to the vision, the feeling of being simultaneously powerful and also more helpless than ever was before, the feeling of great ecstasy and wonder and awe and the loss of placing in time and place.[13] Maslow argues that all human beings are capable of peak experiences and will have a number of peak experiences in life. The 'non-peakers' resist and suppress such experiences and Maslow argues that they should be studied and cultivated. He felt that the willfully induced peak experiences as the characteristic of the self-actualised and it is a state of cognitive blissfulness, the achievement of which requires a long and hard effort and also self-actualisation.

Eupsychian Management

Maslow felt that organisations should be designed in such a way that employees can satisfy their safety, love and self-actualisation needs are met. This he calls 'Eupsychian Management'. If an employee is unhappy with his work he looses the most important means of his self-fulfillment. Maslow argued that the ability of any organisation to satisfy its workers' needs must be assured through study of employee complaints.

An Evaluation

Maslow's theory was criticised mainly on grounds of methodology. Selecting a small number of people, reading about them or talking with them and drawing conclusions about them as self-actualisers is not considered as sound methodology. Dunham noted that in spite of the tremendous amount of research generated by Maslow's theory; it has never been tested adequately as complete theory for a number of methodological reasons.[14] Sophistication and validity of his research data and the order of hierarchy of needs are also questioned. Some criticised that the needs from a lower order to a higher order need not necessarily operate in the same order all the time. His concept of self-actualisation, though attractive, is criticised as vague, imprecise and too general. Thus the criticism against Maslow's theory mostly rests on its lack of sophistication and validity of his research data, dispute over the arrangement of hierarchy of needs, and too general and imprecise nature of the term self-actualisation.

Several researches undertaken on need hierarchy and work motivation gave inconclusive results. Studies by Wabha and Birdwell[15] do not support Maslow's model. Their review of several previous studies lead them to conclude that there are two primary cluster of needs instead of five as suggested by Maslow. They found no support for 'the contention that satisfaction of one level of need will be positively associated with the activation of the next higher level of needs'.[16] Bass and Barrett felt that Maslow's theory has been most interesting and most popular than true.[17] Wabha and Birdwell also noted that "there is no clear evidence that human needs are classified in five distinct categories, or that these categories are structured in a special hierarchy. There is some evidence for the existence of possibly two types of needs, deficiency and growth needs, although this categorisation is not always operative." They noted that the overall attempts to establish evidence of Maslow's hierarchy have failed. Nor is there much to show that the stronger a need, the more likely we are to act to satisfy it.[18]

Vagueness, philosophical connotation and a very generic meaning of the term self-actualisation is another criticism. Cofer and Appley noted that the emphasis on self-actualisation suffers from the vagueness of its concepts, looseness of its language and the inadequacy of the evidence related to its major contentions.[19] The characteristics of self-actualising people, as suggested by Maslow, are also subjected to criticism. Unfortunately Maslow tells us little about the methodology adopted by him to select the cases for study. The list suggested by him also contains several internally overlapping features.[20]

Michael Nash felt that Maslow's theory is interesting but not valid.[21] He characterised the theories of Herzberg and Maslow as "major wrong theories". To him, Maslow's theory is more complex than simply an inside/outside view of the nature of work. "Maslow had a good idea. There is logic to his progression of needs, from the lower order needs (physiological) to the higher order needs (self-actualisation). The needs themselves make sense; they have face validity. We recognise physical needs in ourselves; the need to be with others, and the need to feel that we are doing what we are capable of doing. These needs are present in everyone to some degree at some time. The problem with Maslow's need hierarchy is that it cannot be turned into a practical guide for managers who are trying to make people productive." Maslow was also criticised for ignoring environmental factors like schooling and personal support that can facilitate or impede self-actualisation. His is an individualist theory and does not fit in with the collectivist approaches of cooperation and group action.

Maslow was one of the pioneers and an inspirational figure in the movement to develop personality theories. He inaugurated a fourth force in psychology.[22] He devoted, towards the end of his life, more time and attention to humanistic psychology and human potential movement. Maslow's contribution is a landmark in social-psychological research and he was a forerunner to many like Herzberg and Vroom. Maslow's theory has tremendous impact on modern management approach to motivation[23] and is widely accepted. His contribution to motivation theory, despite criticisms, is substantial and his theories led to further researches in the area of motivation. His theory is more comprehensive and emphasises on esteem and self-actualisation; human values that were previously ignored. He focused on positive experiences unlike Freud who emphasised on negative ones. His theory is useful, as Dunham points out, to assess the need levels of employees and to identify suitable types of rewards and opportunities to improve organisational effectiveness.[24] Maslow identified his particular hierarchy as representative of the total set of humans. He never intended to suggest that every person would have the needs arranged in the same hierarchical pattern.[25] Maslow himself noted that, "We have spoken so far as if this hierarchy was a fixed order, but actually it is not nearly as rigid as we may have implied. It is true that most of the people with whom we have worked have seemed to have these basic needs in about the order that has been indicated. However, there have been a number of exceptions.... There are other apparently innately creative people in whom the drive to creativeness might appear not as self-actualisation released by basic satisfaction, but in spite of lack of basic satisfaction."[26]

In Brief

The contribution of Abraham Maslow can be summarised as:

- Analysis of behaviour through human needs and motivations is a new path in social psychology. Among many contributors to motivation theory. Abraham Maslow (1908-1970), an American Psychologist, is considered the father humanistic psychology and known for his conceptualisation of hierarchy of needs.

- Maslow's contribution in the form of need hierarchy in phenomenal in organisation research and he provided a framework to study and analyse human motivation.

- Maslow arranged human needs in a hierarchy. The lowest needs in the hierarchy are the physiological and security needs and self-actualisation is the higher order need. In between there are social and self-esteem needs which are called middle order needs. The fulfillment of lower order need is a precondition for the higher order need to surface. Maslow calls lower order and middle order needs as deficit needs or "D" needs and self-actualisation as being need or "B" need.

- Self-actualisation, the higher order human need, is a desire for self-fulfillment, actualisation and living a meaningful life. The specific form this need takes varies from person to person. It is a desire to achieve excellence in fields dearer to them. Maslow, based on biographical studies of famous people, developed a list of qualities of self-actualisers.

- Maslow raised the question of who is a self-actualised person and undertook several studies to answer this question. Based on these studies, he identified an exhaustive list of characteristics of self-actualised persons.

- Maslow, conscious of complexity of self-actualisation process, talks of special driving needs of self-actualisers. They include truth, goodness, uniqueness, perfection, justice, meaningfulness, etc. When self-actualisers do not get these needs fulfilled, they develop metapathologies.

- Maslow expounded the concept of peak experiences as exciting moments of life involving feelings of happiness, well-being, and an awareness of transcendental knowledge of higher truth and also considered them the characteristics of the self-actualised.

- Maslow's theory of need hierarchy was criticised on methodological grounds and vagueness of concepts like self-actualisation.

- Despite criticisms, Maslow is a pioneer in social-psychological research and his theory of need hierarchy, with its limitations, has had tremendous impact on modern management approach to motivation.

Notes and References

[1] Maslow, A. H., "A Dynamic Theory of Human Motivation", *Psychological Review*, Vol. 50, 1943, pp. 370-396.

[2] Maslow, A. H., *Motivation and Personality*, New York, Harper & Row, 1954, p. IX.

[3] Ibid.

[4] His books include *Eupsychian Management: A Journal*, Homewood, Irwin-Dorsey, 1965; *The Psychology Science: A Reconnaissance*, New York, Harper & Row, 1966, *Towards A Psychology of Being*, 2nd ed. New York, Van Nostrand Reinhold, 1968.

[5] Maslow, A. H., "A Theory of Human Motivation", in Huneryager, S. G., and Heckmann, I. L., *Human Relations in Management*, Bombay, Taraporevala & Co., 1972, p. 334.

[6] Ibid., pp. 333-334.

[7] See Maslow, A. H., *Motivation and Personality*, op. cit., Ch.5.

[8] Ibid., Ch. 12.

[9] Ibid. p. 211.

[10] http://www.ship.edu/-cgboeree/maslow.html

[11] Maslow, A. H., *Motivation and Personality*, op. cit., pp. 98-106.

[12] See Maslow, Abraham, *Religions, Values and Peak Experiences*, 1964

[13] Ibid, p.164

[14] Dunham, Randall B., *Organisational Behaviour*, Homewood, III. Richard D. Ilwin Inc., 1984, p. 108.

[15] Quoted in Luthans, Fred, *Organisational Behaviour*, New York, McGraw-Hill Company, 1973, pp. 155-156.
op. cit., p. 409.

[16] Ibid.

[17] Bass, Bernard M., and Barrelt, Gerald V., *People, Work and Organisations*, Boston, Allyn and Bacon, Inc., 1981, p.

[18] Quoted in Bass, Bernard M., and Barrelt, Gerald V., op. cit., p. 71.

[19] Cofer, C. N., and Appley, M. H., *Motivation: Theory and Research*, New Delhi, Wiley Eastern Limited, 1980, p. 692.

[20] Ibid. pp. 668-669.

[21] Nash, Michael, *Making People Productive*, London, Jossery, Bass Publishers, 1985, p. 101.

[22] Freudian psychologies constituted the first force; behaviourism as the second; Maslow's humanism and European existentialists the third and the fourth was the transpersonal psychologies.

[23] See Luthans, Fred, *Organisational Behaviour*, New York, McGraw-Hill, 1977, p. 408.

[24] Dunham, Randall B., op. cit., p. 108.

[25] Ibid., p.105.

[26] Maslow, A. H., *Motivation and Personality*, op. cit., p. 98

13

DOUGLAS McGREGOR

P.D. Sharma

Introduction

Douglas McGregor, a social psychologist and a household name in the world of professional managers, will long be remembered for his creative contributions to the art and science of management. Standing in the vanguard of the behaviouralist movement of post-war era, he emerged as a management psychiatrist, who scientifically demonstrated the unrealistic and limiting assumptions of traditional theories of management concerning human nature and the control of human behaviour in an organisational setting. McGregor demonstrably proved that reliance on authority as the primary means of control in industry leads to resistance, restriction of output and indifference to organisation objectives. It creates the problems of refusal to accept authority and ultimately results in inadequate motivation for human growth and organisation development.

(1906-1964)

Life and Works

Douglas Murray McGregor (1906-64) was born in Detroit, Michigan. During his school days he worked as a night clerk and also played the piano. He enrolled for a psychology degree at the College of the City of Detroit - now called Wayne State University - and after two years tried a term at the Oberline in Ohio. At 19, he dropped out of college and to earn a living joined as a gas station attendant in Buffelo, where he rose to the rank of Regional Gas Station Manager by 1930. He obtained bachelor's degree from Wayne State University (1932), and master's (1933) and doctorate (1935) degrees in psychology from Harvard University. He joined as a lecturer at Harvard University in 1935, and after two years in 1937 he moved to MIT to establish Industrial Relations section and also started consultancy work. In 1948, he became President of the Antioch College in Yellow Springs, Ohio at the age of 41 where he spent the next six years.

In recognition of his contribution, the main Antioch College was named as Antioch University McGregor which is more commonly called just McGregor. In 1954, he returned to MIT as a faculty member of the Sloan School of Management.[1] He was consultant to government and industry. He worked as Director of Social Science Research Council, National Training Laboratories and Board Member of the Foundation for Research on Human Behaviour.

McGregor's classic *The Human Side of the Enterprise*[2] marks a watershed in the history of management movement. It is hailed as the most original and seminal book on industrial psychology. The book has a profound influence on management education and practice. McGregor identified approaches of creating an environment within which employees are motivated either through direction and control or through integration and self-control. In numerous articles he made an eloquent plea for a brand 'new social architecture', a new value system to which man and management can gainfully commit themselves for the attainment of professional objectives. His other book *The Professional Manager* is a major step ahead of his unconventional thinking in linking behavioural concepts to organisation behaviour and showing with rare empathy how the human side of the enterprise can be developed through appropriate managerial intervention and understanding. In 1993, he was listed as the most popular management writer of all times along with Henri Fayol.[3]

The Perennial Question in Management

The Human Side of the Enterprise seeks to answer the perennial question 'whether successful managers are born or made'. Facing the question quite squarely McGregor observes:

> It seems clear to me that the making of managers, in so far as they are made, is only to a rather small degree the results of management's formal efforts in management development. It is to a much greater degree the result of management's conception of the nature of its task and of all the policies and practices which are constructed to implement this conception. The way a business is managed determines to a very large extent what people are perceived to have 'potential' and how they develop. We go off on the wrong track when we seek to study management development in terms of the formal machinery of programmes carrying this label.[4]

McGregor's main argument in the book - which is more popularly known for its two important suppositions called Theory X and Theory Y - has been that 'the theoretical assumptions which the management holds about controlling its human resources determine the whole character of the enterprise'.[5] To McGregor, these assumptions also determine the quality of its successive generations of management. Like an organisation psychiatrist, McGregor cherished the conviction that some of the most important problems of management lie outside the realm of improving the selection of managers with technical potential. The top executives, with talent and capacities, contribute very little to industry, especially because they have not learned enough about the utilisation of talent and about the creation of an organisational climate conducive to human growth. To McGregor the key question in the world of top management is [6] "What are your assumptions (implicit as well as explicit) about the most effective way to manage people?" From the answer to this basic question flows the series of meaningful answers to allied questions about the making of managers, the productivity of the enterprise and the other techno-human objectives of the management.

Theoretical Assumptions

McGregor's most creative and lasting contribution has been in the area of theoretical assumptions of management, which he very ably links up with the development of managerial talent and managerial teamwork in an industrial enterprise. His basic hypothesis has been that, 'every managerial act rests on theory',[7] and the frequent invidious comparison of the practical and the theoretical with respect to the management of human resources has been a serious handicap to progress in the field. He is not obsessed with the puerile question whether management is an art or a science. He believed that insistence on the proposition that management is an art 'is a common way of denying the importance of theory to "managerial behaviour". But then, he knew for sure that management was not a science because it served a different purpose. The issue is whether management can utilise scientific knowledge in the achievement of practical objectives with which it is concerned'.[8]

McGregor, as a student of social sciences, is concerned about the use of current social science knowledge for the disposal of misconceptions pertaining to the nature of control in the field of human behaviour. He aptly advances a hypothesis that 'all control is selective adaptation. In engineering, control consists in adjustment to natural law. It does not mean making nature to do our bidding. In the human field, the situation is the same, but many of our attempts to control human behaviour, far from representing selective adaptations are in direct violation of human nature. As managers we strive to make people behave as we wish without concern for natural law. But we should not expect to achieve desired results through inappropriate managerial action in the field than we can or should expect in the field of engineering.'[9] This brings McGregor to the area of methods of influence or control in organisations. He rigorously examines the classical ways of coercion and challenges the validity of the assumptions that underlie behind the authority of the office. Examining the framework of limitations of authority and the psychology of dependence in individual and organisational behaviours, McGregor concludes that 'Human behaviour is predictable but as in physical science accurate prediction hinges on the correctness of underlying theoretical assumptions.... We can improve our ability to control only if we recognise that control consists in selective adaptation to human nature rather than in attempting to make human nature conform to our wishes. If our attempts to control are unsuccessful, the cause generally lies in our choice of inappropriate means. We will be unlikely to improve our managerial competence by blaming people for failing to behave according to our predictions.'[10]

Theory X: The Coercive Compulsions

McGregor was an astute student of human psychology and social behaviour. His empirical researches in organisational conflict and maladjustment in human relations led him to believe that control in human affairs can be viewed as an integration of human behaviour either through coercive compulsion or through motivational self-control. He developed these two assumptions into various hypotheses and quite scientifically tested their validity to propound his theories of managerial control popularly known as 'Theory X' and 'Theory Y'. Any neat dichotomy between the traditional and the modern schools of management thought does not fit in the McGregor's framework of analysis. Rather, it tends to dramatise the fundamental differences of approach to management in terms of emphasis and basic assumptions. McGregor calls his Theory X as the traditional view of direction and control,[11] which is based on some of the assumptions implicit in the literature of organisation and managerial policy and practice. The remarkably pervasive traditional assumptions of Theory X are:[12]

1. The average human being has an inherent dislike of work and will avoid it, if he can;

2. Hence, most people must be corrected, controlled, directed and threatened with punishment to get them to put forth adequate effort towards the achievement of organisational objectives; and

3. The average human being prefers to be directed, wishes to avoid responsibility, has relatively little ambition, wants security above all.

These assumptions, which embody the mediocrity of the masses, have been put somewhat bluntly. They smack paternalism and McGregor by arranging this set of assumptions into a theory has not created any straw man for purposes of demolition, but tried to offer an explanation about the interplay of behavioural factors, which materially influence managerial strategy.

Traditionally known as 'carrot and stick theory', Theory X of McGregor explains the consequences of a particular managerial strategy. It does not describe human nature, although it purports to. The assumptions behind the theory treat man not only as an insecure beast, responding to the language of fear, but as a disliker or avoider of all work under all circumstances. Like axiomatic proverbs about human behaviour, the basic assumptions of managerial philosophy and strategy which have been in vogue, without being tested or verified by any empirical tools of enquiry. McGregor finds these assumptions so unnecessarily limiting that in his judgement they prevent one seeing the possibilities inherent in other managerial strategies. Actually some of the new strategies like decentralisation, management by objectives, consultative supervision, democratic leadership, ultimately prove to be 'new wine in old bottles', especially because the procedures developed to implement these new strategies are in main derived from the same old inadequate assumptions of Theory X about human nature and social behaviour. As a serious researcher on the problems of the human side of enterprise, McGregor felt increasingly disillusioned with widely touted and new fanged theories and approaches because most of them in their essence merely reflected only different tactics in programmes, procedures and gadgets within an unchanged strategy based on Theory X. His conclusion is that 'so long as the assumptions of Theory X continue to influence managerial strategy, we will fail to discover, let alone utilise the potentialities of the average human being'.[13]

McGregor felt that a command and control environment is not effective because it relies on lower needs for motivation. But in modern society these needs are mostly satisfied and therefore no longer motivate. In this situation, one would expect employees to dislike their work, avoid responsibility, have no interest in organisational goals, resist change, etc., thus creating a self-fulfilling prophecy. To McGregor, motivation seemed more likely with Theory Y model.[14]

Theory Y: The Alternate Assumptions of Integration and Self-Control

McGregor discovered the role of emotional commitments of dependence and independence, which stem from a series of universal human experiences. Talking about the psychology of dependence and the limitations of authority in an organisation situation, he finds the classical theory of organisation. Its principles are derived primarily from the study of the military and the Catholic Church and it suffers from ethnocentrism and its underlying assumptions about human behaviour are at best only partially true. Looking positively in the area of human needs and man's psychological quest for their satisfaction, McGregor formulates Theory Y which offers a number of alternate assumptions for the integration of the individual and organisational goals. To him creation of conditions is not control in the usual sense and it does not seem to be a particularly good device for directive behaviour. McGregor emphasises on the need for selective adaptation in managerial strategy, because his studies prove that changes in the population at large, in educational levels, attitudes and values, motivation, degree of dependence and the nature of urbanisation have created both the opportunities and the need for other forms of selective adaptation. He arranged his new set of assumptions about motivation and morale in a theory, which he called Theory Y, perhaps to dramatise the contrast with the major assumptions of Theory X. The assumptions of Theory Y are:[15]

1. The expenditure of physical and mental effort in work is as natural as play or rest;
2. Mass exercises, self-direction and self-control in the services of the objectives to which he is committed;
3. Commitment to objectives is a function of the rewards associated with their achievement;
4. The average human being learns under proper conditions not only to accept but also to seek responsibility;
5. The capacity to exercise a relatively high degree of creativity, imagination and ingenuity in the solution of organisational problems is widely, not narrowly distributed in the population; and
6. Under the conditions of modern industrial life, the intellectual potentialities of the average human being are only partially utilised.

These assumptions point to the fact that the limits on human collaboration in the organisational setting are not limits of human nature, but of management ingenuity in discovering how to realise the potential of human resources. The theory implies that if the employees are lazy, indifferent, unwilling to take responsibility, intransigent, uncreative, uncooperative, the cause lies in the management's method of organisation and control. The central principle implicit in the assumptions of Theory Y is that integration of behaviour is the key process in management, because it results in the creation of conditions conducive for the members to achieve their own goals best by directing their efforts towards the success of the enterprise.[16] It is not easy for any management to perceive the implications of this integration principle, especially because the principle of direction and control implicit in Theory X is firmly built into managerial attitudes with respect to the task of managing human resources. The concept of integration and self-control demands that the needs of the individual and that of the organisation should be recognised. Management by direction and control cannot create commitment, which alone makes available the full resources of those affected by control process. Lesser motivation and lesser degree of self-direction result in costs which when added over a period of time offset the gains obtained by unilateral decision allegedly taken for the good of the organisation.

McGregor calls Theory Y an open invitation to innovation.[17] He does not deny the appropriateness of authority under certain circumstances, but he does deny its appropriateness for all purposes and under all circumstances. His thesis that genuine innovation in management theory and practice requires the acceptance of less limiting assumptions about the nature of human resources which the management seeks to control. More so, the management should exhibit readiness to adapt selectively to the implications contained in new assumptions, which the knowledge of individual psychology and group sociology claims to offer to modern management.

Theory Y in Practice

McGregor attempts a critique of prevailing managerial strategies *vis-à-vis* personnel techniques of the managers while discussing the application of Theory Y. His research in industry indicates a high correlation between the acceptance of responsibility and commitment to objectives. He discovered greater long run advantages in permitting the subordinates to learn by experience than in simply telling them where their planning has been unrealistic or inadequate. It is because the tools for building managerial philosophy are human attitudes and beliefs about people and the managerial role, not just forms and manuals that prescribe them in terms of expectations.[18] Management by integration and self-control does not tack any new set of duties on top of the existing managerial load. Rather it is different, if not a difficult way of fulfilling existing responsibilities. The administrative, informational and motivational purposes of performance appraisal of employees are also served better because intelligent adults take to growth, learning and improved performance only through the language of self-control and integrative behaviour. While testing his Theory Y on practicing managers, McGregor discovered that unilateral direction and control with respect to the administration of salaries and promotions by giving individuals greater opportunities to play an active part in decisions affecting their careers.[19]

The Scanlon Plan

McGregor worked closely with Frederick Lesiaur, who was carrying research on union management cooperation, popularly known as Scanlon Plan at MIT. The Scanlon Plan was not a formula or a set of procedures, but it was a philosophy of management based on theoretical assumptions entirely consistent with Theory Y. The two central features of the Scanlon Plan are[20] loss reduction sharing and effective participation. McGregor found that the proverbial task of 'selling refrigerators to Eskimos' had been also easier in Scanlon companies rather than in other companies selling traditional incentive plans or merit rating programmes. Participation, which grows out of the assumptions of Theory Y offers substantial opportunities for ego-satisfaction of the workers or subordinates and thereby effects motivation toward organisational objectives. The Scanlon Plan research affords a valid testimony to the proposition that 'used wisely' and with understanding, participation is a natural commitment of management by integration and self-control.[21]

Clinton Golden once remarked that, "by and large and over the long run, management gets the kind of labour relations it deserves".[22] The underlying assumptions and theoretical considerations not only influence managerial behaviour, but also the subtle aspects of everyday behaviour which determine the climate of human relationships. These daily manifestations of theory and attitude in turn affect the expectation of subordinates. Organisation research demonstrates that McGregor was right when he stated that, "formal policies, programmes and procedures to be administered and in turn perceived by management reflect this managerial climate of human relationships".[23]

Relevance of Theory Y in Line-Staff Relationship

The big industrial organisations (of today) are operated by the staff. Their knowledge and techniques have profound influence on major decisions they design, and procedures they administer. The line, which represents the central and fundamental authoritative chain of command, is becoming increasingly dependent upon a considerable number of specialised staff groups. The strategies suggested by McGregor in his Theory Y are quite relevant to line-staff conflicts of complex nature, which often result in waste of human resources, friction, costly protective mechanism and lowered commitment to organisational objective. The line managers who seek cooperation within the context of Theory Y can establish relationships with their subordinates, their superiors and their colleagues, which are like those of professionals' *vis-à-vis* his clients.[24] All managers, whether line or staff, have both the line and staff responsibilities. The Theory Y approach, according to McGregor, stresses on teamwork at each level of organisation. It further helps in improving staff-line collaboration of all the available human resources in reaching the best decisions or problem solutions or action strategies.

McGregor believes that one of management's major tasks is to provide a heterogeneous supply of human resources from which individuals can be selected to fill a variety of specific but unpredictable needs. Scientific research in managerial leadership[25] indicates that management should pay more than casual attention to its recruitment practices and promotion policies should be so administered that heterogeneous resources are actually considered when openings occur. Moreover, management development programmes should involve many people within the organisation rather than a select few. Similarly, to groom managerial leaders it is appropriate that management should develop unique capacities and potentialities of each individual rather than common objective for all participants. Operations in the framework of Theory Y can take care of these leadership implications of management theory and practice. It can contribute to the fullest development of potentialities of the employees in their respective roles, which they can fill the best. McGregor recognised that some people may not have reached the level of maturity assumed by Theory Y. They may need, therefore, tighter controls that can be relaxed as the employee develops. [26]

The Professional Manager: From Cosmology to Reality

If *The Human Side of the Enterprise* represents McGregor's concern to educate future managers, *The Professional Manager*,[27] posthumously published, reflects his commitment towards developing the profession of management through bridging its goals, with the aims, values and methodology of behavioural science. Four major themes recur throughout this volume, which McGregor left unfinished before his death. He had a great fascination for theory building and cosmology.[28] From this stems the prediction of social events which in turn is a matter of perception and world view of the individual. McGregor believed that the manager's view of organisational reality exerts profound effect upon managerial acts. They affect achievement of his goals and that of his organisation. In McGregor's view the managerial cosmology should meaningfully address itself to the understanding of the manager's behaviour, his identity and his role perceptions of the industrial organisation.[29] As a researcher McGregor makes a plea that management styles and strategies should be evolved and continuously adjusted in the light of the empirical experience of reality, consistent with the findings of behavioural knowledge. This will make sense and make theory relevant to practice.

The Rehabilitation of Rational Emotive Manager

McGregor realised that emotional reactions, to which most managers are vulnerable, interfere with the managerial perception of reality. To him the culture of management has been generally inhospitable to the expression of natural human responses. This has led to dissonant feelings of guilt often subverting decisions. In *The Professional Manager*, McGregor rehabilitates the rational emotive manager and going beyond the framework of his Theory Y, he places the idea of integration within the mould of transactional concept of power and influence. He argued that

Theory X and Theory Y do not lie at extremes of the scale. In place of representing polar opposites they should be viewed as two different cosmologies.[30] Here McGregor not only re-explained his own epistemological position, but has provided a more concrete description of the implications of various sets of assumptions about man, implicitly contained in Theory Y.

The Concept of Transactional Influence

One of the major contributions of McGregor to management science is his concept of transactional influence.[31] The management of differences or building a managerial team is not a simple matter of managerial power or control. To a professional manager it is actually a challenge of organisation of managerial work. McGregor finds influence as a social phenomenon if mutually oriented. "It cannot be a win-lose affair in which if A gets 100 units, B must get zero or if A gets 90 units, B will have to satisfy with 10 only".[32] McGregor took pains to demonstrate that when certain social elements as trust and mutual support are present, there is no need for concern about 'power equalisation' or the loss of responsibility and status in managerial hierarchy. Throughout his life McGregor kept on responding to this dilemma of his friends and critics, who have been repeatedly telling him that his theories were fine, but they do not work and that they agree with his Theory Y vision of man but that they do not know how to put it into practice. McGregor's answer was that each person must find his own answer. But as a researcher, he certainly developed a conviction that answer to this key issue can provide more bases for human choice. In *The Professional Manager* he discusses in greater detail his views on how management can think about to deal with himself, his role and style, his own power, the issue of control over others, the problem of team work and above all how to manage conflicts creatively.[33]

Working through Differences

McGregor discusses three strategies to deal with the problems of team work and tension in the management of difference in organisations viz., (i) divide and rule, (ii) the suppression of differences, and (iii) working through differences. The first two strategies based on the assumptions Theory X have rendered managerial teams as perpetual liabilities. The professional manager should not only guard himself against mutual antagonism, secrecy, playing politics, currying favour with seniors, but should steer through the differences so that the interplay between members may yield to innovation, commitment to decisions and strengthening of relationships within the group.

An Evaluation

Graham Cleaverly argues that McGregor coined the two terms Theory X and Theory Y and used them to label two sets of beliefs a manager might hold about the origins of human behaviour. He pointed out that the manager's own behaviour would be largely determined by particular beliefs that he subscribes to. McGregor hoped that his book would lead the managers to investigate the two sets of beliefs, invent others, test out the assumptions underlying them and develop managerial strategies that made sense in terms of those tested views of reality. But McGregor was interpreted as advocating Theory Y as a new and superior ethic – a set of moral values that ought to replace the values managers usually accept.[34] McGregor tried in vain to dispel the simplified paradigm of Theory X = Bad and Theory Y= Good that others had imposed on his analysis. [35] Similar observations were made by Edgar Schein when he said: 'In my own contacts with Doug, I often found him discouraged by the degree to which Theory Y had become a monolithic set of principles as those of Theory X, the over-generalisation which Doug was fighting …. Yet few readers were willing to acknowledge that the content of Doug's book made a neutral point or that Doug's own presentation of his point of view was that coldly scientific'.[36] Some criticised McGregor's ideas as being tough on the weaker members of society, those who need guidance and who are not necessarily self-starters. There are conspicuous examples of companies (like Digital Equipment corporations steered by its charismatic founder, Ken Oslen) that followed Theory Y precepts but yet floundered.

The professional and human side of McGregor reveals a very colourful personality of wide vision and scientific temperament. His lifetime mission was to search a model for industry, governments and nations, which would enable the critical decision-makers of future to realise the potential for collaboration, inherent in human nature and human resources, assigned to human groups. His Theories X and Y do not represent any neat categories of human behaviour or human relationships. Rather, they are analytical tools of reference through which managerial behaviour can be analysed, studied, predicted, and still more, corrected in terms of changing social values and organisational goals. The current research in management behaviour has gone a long way "Beyond the Theory Y" but does not in any way belittle the importance of the research work, which McGregor could initiate, pioneer and accomplish in this maiden field of management research. From human side to the professional side, the writings of McGregor indicate a systematic evolution of his ideas and thought, which he was all the time testing and experimenting upon as a behavioural student of management. Most of his ideas obviously seem to be influenced by the dawn of industrial society in the United States, but still more they reflect the impact of post war research in the areas of industrial sociology and management psychology. Like a true researcher, McGregor does not seem to have final answers to the perennial questions, but as an honest student and an erudite scholar of management, his writings represent a mine of ideas from which the theorists of management and practicing managers can dig a great deal to sharpen their tools and readjust their strategies of management for tomorrow. McGregor understood, anticipated and helped point the way to the world what may well emerge as a future model of work, organisations and society that is rooted in core assumptions driving participative, interdependent, authentic, inventive and production relationships.[37]

In Brief

The contributions of McGregor can be summarised as:

- Douglas McGregor (1906-1964), a distinguished social psychologist and management consultant, popularly known for his Theory "X" and Theory "Y", made significant contributions to the understanding of human nature and behaviour in organisations. His classic *"The Human Side of the Enterprise"* is hailed as the seminal work on industrial psychology.
- McGregor raised questions about the theoretical assumptions of management with a firm belief that 'every managerial act rests on theory'. To him the key question in the world of top management is "what are your assumptions (implicit as well as explicit) about the most effective way to manage people?"
- Discussing the nature of control in the field of human behaviour, McGregor advances the hypothesis that "all control is selective adaptation'. He observes that we can improve our ability to control only if we recognise that control consists in selective adaptation to human nature rather than in attempting to make human nature conform to our wishes. If our attempts to control are unsuccessful, the cause generally lies in one choice of inappropriate means.

- Based on his researches in organisational behaviour, McGregor developed two assumptions of human behaviour popularly known as Theory "X" and Theory "Y". The Theory "X" is a traditional way of integration of behaviour in organisations through coercion and compulsion and Theory "Y" is based on self-control and self-regulation of human behaviour. McGregor tried to explain the differences in approach to management in terms of these assumptions.

- McGregor critically examined the prevailing managerial strategies and practices while discussing the application of Theory "Y". His research indicates the effectiveness of Theory "Y" approach.

- Education of future managers was stressed by McGregor and considered that organisation reality is a matter of perception and world view of the individual. From this perceptive he describes the professional manager's education as a journey from cosmology to reality. 'Theory X' and 'Theory Y' are treated as different cosmologies.

- McGregor emphasised the concept of transactional power and influence in management of differences and in building management teams. He recognised the role of rational emotive manager in positively directing human responses.

- McGregor's formulations and theories are criticised for impracticality and over-generalisation.

- McGregor's 'Theory X' and 'Theory Y' may not represent any neat categories of human behaviour and human relationships. They are more analytical tools to analyse and predict human behaviour in organisations. Drawing inspiration from the works of McGregor, many new theories like 'Theory Z' have been developed.

References

[1] http://www.managers?/net.co.uk/Biography/mcgregor.html?; http://en.wikipedia.org/wiki/Douglas?McGregor?

[2] McGregor, Douglas, *The Human Side of the Enterprise*, New York, McGraw-Hill Book Company, 1960.

[3] http://www.economist.com/businessfinance/mgt/displaystory.cfm?story_id=12366

[4] McGregor, Douglas, *The Human Side of the Enterprise*, op. cit., p. iv.

[5] Ibid., p. vii.

[6] Ibid.

[7] Ibid., p. 6.

[8] Ibid., p. 8.

[9] Ibid., p. 9.

[10] Ibid., p. 11.

[11] For an elaboration of the traditional view, see Wright, Bakke E., *Bonds of Organisation*, New York, Harper & Brothers, 1950; and Walker, Charles, *Towards the Automatic Factory*, New Haven, Con, Yale University Press, 1957.

[12] Mayo, Elton, *The Human Side of the Enterprise*, op. cit., pp. 33-34.

[13] Ibid., p. 43.

[14] http//www.envisionsoftware.com/articles/Theory?htm?

[15] McGregor, Douglas, *The Human Side of the Enterprise*, op. cit., pp. 47-48.

[16] For confirmation of the point of view also see, Leavitt, Harold J., *Managerial Psychology*, New York, McGraw-Hill, 1948; and Hertzberg, Frederick, Mausner, Bernard, and Snyderman, Barbara, *The Motivation to Work*, New York, John Wiley & Sons, 1959.

[17] McGregor, Douglas, *The Human Side of the Enterprise*, op. cit., p. 57.

[18] Ibid., p. 75.

[19] Ibid., pp. 90-109.

[20] Ibid., pp. 111-114.

[21] Ibid., p. 131.

[22] Ibid., p.131

[23] Ibid.,p. 144.

[24] Ibid., pp. 157-175.

[25] See Bennis, W., 'Leadership Theory and Administrative Behaviour', *Administrative Science Quarterly*, Vol. 4, No. 3, 1959; Knickerbocker, Irving, 'Leadership: A Conception and Some Implications', *Journal of Social Issues*, Vol. 4, No. 3, 1948.

[26] http://www.envisionsoftware.com/articles/Theory?htm?

[27] McGregor, Douglas, *The Professional Manager*, edited by Caroline McGregor and Warren G.

Bennis, New York, McGraw-Hill Book Company, 1967.

28 Ibid., pp. 30-31.

29 Ibid., pp. 32-42.

30 Ibid., p. 80.

31 Ibid., especially Ch.9, pp. 136-155

32 Ibid., p. vi.

33 Ibid.pp. 183-186.

34 Cleverly, Graham, Managers & Magic, Longman's, 1971 quoted in http://www.wsikipedia.org/with/Douglas?McGregor?

35 http://www.managers?net.co.uk?Biography/mcgregor.html?

36 See Edgar Schein's introduction in McGregor, Douglas, *The Professional Manager*, op.cit.

37 Cutcher-Gershenfeld, Joel, "Introduction to the Annotated Edition" in McGregor, Douglas, *The Human Side of Enterprise: Annotated Edition*, Tata-McGraw Hill, 2006.

14

CHRIS ARGYRIS

C.V. Raghavulu

Introduction

Long before the idea of participative management became a respectable research concern, the writers of the new left had drawn our attention to the phenomenon of widespread discontent and alienation and the increasing irrelevance of mechanistic and technocratic principles as guides to organisational life. They stressed the need for personal freedom and initiative and the dignity of the individual at the work place. The credit for reviving scholarly interest on these aspects, however, goes to Chris Argyris. The reflections of the new left writers and the hypotheses of Argyris - concerning the incompatibility between the prevailing organisational strategies and individual need fulfillment – were based on the same set of objective factors viz., continuously rising level of education in the Western countries, the demands and effects

(July 16, 1923)

of automation - the former requiring greater commitment to work and the latter resulting in a progressive non-involvement of the employee - restlessness in trade unions and the increasingly tenuous relationship between work and satisfaction of material needs. The situation in the West at the turn of the mid-20th century required new forms of organisational adaptation. To promote adaptability, new conceptions of the individual's role in the organisation and the patterning of new relationships were called for. The theories and hypotheses of Argyris, Maslow, McGregor, Likert and other writers belonging to the new management school were a response to such a need.

Life and Works

Born in Newark, New Jersey on July 16, 1923, Chris Argyris joined the Signal Corps in the U.S Army during the Second World War where he became a Second Lieutenant. He went to University at Clark from where he graduated with a degree in Psychology (1947), obtained MA in Psychology and Economics from Kansas University (1949) and Ph.D. in Organisational

Behaviour from Cornell University in 1951. In a distinguished career, Chris Argyris worked as the Beach Professor of Administrative Science and Chairperson of the Department at Yale University (1951-1971) and then moved to Harvard University as James Bryant Conant Professor of Education and Organisational Behaviour (1971). Argyris is currently Director of the Monitor Group in Cambridge, Massachusetts.[1]

Argyris' researches relate to four areas viz., impact of formal organisational structures, control systems and management on individuals; organisational change, particularly executive behaviour; role of social scientist as a researcher and actor and individual and organisational learning. His writings on management and organisational behaviour are voluminous. He authored over 30 books and over 300 articles. Some of his important works include *Knowledge for Action: A Guide to Overcoming Barriers to Organisational Change* (1993), *The Applicability of Organisational Sociology* (1972); *Management and Organisational Development* (1971); *Intervention Theory and Method: A Behavioural Science View* (1970); *Organisation and Innovation* (1965); *Integrating the Individual and the Organisation* (1964); and *Personality and Organisation* (1957).[2] A renowned organisational behaviour theorist, Argyris received numerous awards including honorary doctorates from universities in England, Greece, France, Canada, Belgium, Sweden, Canada and the United States. In honour of his contributions Yale University established Chris Argyris Chair in Social Psychology of Organisations.[3]

Argyris is considered as one of the first generation contributors to the field of organisational development. He defined and vigorously advanced theories and strategies for both individual and orgnisational development.[4] He focuses on the individual's relationship to the organisation and the conflict between the individual's social and psychological needs and the exigencies of the organisation. His writings suggest that the personal development of the individual is affected by the organisational situation. Argyris hopes that if the potential for self-actualisation present in each individual is properly tapped, it can benefit the individual employee as well as the organisation. Unfortunately, current organisational approaches inhibit individual growth, hinder his psychological success and prevent the organisation from reaping the benefits that accrue from the employee's personal development. Argyris' influence on the disciplines of management and public administration is widespread. He trained a large number of teachers, practitioners and consultants who carried the basic ideas of Argyris far and wide. As a consultant and pioneer in the application of the T-group technique his influence on reforms of organisational structures and managerial practices is equally striking.

The Formal Organisation

Argyris argues that there is a basic incongruence between the needs of a mature personality and the requirements of a formal organisation. Bringing together the evidence on the impact of the formal organisational principles upon the individual, Argyris suggests that there is some basic incongruence between the growth trends of a healthy personality and the requirements of the formal organisation. The application of the principles of formal organisation create situations in which: (1) the employees are provided minimal control over their work-day world; (2) they are expected to be passive, dependent and subordinate; (3) they are expected to have a short-time perspective; and (4) they are induced to perfect and value the frequent use of a few shallow abilities. All these characteristics are incongruent to the needs of adult human beings. They are much more congruent with the needs of infant, at least in the western culture. In effect, therefore, organisations are willing to pay high wages and provide adequate seniority if mature adults behave in a less mature manner. Argyris' analysis suggests that this inevitable incongruency increases as (1) the employees are of increasing maturity, (2) as the formal structure is made more clear-cut and logically tight for maximum formal organisational effectiveness, and (3) as one goes down the line of command.

The emphasis on managerial controls make the employees feel dependent on their superiors and fearful of the staff in charge of the various types of controls. For example, employees and superiors tend to perceive controls as instruments of punishment. Similarly, evaluative techniques are perceived as unfair in that they continually accent failures without showing why such failures may be necessary.[5] These conditions tend to increase the probability of the psychology of failure and decrease the probability of psychology of success. In brief, the managerial controls focus on the financial costs the organisation incurs and do not concern themselves with the 'human' costs.

Individual and Group Adaptation

If the formal organisation is defined by the use of such 'organisation' principles as task specialisation, unity of direction, chain of command, and span of control, and if these principles are used correctly, the employees would work in situations in which they are dependent, subordinate and passive towards the leader. They would tend to use few of their abilities. The degree of passivity, dependence, and submissiveness tends to increase as one goes down the line of command and as the work takes on more of the mass production characteristics. As a result, Argyris hypothesises that the formal organisation creates in a healthy individual feelings of failure and frustration, short-term time perspective and conflict. At the same time, it fails to satisfy the higher-order needs of the employees. Apathy, lack of interest and non-involvement are defense mechanisms that might become part of the organisational scenario. To Argyris, the basis of these defenses is the continuous frustration, conflict and failure an employee experiences.

The individual adapts to the impact of the organisation by any one or a combination of behaviours viz., leaving the organisation, climbing the organisational ladder, using defense mechanisms, and becoming apathetic and disinterested. These are all adaptive mechanisms and, therefore, need fulfilling. In order to guarantee his existence, the individual employee also seeks group sanctions. The informal work groups are 'organised' to perpetuate these adaptive processes to reward those employees who follow the informal codes and to penalise those who do not. The individual adaptive acts now become sanctioned by the group, and, therefore, provide feedback to reinforce the continuance of the individual need-fulfilling adaptive behaviour.

Management's Dominant Assumptions

Argyris argues that the top administrators tend to diagnose the problem in a different way. They observe their employees while at work and conclude that the employees are lazy, uninterested and apathetic, money-crazy and commit errors and cause wastage. Management blames the employees and "sees" the disloyalty and disinterest being caused by the employees. It follows logically for management, that if any changes are to occur, the employees must be changed. Thus management initiates programmes to "change peoples' attitudes" and to "make employees more interested in the organisation".[6] The basic action policy that management tends to define to solve the 'problems' actually stems from the logic of the formal organisation and the assumptions about the role of formal leadership. Pressure-oriented leadership style would be adopted by the management. Summarizing the characteristics found in most of the research studies, Argyris concludes that the autocratic and directive leader places the employees in a situation where they tend to be passive, dependent, subordinate, and submissive; focus their activities on the organisation's and the leader's needs rather than the needs of all the followers; and compete with each other for the leader's favour.

Argyris concludes that the impact of directive leadership upon the subordinates is similar to that which the formal organisation has upon the subordinate. Pressure-oriented directive leadership "compound the felony" that the formal organisation commits. Authoritarian leadership, notes Argyris, reinforces and perpetuates the 'damage' created by the organisational structure.

Strategies for Organisational Development

Argyris' approach and prescription for organisational change proceed from the diagnosis of the inadequacy and unimaginative character of the prevailing forms of organisation and managerial controls.[7] He suggests an intervention strategy for organisation development in four core areas. Firstly, the organisation should provide an environment for the development of the individual towards personal or psychological maturity. Secondly, a programme for organisation change should aim at improving the interpersonal competence of the employees. Thirdly, changes must be introduced to transform the traditional pyramidal form of organisation. Fourthly, techniques for programmed learning aimed at individual change should be introduced. Argyris' views about the assumptions and procedures to be followed for applying these strategies for organisational change are discussed below.

(a) Maturity - Immaturity Theory

Argyris observes that there is a basic conflict between the structure of formal organisations and psychological needs of mature adults. In the organisations the employees get frustrated as they are not allowed to function as mature adults. His Maturity-Immaturity Continuum theory proposes that people mature and develop as they grow. The process of maturity from the infant stage was characterised by Argyris to consist of seven components. These are:

1. *From infant passivity towards adult activity* – If the organisations in which the employees work restricts them and forces them to passively perform a narrow scope of work, they tend to become disinterested and frustrated.

2. *From dependence towards relative independence* – If the organisation does not allow the employees to exercise their independence through participation in decisions that affect them, both self-esteem and productivity suffer.

3. *From limited behaviours to much different behaviour* – If the organisation denies the employees the opportunity to play a variety of roles, their motivation decreases and they loose interest.

4. *From erratic, shallow, brief interests to more stable, deeper interests* – If the managers assume that decision-making is their work and do not share with the employees, the decisions will not be synergetic and the employees will feel isolated and disenfranchised.

5. *From short-term perspective to long-term perspective* – If the employees are not allowed to participate and contribute to long-term strategies, employee morale declines and productivity suffers.

6. *From a subordinate social position to an equal or superordinate social position* – Workers react negatively if the organisation treats them as children and do not trust them to behave as adults.

7. *From lack of self-awareness to self-awareness and self-control* – Organisations that fail to provide the necessary opportunities discussed earlier shoot themselves in the foot by not taking advantage of the tremendous potential of the employees.

Since the employees are adults, they should be treated as mature individuals who are capable of accepting responsibility, pursuing long-term interests and concerned about the fulfillment of the higher order needs. According to Argyris' theory of personality, mature individuals would be interested in the constructive release of psychological energy. In this context, Argyris suggests an analytical framework of individual behaviour, linking the concepts of psychological energy, personality needs and abilities. Following Maslow's theoretical model, Argyris suggests that each individual has a set of needs.[8] To quote Argyris:

"Bordering the needs, and in most cases evolving from them, are the abilities. Abilities are the tools, so to speak, with which a person expresses and fulfills his needs. Abilities are the communication systems for the needs to express themselves. Once the energy bubbles over from the needs, it goes 'through' the appropriate ability designed to express the need...".

"Interests are usually a product of a fusion of several needs. This fusion usually comes about at an early age and is unconscious. Interests, therefore, are indicators of the kinds of needs people have. For example, a person with a strong need to be independent, to achieve, and to know things, might make a good scientist."

"The skills that are given to us by inheritance are such skills as finger dexterity and other manual and manipulative skills. Few abilities are inherited. The majority of the more important abilities are learned and developed in interaction with others. This is especially true for such abilities as leadership. There are no born leaders. The personality of a leader is developed, probably during early home life and by the situations in which this personality finds appropriate expression. Ability, in summary, is a function between needs and the environment, thus providing the line of communication for need".[9]

The typical approach to the management of organisations is not geared to the potential satisfaction of individual needs. Nor does it provide challenges to stimulate the employees. The accent in organisational change strategies should, therefore, be upon meeting the needs of mature individuals and providing opportunities to arouse and utilise their full psychological energy.

(b) Improving Interpersonal Competence

Organisations have been emphasising upon improving the competence involving intellectual or mechanical skills. In organisations, ranging from research establishments and hospitals to business firms and civil service, Argyris found that competence involving interpersonal skills has been woefully neglected. Organisations are presumed to be able to function better, the more interpersonally competent their members are. Interpersonal competence refers to the ability to deal effectively with an environment populated by other human beings. Argyris is definitely the most persuasive advocate of the pursuit of the goal of interpersonal competence. He postulates three requirements for the development of interpersonal competence, viz.:

(1) *Self-acceptance*: This refers to the degree to which the person values himself in a positive fashion.

(2) *Confirmation*: By 'confirmation', Argyris meant the reality testing of one's own self-image.

(3) *Essentiality*: This is defined by Argyris as one's opportunity to 'utilise the central abilities and express his central needs'.

In attempting to operationalise the concept of interpersonal competence, Argyris specified several specific kinds of behaviour that he regards as concrete evidence of interpersonally competent behaviour. These four types of behaviour are arranged roughly in order of decreasing frequency of occurrence and increasing potency for contributing to competence. They are:

(1) Owning up to, or accepting responsibility for one's ideas and feelings;

(2) Being open to ideas and feelings of others and those from within one's self;

(3) Experimenting with new ideas and feelings; and

(4) Helping others to own up, be open to, and to experiment with their ideas and feelings.[10]

(c) The Organisational Structures of the New System

Organisations of the future will be a combination of both old and new forms of organisations, according to Argyris. The old pyramidal forms will be more effective for the routine, non-innovative activity that requires little, if any, internal commitment by the employees. However, as the decisions become less routine, more innovative, and as they require more commitment, the newer forms such as the matrix organisation will be more effective. Argyris' detailed prescriptions concerning organisational structures are based on the requirements of the task and the nature of decision-making. Accordingly, he suggests various mixes of the organisation with different pay offs.[11]

Structure I: The Pyramidal Structure

The pyramidal form should be used in the performance of routine operations, in cases where decisions are preceded by widespread agreement, in decisional situations that do not affect seriously the 'rewards and penalty activities' of the organisation or in emergency operations with time-constraints. Further, the pyramidal structure may be more effective if the individual participants do not seek psychological success and prefer to remain apathetic and non-involved.

Structure II: The Modified Formal Organisational Structure

This is close to Likert's 'link-pin' concept which enables a subordinate to be a member of the superior's decisional unit. This structure is more effective because it permits the subordinate's participation with the option for the superior to override the decision made by the group or to go ahead and make his own decision without waiting for the group to decide.

Structure III: Power According to Functional Contribution

Under this structure, each employee has equal opportunity to be provided information, power and controls, depending on his potential contribution to the problem. This strategy may be applied in situations involving teamwork, group incentives, new product development, inter-departmental activities and long-range planning.

Structure IV: The Matrix Organisation

Under this structure, each individual has equal power and responsibility. He has unlimited opportunities to influence the nature of the core activities. A matrix organisation[12] is expected to eliminate superior-subordinate relationships and substitutes for them individual self-discipline. Each individual would have the freedom to terminate as well as to create new activity. A matrix organisation would be rid of internal monopolies, which seem to be the bane of most traditional organisations. It is designed less around power and more around who has the relevant information. Project teams are created to solve specific problems. Each project team is composed of people representing all the relevant managerial functions like manufacturing, engineering, marketing and finance. Each member of the project team is given equal responsibility and power to solve the problem. The members are expected to work as a cohesive unit. The teams remain temporary or permanent, depending upon the nature of the assignment.[13] A matrix organisation may have many teams, as the following chart indicates.

Representatives of	Project 1	Project 2	Project 3
Manufacturing Engineering Marketing Finance			
	Team 1	Team 2	Team 3

Executives in the matrix organisation need to learn many aspects. One important requirement is their awareness of the actual leadership styles to be consistent with the administrative situation. The leader should be able to control 'productive tension', which comes from accepting new challenges, taking risks, for expanding one's competencies, etc. He has to help the employees to understand the internal environment, stretch their aspirations realistically and help them face interpersonal reality. He must also learn to manage inter-group conflicts about constructive aspects. In sum, executive education in the matrix organisation would focus on system effectiveness. The matrix structure enables jobs to be enlarged. Job 'enlargement' facilitates not merely the inclusion of more operations of the same low level, but to expand the use of the individual's intellectual and interpersonal abilities. Under this, each employee can have more control within his sphere of activities and greater participation in decisions about them.

(d) Techniques of Programmed Learning

A programme of education becomes an integral part of organisational development activity. In this, learning focuses on individuals in teams and organisational and system diagnosis, renewal and effectiveness. The concern for effectiveness would be matched by commensurate educational effort. The T-group (T for training) or sensitivity training is one such technique suggested by Argyris for improving the personal effectiveness of employees.

The T-group or Sensitivity Training

The T-group technique consists of a laboratory programme designed to provide opportunities for individual employees to expose their behaviour, give and receive feedback, experiment with new behaviour and develop awareness and acceptance of self and sensitivity to the personalities of others. The T-group also provides the possibilities to learn the nature of effective group functioning.[14] The approach is designed to provide experiences where psychological success, self-esteem, and interpersonal competence can be increased and dependence and control reduced.

It is found that the T-group sessions enable participants to forget hierarchical identities and develop distributive leadership and consensual decision-making. Unlike in the conventional organisational setting, an employee under attack may experiment with aggressive forms of reactions. Among the several positive results Argyris notes from his experiments in laboratory education was the delegation of more responsibilities to lower levels, getting more valid information from the ranks, and making the decisions more freely. Importantly, there are no intermediate relay points in the communication system. They were able to put an end to defensive politicking at meetings and wind milling at the lower levels. The original aim of T-group training was personal growth or promotion of self-insight and the focus was on changing the individuals, not necessarily to change the environment in which they work. Gradually, the same approach is being used extensively to promote organisation improvement. Argyris notes that 'we are not suggesting that organisations be administered like T-groups. However, we are hypothesizing but they should include structures like T-groups for certain selected decisions'.[15]

T-group and Public Administration

Chris Argyris suggests the widespread use of T-group technique or sensitivity training in Public Administration. His assessment of the United States Department of State is illustrative of the pathologies in governmental organisations as well as the need for intervention in organisational socio-emotional processes. According to Argyris, reforms in governmental organisation should aim at providing employees with higher order need satisfaction. This requires a long-range change programme, which would focus on the behaviour and leadership style of the senior participants and the introduction of organisational changes that would culminate in the enlarging of responsibilities and adopting innovative behaviour. Argyris also suggests radical revisions in the personnel practices in order to reduce the system's defenses. It is observed that the characteristics of the US State Department are common to most publicly administered organisations in the West or non-West. While Argyris' recommendations stem from a specific research study, Frederickson considers them relevant to all governmental organisations.[16]

Organisational Learning

One of Argyris's seminal contributions is in the area of organisational learning. He, along with Donald Schon undertook studies and conceptualised the learning processes in organisations. They argue that the organisations are not merely collection of individuals, but there is no organisation without such collections. On the same lines organisational learning is not merely individual learning, but organisations also learn through the experience and actions of individuals.[17] Organisational learning occurs when members act as learning agents for the organisation, responding to changes in the internal and external environments by detecting and correcting errors in organisational theory-in-use and embedding the results in private images and shared maps of organisation. They developed single and double-loop learning. In the former the individuals respond to errors by modifying strategies and assumptions within the organisational norms. In double-loop learning, response to detected error takes the form of joint inquiry into organisational norms *per se* and resolves the inconsistency and makes new norms which can be realised effectively. In both, organisational learning consists of restructuring the theory of organisational action.[18] Argyris and Schon identified several factors that inhibit both individual and organisational learning. They include the disposition not to discuss interpersonal and intergroup conflicts, taboo on public analysis of organisational failures, the desire to avoid direct inter-personal confrontation, etc.[19] They also discuss several intervention models.

Writers on Organisations - A Critique

Argyris is highly critical of the approaches and work of both industrial psychologists and organisational sociologists. While many psychological researchers tended to place the environment (social structure, norms, etc.), in a black box, the organisational sociologists like Blau, Thompson, Perrow, Goldthrope, etc., have ignored much of the research on personality, interpersonal relationships and group dynamics. The latter, while studying organisation as a whole seems to ignore the admittedly critical parts of the organisation. Individual behaviour, small group behaviour and inter-group behaviour represent, according to Argyris, important parts that help to create the whole.[20] Their predominant mode of analysis is the static coorelational mode. The nature of man implicit in their research is one of a mechanistic, closed-system; man is a passive creature with little influence on the organisation. Their concept of man is very close to the one that autocratic and conservative managements have always maintained, namely that people prefer to be market-oriented and economically oriented. They have tended to develop generalisations about the approximate fit between the organisation and the environment that correlate with the management's criteria of success. Finally, Argyris states his own view of organisational reality:

> I would prefer a view of reality where the sociological and psychological level variables interact and reinforce each other. The pure psychological approach tends to lead to views of man that ignore the constraints culture and social structures make and thus results in ignoring the deep psychological issues involved in making a continual choice to give up aspects of one's individuality and autonomy in order to maintain one's uniqueness and freedom.[21]

Critique of Herbert Simon

Hebert Simon's "rational man organisation theory" was criticised by Argyris on several grounds. Argyris considers that Simon's reliance on the descriptive-empirical approach and the concept of 'satisficing man' would support *status quo* in organisational life.[22] Simon's theory, in Argyris' view, excludes variables like interpersonal relations, need for self-actualisation, etc., that are central to organisation behaviour.[23] Further, Simon's reliance on mechanisms of organisational influence as an important source of motivation would tantamount to the view that man can be motivated by the authority system. On the contrary, Argyris asserts, man is basically proactive with potential for self-actualisation. Simon's theory of organisation would have no place for self-actualising individuals. Argyris elaborates and says that the consequences of intendedly rational man concept, in short, is to focus on the consistent, programmable, organised, thinking activities of man; to give primacy to behaviour that is related to goals; to assume purpose without asking how it has developed. Man, as a person who feels, experience chaos; manifests spontaneity; becomes turned-on without planning it or being able to explain it in terms of consistency of conscious purpose; thinks divergently...........is not the primary concern of the intendedly-rational-man organisation theorists.[24] Argyris goes to the extent of bracketing Simon along with the traditional administrative theorists for emphasising the importance of authority structures, for paying insufficient attention to the emotional side of man and for ignoring the hostility, anger and negative feelings of a typical employee towards the organisation and its goals.

A Critique of Argyris

Criticisms of Argyris' theories fall into three broad categories. The first set of criticisms concern Argyris' benign view of man in relation to the organisation; his characterisation of the concept of self-actualisation seem to border to utopia and is without any precise operational indicators. To Simon, self-actualisation is synonymous with anarchy.[25] Simon also takes objection to the view that organisations should be 'be-all and end-all' of self-actualisation; it would be more realistic for organisations to plan for reducing the working hours and enhancing leisure to enable employees to seek self-actualisation. Secondly, Argyris' antipathy to authority is considered to be without any parallel. The view that "structure is devil" is influenced by Argyris' obsession with the need for power.[26] As Simon points out "Argyris...tended to choose de-emphasis of authority elations as the way out, but at the price of neglecting the consequences for organisational effectiveness...what corrupts is not power, but the need for power and it corrupts both the powerful and the powerless".[27]

Thirdly, objections are raised against some of the key propositions of Argyris on methodological grounds. For instance, there is little empirical support in favour of the statement that people in organisations are singularly opposed to authority. On the contrary, there is considerable support to the view that many employees seem to accept authority and organisation goals because such acceptance is in congruence with their values and interests. If employees derive too much negative satisfaction, they would rather withdraw from the organisation. Argyris' assumption that the pursuit of the goal of self-actualisation is a universalistic goal has also been questioned. It appears that not all individuals, under all circumstances, would like to self-actualise themselves and that there are many who feel happier under conditions of directive leadership.

An Evaluation

Argyris has been able to sharpen the various facets of the human relations and participative schools of thought on organisations. His objective is to build healthier organisations and to raise the quality of life in them. Argyris advocates a fundamental transformation of organisations to provide a suitable environment for self-actualisation. He has been pursuing this objective with a missionary zeal, even to the point of transcending the boundaries of the conventional organisational theorist. However, the ideas of Argyris are too contemporary to find a proper place in administrative theory. Some of the propositions are normative and lack empirical validation. It is, therefore, difficult to place his work in a clear historical perspective.

The most important contribution of Argyris is in the realm of interpersonal competence. Much of the research on the interpersonal behaviour of executives would strongly support the idea that the abilities concept does have relevance for the study of personality and interpersonal style to actually influence organisational effectiveness and how interpersonal competence can be thought of as a skill that can be learned. Several studies also indicate the importance of interpersonal competence of upper-level administrators. Argyris' observation concerning the frequent recourse to the use of defence mechanisms, group formation in particular, when the higher-order needs of individuals go unattended, has considerable empirical support. Another lesson that we learn from Argyris is that research on organisations cannot be separated, beyond a point, from action.

In Brief

Argyris' contribution to organisation theory and behaviour can be summarised as:

- Chris Argyris (1923-), belonging to the new management school, is one of the first generation contributors to the field of organisational development. A renowned organisational behaviour theorist and pioneer in the application of T-Group technique, his influence on reform of organisational structures and managerial practices is striking.

- Argyris critically examined the working of formal organisations and advanced theories and strategies for both individual and organisational development. He argues that there is a basic incongruence between the needs of a mature personality and the requirements of a formal organisation. Discussing the basic conflict between the structure of formal organisations and the psychological needs of mature adults, he proposed Maturity-Immaturity theory and the seven components of the continuum.

- He suggests an analytical framework of individual behaviour, linking the concepts of psychological energy, personality needs and abilities. Argyris hopes that if the potential for self-actualisation present in each individual is properly tapped, it can benefit the individual employee as well as the organisation. He suggests intervention strategies for organisation development.

- Argyris emphasises the importance of interpersonal competence in organisational development. He elaborates the requirements and the type of behaviour to improve the interpersonal competencies.

- Discussing about the appropriate organisational structures for realising the self-actualisation potential, Argyris prefers material structures to paramedical structures. He argues that the leadership styles need to be consistent with administrative situations and structures.

- Argyris advocated an ambitious programme of education as an integral part of organisational development activity. The T-Group (T for training) or sensitivity training is one such technique suggested by Argyris for improving the personal effectiveness of employees.

- In the area of organisational learning, Argyris along with Donald Schon, developed single and double-loop learning techniques.

- Argyris is highly critical of the approaches and work of writers on organisations including Herbert Simon and forcefully presents his own view of organisational reality. But his own theories are criticised for taking a benign view of man in relation to the organisation; the antipathy to authority; and lack of empirical evidence.

- Argyris advocates a fundamental transformation of organisations to provide a suitable environment for self-actualisation. Along with his other ideas like interpersonal competence and matrix organisations, this advocacy is of contemporary relevance.

Notes and References

[1] See Smith, M.K. 'Chris Argyris: Theories of Action, Double-loop Learning and Organisational Learning , the Encyclopedia of Education, http://infed.org/thinkers/argyris.htm.

[2] http://www.actionscience.com/argbib.htm

[3] Radhika Warrier, Chris Argyris – A Profile, See ttp://74.125.153.132/s e a r c h ? q = c a che: Bp G X 9 x A G O I J : w w w . business.bgsu.edu/modcompass/articles/c h r i s t h e o r i e s . d o c + r a d h i k a + w a r r i e r + o n + c h r i s +a rgyris&cd=1&hl=en&ct=clnk&gl=in

[4] Ibid.

[5] See Argyris, Chris, *Personality and Organisation*, New York, Harper, 1957, pp. 150-57.

[6] Ibid.

[7] See Argyris, Chris, *Integrating the Individual and the Organisation*, New York, Wiley, 1964, pp. 3-19, and *Management and Organisational Development*, New York, McGraw-Hill Book Company, 1971, pp. 1-27.

[8] For a detailed account of the theory of hierarchy of needs see Maslow, Abraham, *Motivation and Personality*, New York, Harper, 1954.

[9] Quoted in Hampton, D. R., Summer, C.E., and Webber, R.A., *Organisational Behaviour and the Practice of Management*, Glennview (III.) Scott, Foreman and Co., 1968, p. 139.

[10] Argyris, Chris, *Intervention Theory and Method: A Behavioural Science View*, Reading (Mass), Addison-Wesley, 1970, p. 40.

[11] See Argyris, Chris, *Integrating the Individual and the Organisation*, op. cit., pp. 197-214.

[12] The matrix structure was originally developed in the US aerospace industry. Along with several other organisation theorists Argyris became a strong advocate of the matrix structure. See Knight, K., "Matrix Organisation: A Review", *The Journal of Management Studies*, 1976 (13), 2, pp. 111-30.

[13] Argyris, Chris, "How Tomorrow's Executives Will Make Decision", *Think*, Nov.-Dec. 1967, pp. 18-22, published by IBM.

[14] The method was originally developed in 1947 by Bradford, L. P., Benne, K. D., and Lippitt, R., See their book T- *Group Theory and Laboratory Method*, New York, Wiley, 1964; Summer, C. E. 'Strategies for Organisation Design", in Kilmann, R. H., Pondy, L. R., Slevin, D. P., (Eds.), *The Management of Organisation Design*, Vol. I, New York, North Holland, pp. 103-39. Also see Argyris, Chris," A Brief Description of Laboratory Education", *The Training Directors Journal*, Vol. 17, No. 10, October,1963, pp. 5-8.

[15] Argyris, Chris, "A Brief Description of Laboratory Education", op. cit., p. 5.

[16] Frederickson, H.G., "Toward a New Public Administration", in Frank Marini (Ed.), *Toward a New Public Administration: The Minnow Brook Perspective*, Scranton, Chandler, 1972, p. 328.

[17] Argyris, Chris, and Schon, Donald A., *Organisational Learning: A Theory of Action Perspective*, Reading, Massachusetts, Addision-Wesley Publishing Company, 1978, p.9.

[18] Ibid. Specially chapter 1, pp.8-29.

[19] Ibid., p.43.

[20] See Argyris, Chris, *The Applicability of Organisational Sociology*, Cambridge, Cambridge University Press, 1972, pp. 70-83.

[21] Ibid., p. 72.

[22] For details about the controversy between Argyris and Simon see Argyris, Chris, "Some Limits of Rational Man Organisation Theory", *Public Administration Review*, Vol. 33, No. 3, (May-June 1973), pp. 253-67; Simon, H.A., "Organisational Man: Rational or Self-Actualizing", *Public Administration Review*, vol. 33, No. 4 (July-August 1973), pp. 346-53; and Argyris, Chris, "Organisational Man: Rational and Self-Actualizing", *Public Administration Review*, op. cit., pp. 354-57.

[23] Argyris, Chris, "Some Limits of Rational Man Organisation Theory", op. cit., p. 253.

[24] Ibid., p. 261.

[25] Simon, H.A., "Organisational Man: Rational or Self-Actualizing", op. cit., p. 352.

[26] Ibid., p. 348.

[27] Ibid., p. 349.

15

FREDERICK HERZBERG

V. Lakshmipathy

Introduction

Motivation to work has been receiving increasing attention from both those who study organisation and also those who manage them. The traditional simplistic prescriptive guidelines concerning the 'economic man' are no longer considered adequate in understanding human behaviour. There are several factors that account for the growing importance of motivation viz., growing complexity of behavioural requirements in modern complex organisations, ever tightening constraints placed on organisations by unions and governmental agencies, increasing competition, lobbying, changing nature of technology, corporate objectives of organisations and the increasing emphasis on human resources and their management. It is in this context the conceptual contributions of Frederick Herzberg gains significance in the literature of public administration.

(1923-2000)

Life and Works

Frederick Irving Herzberg (1923-2000) was born in Lynn, Massachusetts. He joined the City College, New York in 1939 but his studies were interrupted by the Second World War when he enlisted as a non-commissioned officer in the US Army where he won the Bronze Star for valour. As a patrol sergeant, he was a firsthand witness of the Dachau Concentration Camp and he believed that this experience, as well as the discussions he had with other Germans living in the area was what triggered his interest in motivation. On return from the army he completed his BS degree in 1946 and went on to take MS and Ph.D in psychology from the University of Pittsburgh. He worked as a Research Director of Psychological Services at Pittsburgh (1951-57), Professor of Psychology at Case Western Reserve University in Cleveland (1957-72) and Professor of Management at the College of Business, University of Utah (1972-95) until retirement. At

Case Western Reserve University he established the Department of Industrial Mental Health. [1] His publications include *The Motivation to Work (1959), Work and the Nature of Man (1966)* both along with B. Mausner and B. Snyderman, *The Managerial Choice* (1982) and *Herzberg on Motivation* (1983). [2]

A renowned psychologist, pioneer of job enrichment concept and one of the most influential management teachers and consultants in the post world war period, Herzberg is the originator of motivation-hygiene theory and was called the father of job-enrichment. He became an icon and a legend among post-war visionaries such as Maslow, McGregor and Drucker. His article "One More Time, How Do You Motivate Employees?" published in *Harvard Business Review* in 1968 seems to have sold over 1.2 million reprints in less than two decades. [3] In 1995 the International Press announced that his book *Work and the Nature of Man* was listed as one of the ten most important books impacting management theory and practice in the twentieth century. Herzberg was a consultant for many multinationals both in the United States and foreign governments. He was among the first American consultants to study workers in the Soviet Union and worked extensively in Israel and Japan.

Studies on Motivation

Influenced by the writings of Abraham Maslow, Douglas McGregor and Chris Argyris, Frederick Herzberg became interested in analysing the relationship between meaningful experience at work and mental health. He believed that all individuals have two sets of needs viz., to avoid pain and to grow psychologically. The Motivation-Hygiene theory grew out of the studies Herzberg conducted on two hundred and three accountants and engineers, chosen because of the profession's growing importance in the business world, in and around Pittsburgh, Pennsylvania. His study revolved basically around two issues, i.e., identification of the events which resulted in marked improvement in individual's job satisfaction; and conversely the events that have led to marked reduction in job satisfaction. He used the critical incident method to collect data. The interviewers asked the respondents "think of the time when you felt exceptionally good or exceptionally bad about your present job or in other jobs you have had". The time frame could be either the 'long range' or the 'short range'. Based on the responses, he probed further and developed his Motivation-Hygiene theory.

Herzberg's study was based on open questioning and very few assumptions to collect and analyse the details of 'critical incidents' as recalled by the respondents. This methodology was adopted by him first in his doctoral study at the University of Pittsburg. This open interviewing method gave far more meaningful results than the most popular, convenient and conventional closed or multiple-choice or extent-based questions, which assume or prompt a particular type of response. A significant aspect of his study is that Herzberg undertook extensive preparatory work prior to his study in 1959 by scrutinising and analysing the methodologies and the results of 155 studies undertaken previously on job attitudes carried out between 1920 and 1954. The level of preparation and the critical incident method as well as the depth of care and analysis after the study helped Herzberg to produce a powerful and sophisticated work.[4] Herzberg expanded his motivation-hygiene theory in his subsequent books. Significantly, Herzberg commented 25 years after the publication of his theory that the "original study has produced more replications than any other research in the history of industrial and organisational psychology".[5]

Before the Herzberg's studies, managements in general used to concentrate on improving the hygiene factors i.e., whenever there was a problem they attempted to 'solve' it by hiking pay, giving additional fringe benefits and by improving the working conditions.

But unfortunately, these simplistic solutions could not always succeed in motivating the employees. Herzberg's theory, apart from explaining the problems of motivation, also opened the eyes of managements to have a closer look at all the motivational factors instead of only concentrating on hygiene factors.

Two-Factor Theory

Herzberg's two-factor theory identified five strong determinants of the job satisfaction and five of job dissatisfaction, which are a totally different set of factors. They are presented in chart 1.

Chart 1: Herzberg's Two-Factor Theory

Hygiene Factors	Motivation Factors
Company policy and administration	Achievement
Supervision	Recognition
Salary	Work itself
Interpersonal relations	Responsibility
Working conditions	Advancement

Herzberg found duality of attitudes about work experience in the responses of workers on their jobs. Job experiences leading to favourable reactions most often were related to the context in which the job performed, that is, the surroundings and the factors on the periphery of task content. As against this, factors causing unfavorable responses were found to be related to avoidance of discomfort. Again the factors causing good responses are related to personal growth, or fulfillment of psychological needs. Herzberg labelled the factors associated with the growth and the task content of the job as 'satisfiers' and factors associated with pain avoidance and the "context/surroundings" of the job were labelled dissatisfiers.

Satisfiers

The factors identified as satisfiers, which perform the role of motivators in jobs, are as follows:

Achievement: The personal satisfaction of solving problems independently, completing task, and seeing the results of one's efforts.

Recognition: Positive acknowledgement of the task completed or other personal achievement, rather than generalised "human relations" expression of rewards.

Work itself: The task content of the job and relative interest, variety, challenge, and freedom from boredom.

Responsibility: Being entrusted with full responsibility and accountability for certain tasks, or the performance of others, and having control over deciding how and when tasks are to be done.

Advancement and Growth: Advancement to a higher order of task to perform. A sense of possibility for growth and advancement as well as actual satisfaction from new learning; being able to do new things.

Dissatisfiers

The potential dissatisfiers, or "hygiene factors" - using an analogy to the medical use of the term, meaning preventive and environmental - are salary, company policy and administration, supervision, working conditions, and interpersonal relations. Hygiene factors, such as working conditions, company administration, salary, supervisory relations, and benefits and services are envisioned as environmental elements that have little or no relationships to the motivation of specific job-related behaviour. The factors that can motivate a man to work harder according to Herzberg include elements such as the work itself, achievements, recognition, advancement and responsibility. These latter factors determine how an employee feels about his job, whereas hygiene factors only determine how a worker feels about his company or organisation in general. Expressed somewhat differently, motivation factors are related to job context. In addition, Herzberg argued that an employee is either dissatisfied or not dissatisfied with hygiene factors, and he is either satisfied or not satisfied with motivational factors. The implication being satisfaction and dissatisfaction are separate continuums and not the opposite of each other. Instead, a neutral state exists as contrary to job satisfaction and job dissatisfaction. A worker is either satisfied or not satisfied (neutral) with motivational job factors. Similarly, an employee is either dissatisfied or not dissatisfied (neutral) with hygienic factors.

Herzberg's rationale helps to explain why a worker may hate his job and yet remain with the organisation or love his job and yet quit the organisation. This is because separate types of factors influence these two separate and distinct feelings. The elements that determined how an employee feels about his job are the motivational factors; the variables that influence how a worker feels about his organisation are the environmental or hygiene factors. Hygiene factors must be adequate, or employees will not be attracted to an organisation. But when employed, manipulating hygiene factors cannot motivate a worker to do a better job.

Each set of factors are rarely involved in contributing to the other and each set is independent of the other. What is important is that dissatisfiers only produce short-term changes in human attitudes and satisfiers produce long-term attitudes. Dissatisfiers describe man's relations with context and environment in which he does the job. They only serve to prevent job dissatisfaction and have very little effect in creating positive job attitudes. On the other hand, satisfiers are related to what one does, i.e., job content, nature of task, and growth in task capability, etc. They are effective in motivating the individual for superior performance. Herzberg calls hygiene factors as dissatisfiers and maintenance factors whereas satisfiers are called motivators and growth factors.

The motivation and hygienic factors are separate and distinct and they are not opposite or obverse of each other. For example, opposite of job satisfaction is not job dissatisfaction but only indicates there is no job satisfaction. Similarly, opposite of job dissatisfaction is not job satisfaction, but only indicates that there is no job dissatisfaction. Therefore, these two are made up of two unipolar traits, each contributing very little to the other. The three key principles of the motivation-hygiene theory are:

1. The factors involved in producing job satisfaction are separate and distinct from the factors that lead to job dissatisfaction. Growth occurs with achievement and achievement requires a task to perform. Hygiene factors are unrelated to tasks.

2. The opposite of satisfaction on the job is not dissatisfaction; it is not merely no job satisfaction. Satisfaction and dissatisfaction are discrete feelings. They are not opposite ends of the same continuum. Herzberg described them as "unipolar traits".

3. The motivators have a much long-lasting effect on sustaining dissatisfaction than hygiene factors have on preventing dissatisfaction. The motivators in a work experience tend to be more self-sustaining and are not dependent upon constant supervisory attention. Hygiene needs, however, are related to things for which our appetite is never satisfied completely. Applications of hygiene improvement must be constantly reapplied, since

the need for them always recurs, usually with increased intensity. Hygiene must always be replenished. Most methods used in work-related organisations to "purchase" motivated behaviour over the years have appeared to be ineffective, since the traditional motivation problems still exist. This is the inevitable result because only things that surround the work itself were being improved, and these things have no lasting effects on the motivation of workers.

Hygiene and Motivation Seekers

After explaining the significance of motivation and hygiene factors, Herzberg divides the people working in organisations into two groups and calls them 'hygiene seekers' and 'motivation seekers'. Chart 2 explains the characteristics of both hygiene and motivation seekers. Successful hygiene seekers will have two types of impact on the organisation. Firstly, they will lead the organisation to 'as is where is' as they are more motivated to external reward than internal. Borrowing the terminology from the army, Herzberg equates them as 'barrack soldiers'. Secondly, they instill their own motivational attitudes in their subordinates and set extrinsic reward atmosphere in the organisation. Often their influence can be out of proportion to their long-term effectiveness. Thirdly, a hygiene seeker, even after fulfillment of hygiene needs, may not get motivated. Inadequate pay, no doubt, contributes to dissatisfaction but more pay is no guarantee for more productivity. As Paul and Robertson have noted, 'no amount of environmental improvement can compensate for task impoverishment'. If our concern is to motivate people, we must look at the task we ask them to do. Emphasis on hygiene factors would lead to impede creativity, absenteeism, frequent occurrence of failures and restriction or elimination of opportunity for initiative and achievement.

Chart 2: Characteristics of Hygiene and Motivation Seekers

Hygiene Seeker	Motivation Seeker
1. Motivated by nature	1. By the nature of the task
2. Chronic and heightened dis-satisfaction with aspects of job content. E.g. Salary, job security, fellow employee	2. Higher tolerance for poor hygiene factors
3. Overreaction with satisfaction to improvement in hygiene factors-	3. Less reaction to improvement in hygiene factors.
4. Short duration of satisfaction	4. Similar
5. Over reaction with dissatisfaction when hygine factors are not improved	5. Milder discontent when hygiene factors need improvement
6. Realises little satisfaction from accomplishment	6. Realises greater satisfaction
7. Shows little interest in the kind and quality of work he does	7. Shows capacity to enjoy the kind of work he does
8. Cynicism regarding positive virtues of life work and life in general	8. Have positive feelings towards work and in general
9. Does not profit professionally from experience	9. Profits professionally from experience
10. Prone to cultural noises: a) Ultraliberal b) Ultra conservative - Parrots most philosophy c) Acts more like topmost than the topmost does	10. Belief systems - sincere and considered
11. May be successful on the job because of talent	11. May be an over achiever

To an organisation, it is easy to motivate through fear of hygiene deprivation than to motivate in terms of achievement and actualising the goals. Such a policy would be injurious to the long-term interests of the organisation. Therefore, it is desirable to focus emphasis on motivating the people. For this, Herzberg suggests job enrichment and vertical overloading as the important means.

Job Enrichment

Motivation-hygiene theory holds that management must provide hygiene factors to avoid employee dissatisfaction but also factors intrinsic to the work itself so that the employees are satisfied with their jobs. Herzberg argued that *job enrichment* is required for intrinsic motivation and this is a continuous management process. According to Herzberg:

- The job should have sufficient challenge to utilise the full ability of the employee;
- Employees who demonstrate increasing levels of ability should be given increasing levels of responsibility; and
- If the job cannot be designed to use an employee's full abilities then the organisation should consider automating the task or replacing the employee with one who has a lower level of skill. If a person cannot be fully utilised then there will be a motivation problem.[6]

The term 'Job Enrichment' designates a technique used by managers to maximise in workers the internal motivation to work, which is the true source of job satisfaction. Basically a concept founded on the work of Frederick Herzberg, job enrichment has been significantly augmented by work done at Yale University. The job-enrichment concept designates a production and profit-oriented way of managing, as well as a means of making work experience meaningful for the people. It is based on the premise that people are not motivated by what is externally done to them by management with rewards, privileges or punishment, nor by the environment or context in which they perform their work. People develop lasting motivation only through their experience with the content of their jobs - the work itself.

Such factors as pay, fringe benefits, the work environment, working conditions, and the quality of supervision cannot be ignored or given only token attention. Dissatisfaction with the factors can have a severely debilitating effect on a workforce. Caring properly for these needs can result in absence of dissatisfaction. But generating motivation in workers requires doing something with what they do in their work. Managers in recent years have been witnessing high-velocity change and turmoil in the patterns of employee behaviour, and are forced to cope with a host of problems including high turnover or quit rates, absenteeism, tardiness, union grievances and work stoppages, high training costs, poor production quality, and low rates of production. Job enrichment was designed to eliminate such problems, thereby benefiting both the employee and the employer.

Job Loading

In attempting to enrich an employee's job, Herzberg contends that management often merely succeeds in reducing the man's personal contribution, rather than giving him an opportunity for growth in his existing job. He calls this "horizontal job loading", as opposed to "vertical loading"' which provide motivation factors. Horizontal loading, in his view, is what has mostly been wrong in earlier programmes centered on job enlargement. He gives some examples of this approach, [7]with some tart observation:

- Challenging the employee by increasing the amount of production expected of him. If he tightens 10,000 bolts a day, see if he can tighten 20,000 a day. "If the job is already zero in motivation, multiplying zero by anything still equals zero."
- Adding another meaningless task to the existing one, usually some routine electrical activity. "The arithmetic here is adding zero to zero."
- Rotating the assignments of a number of jobs that really should be enriched. This means, for example, washing dishes for a while, and then washing silverware. "The arithmetic is substituting one zero for another zero".
- Removing the most difficult parts of the assignment to free the worker to accomplish more of the less challenging assignments. "This traditional industrial engineering approach amounts to subtraction in the hope of accomplishing addition."

Herzberg concedes that all the principles of motivation through job enrichment have not worked out as yet, but he offers the seven-point checklist shown in Exhibit I as a practical guide for anyone who wishes to re-examine the motivator factors in the jobs over which he has control.

Opportunities in Job Enrichment

Job-enrichment has been described as "the art of reshaping jobs". Quantitative measures of production rates, quality, and job attitude have been carefully made in many applications. Improvements have amply demonstrated the validity of changing job content to effect increased motivation.

The Process of Enriching Jobs

Herzberg describes a ten-step process that the managers may keep in mind in motivating their employees. They include:

1. Select the jobs where attitudes are poor, hygiene is becoming costly and motivation will make a difference in performance.
2. Approach the jobs with the conviction that they can be changed.
3. Brainstorm a list of changes that may enrich the jobs, without concern for their practicality.
4. Screen the list to eliminate the suggestions that involve hygiene than motivation.
5. Screen the list for generalities viz., 'give them more responsibility', that are rarely followed in practice.
6. Screen the list to eliminate suggestions for horizontal loading.
7. Avoid direct participation by employees whose jobs are to be enriched.
8. In the initial attempts of job enrichment, two equivalent groups should be chosen - one as a experimental group and other as a control group.
9. Be prepared for a drop in performance in the experimental group initially as a change over to a new job may lead to a temporary reduction in efficiency.
10. Expect the first line supervisors to experience anxiety and hostility over the changes that are being made.

These experiments will enable the supervisory functionaries to identify functions they have neglected in the past and to devote time to review colleague's performance and administering through training.[8]

The Module of Work and Vertical Loading of the Job

Among the best ways to set up individual responsibility is to seek natural modules of work, which can be individually assigned. A work module can appear in many forms. In general, a module is a set of related tasks, which contribute in sequence to the completion of some function or turning out some completed item. The module of tasks can be more meaningful if it is related to some natural unit of work for which an individual has continuing responsibility.

Natural units of work may have geographic, alphabetical, or numerical grouping or other identity. That identity may also be related to serving some recipient or group of recipients. When a natural work module is first identified it may be performed by several people doing fragments of the full module with no one singly responsible for the whole. To the greatest degree that is practical, each individual is given the full process to perform. In effect, a sense of "proprietorship" can and should be developed.

The responsibility is full and individual. In one key punch job, for example, the operators were given a module of work by having them prepare all cards from a certain geographic area or for certain kinds of reports rather than whatever cards happened to come along next.

The principle of vertical loading involves process loading into a job, additional tasks and responsibilities which can deliver more satisfaction than the tasks in the job to begin with. This is very different from adding more tasks which may be varied but have essentially no greater interest and responsibility and are most often found above in the supervisory job or a job at a higher level of complexity.

Direct Feedback: The process of feedback is highly important in the enriching process. It affects the recognition motivator. The most effective feedback occurs in the transaction between employee and the task rather than in the usual transaction between employee and the supervisor. Effective feedback has these characteristics:

- It is related to task performance, not personal characteristics.
- It is given on an individual rather than group basis.
- It occurs at short intervals.
- It is given direct from the task to the employee, not through the supervisor.

This is not intended to imply that supervisory feedback is ineffective or waste of time. Most people desire it, and such interpersonal feedback on performance can be of great value when done well. Direct feedback is not fettered with interpersonal problems and is less complicated.

Soon after the completion of a task, a worker should be learning through task feedback how well he is doing, where he stands, and what he is worth. Then he should have the opportunity to do something about it himself. This is usually accomplished by making him responsible for changes and adjustments in his process and for correcting his own errors.

Once a new responsibility is given, the supervisor must give consideration to what his response will be if the employee fails with it. Some failure must be expected. The supervisor should help the employee correct the error, examine why it occurred, and assist in planning to prevent recurrence. This kind of individual coaching becomes a major supervisory function, which ushers in a new way of life for many supervisors.

Referring to the model, the Exhibit 1 elaborates on the job-dimension and implementation components:

Task Combination: Combining tasks to a complete task module have a high degree of potential. This will provide additional interests, challenge, and a feeling of responsibility for the whole piece.

EXHIBIT: I

The Work Effectiveness Model

Diagnostic Tools

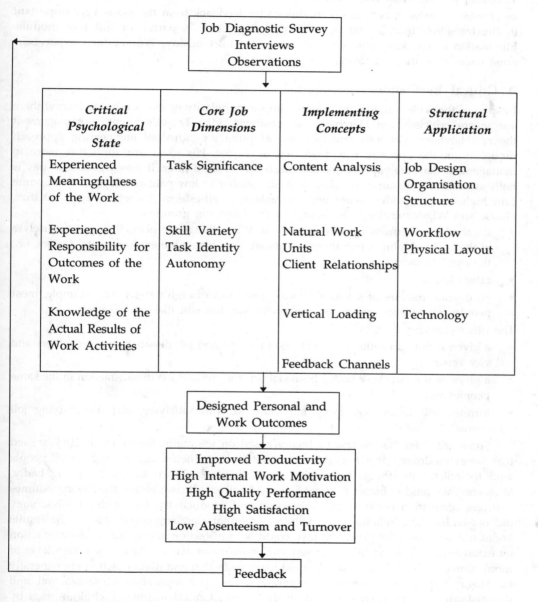

Critical Psychological State	Core Job Dimensions	Implementing Concepts	Structural Application
Experienced Meaningfulness of the Work	Task Significance	Content Analysis	Job Design Organisation Structure
Experienced Responsibility for Outcomes of the Work	Skill Variety Task Identity Autonomy	Natural Work Units Client Relationships	Workflow Physical Layout
Knowledge of the Actual Results of Work Activities		Vertical Loading	Technology
		Feedback Channels	

Job Diagnostic Survey
Interviews
Observations

Designed Personal and
Work Outcomes

Improved Productivity
High Internal Work Motivation
High Quality Performance
High Satisfaction
Low Absenteeism and Turnover

Feedback

Natural Work Units: Designing the work according to a logical group that is aligned with the mission allows for the personal feeling of responsibility. Workers start to identify with this group and behave accordingly.

Client Relationship: Where natural work units are groupings by customers - for example, billing or accounts receivable—the engendered sense of responsibility leads the workers to form a "client relationship" with the accounts. They start to call them "my customers" and take on a strong attitude of ownership

Vertical Loading: This pushing of responsibilities down higher levels and giving the workers more control make for increased responsibility. This should be done selectively according to individual competence.

Feedback Channels: Setting up conditions for feedback from the job is very important in the transition from a 100 per cent checking job to a partial or full task module. Elimination of checking without feedback might hurt quality. Workers and supervisors must know how they are doing.

A Critical Evaluation

In spite of the wide ranging application and the popularity of the two-factor theory, there are severe criticisms on Herzberg's propositions. Like Taylor's scientific management theory, Herzberg was also criticised for adopting an industrial engineering approach though from the opposite way than that of Taylor. His ideas are applicable more to management than the supervisors and much less to shop floor. It was argued that pay is both satisfier and dissatisfier; particularly dissatisfier to low paid employees, at the same time higher pay provides recognition and enhances self-esteem. Therefore, it is a satisfier. House and Wigdor criticise the theory on the following grounds:

* the theory is methodologically egg-bound. When things are okay, they put themselves in the best light, but when things go wrong they blame the environmental factors, i.e., the hygiene factors;
* rater bias; and
* no overall measure of satisfaction was used in Pittsburgh's study. For example, most people may dislike certain features of the job, but still like the job itself.

The other elements of criticism are:

* a given factor can cause job satisfaction for one and job dissatisfaction for others and vice-versa;
* a given factor can cause both job satisfaction for one and job dissatisfaction in the same people; and
* intrinsic job factors are more important to both satisfying and dissatisfying job events.

Some criticised the Herzberg's theory based on the methodology used. They argued that the methodology does not address the notion that when things are going well people tend to look at the things they enjoy about their job. When things are going badly, however, they tend to blame external factors. Another criticism is that the theory assumes a strong correlation between job satisfaction and productivity. Herzberg's methodology did not address this relationship. [9] Others argue that Herzberg could observe the results because it is natural for people to take credit for satisfaction and to blame dissatisfaction on external factors. In addition, job satisfaction does not necessarily imply a high level of motivation or productivity.[10] King argued that satisfaction and dissatisfaction are generally no longer considered to exist on separate scales. The separation of satisfaction and dissatisfaction has been shown as an artifact of the Critical Incident Technique used by Herzberg to record events. On the other hand, Hackman and Oldham felt that the theory does not allow for individual differences, such as a particular personality trait, which would affect individuals' unique responses to motivation or hygiene factors.[11] Some behavioural scientists also point out the inadequacies in the need hierarchy and motivation-hygiene theories viz., these theories contain the relatively explicit assumption that happy and satisfied workers produce more; statistical theories are concerned with explaining 'average' behaviour and the employees in their pursuit of status might take a balanced view and strive to pursue several behavioural paths to achieve a combination of personal status objectives.[12]

It is argued that respondents did not like to appear greedy and therefore, ranked pay very low, whereas in studies of Lawler pay was ranked as satisfier. Studies by Shepard and Herrick confirmed Herzberg's conclusions. Similarly, it was argued that after the initial years in employment, job satisfaction decreases but the worker continues to work for a living.

The main criticism of the motivation-hygiene concept is that initially it interpreted job and company employment factors to be totally distinct and a separate set of entities. Today, it is recognised that these factors at times can be both "motivators" and "hygienic" in nature. Money seems to be a motivator in many work situations, especially those in which the employee is earning a relatively small total annual income. Motivators and hygienic factors also may vary on jobs at different organisational levels.

Vroom argued that no one has investigated whether Herzberg, Mausner and Snyderman's results could be an outcome of an attribution process. Some relevant studies do indicate that this process may account for the observed data. Barry M. Staw noted that when individuals are led to believe their performance has been successful, they tend to attribute various pleasing characteristics to the work group. Others showed that regardless of the supervisor's behaviour, manipulated to be structuring or considerate, when a work group does well it tends to see the leader as considerate. In short, people select characteristics on the basis of their outcomes.

Methodology adopted in any study has a bearing on the conclusions emanating from the study. One criticism against Herzberg's theory is the methodology adopted. Schwab and others have adopted same methodology as that of Herzberg but they obtained results different from what the two-factor theory would predict.

In spite of the criticism on two-factor theory, many based upon empirical researches; it is unquestionable that Herzberg's contribution to work motivation is substantial. He focused attention on the significance of job content in motivation, which was a neglected factor earlier. The concept of job enrichment is certainly one of his better-known contributions. Herzberg's theory is largely responsible for the practice of allowing employees greater responsibility for planning and controlling their work as a means of increasing motivation and satisfaction.

Herzberg's ideas, it is argued, relates to modern ethical management and social responsibility. He understood well and attempted to teach the ethical management principles that many leaders today - particularly in business organisations - still struggle to grasp. In this respect Herzberg's concepts are just as relevant today as when he first suggested, except that the implications of responsibility, fairness, justice and compassion in business are global. It is also argued that Herzberg was essentially concerned with people's well-being at work. Underpinning his theories and teachings he was basically attempting to bring more humanity and caring into the workplace than only to improve organisational performance.[13] The significance of the theory can be understood from the fact that by 1968, according to Herzberg, the two-factor theory was replicated sixteen times in a wide variety of situations and corroborated with the studies using different procedures which agreed with Herzberg's original findings relating to intrinsic employee motivation making it one of the most widely replicated studies on job attitudes.[14] Notwithstanding the criticisms, Herzberg's contribution to work motivation is substantial. He drew attention to the importance of job content and job enrichment to work satisfaction.

In Brief

The contribution of Herzberg can be summarised as:

- Frederick Herzberg (1923-2000), pioneer of job enrichment concept and motivation-hygiene theory, is one of the most influential management consultants. Among his writings, *Work and the Nature of Man* was rated as one of the influential book on management in the 20th century.

- Herzberg conducted studies using 'critical incidents' method and developed theories of motivation-hygiene and job-enrichment.

- Herzberg found in his studies duality of attitudes and called them dissatisfiers and satisfiers. The dissatisfiers are called as 'hygiene factors' and satisfiers 'motivational factors'. Expressed differently, the variables that influence how a worker feels about his organisation are the environmental or hygiene factors and the elements that determine how an employee feels about his job are the motivational factors.

- Herzberg in his two-factor theory identified job satisfactions and job dissatisfactions and considered them as totally different set of factors. The implication being an employee is either dissatisfied or not satisfied with hygiene factors and is either satisfied or not satisfied with motivational factors. These two factors are on a separate continuum and not opposite of each other.

- Herzberg divides people working in organisations into two groups and calls them 'hygiene seekers' and 'motivation seekers' and also explains their characteristics. The impact of hygiene seekers and motivation seekers on organisations is also elaborated by Herzberg.

- Herzberg argues that 'Job Enrichment' is a technique to maximise in individual workers internal motivation to work and to enhance job satisfaction. Realisation of employees' full potential is one of the objectives of job enrichment and the process is described as 'the art of reshaping jobs'.

- The process of enriching jobs has also been described in detail by Herzberg. Among others he considers module of work, vertical loading of the job and feedback as an important means of job enrichment.

- Herzberg's two-factor theory is criticised based on methodology and conclusions. Many consider the existence of separate scales of satisfaction and dissatisfaction as not valid. It is argued that same factors may be satisfiers and dissatisfiers depending on the levels of work and context of work.

- Herzberg's work resulted in more focus on significance of job content in motivation. His concept of job enrichment has played an important role in practices of allowing employees greater responsibility for planning and controlling their work as a means of increasing motivation and satisfaction.

Notes

1. Benedict S. Grigaliunas and Herzberg, Frederick, "Relevancy in the Test of Motivation-Hygiene Theory", *Journal of Applied Psychology*, February 1971, pp. 73-79.

2. Lindsay, C. A., Marks, E., and Gorlow, L., "The Herzberg Theory: A Critique and Reformulation", *Journal of Applied Psychology*, August 1967, pp. 330-339.

3. Schwab, Donald P., William De Vitt, H., and Cummings, Larry l., "A Test of the Adequacy of the Two-Factor Theory as a Predictor of Self-report Performance Effects", *Personal Psychology*, Summer 1971, pp. 293-303.

4. Ford, Robert N. *Motivation Through the Work Itself*, New York, American Management Association, 1969.

5. Hackman, J. Richard and Oldham, Greg R., *Work Redesign*, Reading, Mass., Addison Wesley, 1980.

6. Hackman, J. R. and Oldham, G. R., "Motivation through the Design of Work; Test of a Theory" (Tech. Rep. No. 6), New Haven, Conn., Yale University, Department of Administration Sciences, 1974.

7. Waters, L. K., and Waters, Carrie Wherry, "An Empirical Test of Five Versions of the Two-Factor Theory of Job Satisfaction", *Organisational Behaviour and Human Performance*, February 1972, pp. 18-24.

8. Scott, Myers, M., *Every Employee a Manager*, New York, McGraw-Hill, 1970.

9. Nathan A. King, "A Clarification and Evaluation of the Two-Factor Theory of Job Satisfaction", *Psychological Bulletin*, July 1970, p. 18.

10. Paul, W. J. Jr., Robertson, K. B., and Herzberg, F., "Job Enrichment Pays Off", *Harvard Business Review*, March-April, 1969, pp. 61-78.

11. Bockman, Valerie M., "The Herzberg Controversy", *Personnel Psychology*, Summer 1971, pp. 155-189.

12. Vroom, Victor H., *Work Motivation*, New York, John Wiley and Sons, Inc., 1964.

13. Walters, Roy W., and Purdy, Kenneth L., "Job Enrichment Programs", in Heyel, C., ed., *Handbook of Modern Officer Management and Administrative Services*, New York, McGraw-Hill, 1972.

14. Walters, Roy W., *Job Enrichment for Results*, Reading, Mass., Addison Wesley, 1975.

References

[1] See http://www.lib.uwo.ca/programs/general business/herzberg.html; http://www.nytimes.com/2000/02/01/business/f-i-herzberg-76-professor-and-management-consultant.html; See also The Encyclopedia of the History of American Management-MorganWitzel, http://www.siop.org/tip/backissues/TipApril00/31Obituaries/html,16April2001

[2] Herzberg, Frederick, Mausner, Barnard, and Snyderman Barbara Bloch., *The Motivation to Work*, New York, John Wiley and Sons, Inc., 1959; Herzberg, Frederick, *Work and the Nature of Man*, Cleveland, The World Publishing Company, 1966.

[3] Herzberg, Frederick, "One More Time: How Do You Motivate Employees?" *Harvard Business Review*, Vol.46, No.1, Sep.-Oct., 1987, pp.109-120.

[4] http://www.businessballs.com/herzberg.htm (Retrieved on 21st August, 2009)

[5] Ibid.

[6] http://www.netmba.com/mgmt/ob/motivation/herzberg/ (Retrieved on 21st August, 2009)

[7] Herzberg, Frederick, "One More Time: How Do You Motivate Employees?", opp.cit., p.114.

[8] Ibid., pp.116-117. See also Miner, John B., *Organisational Behavior: From Theory to Practice*, Vol. 4, New York, M.E. Sharpe. Inc.,2007. Ch.5.

[9] See http://www.mindtools.com/pages/article/newTMM_74.htm (Retrieved on 21st August, 2009)

[10] http://www.netmba.com/mgmt/ob/motivation/herzberg/ op.cit.

[11] Ibid. See also Luthans, Fred, *Orgnisational Behavior*, New York, McGraw-Hill Book Company, 1977, pp.411-413

[12] http://en.wikipedia.org/wiki/Two-factor theory (Retrieved on 21st August, 2009)

[13] See http://www.businessballs.com/herzberg.htm, op.cit.

[14] http://en.wikipedia.org/wiki/Two-factor theory, op.cit.

16

RENSIS LIKERT

P. Seshachalam

Introduction

The human relations school in administrative theory was initially developed to counter the effects of "efficiency engineering" through scientific management and the apparent degradation of man as an appendage to the machine. In later years, its scope has been widened to emphasise the importance of people creating, operating and influencing organisations and management processes. This school believes that organisational effectiveness depends upon the quality of relationships *inter se* among people in the organisation and managerial ability lies in developing 'interpersonal competence among members to support collaborative effort at all levels of the organisation'. The scope of behavioural studies extends from individual personality and motivation dynamics to organisation culture and climate and their impact on work performance, job satisfaction

(1903-1981)

and organisation effectiveness and development. Likert's 'Management Systems I-IV' represents a major breakthrough in the researches in this field. He is known for his studies on organisation and analysis of management styles. He developed Likert's Scale as part of his thesis work to measure attitudes and the Linking Pin Model.

Life and Works

Rensis Likert (1903-1981), an American organisational psychologist, educator and management theorist, was born in Cheyenne, Wyoming. He received B.A. in sociology from the University of Michigan, Ann Arbor (1926) and Ph.D (1932) from Columbia University. He started his teaching career as an Instructor at New York University, became assistant professor in 1935 and spent a year (1935-36) on the faculty of Sarah Lawrence College in Bronxville, New York. He worked as Head, Division of Program Surveys, Bureau of Agricultural Economics in the U.S.

Department of Agriculture, Washington, D.C, Research Director for Life Insurance Agency Management Association (1935-39) and Director of the Morale Division of the U.S. Strategic Bombing Survey (1944-1946) during World War II. He worked as Professor of Psychology and Sociology at the University of Michigan during 1946-1970. At Michigan, he founded the Survey Research Centre in 1946 which evolved into the Institute for Social Research with him as the Director. After retirement he became Director Emeritus. In 1971, he formed Rensis Likert Associates in Ann Arbor and continued his studies and consultancy relating to management systems and styles in numerous corporations.[1]

Research on Management Practices

Likert and his associates carried out extensive research on management practices in American business and government. The comprehensive studies conducted by a team of about 40 researchers over a period of twenty-five years at a cost of $15 millions compare favorably with the famous Hawthorne studies. They were conducted in a wide variety of situations like industrial and commercial firms, railways, hospitals, schools and voluntary organisations and covered unskilled workers in factories to top scientists in research laboratories. His major works include *New Patterns of Management; The Human Organisation;* and *New Ways of Managing Conflict.*[2] His books were extremely popular in Japan and their impact can be seen across modern Japanese organisations.

Likert was actively associated with the National Academy of Public Administration, American Psychological Association and American Statistical Association. He received the Paul D. Converse Award from the University of Illinois, James A. Hamilton Award and awards from the Organisation Development Council, McKinsey Foundation, Society for the Advancement of Management, Professional Achievement Award from the American Board of Examiners of Professional Psychologists and Outstanding Achievement Awards from the American Society for Training and Development and the American Association for Public Opinion Research. [3]

Likert, through his wide-ranging research identified the forces accelerating the pressure for high performance in American business organisations. Some of the forces listed by him include[4] growing competition from the industrially developed countries for world markets; resistance to pressure and close supervision and rising trend towards giving the individual more freedom and initiative; significant increase in the educational level of labour force and consequent change in employee attitudes and expectations of participative styles; increasing concern for the mental health and fulfillment of the personality needs of emotionally mature persons in business and government organisations; and increasing need for more complex systems of organising human efforts to meet the demands of more complex technologies and larger and diverse enterprises. Likert believed that the body of knowledge of social sciences can pave the way to frame a generalised theory of organisation and management. He propounds three distinctive concepts pertaining to supervision, management systems, and dynamics of interpersonal relationships.

Supervisory Styles

Recognising the climate for better performance, Likert and his associates explored the characteristics of high performance units as contrasted to low performance units. They addressed questions such as,[5] Why do some managers get better results than others? What do effective managers do that dissipative managers do not? How to measure effectiveness of a manager? What criteria exist or can be developed to measure results? Are objective and factual measures reliable or are they misleading? Likert classifies supervisors into two categories viz., job-centered and employee-centered. The primary concern of the first category of supervisors is to ensure performance of assigned tasks and maintenance of prescribed standards. The characteristics of such supervisors are that they:[6]

- exert heavy pressure to get work done;
- have little confidence in the subordinates;
- exercise close and detailed supervision;
- allow little freedom to subordinates; and
- are punitive and critical when mistakes occur.

On the other hand, the supervisors in the second category are primarily concerned with the human aspects of their subordinates and effective team building for high task performance. The characteristics of supervisors in this category[7] are that they:

- exert little pressure on subordinates;
- earn and get the confidence and trust of their subordinates;
- increase the achievement motivation of subordinates and encourage them to accept high performance goals through group decision processes;
- exercise general rather than detailed supervision, and allow subordinates to schedule their own pace of work; and
- help subordinates when mistakes and problems occur.

Even if the characteristics of high and low performing managers can be identified, it will still be necessary to ascertain whether such characteristics are the cause or effect of their work environment. It is argued that high performing managers are humane to their subordinates, and low performing managers are compelled to get tough with their subordinates to achieve better results. To resolve this dilemma, Likert and his colleagues conducted a series of experiments in which high and low performing managers were changed into each other's jobs. While high performing managers succeeded in improving the performance of low production units, low performing managers placed in high production units brought down their output over a span of time.

Likert underlines the time factor in managing change. Heavy pressure exerted by supervisors may produce good results for a short while. But group performance is bound to go down with increasing resentment against the sustained exercise of authority. On the other hand, moulding employee attitudes for positive achievement of organisational goals through effective team building will take some time before making any impact on group performance. Either process is likely to take about two years.

Likert recognises that effective supervision is an adaptive and relative process. It needs constant adaptation to the background values, expectations and interpersonal skills between subordinates, peers and superiors. It is relative to the situation. His concept of leadership comes close to that of Mary Parker Follett. He quotes Jenkins approvingly in this regard:[8]

"Leadership is specific to the particular situation under investigation. Who becomes the leader of a given group engaged in a particular activity or leadership characteristics in a given case are functions of the specific situation including the measuring instruments employed. Related to this conclusion is the general finding of wide variations in the characteristics of individuals who become leaders in similar situations and even greater divergence in leadership behaviour in different situations".

Supportive Relationships

Based on his assessment of managers of high performance, Likert postulated his principle of supportive relationships as an organising concept. He states: [9] "The leadership and other processes of the organisation must be such as to ensure a maximum probability in all interactions and all relationships with the organisation. Each member will, in the light of his background, values and expectations, view the experience as supportive and one which builds and maintains his sense of personal worth and importance". He conceives of an interaction-influence system to maximise skills, resources and motivation of individuals at different levels of the organisation. Such a system would facilitate integration of organisational and managerial processes such as coordination, communication, decision-making, direction, etc. The effectiveness of these interdependent processes rests on the efficacy of the interaction-influence system and in turn determines the capacity of the organisation to optimise the skills, abilities and resources of individuals and workgroups. According to Likert, an organisation operating on an ideal interaction-influence system will reveal some of the following characteristics:[10]

- Each member will find his personal values, needs and goals reflected in those of the workgroups and organisation as a whole;

- Every member of the organisation would be identified with the objectives of organisation and the goals of his workgroup and see the accomplishment of them as the best way to meet his own needs and personal goals;

- Pressures for high performance goals, efficient methods, and skill development come from the members themselves. The anxieties associated with hierarchical pressures in traditional organisations will be conspicuous by their absence;

- Authentic and sensitive communication processes within and between workgroups would ensure spontaneous and accurate information flows to providing rational basis for individual and group decisions and actions at all points in the organisation;

- Every member of the organisation will be able to exert his influence on decisions and actions of the organisation. The amount of influence exerted by any individual will be proportionate to the significance of his ideas and contributions and not necessarily related to his position in the formal organisation; and

- Cooperative motivation, communication and decision processes will enable each member in any part of the organisation to exert his influence, contribute his ideas, skills, resources and improve the total capacity of the organisation for problem-solving and goal-fulfillment.

It is important to recognise that the ideal interaction-influence system of the kind envisaged by Likert is a far cry in the traditional hierarchical organisations. The conventional one-to-one relationships between superiors and subordinates can hardly be expected to be the breeding ground for the development of optimal interaction between members of the organisation. Further, one-way top-down communication and exertion of influence from above and minimal opportunities for upward and horizontal communication precludes development of well-knit work-groups and cross-fertilisation of ideas, skills and resources for effective problem solving in traditional organisations.

Linking Pin Model

The Linking Pin Model or organisation structure conceived by Likert is expected to remove the hurdles found in traditional hierarchies and facilitate the growth of interaction-influence system. The salient feature of his model is that each individual in the organisation has twin roles in two overlapping groups as shown in chart 1. He is a member of a higher-level group and leader of a lower-level group. Group functions and processes become far more important than individual roles in this model. They grow upwards from the organisational base in sharp contrast to top-down management of classical organisation.

Chart 1: Linking Pin

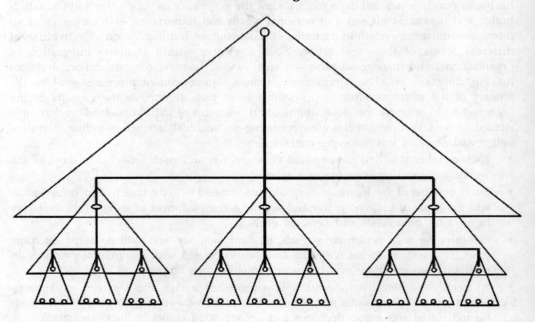

Source: Rensis Likert, *New Patterns of Management, p.105*

In developing his model Likert reinforces the upward orientation with horizontal linkages. He illustrates with examples of (a) subordinates serving as linking pin for horizontal coordination, (b) vertical overlapping group linkages of line and staff departments, (c) vertical overlapping linkages of product departments, and (d) multiple-overlapping group structures with horizontal as well as vertical linkages.[11] Emphasis on processes within a functional group needs to be distinguished from mindless superfluous multiplication of committees, as adjunct to the staff line organisation. No overlapping workgroups should exist than are absolutely necessary to perform the linking process. Meaningfully exploited, multiple linkages provide additional channels to share information and influence. They become the link pins to hold the organisation together.

Management Systems 1-4

The most important contribution of Likert lies in his conceptualisation of different systems of management along a continuum. He identifies four distinct points along the continuum for purpose of illustration of the characteristics of each of the management systems. He labels these points as exploitative-authoritative, benevolent-authoritative, consultative, and participative.[12] However, he did not see them as isolated categories but as blending into one another with many intermediate patterns along the continuum. The four management systems are arrayed along the two important dimensions. The first is the type of authority or control an organisation exercises over its members. The second relates to the operating characteristics of the organisation and the motivational forces used to control and coordinate the activity of the people in the system and the kinds of attitudinal responses evoked from them. The operating characteristics include leadership, motivation, communication, interaction, influence, decision-making, goal setting, goal performance and control analysed. Such operating characteristics are juxtaposed over the four types of the management systems.[13]

Likert brought a new dimension to organisational development theory. Likert's four systems of management describe the relationship, involvement and roles between management and subordinates in industrial settings. The four systems are a result of the study undertaken with the high productive supervisors and their team of an American Insurance Company. Later on, he and Jane G. Likert revised the systems to apply to educational settings. Likert delineated the characteristics of high and low-performing organisations and identified the problems with traditional organisational structures. Likert emphasised a management style in which people are likely to implement the decisions if they had a role in their making. This theory supports the idea that the key to positive interaction consists of maintaining an individual's self worth and importance. Working towards organisational objectives can help individuals realise their personal goals.

Exploitive-authoritative System - 1

Likert's first system is characterised by goal setting and decision-making by the top management and communications flow downwards. The subordinates do not participate in the decision- making process. In this management system the subordinates are not trusted by the management and the employee's job is to abide by the decisions of the managers. The organisation is concerned only about completing the work. It uses fear and threats and sporadic rewards to make employees complete the work assigned. There is no teamwork involved.

Benevolent-authoritative System - 2

As in the exploitive-authoritative system, decisions are made at the top of the organisation and management. Employees, however, are motivated through rewards for their contributions rather than fear and threats. Information flows from subordinates to managers but it is restricted to what management wants. The system is based on master-servant relationships between management and employees. More rewards are given than in System 1. There is slightly better upward communication and employees are given marginal autonomy.

Consultative System - 3

In this management system, the employees are consulted by management before taking decisions and their involvement in the decisional process exists. Though the management takes the major decisions, there is a greater flow of information than in a benevolent-authoritative system from subordinates to management. Though upward communication is encouraged, employees are cautious not to send unfavorable information. In this system, managers partly trust subordinates, use both rewards and involvement of employees to inspire motivation, foster a higher level of responsibility for meeting goals and inspire a moderate amount of teamwork.

Participative System - 4

Participative management systems are characterised by complete confidence and trust in their employees, open communication flows and the employee participation in the decision process.

Subordinates freely express their views and teamwork exists. There is collective responsibility for meeting organisational goals and objectives and collaborative teamwork exists. Employees are offered rewards for achieving collectively determined goals.

System 4 is considered to be the most productive and ideal. When combined with good management and achievable goals, this system is expected to result in better production, higher motivation, and more profit than the other systems. Likert favoured System 4, because of its commitment to giving the decision-making power to the employees who are trusted by the management and do not hesitate to share feedback and opinions. It is to each employee's advantage to share expertise and information that could help others in the organisation. The three basic concepts of Likert's System 4 are the principle of supportive relationships, group decision-making and methods of supervision, and high performance goals for the organisation.

Likert points out that the component parts of the management system should be internally consistent with the overall pattern and philosophy of the organisation. Thus, an exploitative-authoritative system displays a steep hierarchical structure, centralised decision-making, top-down communication, tight supervision, man to man rather than group to group relations, performance under pressure, and low degree of employee motivation. On the other hand, the participative management system displays overlapping structures, cross-functional linkages, group decision processes, open and authentic three-way communication (up, down and lateral), adaptive supervision and individual and workgroups with a high degree of achievement motivation (Systems 1 & 4).

The intermediate forms of management Systems 2 and 3 reveal transitory characteristics of progression from management System 1 and 4 over a period. In System-2, management orientation is still authoritative, but becomes less exploitative and more benevolent towards the members of the organisation. In System-3, exercise of authority is broad based with delegation of power to middle levels and consultations with affected interests at lower levels. To the extent motivation, communication and involvement of subordinates replace reliance on exercise of formal authority; consultative management systems will be well set to move forward to the Management Systems 4.

After describing the salient features of his four systems of management deduced from the empirical research, Likert is somewhat equivocal in stating that the operational characteristics of one system cannot be grafted abruptly to another. Illustrating the management systems further he states that in an authoritative system decisions are taken at the top and the organisation requires more number of dependents than leaders. On the other hand, in a participative system, decision-making is decentralised and requires emotionally stable persons and a large number of leaders. Each form of organisation to function at its best requires individuals and skills of interaction on the part of leaders and follows to suit the particular system. And again each system tends to produce and perpetuate people to function effectively within the system. In each system communication and motivation processes will be tailor-made to fit their unique decision-making style. Any attempt to switch processes of one system abruptly to the other is bound to impair the total system's effectiveness. Nevertheless, Likert pleads for a gradual change from System 1 to System 4.

Likert marshals empirical evidence to show the prevalence of Systems 1 and 2 management practices in low performance units, and Systems 3 and 4 management practices in high performance units. Even if the former occasionally produce high performance, such performance is short lived. On the other hand, the latter ensures high level of performance over fairly longer periods. Further, the high level performance achieved by System-1 management is generally under considerable stress and strain contributing to deterioration if not breakdown, in employee morale. On the contrary, the high level performance realised by System-4 management is under more durable conditions of achievement motivation of individuals leading to their self-actualisation. Why do most organisations fail to recognise the advantages of management Systems 3 and 4 and persist with system 1 and 2 practices? To Likert, it is mainly because of the widely prevalent notion among managers that consultative and participative methods can be used only after high performance has been achieved. Therefore, top managements have a tendency to persist in System 1 and 2 practices.

Likert finds fault with the prevailing accounting methods and measures of efficiency rating purely in terms of financial costs, profits and turnovers. He feels that the costs of running the most important asset of organisation - its managers and workers - are equally important. He emphasises the need to recognise the monetary value of human resources in organisations. Good managers and workers joining or leaving organisation should be considered as increasing or decreasing the assets of that organisation. Therefore, in calculating the value of human resources, Likert suggests that the variables like level of intelligence and aptitude, communications and control, level of motivation, capacity to achieve coordination, capacity to use experience to introduce innovations, etc., should be taken into account.[14] The cost of training is conventionally regarded as avoidable and its value in human asset building is not fully appreciated. Likert, therefore, pleads for better methods of accounting total cost and total assets of an organisation.

Science-based Management

Likert suggests on the need to monitor the state of the organisation and its internal management system at periodic intervals or stages of growth. He proposes a scheme of evaluation for the causal, intervening and end-result variable, affecting organisational climate and performance. He claims that social sciences, using the methods of mathematics and statistics, can develop methodologies for measurement of the state of human resource and predict the cause and effect of intervening variables. But socio-metric measurements of casual, intervening and end-result variables may not always establish reliable relationships to provide firm basis for management action. Explicating the relationships between casual, intervening and end-result variables, Likert postulates two hypotheses relating to the Management Systems 1, 2 and 4.[15] The first hypothesis is that if a manager has well organised plan of operation, high performance goals, high technical competence and if the manager manages by System 1 or 2, using direct hierarchical pressures, his organisation will display less group loyalty, lower performance, greater conflict, less cooperation, less technical assistance to peers, greater feelings of unreasonable pressure, less favourable attitudes towards manager and lower motivation to produce. Such organisations will attain lower sales volume, higher sales costs, and lower quality of business sold and lower earnings. The second hypothesis is that if the manager manages by System-4 using the principles of supportive relationships, group methods of supervision and other principles the organisation will display greater group loyalty, higher performance, greater cooperation, more technical assistance to peers, less feeling of unreasonable pressure, more favourable attitudes towards manager, and higher motivation to produce. Such organisations will attain higher business sales volume, lower sales costs, higher quality of business sold, and higher earnings.

Likert tested these hypotheses through research and confirmed the effects of changes in causal variables on intervening variables and end-result variables.

The science-based management has its appeal to social scientists but managerial action in practice is guided more by organisation, history, experience, perceptions and perspectives. Most practicing managers have neither the time nor inclination to undertake analytical exercises or at least document their experiences of critical phases in organisation life. External research, training and consulting agencies can aid the managements in this task. But they will have their own problems of hindsight or foresight and the analytical tools they bring to their analysis may be inadequate, if not unreliable. The importance of the role of scientific management theories, concepts and practices, lies in further research and perfection of analytical tools and training methodologies.

Applications of System-4

Research and experimental studies conducted in a variety of organisations have convinced Likert about the validity of System-4 management for realising high performance goals. He visualises the possibility of all organisations practicing System 1, 2 and 3 eventually shifting to System-4. Likert opines that his System-4 model provides a useful framework to guide all types of organisation development efforts.[16] He feels that uncoordinated and piecemeal efforts such as team building, job enrichment, sensitivity training, participative decision-making and management by objectives will not pay high dividends unless they are integrated into an overall strategy of changing the management system. To guide the efforts of human resource development, the management system should possess the following characteristics:[17]

- The system should have been discovered by rigorous, quantitative research. This research should have demonstrated that the model management system yields the best performance and other desirable results in most working situations;

- It should be possible to define the management system by means of a limited number of measurable dimensions;

- Such dimensions should have closer relationships to end-result variables such as productivity and employee satisfaction than other organisational dimensions;

- Efficient procedures and instruments to measure these key organisational dimensions should be available; and

- There should be ample research findings to show that as organisations shift towards the management system, there is a corresponding improvement in performance and other desired outcomes. The research should demonstrate that these results occur in different kinds of industries and work situations.

Likert claims that his System-4 model fulfills all the above specifications. It has been defined by a limited number of key human organisational dimensions. These dimensions have been identified after extensive research and were found to be correlated with performance across a wide variety of organisations. Efficient instruments are available to measure the key dimensions of any human organisations. A sizable number of studies in different kinds of work situations have found that as organisations shift closer to System-4, there is a corresponding improvement in performance and increase in other desired results. To Likert, another useful aspect of the System 1-4 models for human resources development purposes is the recognition that certain human organisational dimensions are causal in character. Causal variables are those which are capable of being influenced or altered by the leadership and which, when altered, produce corresponding changes in the intervening variables and, in turn, in the results that the organisation achieves.

Using survey feedback method, Likert proposes an organisational improvement cycle comprising of five steps.[18] They are:

- Establishing an ideal model (System 4);
- Measuring the organisation's scores on key dimensions of ideal model;
- Analysing and interpreting scores based on their relationship to the ideal model and preparing diagnosis of organisational strengths and weaknesses;
- Based on this diagnosis, preparing an action plan to build on strengths and correct weaknesses concerning structure, leader and subordinate behaviour, organisational climate; and
- Implementation of the action plan.

Likert lays down guidelines for using the proposed organisational improvement cycle. They are:[19]

- Focus the action efforts on the causal variables, such as leadership behaviour and structure. Do not try to change by direct action the intervening variables such as motivation and control. If the causal variables are improved, there will be subsequent improvements in the intervening variables;
- Move from System 1 to 4 gradually and do not attempt one big jump as both leaders and members of the organisation lack the skills for interaction and adaptation and many find it difficult to make a sudden, sizable shift from System 1 to 4.
- Involve those whose behaviour has to be changed to bring the desired improvement, in planning the action to be taken. Involve all the persons affected in all the steps of the improvement cycle;
- Use objective, impersonal evidence as much as possible in the action planning process;
- As far as possible, ensure the initiative and active participation of those in the most powerful and influential positions in the improvement programme; and
- Conduct the action planning in a supportive, helpful atmosphere.

The guidelines have utility for the application of System-4 concept of organisation improvements. However, Likert was conscious of the problems involved in adapting System-4 to all organisations. This is clear when he says that differences in the kind of work, in the traditions of the industry and in the skills and values of the employees of a particular organisation require quite different procedures and ways to apply appropriately the basic principles of System-4 management.[20] Actual realisation of System-4 conditions of management, therefore, depends on the complex interplay of factors and forces at work in real organisation life.

Managing Conflicts

In his search to evolve new patterns of management based on cooperative and supportive relationships, Likert focused attention on new ways of managing conflict. For, in the capitalist mode of production conflict is inherent in management-worker relations and manifests in several forms. Likert himself refers to the nature of this conflict when he states that "There is ample evidence in the mass media and elsewhere that bitter, unresolved conflict is widespread and increasing in frequency. It occurs at all levels of society; among nations and within nations, among organisations and within them". Likert defines conflict, 'as the active striving for one's own preferred outcome, which if attained, precludes the attainment by other of their own preferred outcome, thereby producing hostility'.[21] He differentiates two kinds of conflicts - substantive and affective. Substantive conflict is rooted in the substance of the task and affective conflict is derived from the emotional, affective aspects of interpersonal relations. Likert considers methods to handle substantive conflict even in situation where the presence of affective conflict makes this task more difficult. The widely prevalent win-lose strategies of conflict resolution in organisations distort the perceptions of individual and groups, maintain a polarised adversary orientation at all times and escalate the costs of chronically defeated groups to organisations. In conflict situations, leadership migrates to the aggressive, relegating the emotionally mature to the background.[22]

An Evaluation

The central features of System-4 viz., supportive relationships, group methods of decision-making and supervision, high performance goals and achievement motivation contribute to better forms of human organisation. It is only to be hoped that human organisations will move increasingly towards this ideal-rational system of management. The linking pin model is often accused of doing nothing more than drawing triangles around the traditional hierarchical structures. It is also criticised as slowing down the process of decision-making.[23] Notwithstanding these criticisms, the linking pin model has its own advantages. It fosters the upward and horizontal linkage in contrast to the only downward orientation of classical structure and strengthens the cross-functional linkages in complex organisations. But the questions are: How do we push the Management Systems 1 and 2 towards 3 to 4? What holds up the transformation of the Management Systems? Why does top management revert to management practices of System 1 and 2 in the face of a crisis? Is crisis management by itself a reflection of the breakdown in supportive relationships, group decision processes and performance goals? If that be so, is System-4 management fallible? How can one ensure the evolution and enduring success of System-4 management? Can organisation systems and management practices be isolated from the cultural constraints and social values? If social organisation is hierarchical and its orientation is authoritarian, will it not also permeate organisation structures and management processes? So long as the power dominates modern organisations, participative management remains in the realm of utopia. Again if conflict is inherent in the competing values, needs and expectations of individuals and groups in organisations, how does one realise the supportive relationships and other desirable features of System-4 management?

Despite criticisms, Likert pins his faith in System-4 leadership and interaction-influence networks to diffuse conflict situations and replace win-lose strategies of conflict resolution by win-win strategies, wherein all parties to conflict stand to gain leaving no one frustrated and embittered. System-4 structures and processes help to de-emphasise status, depersonalise problem-solving and use power to resolve conflict constructively instead of suppressing them.[24] The System-4 concepts hold out prospects of development of advanced forms of human organisation. Some critics may underplay the importance of 'new patterns of management' as little more than summary of good management practices. But Likert's most important contribution to management thought and practice is his systematic analysis of good management practices and extending their frontiers of knowledge and application. He earned his place among management thinkers and researches for laying the empirical foundations for the development of management science.

In Brief

Likert's contribution may be summarised as:

- Rensis Likert (1903-1981), an American organisational psychologist, educator and management theorist is known for his studies on organisation and management styles.

- Making detailed study of supervisory styles, Likert classified supervisors into two categories viz., job-centered and employee-centered. The job-centered supervisor's focus is to ensure the performance of assigned tasks and maintenance of prescribed standards and employee-centered supervisor is more concerned with human aspects of their subordinates and effective team building for high task performance. He recognises that the effective supervision is an adaptive and a relative process.

- Likert postulates supportive relationships as a contributing factor of high performance of management. He conceives of an interaction-influence system to maximise skills, resources and motivation of individuals at different levels of organisation and elaborates the characteristics of the system.

- To overcome the difficulties of traditional system and to facilitate the growth interaction-influence system, Likert suggested Linking Pin Model. In this model each individual in the organisation has twin roles in two overlapping groups.

- The most important contribution of Likert is the conceptualisation of different systems of management along a continuum as "Management Systems 1-4". He labels them as exploitative-authoritative, benevolent-authoritative, consultative and participative. These systems are arranged along the type of authority and operating characteristics.

- Likert considers System 4 as an ideal model of management and suggests applications for transfer of systems from System 1 to System 4. He proposes improvement cycle with elaborate guidelines for the application of organisational improvement. Likert suggested internal management and monitoring systems based on causal, intervening and end result variables.

- In his search to evolve new patterns of management based on cooperative and supportive relationships, Likert focused attention on new ways of managing conflict.

- Management systems model of Likert is criticised for lack of contextual sensitivity. His linking pin model is often accused of doing nothing more than drawing triangles around the traditional hierarchical structures and slowing down the process.

- Likert's most important contribution to management thought and practice is his systematic analysis of good management and extending their frontiers of knowledge and application.

Notes and References

1 See http://www.bookrags.com/biography/ rensis-likert-soc/ and http://en.wikipedia.org/wiki/Rensis_Likert

2 Likert, Rensis, Likert, Jane Gibson, *New Ways of Managing Conflicts*, New York, McGraw-Hill Book Co., 1976.

3 See http://www.bookrags.com/biography/ rensis-likert-soc/

4 See Likert, Rensis, *New Patterns of Management*, New York, McGraw-Hill Book Co; 1961, pp. 1-3.

5 See Pollard, Harold. R., *Developments in Management Thought*, London, Heinemann, 1974, p. 236.

6 Ibid., p. 239.

7 Ibid., pp. 239-240.

8 Jenkins, W. O., "A Review of Leadership Studies with Particular Reference to Military Problems", *Psychology Bulletin*, 44 (1), pp. 54-79; Quoted in Likert, Rensis, *New Patterns of Management*, op. cit., p. 90.

9 Ibid., p. 103.

10 Ibid., pp. 181-183.

11 See Likert, Rensis, *The Human Organisation: Its Management and Value*, New York, McGraw-Hill Book Co., 1967, pp. 164-69.

[12] See Likert, Rensis, *New Patterns of Management*, op. cit., pp.222-236.

[13] Likert has constantly refined the operating characteristics of the four management systems. This is reflected in the development of questionnaires incorporated in his successive publications.

[14] Likert, Rensis, *The Human Organisation: Its Management and Value*, op. cit., p. 148.

[15] See Pollard, Harold. R., *Further Developments in Management Thought*, London, Heinemann, 1978, p. 168.

[16] See Likert, Rensis, "An Improvement Cycle for Human Resource Development", *Training and Development Journal*, July, 1978, Vol.32.No.7.pp.16-18.

[17] Ibid., pp. 16-17.

[18] Ibid., p. 17.

[19] Ibid., pp. 17-18.

[20] Likert, Rensis, *The Human Organisation: Its Management and Value*, op. cit., p. 192.

[21] Likert, Rensis, Likert, J. C., *New Ways of Managing Conflicts*, op. cit., pp. 7-8.

[22] Ibid., pp. 56-69.

[23] Luthans, Fred, *Organisational Behaviour*, New York, McGraw-Hill Company, 1973, pp. 155-156.

[24] Likert, Rensis, Likert, Jane Gibson, *New Ways of Managing Conflicts*, op. cit., pp. 107-57, 269-86.

17

FRED W. RIGGS

V.S. Prasad
K. Murali Manohar

Introduction

The dynamics of post war modernisation and development became more complex with the emergence of the concept of welfare state and consequential expansion in the functions and responsibilities of the state. This was compounded by the changing nature of science, communications and technology. In this context, public administration has a crucial role to play. Development and modernisation of society, and the efficiency of the government, to a large extent, depends on the capacity of the administrative system and its ability to make and implement policies and plans. The administrative theories and models acquire significance in this context. It was assumed that transfer of administrative models of developed countries, with few modifications, would meet the demand. But soon it was realised that such approach was defective and needed more appropriate models to meet the emerging

(1917-2008)

development challenges of the new nations. Fred Riggs, who developed analytical models and approaches to study public administration in a comparative perspective, is a pioneer in this field and occupies a very prominent place in administrative model building.

Life and Works

Fred Warren Riggs (1917-2008), born in Kuling, China, initially went to the University of Nanking, China (1934-35). Later he went to the United States to study journalism and political science to become a foreign correspondence which was thwarted due to economic depression. He obtained BA from the University of Illinois (1938), MA from Fletcher School of Law and Diplomacy (1941) and Ph.D in Political Science from Columbia University (1948). Riggs started his academic career as a lecturer in the City University of New York (1947-48) and moved on to hold important positions at several leading institutions. He worked as Research Associate, Foreign Policy Association (1948-1951), Assistant to Director, Public Administration Clearing House, New York (1951-55), Arthur F. Bentley Professor of Government, Indiana University (1956-1967), Director, Social Science Research Institute, University of Hawaii (1970-73), Professor of Political Science, University of Hawaii (1967-1987) and after retirement as Professor Emeritus, University of Hawaii until his death in 2008. Riggs worked as Visiting Professor at the City University of New York (1974-75), Institute for Social Studies, The Hague (1972), Massachusetts Institute of Technology (1965-66), University of the Philippines (1958-59), Visiting Lecturer, National Officials Training Institute, Korea (1956), and Yale University (1955-56).

Riggs received several honours and awards including Dwight Waldo Award for Lifetime Achievements in Public Administration, American Society for Public Administration (1991), Order of the White Elephant by the King of Thailand, Bangkok (1983), Fellow, Center for Advanced Study in the Behavioural Sciences, Stanford (1966-67) and Senior Specialist, East-West Center, University of Hawaii (1962-1963). Riggs was associated with several professional organisations including American Society for Public Administration, National Academy of Public Administration, International Political Science Association, International Sociological Association, American Political Science Association, Association for Asian Studies, International Institute for Terminology Research, Society for Comparative Research, etc., He chaired several committees and working groups relating to social sciences including Comparative Administration Group, American Society for Public Administration (1960-1971) and was member of editorial boards of Public Administration Review and various other journals at different points of times.[1] Riggs published a number of books and papers[2] and his writings were translated into many languages including Italian, French, Korean, Portuguese, Russian, and Spanish. He lectured in every continent. As Heady has observed 'mere acquaintance with all his writings (on comparative theory) is in itself not an insignificant accomplishment'.[3] Riggs' creative scholarship in the field of comparative public administration brought him worldwide recognition and he contributed to the development of public administration in India, Indonesia, Korea, the Philippines, Taiwan, and Thailand.

Model Building

Administrative theories and models, mostly developed before the Second World War, were generally the offshoot of industrial revolution. These theories originated in the western countries, mainly in the United States of America. The developing countries of Asia, Africa and Latin America, which adopted western administrative models, found the models developed in particular environments to suit particular systems were not useful and valid for all systems. The models were found to be more suitable to maintain the existing systems than for changing the systems, which is the priority task of all developing nations. These models and theories also failed to help in understanding the administrative systems in the developing countries. It is in this context that the need for developing new concepts arose and the result is the emergence of the concept of comparative public administration, which emphasised on cross-cultural and cross-national administrative studies. In the study of comparative public administration Riggs identified three broad trends, viz., normative to empirical, ideographic to nomathetic, and non-ecological to ecological. The major focus of an empirical study is to arrive at inferences on the basis of extensive field study instead of normative descriptions. Ideographic approach concentrates on the 'unique cases or case study' of a single agency or country. On the other hand, the nomathetic approach seeks generalisation, laws, hypotheses that assert regularity of behaviour and correlations with variables.[4] Further, Riggs emphasised the need to study administrative systems in an ecological perspective so as to gain a comprehensive and a in- depth understanding of the administrative dynamics.

Riggs depended on the concepts developed in other subjects to explain the ecology of public administration. He borrowed concepts from sociology, physics, and biology to propose new theories and models in public administration. He also extensively borrowed a number of new words from other subjects, apart from coining a few to convey his ideas. That is why it is aptly said that the terms used by Riggs to explain his models are peculiarly Riggsian. Riggs used three important analytical tools to explain his administrative theories, viz., ecological approach, structural-functional approach and ideal models.

Ecological Approach

Administration and its environment influence each other and an understanding of the dynamics of this process is necessary to understand administration. This approach is termed ecological, a term borrowed from biology. It deals with the science concerned with the interrelationship of organisms and their environment.[5] It is concerned with the interplay of living organisms and their physical and social environment and how organisms and environment are kept in balance for survival and other important objectives. The ecology of public administration, being the interaction of administration and its environment, requires a deeper understanding of the society and the various factors affecting its functioning. The ecological approach in the study of public administration was initiated by Gaus,[6] Robert A. Dhal[7] and Robert A. Merton[8] long before Riggs. But it was Riggs who made a distinctive contribution to this approach.[9] 'Ecology of public administration', according to J. M. Gaus, includes the study of 'people, area or property, physical and social technology wants of the people, thoughts, individuality and emergency conditions'.[10] Developing the concept further, Riggs analysed the relationship between the administration and economic, social, technological, political and communication factors in a larger perspective. He explained illustratively how environmental conditions influence administrative system, on the basis of his studies in Thailand and Philippines.[11]

Structural-Functional Approach

In analysing the administrative systems from the ecological point of view, Riggs mainly used structural-functional approach. Talcott Parsons, Robert Merton, Almond, etc., are the other thinkers who adopted this approach in their works.[12] This approach envisages that in every society certain important functions have to be carried out by a number of structures with the application of certain specified methods. Structures may mean the administrative or other mechanisms by which the functions are discharged. Thus, the structural-functional approach is a method of analysing the functions that are carried out in a society, the structures that are responsible to discharge the functions and the methods that are adopted in undertaking the functions. According to Riggs, in every society five important types of functions are discharged viz., economic, social, communication, symbolic and political.[13] The same set of functional requisites applies to an administrative sub-system in which various structures carry out a number of functions in a specified manner. A study of these structures, functions and methods to understand the phenomena is the structural-functional approach.

Ideal Models

Riggs developed ideal models to analyse the administrative systems of developing countries. Models are useful in the development of public administration as a subject from the normative to empirical study. Riggs first used his much-published models in 1956, by classifying the societies into Agraria and Industria, i.e., agricultural and industrial societies. These models were developed keeping in view the societies of Imperial China and the United States of America. To him all societies transform from Agraria to Industria at a given point. Riggs identified the structural features of Agraria and Industria.[14] They are:

Agraria	Industria
1. Ascriptive values	Achievement norms
2. Particularistic	Universal
3. Diffuse pattern	Specificity
4. Limited social and spatial mobility	Higher social and spatial mobility
5. Simple and stable occupational differences	Well developed occupational patterns
6. Existence of differential stratification system	Existence of egalitarian class system

Riggs developed an equilibrium model named 'transitia' representing the transforming societies in 1957. The 'transitia' represents the transitional stage between Agraria and Industria and possesses the characteristics of both Agraria and Industria. But Agraria-Industria was criticised as having many limitations which are briefly summarised as follows:[15]

- The typology is not helpful in studying the transitional societies, i.e., those societies which are moving from the agrarian to the industrial stage;

- The system does not provide sufficient mechanism to analyse mixed societies, since modern societies always have some agrarian features;

- The typology assumes a unidirectional movement from agraria to industria; and

- The models give very little emphasis to the analysis of the environment of the administrative system.

Responding to these limitations and criticisms, Riggs developed another set of models, discarding old ones, to analyse the administrative systems in developing countries. The fused-prismatic-diffracted model is the result of this effort. The ideal models of Riggs such as fused, prismatic and diffracted are hypothetical assumptions aimed at analysing the pre-historic, developing and developed societies. The process of transition of a ray through a prism is taken symbolically to explain the process of transformation of a society. The starting point of the ray is termed as fused, the process of internal vibration of the ray within the prism is called prismatic and finally when the rays come out of the prism it gets diffracted to project a rainbow and this process is called diffraction. On the same analogy, various social systems in the early stages of development would be fused, in the transitional stage prismatic, and finally, at the end they would be in a complete diffracted stage as explained by Riggs.

Riggs created models on the basis of structural and functional approach. Accordingly, in a fused society a single structure carries out various functions. Contrary to this, in a diffracted society separate structures are created to carry out specific functions. But between these two there exist a number of societies, in which the characteristics of both fused and diffracted societies exist side by side. These are called prismatic societies. However, Riggs emphasises that no society can be exclusively called fused or diffracted; all societies are generally prismatic in nature. The character of every society and their relation to the fused or the diffracted society depends on the nature of its various structures and the functions. Riggs explains this by using a scale given in Fig. 1.

Fig. 1.

X S	T X P	A X
Fused	Prismatic	Diffracted

In fig. 1, the letter X is placed at three positions on the scale to suggest where pure or ideal types of the fused, prismatic and diffracted models might be located. Riggs says: "if we could average the characteristics of real societies, we might be able to place them on the same scale, and I would suggest that traditional Siam might be put where I have placed the letter S, modern Thailand near T. P would represent the Philippines and A, America. Of course, these are speculative guesses and not the result of any exact measurement, but I believe that this method lands itself to quantification".[16] The table indicates the broad characteristics of fused, prismatic and diffracted societies.[17]

Table 1

Fused	Prismatic	Diffracted
Particularism	Selectivism	Universalism
Ascriptive values	Attainment	Achievement
Functionally diffuse	Poly-functionalism	Functional specificity

Riggs attempted to explain various societies by using the concept of 'multi-functionality' of social structures. He termed 'functionally diffuse' societies 'fused' and 'functionally specific 'diffracted'. He further pointed out that an intermediate society between these two extremes is 'prismatic' - his most popular model. These 'fused-prismatic-diffracted' models, Riggs very emphatically said, are designed to be 'ideal' types not to be found in any actual society, but perhaps approximate to some, useful for heuristic purposes and as an aid in the organisation of data.

Riggs further explained his model societies by making use of Parsonian pattern of variables and formed his hypothesis to test and understand various societies. He said that diffracted societies would rank high in terms of universalism and achievement orientation, a fused society high in particularism and ascription, and the prismatic society is characterised as an intermediary between these two by 'selectivism' (scales between universalism and particularism), 'attainment' (stands between achievement and ascription), and poly-functionalism (stands between functional specificity and functional diffuseness). Riggs in his wide-ranging analysis touched on various social, cultural and political sub-systems with a detailed examination of connected issues and problems using a number of models. But his primary interest has been to illuminate administrative problems in transitional or developing societies.[18] In his entire analysis, he made use of the fused and diffracted models as tools to explain the prismatic phenomenon of developing countries.

Fused Model

Riggs selected Imperial China and the pre-revolutionary Siamese Thailand as examples to represent his concept of fused society. These societies have no classification of functions and a single structure carries out a number of functions. These societies heavily depend on agriculture with no industrialisation and modernisation. Their economic system was based on law of exchange and barter system, which Riggs calls as 'redistributive model'. The Royal Family plays a very important role in the administration of the country. The king and the officials nominated by him carry out all the administrative, economic and other activities. No separate structures exist to manage the economic and administrative affairs. The relations between the government and the people are generally at low ebb. People pay respect to the King through service and presentation of material goods, without expecting anything in return. The government is not responsible and accountable to the people though public has an obligation to respect the government.

The family played a prominent role in the Siamese kingdom. It used to carry out a variety of economic, political and social functions. The family apart from providing base on the social structure also stands at the apex of the administration. Influenced by this, the administration in these societies strives to protect the special interests of the family and certain sects rather than aim at universal happiness and development. The administrative system is based on structure of the family and special sects and it continues to help to preserve the system. Generally these societies tend to be static with no developed communication systems. The people would have no demands and never hope to raise any issue with the government. The king and his nominees enjoy the coercive and absolute powers and they generally use their powers to protect their personal interest. These societies do not differentiate between justice and injustice, formal and informal set-ups and governmental and non-governmental activities. Ascriptive values play a predominant role in the society, and the behaviour of the people would be highly traditional. Age-old customs, beliefs, faith and traditional ways of living enable the people to live together and control their behaviour.

Diffracted Model

These societies are based on universalistic principles with no differentiation in treatment. There is a high degree of specialisation and each structure carries out a specialised function. Ascriptive values cease to exist, giving way to the attainment values in the society. The society would be highly dynamic and diffracted. Here exist open class structures represented by various associations, which play a prominent role in achieving rational results in the society. All organisations and structures in the society are created and based on scientific rationale.

The economic system is based on market mechanism. The influence of market has both direct and indirect effect on the other facets of the society. Riggs called it 'marketised society'. Various associations discharge different functions. Communications and technology are highly developed and governments give top priority to maintain cordial public relations. Governments would be responsive to the needs of the people and protect human rights. People would bring pressure on the government to get their things done and control its behaviour to a great extent. Government officers have no coercive and absolute powers. Public pay attention and give respect to the laws of the nation on their own. This facilitates the government to implement the laws and discharge its responsibilities without any difficulty. There would be a general consensus among the people on all basic aspects of social life.

Prismatic Model

Riggs concentrated all his efforts to explain in detail the prismatic model - the focal point of his models. According to Riggs, the prismatic society is one, which has achieved a certain level of differentiation; specialisation of roles that is necessary for dealing with modern technology, but has failed to integrate these roles. The prismatic society shares the value-patterns of both fused and diffracted societies. Riggs identified three important characteristics in prismatic society viz., heterogeneity, formalism, and overlapping.

Heterogeneity

The existence of a high degree of heterogeneity is the main characteristic of a prismatic society. Heterogeneity refers to 'the simultaneous presence, side by side, of quite different kinds of systems, practices and viewpoints'.[19] Due to the parallel coexistence of a diametrically opposite viewpoints and practices, the social change in a prismatic society would be inconsistence, incomplete and irresponsive. The heterogeneity also extends its Damocle's sword straight on the administrative system.

There are, in a prismatic society, urban areas with 'sophisticated' intellectual class, western style offices and the modern gadgets of administration. There also exist a well-developed communication system, skyscrapers, and specialised agencies to discharge various social, political, economic and technical services. On the other hand, in rural areas, people lead a highly traditional life with no facilities of modern living like use of telephones, refrigerators, etc. The village 'elders' combine various political, administrative, social, economic and religious roles.[20] Heterogeneity exists in all walks of life presenting a paradoxical picture. In the field of education, society pays high premium on the western type of education but equally proves susceptible to traditional gurukulas. Hospitals with all modern facilities giving allopathic treatment coexist with ayurvedic, unani, homoeopathic and naturopathic centres. Such a coexistence of contrasting systems pulling the society in different directions makes it difficult to draw generalisations.

In prismatic societies, political and administrative offices enjoy enormous influence, power and prestige and help in making money. Although equal opportunities exist for all, only some are privileged enough and hope to get the jobs in higher echelons. Those who fail to get jobs would waste no time in forming 'pressure groups' against the government and start agitation on some pretext or the other. Despite the existence of a government duly elected through democratic processes, it would not be in a position to control the people. The people in power would make all efforts to protect their interests and stick to power. Thus, there is always a misunderstanding and misrepresentation of facts giving rise to tensions and instability in the society.

The problem becomes complicated in a poly-communal society where different communities try to pull the society in different directions in furtherance of their own sectional interests. This is evident in almost all the developing countries of Asia, Africa and Latin America. Lack of integration thus forms the basic feature of a prismatic society. All these disparities and differentiations in almost all aspects of life not only influence the working of the administrative system and condition its behaviour but would also create a number of problems to the administration. The ruling class would normally try to protect the interests of 'haves' and ignore the interests of 'have nots', which, according to Riggs, would create a revolutionary atmosphere in society.

Formalism

Formalism refers to 'the extent to which a discrepancy exists between the prescriptive and descriptive, between formal and effective power, between the impression given by the Constitution, laws and regulations, organisation charts and statistics and actual practices and facts of government and society'.[21] In other words, it means the degree of discrepancy or incongruence between the formally prescribed and effectively practiced norms and realities and the existence of discrepancy between the 'stated objectives' and 'real performance'. Greater the discrepancy between the formal and the actual, more the formalism in a system. The fused and diffracted societies have a relatively high degree of realism in comparison to a prismatic society where there is a high degree of formalism.

Though the laws, rules and regulations prescribe the style of functioning of the government officials, there are wide deviations in their actual behaviour. The officers sometimes stick to the rules and sometimes overlook and even violate them. This behaviour is caused by the lack of pressure on the government towards the programme objectives, the weakness of the social power to influence the bureaucratic performance and a great permissiveness for arbitrary administration.[22] Thus, the behaviour of the government officials and bureaucrats would be highly unpredictable, inconsistent and depends on the situational variables. The reasons for such a type of behaviour may be ascribed either to the natural inclination of the employees towards collecting easy money or to the existence of chances for maladministration. Thus, generally formalism in administration paves the way for corruption in society.

Formalism exists in all aspects of social life. Generally the laws relating to social and cultural aspects of life are not respected and adhered to. They exist only in the record rooms of the government, and the government is not serious about their implementation. To quote a few instances in India, prohibition laws are respected more in violation than in observance. The town planning regulations are more violated than observed. Such hypocrisy in social life is generally found to be a rule rather than exception in almost all the developing countries.

While explaining the dimensions of formalism, Riggs also mentions about the constitutional formalism which refers to the gap between the constitutional principles and their actual implementation. This can be found in India. For instance, according to the Constitution, the chief ministers are to be elected by the members of the majority party in the State Assembly and the council of ministers to be chosen by the chief minister. But in practice, in most cases the central party leadership plays a decisive role in these matters.[23] The Constitution legally vests the governance in the hands of elected representatives but in practice the real governmental power and influence are wielded by some individuals or groups outside the Parliament. The Constitution entrusts law-making responsibility to legislators but in reality they spend only a little time in law making. They concentrate more in power politics, ignoring their legislative responsibility. This facilitates the bureaucracy, in the prismatic societies, to play a major role in law making. The bureaucrats even form groups or align themselves with various political leaders, due to the factions within the ruling party or within the Council of Ministers. Thus formalism exists in all aspects of social life in a prismatic society.

Overlapping

Overlapping refers to 'the extent to which formally differentiated structures of a diffracted society coexist with undifferentiated structures of a fused type".[24] In administrative system what is described as administrative behaviour is actually determined by non-administrative criteria i.e., by political, social, religious or other factors.[25] In a fused society, traditional structures perform almost all kinds of functions and the problem of overlapping does not arise, because in such a society whatever is formal is also effective. However, in a prismatic society, although 'new or modern' social structures are created, in essence the old or undifferentiated structures continue to dominate the social system.[26] Though formal recognition is given to new norms and values which are generally associated with diffracted structure, in reality they are paid only lip-sympathy and are overlooked widely in favour of traditional values associated with fused societies. Thus, in a prismatic society, the parliament, the government, offices, market, schools, etc., perform various administrative, political, and economic functions. In reality, their behaviour is governed and influenced by traditional organisations like family, religion, caste, etc. Overlapping in a prismatic society manifests in several noticeable dimensions in various fields and these are conceptualised as nepotism, 'poly-communalism', 'clects', poly-normativism, and lack of consensus and separation of 'authority' from 'control'.[27]

Sala Model: Administrative Sub-System of a Prismatic Society

Prismatic society is characterised by various economic, social, political and administrative sub-systems. Riggs termed the administrative sub-system as 'Sala Model'. In a differentiated society its counterpart is 'Bureau' or 'Office' and in a fused society it is termed 'Chamber', and each have features of their own. The Spanish word 'Sala' has a variety of meanings, such as government offices, religious conference, a room, a pavilion, etc. The word 'sala' is also generally used in East Asian countries more or less with the same meaning.[28] Sala has certain features of diffracted 'bureau' and fused 'chamber'. However, the 'bureau' features of sala do not stand well to represent its basic character. The heterogeneous value system and the traditional and modern methods of the prismatic society reflect in its administrative dealings and functional management. The administrative rationality and efficiency found in bureau are absent in sala.

In a prismatic society, nepotism and favouritism play a very important role in the appointments to various administrative positions and in performing administrative functions. In a diffracted society, the considerations of kinship are kept away from the administrative behaviour and the exercise of governmental power. In a fused society the politico-administrative system has a patrimonial character, and therefore, provides dominant importance to kinship or family. In a prismatic society, on the other hand, besides the super-imposition of new formal structures on family and kinship, the universalisation of laws is disregarded. Though, patrimonialism is officially proscribed, in reality it is widely practiced and it reflects in all administrative practices. The 'Sala' officer gives priority to personal aggrandisement than to welfare. His behaviour and performance are influenced by parochialism as a result of which the rules and regulations are not applied universally. A few get more benefits from the government programmes ignoring the interests of a large number of others.

Poly-communalism also creates certain administrative problems. Theoretically speaking, the government officers have to implement the laws without any favouritism and discrimination. But a government official would develop a greater sense of loyalty towards the members of his own community than towards the government. In this process, a dominant minority community gains a high proportion of representation in matters of recruitment, while creating dissatisfaction among the larger number of people. To diffuse the situation and protect the interests of other minorities 'quota' or 'reservation' systems are adopted to provide some sort of proportional representation to all communities in administration. However, such arrangements would lead to compartmentalisation and mutual hostility among various communities, which may further generate non-cooperation and increase tensions among the rival communities working in various government agencies. This situation, however, is not peculiar to developing countries alone. 'The Whiteman-Negro' relations in Southern America also relates to the same problem.

Family, community and caste play a decisive role in society and there is simultaneous growth of new groups. Riggs called them as 'Clects', which are typical prismatic groups making use of modern, associational methods of organisation, but retain diffuse and particularistic goals of a transitional type.[29] Thus, clect combines the features of 'club' of the diffracted society and the 'sect' of the fused. 'Clects' represent exclusively the people of a particular community or group, and government officials belonging to that category serve only the members of their respective 'clects' more effectively by ignoring others. Sometimes the sala or one of its agencies develop close relations with particular clects, or start functioning like a clect in itself. As a result, the clects continue to maintain close links with a particular group and function primarily in their interest and pay lip service to achievement and universalistic norms.[30]

In a prismatic society the traditional behaviour pattern coexists with 'new' sets of norms. As a result of overlapping of the 'formal' and the 'effective' standard of conduct, prismatic society's social interactions are characterised by a lack of consensus on the norms of behaviour.[31] Sala officials may have entered service through higher educational qualifications and competitive examinations, but in regard to the matters of promotion and career development, they depend largely on ascriptive ties, as also the support of seniority, or on the influence of senior officers. These officers claim to apply modern norms in their behaviour, but are indifferent and reject all inconvenient norms in their day-to-day functioning. The public also takes the example of sala officials in their behavioural pattern and in general, plead for the strict observance of rules and regulations. But when their personal issues are involved they would either try to break the rules or plead for exemption in their favour.

While referring to overlapping in the power structure of a prismatic society, Riggs observes that it consists of a 'highly centralised and concentrated authority structure overlapping a control system that is highly localised and dispersed'.[32] There exists a separation of 'authority' (officially sanctioned or legitimate power) and 'control' (real but unofficially permitted of illegitimate power). In practice, the *de jure* 'authority' succumbs to the *de facto* 'control'.[33] The authority of the sala overlaps with the society's control structures which are based on poly-communalism, clects and poly-normativism.[34] A number of structures behave in a peculiar fashion and many a time even act against the very purpose for which they were created. Sometimes structures lacking primary orientation towards administration carry administrative functions along with other concrete structures responsible for it. Such an overlapping influences the relationship between politicians and administration.

Riggs termed the prismatic society as 'unbalanced polity' in which bureaucrats dominate the politico-administrative system despite the political leader's constitutional powers. As a result, the sala officials play a more dominant role in decision-making processes in a prismatic society than the officials in a diffracted society. Due to such a concentration of powers in the hands of bureaucrats, there would be lack of response to the people's needs and wishes. In such a situation strengthening of public administration in developing societies is likely to impede political development. He further pointed out, that such a weak political system and leadership fail to control the bureaucracy and consequently the legislature, political parties, voluntary associations and public opinion also become ineffective.

The strengths and weaknesses of any political leader in power varies with his ability to reward and punish the administrators. A weak political leader may fail to recognise the services of any official and reward him suitably for achieving the organisational goals, and at the same time an inefficient official may escape punishment for his failures. As a result a talented sala official tends to spend most of his time for self-aggrandisement and for the promotion of personal interests and in the process inefficient officials may go scot-free. Since the performance of the government depends on the level of output of the sala official, Riggs says, there is a close link between bureaucratic behaviour and administrative output; the most powerful a bureaucrat is, the less effective he is as administrator. As a result, the sala is characterised by nepotism in recruitment, institutionalised corruption and inefficiency in the administration of laws and by the motives of gaining power for protecting its own interest.[35]

The Bazar-Canteen - Prismatic Economy

Riggs termed the economic sub-system of a prismatic society 'bazar-canteen'. In a diffracted society the economic system operates depending on the market factors of supply and demand and economic considerations alone govern the market. In contrast, in a fused society, 'arena factors' - religious, social, or familial considerations - determine the economic transactions and the question of price scarcely arises. In a prismatic society, both the 'market factors' and 'arena factors' play side by side. Both economic and non-economic factors interact and influence the economic structures. Under such conditions it is not possible to determine common price for a commodity or service. Besides, the 'price indeterminacy', foreign domination on the economic system, a small section of people enjoying all benefits with control over economic institutions and exploiting large number of people, are some of the other features of 'bazar-canteen' model. This gives place to bargaining in regard to fee and tax-payments, rebates and bribes. This further influences the financial administration and ultimately destroys the economic system.

In a diffracted society everyone gets the services on equal basis without discrimination and favouritism. In the same manner employees get their emoluments and remuneration in proportion to their work turnout, service, and its market value. But in a prismatic society, the relationship between the public official and their clientele would be in terms of buyer-seller relationship. The price for the service is determined by the nature of relationship between the public servants and their clientele. The price varies from place to place, time to time and person to person. The price of any commodity or service depends on the family contacts, kinship, individual relationship, bargaining power and politics. Services are guaranteed and sold to the members of the 'clects' and dominant communities at reduced prices and members 'outside' the clects and minority community are charged higher prices. Thus, the economic structures in a prismatic society behave like a 'subsidised' canteen to the members of the privileged groups and politically 'influential' persons having access to the canteen. Conversely it behaves like a 'tributary' canteen, where they charge higher prices to the members of less privileged, politically non-influential or members of the 'outside' groups.

The state of price-indeterminacy in a prismatic society further deteriorates the economic conditions, encourages black-marketing, hoarding, adulteration, etc., and ultimately leads to high level of inflation. In such a situation the sala official would try to encash it by developing contacts with foreign businessmen and misuse foreign exchange for private purposes. This would generally lead to exploitation, poverty, and social injustice in a prismatic society. The wage relations in a prismatic society also depends on family relations. A good number of public officials receive higher pay and salaries without doing any work. Generally, the gap between the lowest and the higher wages would be very wide and those people who draw less pay will have to do more work. In such a situation, low wage earners would be inclined to increase their incomes through illegitimate means. This affects the norms of officials conduct, which in turn, affects the economic sub-system of a prismatic society.

In a prismatic society the 'market factors' are developed without proportionate increase in the capital. Production does not increase and society would give less value to trade and commerce. Native businessmen lose interest and foreigners and the migrant minorities provide the capital and conduct business. They slowly try to extend their influence to political and administrative spheres and corrupt them to achieve their personal ends. Thus, the economic sub-system in a prismatic society ultimately influences the public officials and is influenced by its governing factors.

Change in a Prismatic Society

The pace of development in any society depends mainly on the availability of favourable conditions for change in the system. The western societies witnessed relatively longer time-span for their development and were able to adjust their behaviour gradually to the desired patterns. In the process of development they experienced less formalism, heterogeneity and overlapping, than the contemporary transitional or developing societies. Generally, in a prismatic society the pressure for change comes from both internal and external sources. If pressure is primarily external (foreign technical assistance programmes), it may be called 'exogeneous' change and if the pressures are primarily internal (normally by administrative reforms) it may be called 'endogenous' change. And if the change is the result of both external and internal pressures, it is termed as 'equi-genetic'. Riggs explained the dilemma of change in the manner that the more exogenetic the process of diffraction, the more formalistic and heterogeneous its prismatic phase; the more endogenetic, the less formalistic and heterogeneous. Thus, greater the formalism, heterogeneity and overlapping, greater the state of 'exo-prismatic' and the lesser the 'endo-prismatic' character of change. Such a difference occurs because, with endogenetic change, 'effective' behaviour precedes the creation of new formal institutions, but in an exo-genetic transformation the sequence is reversed. Paradoxically, in their bid to absorb the externally induced change in the shortest possible time, prismatic societies face the possibilities of higher formalism, heterogeneity and 'the severity of evolutionary tensions'.

Concept of Development

Riggs defined development as 'a process of increasing autonomy (discretion) of social systems, made possible by rising level of diffraction'. 'Discretion', he observes, is the 'ability to choose among alternatives' while diffraction refers to the degree of differentiation and integration in a social system.[36] Ecologically, development is increasing the ability to make and carry out collective decisions affecting the environment.[37] Riggs considered differentiation and integration as the two key elements in the process of development. Differentiation means existence of a situation in which every function has a corresponding specialised structure for its performance. Integration means a mechanism to tie together, to link-up, to mesh and to coordinate the various kinds of specialised roles.[38] The levels of differentiation and integration represent diffracted and prismatic conditions of development. If the society is highly differentiated and poorly integrated, it is prismatic. Diffraction leads to development and the higher the level of differentiation and integration, the greater the level of development, and the lower their level, lesser the development. In the same way the level of malarrangement between differentiation and integration results in the different levels of prismatic conditions. Riggs explained the differentiation and integration correlations and resultant diffracted and prismatic conditions as shown in Fig. 2.

Fig 2: Differentiation and Integration

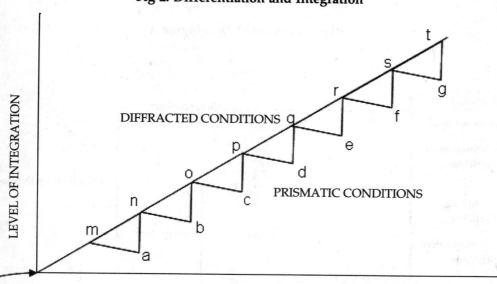

a to g = Prismatic Conditions; m to t = Diffracted Conditions

Source: Administrative Change, Vol. 2, No.2, Jan-June, 1975.

Riggs drew two lines of coordination and each between the changing levels of differentiation and integration. He pointed out a diagonal between representing the ideal level of integration required to handle the complexities involved in coordinating differentiated roles while providing sufficient autonomy for each role to be carried successfully and its distinctive functions. Thus, the line m, n.....t represent a condition that is more diffracted than situations symbolised below the line a, b...g. On this scale the extremes represent mere hypothetical constructs, but the intermediate points come closer to characterise empirical realities.

Riggs also hypothetically presented imaginary societies, which are becoming more and more differentiated without successfully mastering the problems posed by these changes through its integrative mechanisms. The shift from 'n' to 'b' or 'p' to 'd' in the graph represents this condition. The fact of having a variety of differentiated roles can lead to greater confusion and chaos - unless the specialised roles are carefully coordinated with each other. There must be a mechanism to tie together different kinds of specialised roles. Integration, thus, becomes a highly essential part of the whole scheme. "Surely", Riggs observes, "it is much easier to train people to perform the specialised roles of modern government than it is to integrate these roles, to link them up together". Development would be possible only when the roles are carefully integrated. Riggs further explains his concept of development by analysing the factors affecting differentiation and integration. Fig: 3 facilitates a better understanding of his concept of development.

Fig: 3

Riggs' Concept of Development

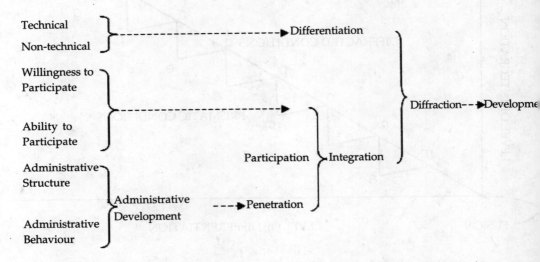

The level of differentiation in any country depends on the technological and non-technological factors. The more the development of technology, the higher the level of differentiation. The integration depends on two important factors viz., penetration and participation. Penetration is the ability of a government to make and carry out decisions throughout the country. Participation is the receptivity to law and the willingness to help carry out the laws and the policies which the government has formulated. Participation, thus, has two important elements viz., willingness and ability of the people to participate. The more the willingness and ability to participate on the part of the people, the higher the level of participation in governmental affairs. Thus the penetration and participation facilitate the integration of differentiated structures resulting in development.

A Critique

Extensive references made to the views of Riggs in the literature of Public Administration itself are an indication of his tremendous influence on the discipline. There cannot be any study of comparative public administration and development administration without a reference to Riggs. But Riggs, like many other administrative theorists, was subjected to severe criticism. Riggs liberally coined new words to explain his concepts. In addition, he also gave different meanings to a number of words already in use. There is no harm in coining new words when the existing vocabulary fails to convey the meaning and clarify the concepts. There is also nothing wrong if one gives his own meaning for the effective expression of his views. But free use of new words, and using them with different meanings may create confusion instead of clarifying the concepts.[39] Riggs in his enthusiasm to give a scientific temper to his models, borrowed most of his terminology from physical sciences. But by mere use of new words borrowed from physical sciences, administration cannot become a science.[40] Sometimes the usage of new words may even mislead readers.

Sisson, who is very critical of Riggs' models and his terminology, says that to understand the writings of Riggs one has to read them three times. First time to understand his language, second time to understand his concepts and third time to know whether there is anything really to learn.[41] Chapman, commenting on this aspect, writes that Riggs should have prepared his own dictionary to explain his terminology.[42]

Hahn-Been Lee doubts the utility of the prismatic and sala models, in view of the administration's focus on social change. Lee feels that Riggs' models are not helpful to know the process of social change in development. He considers Riggs' models as equilibrium models. Equilibrium models would only facilitate in preserving the system but not introducing any change in the system. Lee concludes that the models of Riggs are not very useful when the objective of administration is to change the system, rather than its maintenance.[43]

Richard A. Chapman emphasises that one should have an open mind in analysing the Riggsian models and see how far they would be useful to understand Public Administration. Although Riggs adopted an interdisciplinary approach to analyse social systems, he has not fully worked out the implications of his theory for Public Administration. Models are intended to be heuristic devices, valuable as aids to understand complex social phenomena. In applying Riggs' models to particular societies, the problem of measurement comes. In the absence of a measuring scale, the identification of prismatic or diffracted societies becomes very difficult. As the reader carefully follows Riggs' analysis, there may be a tendency for him to associate prismatic conditions with every situation he knows. Similarly, Daya Krishna says, when the fused and diffracted societies are imaginary, all the societies are to be classified as prismatic at various levels of low, middle and high. But when scales to measure the levels of 'prismatism' are lacking, the 'low', 'middle' and 'high' words have no relevance. Riggs' models are mostly based on certain assumptions. But in the absence of empirical evidence the validity of such assumptions are highly questionable. Daya Krishna[44] mainly directs his attack with a view to examine how far the Riggs' models are useful to analyse the development processes and points out that his prismatic model serves no purpose to find out the stages in the process of development. When change is inevitable in any society, according to Daya Krishna, Riggs' diffracted model is impracticable. Diffracted society represents the equilibrium state and stands for the stability and preservation of the system. To Daya Krishna diffracted society is not a desirable society.

When Riggs assumes that America also is set to become a prismatic society, Daya Krishna finds no logic in the three-fold classification of the societies in the background of the concept of 'development'. If America is a prismatic society and economically backward Egypt a diffracted society, Daya Krishna feels that all developing countries in the world would like to continue to be prismatic societies. Riggs considered differentiation and integration as two important ingredients of development. But it is a difficult task to identify the desirable level of differentiation and integration required for development. Riggs' preference for societies with low but equitable level of differentiation and integration to those with high level of differentiation and low level of integration, according to Daya Krishna, stands as an obstacle to development. Lack of international perspective in his approach to development is another limitation of Riggs' concept. In a competitive world, the higher-level prismatic society may exploit the lower-level diffracted society. In Daya Krishna's view, Riggs failed to recognise the role of outside or external forces in the process of development. Daya Krishna also feels that the Riggs' view of integration as the result of a penetration and participation cannot be relevant to all situations.

He says that people's participation is also possible even in dictatorial regimes and hence, mere participation cannot be considered an important variable of integration. Riggs also failed to take into consideration the social aspects besides scientific and technological reasons for differentiation. The feeling that the social equilibrium will be disturbed only because of scientific and technological reasons is far from convincing.

Adoption of a wrong analytical tool borrowed from physical science in explaining the social systems was criticised by Tilman. When interdisciplinary approach is adopted, it is the primary responsibility of the researcher to select a most suitable analytical approach. Ecological models generally explain the motives of administrative behaviour. In the whole process, administration also plays an important role to influence its environment. Administration is also a tool for social change and it influences the society in different ways at different times. But Riggs has completely neglected this aspect.

Prismatic model mainly describes developing societies but fails to explain the place of administration in the society. The main reason for it was the failure on the part of Riggs to analyse the 'internal dynamics of the society'. In prismatic society, the character of each social structure is distinct and also an independent variable. There is wide disparity and distinction in the relation of social, economic, political and administrative system of a society. Riggs has failed to recognise these distinctions. Not much work has been done in the relationship between the diffracted characters and fused characters in a prismatic society. Due to this gap, the conclusion that formalism leads to the concentration of power in the hands of bureaucracy, which in turn leads to inefficiency in administration is arrived in haste and without any proper empirical evidence.

Arora opines that overlapping exists equally in diffracted societies as in prismatic societies, but the reasons may be different. An examination of reasons would be very useful and provide guidance to administrative actions. Riggs has only highlighted the negative impact of overlapping but did not examine the positive aspects, which may provide healthy competition among various administrative sub-systems and increase efficiency in the administration.

The very concept of prismatic model has a negative character. It looks as though, the conditions of developing countries were analysed through the western values and concepts. Commenting on this aspect, Michael Monroe observed that Riggs examined the conditions in developing countries while taking America as a standard society. Riggs did not give any importance to the positive character of prismatic society as much as he did to the negative characters. He projected formalism, as a negative aspect and highlighted all its bad effects. But it is also true that sometimes there would be more benefits to the people if the rules and regulations are not strictly followed. Administration may move fast if certain rules are not strictly observed. In countries like India, if there is proper leadership, formalism may play a very positive role in carrying out the works in time.[45] In a sense, Riggs' implication that formalism is dysfunctional in most or all circumstances represents a 'non-ecological' viewpoint. To counterbalance the Riggsian concept of negative formalism, Valson presented the concept of positive formalism.[46] Riggs also failed to give enough attention to the operation of internal forces, which are important in the functioning of any system.

An Evaluation

Classical organisational theories mainly emphasise on organisational principles and behavioural theories concentrated on human behaviour in the organisation. But ecological theories emphasise the interaction of administration and its environment. Both in content and analysis, Riggs' ecological approach touches a wider horizon, and takes an integrated approach of administrative system. His approach and models help us in understanding the administrative process in developing countries. Although his administrative models are difficult to find in practice, they help us in understanding the realities. Sala model provides an opportunity to analyse and understand the administrative system in developing countries. It also facilitates to conduct further studies based on empirical and ecological approaches.

As Chapman has correctly observed that in spite of many limitations, Riggs models may deepen our insight into some of the underlying problems of public administration in transitional societies. In some ways the prismatic model may be analogous to principles in administration. The principles may not be universal truths and they may have the defect of proverbs, that they occur in contradictory pairs, but this does not mean that principles are worthless; indeed they may be particularly useful as criteria for describing and diagnosing administrative situations. In a similar way Riggs' approach and models may be considered as sophisticated tools for describing and diagnosing administrative situations.[47]

In Brief

Fred Riggs' wide ranging contributions to administrative theory can be summarised as:

- Fred W. Riggs (1917-2008), a pioneer in administrative model building and comparative administration studies, is known for his studies of administrative systems in developing societies in a broader ecological and developmental perspective. In his book, *The Administration in Developing Countries* Riggs presented his popular model, theory of prismatic societies.

- Riggs considered comparative public administration, which emphasises cross-cultural and cross-national administrative studies, as more appropriate to the understanding of administrative systems in developing countries. He identified three broad trends, viz., normative to empirical, ideographic to nomathetic and non-ecological to ecological in the study of comparative public administration.

- Riggs used three important analytical tools to explain his administrative theories, viz., ecological approach, structural-functional approach, and ideal models.

- Riggs developed certain ideal models to analyse the administrative systems of developing countries. Initially, Riggs developed Agraria-Industria model to describe agricultural and industrial societies. Responding to criticisms of the model, he developed another set of models to describe pre-historic, developing and developed societies and called them fused, prismatic and diffracted models respectively. These models are based on the basis of structural and functional approach. He termed 'functionally diffuse' societies as 'fused' and 'functionally specific' as 'diffracted' and the intermediate societies between these two extremes as 'prismatic'. The prismatic is his most popular model characterised by heterogeneity, formalism and overlapping.

- The administrative sub-system of prismatic society is called a 'Sala' and the economic sub-system is called a 'Bazaar Canteen'.

- Riggs in discussing reforms and changes in prismatic societies identified 'exogenous', 'endogenous' and 'equi-genetic' factors responsible for changes.

- Riggs examined the conditions of prismatic society from a development perspective. He defined development as a process of increasing autonomy of social systems made possible by raising the level of diffraction. To him, differentiation and integration are the two key elements in the process of development.

- The criticism of Riggs models include confusion from the use of new terms and giving new meaning to the terms already in use; focus of models is on equilibrium than on change; problems of measurement in the identification of prismatic societies; difficulties in identifying the desirable levels of differentiation and integration required for development; examination of developing societies with American society as a standard.

- In spite of many limitations and criticisms, Riggs' models deepen our insight into some of the underlying problems of public administration in developing societies. Even if ideal types are not to be found in reality, they are considered useful for heuristic purposes.

Notes and References

1. See http://www2.hawaii.edu/~fredr/6-vita6a.htm. See also Tummala, Krishna K., "An Ode to Fred," *Public Administration Review*, Nov.-Dec., 2008, Vol.68, No.6, 2008, pp. 973-976.

2. For a list of Riggs's publications see http://www2.hawaii.edu/~fredr/checka.htm

3. Heady, Ferrel, "Comparative Public Administration: Concerns and Priorities", in Heady, Ferrel, and Stokes, Sybil L., (Eds.), *Papers on Comparative Public Administration*, Ann Arbor: Institute of Public Administration, the University of Michigan, 1962, p. 4.

4. See Riggs, Fred W., "Trends in the Comparative Study of Public Administration", *International Review of Administrative Sciences*, Vol. XXVIII, No. 1, 1962, pp. 9-15.

5. Bews, J. W., *Human Ecology*, London, Oxford University Press, 1935, p. 232.

6. Gaus, John M., *Reflections on Public Administration*, Alabama, University of Alabama Press, 1958, pp. 1-19.

7. Dahl, Robert A., ."The Science of Public Administration: Three Problems", *Public Administration Review*, Vol. VII, No. 1, 1947, pp. 1-11.

8. Dahl, Robert A., "Technical Assistance: The Problem of Implementation", *Public Administration Review*, Vol. XII, 1952, p. 266.

9. See Riggs, Fred W., *The Ecology of Public Administration*, Bombay, Asia Publishing House, 1961.

10. Gaus, John M., op. cit. p. 9.

11. See Riggs, Fred W., *The Ecology of Public Administration*, op. cit.

12. See among others, Parsons, Talcott, *The Social System*, Glencoe, Illinois, Free Press, 1957, Merton, Robert K., *Social Theory and Social Structure*, Glencoe, Illinois, Free Press, 1951: Almond, Gabriel A., and Coleman, James S., (Eds.), *The Politics of Developing Areas*, Princeton, Princeton University Press, 1961.

13. Riggs, Fred W., *Administration in Developing Countries: The Theory of Prismatic Societies*, Boston, Houghton Mifflin Co. 1964, p. 99.

14. Riggs, Fred W., "Agraria and Industria: Towards a Typology of Comparative Public Administration", in Siffin,William J., (Ed.), *Toward a Comparative Study of Public Administration*, Bloomington, Indiana University Press, 1957, pp. 23-116.

15. Ticknet, F. J., "A Survey and Evaluation of Comparative Research", *Public Administration Review*, Vol. XIX, No. 1, 1959, pp. 19-25; Milne, R. S., "Comparisons and Models in Public Administration", *Political Studies*, Vol. X, No. 1, 1962, pp. 1-14.

16. Riggs, Fred W., *The Ecology of Public Administration*, op. cit. p. 95.

17. See Arora, Ramesh K., *Comparative Public Administration: An Ecological Perspective*, New Delhi, Associated Publishing House, p. 110.

18. Ibid.

19. Riggs, Fred W., *The Ecology of Public Administration*, op. cit., p. 91.

20. Arora, Ramesh K., op.cit., pp.110-111.

21. Riggs, Fred W., *The Ecology of Public Administration*, op. cit., pp. 91-92; See also B.S. Bhargava,"Riggs's Concept of Formalism," Prashasnika, Vol.VI.No.4.,Oct.-Dec., 1977, pp.4-11.

22. Riggs, Fred W., "The 'Sala' Model: An Ecological Approach to the Study of Comparative Public Administration", *Philippine Journal of Public Administration*, Vol. VI, 1962, p. 5.

23. Ram Reddy, G., and Ravindra Prasad, D., "Personnel of the Council of Ministers", in Ram Reddy, G., and Sharma, B. A. V., (Ed.), *State Government and Politics: Andhra Pradesh*, New Delhi, Sterling Publishers, 1979.

24. Riggs, Fred W., "The 'Sala' Model: An Ecological Approach to the Study of Comparative Public Administration", op. cit., p. 6.

25 Riggs, Fred W., *The Ecology of Public Administration*, op. cit., p. 92.

26 Arora, Ramesh K., op. cit., pp. 112.

27 Some of these concepts are discussed later in this chapter.

28 Sanskrit word 'Shala' also denotes the same meaning and is used for 'Patashala' (School), 'Kalashala' (College), 'Vaidyashala' (Hospital), 'Dharmashala' (Guest-house), etc.

29 Riggs, Fred W., *The Ecology of Public Administration*, op. cit., p. 126.

30 Arora, Ramesh K., op. cit., p. 113.

31 Ibid., p. 115.

32 Riggs, Fred W., "The 'Sala' Model: An Ecological Approach to the Study of Comparative Public Administration", op. cit., p. 14.

33 *de jure* authority here means the officially sanctioned legitimate power and *de facto* control means the 'real' but unofficially permitted or illegitimate power.

34 Arora, Ramesh K., op. cit., p. 116.

35 Ibid.

36 Riggs, Fred W., "The Idea of Development Administration", in Edward W. Weidner, (Ed.), *Development Administration in Asia*, Durham, N. C., Duke University Press, 1970, pp. 25-72.

37 Riggs, Fred W., "Further Considerations on Development", *Administrative Change*, Vol. 4, No. 1, July-December 1976, p. 2.

38 Ibid., p. 3.

39. Chapman, Richard A., "Prismatic Theory in Public Administration: A Review of Theories of F. W. Riggs", *Public Administration*, Vol. 44, Winter, 1966, p. 418.

40 Kishan Khanna, "Contemporary Models of Public Administration: An Assessment of their Utility and Exposition of Inherent Fallacies", " *Philippine Journal of Public Administration*, Vol. XVIII, No. 2, April 1974, p. 103.

41 Quoted in Ibid., p. 105.

42 Chapman, Richard A., op. cit.

43 Lee, Hahn-Been , "From Ecology to Time", *International Review of Administrative Sciences*, Vol. XXXIII, No. 2, 1967, pp. 1-13.

44 For details of Daya Krishna's criticism see his "Shall we be Diffracted? A Critical Comment on F. W. Riggs' Prismatic Societies and Public Administration", *Administrative Change*, Vol. 2, No. 1, June 1974, pp. 48-55 and "Towards a Saner View of 'Development': A Comment on F. W. Riggs' Comment", *Administrative Change*, Vol. 3, No. 2, Jan-June, 1976, p. 19-26.

45 See Arora, Ramesh K., op. cit., p. 119.

46 Valson, E. W., "Positive Formalism: A Desideration for Development", *Philippine Journal of Public Administration*, Vol. XII, 1968, pp. 3-6

47 Chapman, Richard A., op. cit., p. 427.

18

YEHEZKEL DROR

G. Haragopal

Introduction

Yehezkel Dror's inclusion in a volume of administrative thinkers is not only unconventional but a bit adventurous too. This attempt completes the circle started by Woodrow Wilson who vehemently pleaded for the dichotomy of administration and policy. Although the dichotomy appeared to be real and caught the imagination of some of the administrative thinkers, it did not last long. The administrative system cannot be isolated from the larger political system, as the latter influences the tone and tenor of administration. Public administration, therefore, both as a profession and as a discipline, cannot and should not be treated as independent of its political context. It is in this light that the students of public administration need to be introduced to the concept of policy science, which not only widens their intellectual horizons but also enables them to integrate the fragmented knowledge. Dror is widely regarded as the world's foremost pioneers of modern public policy studies.

(Born in 1928)

An accelerated thrust of knowledge in all branches has resulted in increasing specialisation. The need for specialisation arose not because each area had its own distinct boundaries but the time at the command of a single human being was awfully inadequate to cope up with the fast growing information. Specialisation, bordering narrow isolation, is dangerous as it renders both the knowledge and its possessor ineffective. Dror through his concept of policy science attempted to avoid this peril present among the social sciences in modern times. This remarkable attempt is not only very timely but is also capable of restoring the perspective.

Life and Works

Yehezkel Dror (1928) born in Vienna, Austria migrated to Israel in 1938 and was educated in Jerusalem at Hebrew and Howard universities. He obtained B.A (1953) and Magister

Juris (1954) from the Hebrew University and LLM (1955) and S.J.D., (1957) from the Harvard University (1957). He joined the Political Science Department of Hebrew University of Jerusalem, Israel in 1957 where he is at present Professor of Political Science and Wolfson Chair Professor of Public Administration, Emeritus.[1] In his long career, Dror worked in senior positions in Israeli Government including as Senior Policy Planning Advisor in the office of the Defense Minister, and the Prime Minister's Office, chairman and member of public service commissions dealing with various policy issues, founder-president of the Jewish People Policy Planning Institute (2002- 2008), etc.

Dror's professional experience includes visiting professorships and policy consultancies at universities and government institutes in several countries including Advanced Study in the Behavioural Sciences, Palo Alto (1962-1963); Woodrow Wilson Center, Washington, D.C., (1981); Center for Advanced Study, Berlin (1981-1982); European Institute of Public Administration, Maastricht (1989-1991), etc. As an international consultant on behalf of the United Nations, Organisation for Economic Cooperation and Development, the European Union and at the invitation of governments, Dror worked in several countries on policy planning, capacity to govern and state craft. He was Fellow, World Academy of Art and Science and European Academy of Sciences and Arts, etc. He was a member of the Club of Rome and International Institute of Strategic Studies, London and worked as a senior professional staff member at the Rand Corporation in California and New York (1968-70).[2] For senior politicians and policy-makers he organised workshops on policy planning and capacity to govern in over forty countries.

Dror's publications include[3] *Public Policymaking Reexamined* (1968); *Design for Policy Sciences* (1971); *Ventures in Policy Sciences* (1971); *Crazy States: A Counterconventional Strategic Issue* (1971): *Policymaking Under Adversity* (1986); *The Capacity to Govern: A Report to the Club of Rome* (2000). He is currently working on *The Superior Ruler: Mirrors for Future-Weaving Governor,* a mentoring book for top level politicians and chief executives; *Global Leviathan* on a global regime confronting evil equipped with weapons of mass killing and *Grand Strategy Crafting* a text for high-level strategic planning professionals. His books were published in several languages.

Dror is a recipient of several awards including First Annual Harold Lasswell Award of Policy Studies (1983); Thomas R. Dye Award for outstanding service to the Policy Studies Organisation (1997); Landau Prize for outstanding contributions to social sciences (2002), Israel Prize in Administrative Sciences for outstanding original scientific and applied work in policy- making, capacities to govern and strategic planning (2005) and Rosolio Award for his contributions to the advancement of the study and practice of Public Administration in Israel (1965).

Knowledge Systems and Public Policy

Dror strove to integrate administration and policy for better policy-making. Taking a curative approach to fragmentation and specialisation, Dror's 'policy science' developed models that challenged the modern dispersion of the social sciences. He believed that by nurturing the 'organised dreaming' of its members, organisations could develop new research designs, could broadly conceptualise discrete policy issues and thereby solve current and future social problems. Dror's version of policy sciences capitalises on the epistemological development of politicians; changes in political, cultural and educational spheres and inter-governmental participation of the public in public policy-making. Advanced studies in public administration will make contributions in all these areas.

Dror made a mark in public administration through his outstanding publication *Public Policy Re-examined*. This book launches a call for rational public policy formulation but has become a statement of Dror's refusal to acknowledge that incrementalism is justified when knowledge is scanty. Dror includes an ideal model for policy-making in his study, suggesting its replacement of normative models that help evaluate policy-making for flaws but fail to meet the required challenges. The study includes three central elements: identifying problems and resources, evaluating and revising policy production systems and determining policy-making strategies. Overall, Dror foregrounds the "gap between the ways individuals and institutions make policy and the available knowledge of how policies can best be made" in his theoretically constructed project, the revised version of which appeared as *Policy-making Under Adversity*.[4]

Dror, while taking stock of the existing knowledge for human action, divided the knowledge into three levels: knowledge relevant to the control of the environment, knowledge relevant to control society and individuals and knowledge concerning the control of the controls themselves that is meta-control.[5] Of these three levels, knowledge about control over environment relatively is the most advanced area owing to scientific and technological advancement. Knowledge about control of society and individuals has not developed highly although it registered some progress. But the knowledge about control over controls is the least developed of all and is scarcely recognised as a distinct focus for research. The necessity to be acquainted with the knowledge of the design and operation of the control mechanism itself is of serious consequence to the future of mankind.

The deep urge and increasing capacity of human beings in the twentieth century to mould their destiny by choice is too evident. There has been a scarcity of knowledge about various dimensions of society since the beginning of human history. The design and operation of the overall social control system, which Dror describes as societal direction system, is one such area. Dror lamented that this blind area in human knowledge always caused suffering and tragedy in terms of human values. But the gravity of the tragedy is all the more severe in modern times when the society is subjected to innumerable stringent controls. The available knowledge such as nuclear bomb, ecology, poisoning techniques, predicting the gender of the children, genetic engineering, stimulating altered states of consciousness, emotional controls, etc., place immense power in the hands of controlling authority. It is this dangerous development that makes the societal direction system extremely crucial.

Limitations of Knowledge in Policy Making

The changes required in societal direction system are multidimensional in character. It is not only that the existing gaps in the body of knowledge are to be filled up, but what is urgently needed is a new value and belief system in view of the global role of controlling man. Unfortunately, the scientific knowledge is triggering change without supplying new values and belief systems. Therefore, this knowledge should enable the societies to raise the level of rationality as an important component of the societal direction system. This, in turn, would help in improving the public policy-making system, which constitutes the dominant of the societal direction system as a whole. This analysis led Dror to propound the following law: "While human capacities to shape the environment, society and human beings are rapidly increasing, policy-making capabilities to use those capacities remained the same."[6] It is not that no effort to improve public policy-making is made. The inter-disciplines such as operations research, systems analysis, organisational theory, strategic analysis, and general system theory are a testimony. It is also evident that even traditional disciplines like economics, psychology and political science are moving in this direction. The endeavours to develop scientific knowledge in the area of policy-making, according to Dror suffer from the following weaknesses:[7]

- The present research is adopting micro approach which has very limited relevance to the policy-making system;

- Knowledge is disjointed causing fragmentation and ignoring systems analysis approach;
- It focused more attention on the component of rationality, remaining oblivious to extra-rationality;
- In the policy-making improvement measures, there has been too much of incrementalism without any effort for the new designs (Nova Design).
- The concern for improving the policy-making has been so narrow that it has neglected critical elements such as politicians;
- The dichotomy between the behavioural approach and normative approach prevented a comprehensive approach in understanding and improving the policy-making system as a whole;
- In the normative approach no new devices are developed to handle qualitative variables;
- In the behavioural approach, there has been indifference to prescriptive methodology whereby the knowledge can be applied to practical problems of the society;
- Policy-making study has not been able to utilise knowledge from different disciplines because of conventional nature of research.

All these weaknesses, with many others, have generated knowledge, which is too inadequate for effective public policy-making. Therefore, there is a need to build a new body of knowledge with greater integration of different concepts. It is this endeavour that gave birth to policy-sciences - a new area of enquiry. Policy science as a separate field is necessary and essential to accelerate the development of policy knowledge and to use it for better policy-making. It is also useful for advanced research and training and to recruit and train professional policy scientists and policy-makers.[8]

Emergence of Policy Sciences

The policy sciences are emerging from a number of efforts. First, pressure of problems - environmental, urban, public order, demands for new forms of participation, new patterns of international cooperation, etc., - encouraging and even pushing a policy approach. The American experience - which established a number of policy research organisations like the Hudson Institute, the Woodrow Wilson Foundation, etc., is providing an impetus and is encouraging policy studies in many other countries. Science policy has received considerable attention in the recent past. Now, in many countries, there is a tendency to move from science policy to policy research using science and scientific methods. Thus the science policy is leading the way towards policy research. The imperatives of administrative reforms have also led the way for increased policy studies.[9] The interest shown by a number of outstanding social scientists in policy studies and offering of courses on the subject in a number of universities have also contributed to the growth of policy sciences as a separate field of study.[10]

Although these developments do indicate the emergence of a new science, Dror fears that it may not be allowed to come up at all because of the existing "academic and political culture". Further, it is doubtful whether the intellectual capacities of man are adequate to meet the new challenge. However, in order to give a fair trial to the efforts already stated, Dror suggests some new paradigms of the policy sciences which are as follows:[11]

1. The main concern of policy sciences is the understanding and improvement of macro-control systems and especially the public policy systems. This includes policy analysis, alternative innovations, master policies (mega policies) evaluation and feedback, improvement of meta policy (policy about policy-making), etc.

2. Policy sciences would break the barriers and traditional boundaries between various social science disciplines including behavioural sciences and decision disciplines. Further, they would integrate knowledge and build-up a supra-discipline focussing on public policy-making. In this attempt even the knowledge relevant in physical and life sciences would be drawn.

3. Policy sciences would also bridge the gulf between pure and applied research. The real world would be the main laboratory of policy sciences and it is in this laboratory the relevance and practicability of the most abstract theories would be tested.

4. Policy sciences would accept tacit knowledge and personal experience as an important source of knowledge. Efforts would be made to distill the tacit knowledge of policy practitioners in the building up of policy sciences. It is this approach, which would distinguish policy sciences from contemporary normal sciences.

5. Policy sciences, unlike the normal sciences, would be sensitive to the difficulty of achieving "Value Free Sciences". As a result they would attempt to explore value implications, value consistencies, value costs and behavioural foundations of value commitments. Policy sciences would also present alternative features with their value contents. For this purpose they would encourage "Organised creativity". In the whole process they would breach the solid wall separating contemporary sciences from ethics and philosophy of values and build-up an operational theory of values.

6. Policy sciences reject the "a-historic approach" as it is very time sensitive. They emphasise historic developments on the one hand and the future dimensions on the other hand, as a central context for improved policy-making.

7. Policy sciences discard the take-it-or-leave-it attitude of behavioural sciences. They are committed for increased utilisation of knowledge in actual policy-making and in preparing professionals to serve in positions throughout the societal direction system.

8. Policy sciences recognise the crucial role of extra-rational processes such as "creativity, intuition, charisma and value judgement" and of irrational processes such a "depth motivation". They would make an attempt to build up systematic knowledge and structured rationality to be applied to the design and operation of societal direction system.

Some Implications of Policy Sciences

The emergence of policy sciences will have far-reaching implications such as transfer of some major research and teaching functions from universities to research organisations; the participation of the experienced politicians and executives in scientific activities; interaction between universities and policy research organisations; novel teaching designs, etc. Further from the social point of view, it brings about a basic change in the age-old dilemma of knowledge and power, which in turn affects social and political power.

Policy sciences are unique as it deals with the internal processes of policy-making and presumes that it would enable the policy-maker to arrive at the right decision. In contemporary normal sciences, unlike policy sciences, inputs are taken into account in policy-making but do not open up the black box of how policy decisions are made. Therefore, the quality of policy-making system is directly proportionate to the increase in the policy science knowledge. It does not mean that it would tamper with the political processes but help it by offering clear-cut alternatives from which political system can pick up an alternative of its choice. Dror anticipates the following far-reaching implications in the growth of policy sciences:[12]

1. The knowledge of policy sciences will be utilised for consideration of issues, exploration of alternative and clarification of goals.

2. It would encourage explicit mega policy decisions, which would include factors such as degree of acceptable innovations in policies, extent of risk accepted in policies, a preferable mix between comprehensive policies (which aim at breakthrough accompanied by temporary disequilibration).

3. Comprehensive mega policies are encouraged so that discrete policy issues are considered within a broader context of basic goals, postures and directives.

4. Policy sciences would be too willing to learn by systematic evaluation of past policies.

5. Policy sciences would devote greater attention to better consideration of the future. This would include organisations, units and staff who would be examining the alternative images of the future in all policy considerations.

6. Policy sciences in order to encourage creativity would support individuals and organisations engaged in adventurous thinking and 'organised dreaming'. This would be achieved by seeing to it that the creative minds do not get locked up in the contemporary policy-making process and protects them from organisational conformity pressures. It would also examine the utility of creativity, amplifying devices and chemicals in stimulative innovating thinking.

7. The policy sciences envisage the establishment of multiplicity of policy research organisations to work not only on main policy issues but also to help the government, legislature and the public at large.

8. Policy sciences would believe in extensive social experimentation for finding solutions to present and emerging social issues. For this purpose new research designs are to be invented. For that, the necessary political and social climate for experimentation will have to be created.

9. Institutional arrangements would be made to encourage possibilities of long-range advancement of humanity through genetic policies. It would also attempt changes in basic social institutions such as the family.

10. Policy sciences expect that the individual decision-makers in the times to come will have to bear the major brunt of work. Therefore, it is necessary to encourage one-person-centred high-level decision-making. Contemporary research has neglected this area completely. In this research, the personal characteristics, tastes and needs of individual administrators will be adequately taken care of.

11. Policy sciences would also devote considerable attention to improve the politician, as it believes in new symbiosis between power and knowledge. Unless politicians are adequately equipped with knowledge, improvement in policy-making cannot be expected.

12. Policy sciences would also endeavour to advance citizen participation in public policy-making. All the modern tools provided by science and technology such as television, computers would be used to enable public participation in decision-making.

13. Public participation in decision-making depends largely on the quantum of their enlightenment. To meet this challenge, radical Nova design of adult education is required. These designs will involve developing new techniques for presenting and analysing public issues in the mass media and facilitate greater communication between public opinion and public policy-making process. Training tools would include case studies, policy games and individual policy exploration programmes. Through these programmes

adult education for policy-making would be strengthened. Incentives for participation in policy-oriented educational activities will be provided for. It is in these areas a large-scale research activity will have to be initiated.

14. Policy sciences would also go to the extent of molding the children - the future citizens for policy-making roles. For this purpose, the school education will have to be recast in such a way that it would expose the children to all the social dynamics which would increase their capacity to withstand and handle the social change. This would involve changes in the school curriculum and teaching methods. For instance, a subject like History should illuminate the policy issues involved in the historic evolution of man. A subject like Mathematics should be taught with problem-solving approach with more emphasis on the probability theory. New subjects should be included which would highlight explicitly the policy problems and policy analysis.

15. Policy sciences would expect changes from politics, the public and education. It would involve a major change in the contribution of scientists in policy-making. The scientists should not only concentrate on their areas of specialisation but also be concerned with matters such as judgement on values to be pursued, value priorities, judgement on risks to be taken and judgement on time preferences, etc. The scientists, to be more useful to the policy sciences should base their knowledge not only on the basis of facts but also on social relevance and far-reaching effects on man's future.

Policy sciences, thus hope to improve policy-making and decision-making, which remain largely underdeveloped. This would help man, in the ultimate analysis, to shape his future by choice and not by chance. This could be achieved by greater integration of knowledge. But the whole process will encounter many difficult challenges as it plans to revolutionise all the assumptions on which knowledge is based. Therefore, it involves the large-scale effort on the part of the scientific community and policy practitioners.

Models of Public Policy-making

In Dror's analysis of public policy-making, models occupy an important place. Dror considers the normative model as a tool for systematically analysing public policy-making, as a basis for the criteria and standards needed to evaluate policy-making, and as a guide for formulating effective proposals for any improvements that are found to be desirable.[13] Dror examines existing normative models critically and suggests that they fall short of the requirements. He identified six normative models of policy-making: 1) the pure-rationality model; (2) the 'economically rational' model; (3) the sequential decision model; (4) the incremental change model; (5) the satisfying model; and (6) the extra-rational process model. Dror's critical survey of the six models is beautifully summarised by V. Subramaniam as follows:[14]

The pure-rationality model comes in for most detailed criticism. Its first step, namely, establishing a complete set of operational goals is 'politically' more difficult than general goals and then letting operational goals evolve themselves. As a result politicians abdicate this to administrators who are timid and conservative. The next two steps, namely, making a complete inventory of values and resources and preparing a complete set of alternative policies are even more difficult with the present manpower allocated to policy-making. The next three steps, newly preparing a valid set of predictions of cost and benefit for each alternative, calculating the net differential expectation for each and then choosing the best are indeed extremely difficult. The steps from four to six are at all attemptable only for certain quantifiable problems in transportation of business policy. The economically rational model may be dubbed as the pure-rationality model with a tack on it "as far economically possible". The sequential decision model with a tack on it involves trying out two alternatives till one proves obviously better than the other less than half way through the trial. The total cost of carrying out the alternative finally chosen and a part of the other on trial is quite often less than the risk of choosing the second one only. The incremental model of step-by-step decision-making using past-experience—advocated by Lindblom comes in again for very sharp criticism. It can possibly succeed only when the future is ridiculous in the present world situation. It conforms, however, to actual behaviour in so far as the average policy-maker depends on the past to study the future as well as to avoid discord arising from any radical change. The satisfying model is essentially Simon's satisficing model of the normal human being choosing the first satisfactory alternative without going further. The extra-rational model is no model as such but is brought in to emphasise the need to use extra-rational abilities.

As normative models have many limitations, Dror suggests the optimal model integrating and supplementing the strength of various models, at the same time avoiding their weaknesses.[15] He claims his optimal model to be a fusion of the economically rational model with the extra-rational model. The optimal model according to Dror has five major characteristics. They are: (1) it is qualitative not quantitative; (2) it has both rational and extra-rational components; (3) it is basic rationale to economically rational; (4) it deals with metapolicy-making and (5) it has much built-in feedback.[16] The optimal model has three major stages viz., metapolicy-making, policy-making and post-policy-making. Each of the stages is closely interconnected by channels of communication and feedback. Each of the stages, in turn, has a number of phases.[17] The metapolicy-making has seven such phases viz., (a) processing values; (b) processing reality; (c) processing problems; (d) surveying, processing and developing resources; (e) designing, evaluating and redesigning the policy-making system; (f) allocating problems, values and resources and (g) determining policy-making strategy. The policy making stage also has seven phases, viz., (a) sub-allocating resources; (b) establishing operational goals with some order of priority for them; (c) establishing a set of other significant values; (d) preparing a set of major alternative policies; (e) preparing reliable predictions of benefits and costs of the alternatives; (f) comparing the predicted benefits and best ones, and (g) evaluating the benefits and costs of the best alternatives and deciding whether they are good or not. Finally the post-policy-making stage has three phases, viz., (a) motivating the execution of the policy, (b) executing the policy, and (c) evaluating the policy-making after execution. All these seventeen phases are interconnected with a complex network of communication and feedback channels, which Dror considers a separate phase of his optimal model. Dror also considers the structural framework of public policy-making and identifies a number of essential structural requirements for his model to be effective.[18]

Barriers to Policy Sciences

Policy science, which is emerging as a separate field, is encountering many problems hindering its growth.[19] A careful study of barriers to policy science is not only interesting but essential for overcoming them. In particular, Dror identifies five specific barriers viz.,:[20]

1. Lack of belief in the ability of science to be of help in the policy-making process, which is regarded quasi-mystically as an art and which is monopolised by the 'experienced politician and decision-maker;'

2. Strong taboos and ritualistic attachments to institutions and beliefs which are expected to be undermined or when policy sciences develop;
3. Socio-cultural distance between scientists and policy-makers;
4. Bewilderment at the contradictory conclusions arrived at by equally reputable scientists and therefore, a tendency to ignore scientific contribution as a whole; and
5. Bad experience with scientists and with science contributions to policy-making.

In addition to the above, the two main interrelated socio-cultural barriers to policy sciences in the United States and in most other western countries appear to be fear of the policy-making roles of science and the beginning of an anti-intellectual and anti-rational movement. The fear that scientists may take over and become a new compact ruling class-apprehensive of scientocracy, is expressed in the form of 'Managerial Revolution', 'technocracy', 'meritocracy' and 'technopolis'.[21] Another important barrier to policy studies in many countries is university conservatism. Universities are dominated by juridical approach and absence of advanced social sciences. This hinders the development of the academic and professional infrastructure essential for policy sciences.[22] The highly ideologised university where the academic pluralism is used to demand academic status for representatives of radical ideologies is another barrier. Most radical ideologies reject policy studies and research, as a servant of the corrupt establishment delaying the needed revolution by constituting a palliative.[23] Scarcity of persons who are qualified to engage in policy research is another variable hindering the development of policy sciences.[24]

On Becoming a Policy Scientist

Dror, based on his long years of intense interest and work in policy-making and its improvement, suggests nine desiderata to the striving policy scientists. They are:

1. Gain historic and comparative perspectives;
2. Know policy-making realities;
3. Study your society in-depth;
4. Take up grand policy issues;
5. Move into metapolicy-making;
6. Build up an appropriate philosophy of knowledge and action;
7. Broaden methodologies;
8. Multiply disciplinary base; and
9. Be careful about your professional ethics.[25]

The desiderata presented above, is no doubt, formidable, if not prohibitive. There are no easy ways of becoming a full-fledged policy scientist from the present state-of-the-art policy sciences. Dror offers, therefore, five operational recommendations to aid and guide those who intend to become policy scientists. They are: read a lot and broadly; work on diverse issues; experience different work locations; spend some years in another culture; and study a major language.[26] Dror was clear that to become a policy scientist one's skills and qualifications are important to advice on critical decisions. "To be satisfied", Dror opines, "is irresponsible; to appear to be more, to oneself or others; is reckless". After mastering, at least partly, the steps listed above, the policy scientist must face more difficult requirements such as building upon appropriate personal *weltanschauung*, in addition to further forging one's mind.[27]

Capacity to Govern

The inadequacies of the present day forms of governance are being increasingly recognised due to distrust of governments, money dominated elections, failure of governments to find policy options on major issues, etc. The civil society, private sector and non-government organisations, however important, are not able to compensate the government's incapacity to shape the future. Dror argues that the contemporary governments are obsolete and proposes changes in values, structures, staffing, public understanding and political culture to equip the governments to meet the challenges of the 21st century. He identifies ten characteristics of global change viz.[28]:

1. Rapid non-linear change;
2. Increasing uncertainty and complexity;
3. Golbalisation;
4. Multiplying complexity;
5. Powerful global actors;
6. Co-existence of growing prosperity and increasing inequality;
7. Intense frustrations, trauma, dependency and unrest;
8. Likelihood of harm and evil;
9. Conflict and violence; and
10. All the changes leading to mutations.

Dror further says that the "Humanity is undergoing transformations and approaching phase transitions with a large potential for both good and bad – even evil – outcomes. The actual trajectory into the future will be significantly influenced by both action and inaction on the part of governance, including critical choices that no other social institution can or should make. However, present governance is not equipped for weaving the future for better. Therefore, radical governance redesigns are essential in order to upgrade capacities to govern and, in particular, to influence the future for better."[29] Upgrading capacities to govern depends a lot on changes in underlying political cultures that are unlikely to come about on their own. Therefore, the governments must engage in political culture architecture, including moral education.[30]

Dror distinguishes between 'ordinary tasks of governance' and 'higher order tasks'. The former include service delivery, maintaining public order, etc., that are receiving attention in 'new public management' and 're-inventing government'. Any failure in fulfilling these tasks seriously undermines the very fabric of society and governance and therefore they are very important. Higher order tasks of governance should receive more attention and priority. Even the well performing governance systems need to be redesigned in the context of transformations that is taking place across the globe to meet the future needs. The redesign of governance systems depends on the specific situation of each country.

A Critical Evaluation

Dror's proposition for the development of a new discipline of 'Policy Sciences' is a bold attempt at integration of knowledge. But the total approach tends to be academic in perspective with poor operational utility. It is paradoxical that Dror on the one hand attacked pure academic approach but made his argument for a new science equally academic. Dror started with an observation that control systems developed so far are feeble which is considered to be disastrous to the future of man. Although this is the starting point there is unpardonable departure resulting in more of policy analysis than a concentrated discussion on improving societal direction systems. Dror failed to establish any valid correlation between improvement in public policy-making and societal direction systems.

Dror's call for the use of extra-rational abilities in his optimal model is criticised from the standpoint of the present state of administrative studies. Dror did not pay attention to the problem of controlling the extra-rationally able person from controlling and destroying others. He deals with the problem somewhat casually thus giving a handle to the counter-reformists, who are ready to credit the administrator 'with a feel for things' and 'the art' of administration.[31]

Dror's major contribution is metapolicy-making. From this he goes over to describe the existing structure but fails to underpin the problem of special research into deliberate structural change and their impact on policy. Research in this area is very essential as the existing literature only concentrates on resistance to change and not how to bring changes in the structures.[32]

Dror's discussion on policy sciences is conditioned mostly by the experience of western societies and Israel. But an analysis of such a comprehensive subject cannot be complete without adequate examination of experiences of the third world countries. Dror's discussion suffers from vagueness and repetition. This could be partly because of his hastiness to develop a new science and partly due to 'over commitment' to the concept.

Dror views policy sciences as a response to face the challenge of shaping the future through improved knowledge, structural rationality and organised creativity. As the purpose of policy sciences is to contribute to the improvement of public-policy-making, policy sciences as supradisciplinary effort based on behavioural sciences and management studies, has an immense contemporary relevance. Although the analysis of Dror suffers from certain shortcomings the whole approach has immense academic relevance to the students of social sciences. It is a bold attempt to break the artificial barriers created to knowledge. A stage has reached where social phenomenon must be examined by social scientists in its totality. Policy sciences are a significant and right step in this direction.

In Brief

Yehezkel Dror's wide ranging contributions to policy studies in the wider context of public administration can be summarised as:

- Yehezkel Dror (1928), a distinguished scholar and a policy consultant, is widely regarded as the world's foremost pioneer of modern public policy studies. He made a mark in public administration through his outstanding contributions to policy studies.
- Elaborating on the nature of knowledge for human action, Dror divided knowledge into three levels: knowledge relevant to control over environment; knowledge relevant to control society and individuals and knowledge concerning the control over controls. Dror calls the knowledge of control over controls as societal direction system and considers it the least developed of all knowledge systems.
- Dror considered public policy-making as a dominant component of the societal direction system and identified the weaknesses of scientific knowledge in the area of policy-making. These weaknesses resulted in inadequate knowledge for effective policy-making.
- Dror identified various sources for the emergence of policy sciences and suggested elements of new paradigm of policy sciences.

- Dror anticipated far-reaching implications with the growth of policy sciences. He believed that by nurturing the 'organised dreaming', policy sciences could solve current and future social problems.

- In Dror's analysis, public policy-making occupies an important place. He examines existing normative models critically and considers that they fall short of the requirements. He suggested 'optimal model' integrating and supplementing the strengths of various models. Dror elaborated the characteristics, major stages and phases of his optimal model.

- Dror identified barriers to policy sciences. Among others, he particularly mentions anti-intellectual, anti-rational movements and university conservatism as barriers to the growth of policy sciences. He suggests a number of desiderata to the striving policy scientists in the context of wide ranging global changes.

- Dror's views on policy sciences are criticised for their vagueness, repetition and academic orientation with limited operational utility. His failure to establish any valid correlation between improvement in public policy-making and societal direction is also criticised.

- Dror has made a bold attempt to integrate knowledge systems for societal direction through public policies. Dror's public policy studies approach has widened the intellectual horizon and social relevance of public administration studies.

Notes and References

1 See http://www.amazon.com/YehezkelDror/ e/B00IHPE3GE; See also, http://public-policy.huji.ac.il/eng/staff-in2.asp?id=119&pageid=112; and Wigfall, Patrice Moss, and Kalatari, Behrooz, *Biographical Dictionary of Public Administration*, Greenwood Press, 2000, pp. 28-29.

2 Ibid.

3 Dror, Yehezkel, *Public Policymaking Re-examined*, Scranton, Pennsylvania, Chandler Publishing Company, 1968; Dror, Yehezkel, *Design for Policy Sciences*, New York, American Elsevier Publishing Company, Inc., 1971; Dror, Yehezkel, *Ventures in Policy Sciences: Concepts and Applications*, New York, American Elsevier Publishing Company, Inc., 1971; Dror, Yehezkel, *Policymaking Under Adversity, New Brunswick, Transaction Books, 1986*; Dror, Yehezkel, *The Capacity to Govern: A Report to the Club of Rome*, London, Frank Cass, 2000. For a list of his recent publications see http://public-policy.huji.ac.il/eng/staff-in2.asp?id=119&pageid=113.

4 Dror, Yehezkel, *Policymaking under Adversity, op.cit.*

5 Dror, Yehezkel, *Ventures in Policy Sciences: Concepts and Applications*, op. cit., p. 9.

6 Ibid., p. 11.

7 Ibid., p. 11-12

8 Dror, Yehezkel, *Public Policymaking Re-examined*, op. cit., p. 241.

9 Dror, Yehezkel, "Policy Sciences: Some Global Perspectives", *Policy Sciences*, Vol. 5, No. 1, March 1974, pp. 83-85.

10 Dror, Yehezkel, *Ventures in Policy Sciences*, op. cit., pp. 12-13.

11 Ibid., pp. 14-16. See also Yehezkel Dror, *Design for Policy Sciences*, op. cit., pp. 49-54.

12 Dror, Yehezkel, *Ventures in Policy Sciences*, op. cit., pp. 16-24. See also Dror, Yehezkel, Dror, Yehezkel, *Design for Policy Sciences*, pp. 123-135.

13 Dror, Yehezkel, *Public Policymaking Re-examined*, op. cit., p. 130.

14 Subramaniam, V., "Dror on Policy Making", *The Indian Journal of Public Administration*, Vol. 16, No. 1, Jan-March, 1970, pp. 86-87. See also Dror, Yehezkel, *Public Policymaking Re-examined*, op. cit., pp. 129-153.

15 Dror, Yehezkel, *Public Policymaking Re-examined*, op. cit., pp. 131-132.

16 Ibid., pp. 154-162.

17 Ibid., pp. 163-196.

18 Ibid., pp. 197-213.

19 For a detailed discussion of barriers hindering the development of policy sciences see also Dror, Yehezkel, *Public Policymaking Re-examined*, op. cit., pp.225-240; and *Design for Policy Sciences*, op. cit., pp. 33-50.

20 Dror, Yehezkel, *Design for Policy Sciences*, op. cit., pp 37-38.

21 Ibid., p. 39.

22 Dror, Yehezkel, "Policy Sciences: Some Global Perspectives", op. cit., pp. 85-86.

23 Ibid., p. 86.

24 Ibid., p. 87.

25 See Dror, Yehezkel, "On becoming More of a Policy Scientist", *Policy Studies Review*, Vol. 4, No. 1, August, 1984, pp. 13-18.

26 Ibid., pp. 18-19.

27 Ibid., p. 19.

28 Dror, Yehezkel, *The Capacity to Govern*, op.cit., p.39.

29 Ibid., p.63.

30 Ibid., p.60.

31 Subramaniam, V., op. cit., p. 96.

32 Ibid.

19

DWIGHT WALDO

Y. Pardhasaradhi

Introduction

Dwight Waldo is very closely associated with the history and theory of public administration than any other thinker. A 'chronicler', a leading 'philosopher-historian-theoretician', and a 'defining figure' of public administration, his contribution to the discipline of public administration has been outstanding. He was interested not only in virtually every facet of administrative studies and learning, but also in the larger aspects of social world which shape and are themselves shaped by the administrative centres of the governments. Waldo had very significant influence on the teaching and theory of public administration during the second half of the twentieth century. This is evident from the observations of Carroll and Frederickson when they said that "To study public administration today is to have been taught by Dwight Waldo. To do research in

(1913-2000)

public administration is to have been taught by Dwight Waldo. To practice public administration today is to have been taught by Dwight Waldo."[1] He influenced curriculum and pedagogy, and he influenced how those who teach public administration see and understand the field. He set the standards for contemporary consideration issues of bureaucracy in a democratic government. He also set standards for the quality of writing, for clarity of elaboration, and for moving academic public administration from just knowledge to understanding. [2]

Life and Works

Clifford Dwight Waldo (1913-2000) was born in DeWitt, Nebraska.[3] After high school, Waldo joined Wesleyan College in Peru, Nebraska from where he received his B.A in (1935). He looked for a job as a teacher, but unable to get in the throes of the Great Depression, he accepted the job of reading papers at the University of Nebraska - Lincoln and enrolled in the master's programme in political science. After receiving a master's degree (1937) from the University of Nebraska, he joined as a Cowles Fellow at Yale University. He worked as an instructor in the Political Science department (1941-42) and while on the job worked for his Ph.D and obtained the degree in 1942. The initial focus of his dissertation was on "Theories of Expertise in the Democratic Tradition" intended to address the question of how much democracy should be yielded to experts.[4] But the scope of the thesis changed over time and finally it was titled as 'Theoretical Aspects of the American Literature in Public Administration'.

Waldo, an unintended bureaucrat, worked as a Price Analyst for the Office of Price Administration (1942-44) and later as Administrative Analyst (1944-46) in the Bureau of the Budget at Washington, DC. During these four years he gained insights into public administration and its working which probably laid the foundations to his later contributions. After the Second World War, Waldo joined the University of California at Berkeley as an assistant professor. Waldo helped to establish a Graduate School of Public Affairs and contributed to changing the University Bureau of Public Administration to that of the Institute of Governmental Studies, and served as its Director from 1958-1967. Later, he went to Italy on a project to improve Italian administration, an experience that made him aware of the limitations of 'principles' of administration.[5] In 1967, he moved to Syracuse University to become Professor of Political Science and Albert Schweitzer Professor of Humanities in the Maxwell School of Citizenship and Public Affairs. This is one of the ten "Super professorships" created by the New York State that year. In 1979, he retired as professor emeritus from Syracuse and spent the next two years at the Woodrow Wilson International Centre for Scholars of the Smithsonian Institute. He remained professionally active and was a member of many prestigious associations, both national and international, until his death on 27th October, 2000 at the age of 87.

Waldo wrote extensively – books, monographs and articles. The publication of *The Administrative State*, a revised version of his doctoral dissertation, made him a *'pariah'* in the public administration discipline. His other significant publications include *The Study of Public Administration* (1955), *The Novelist on Organisation and Administration* (1968), *Public Administration in a Time of Turbulence* (1971), *Democracy, Bureaucracy and Hypocrisy* (1977), *The Enterprise of Public Administration* (1980), *Bureaucracy and Democracy-A Strained Relationship* (unpublished manuscript with Frank Marini, 1999). A gleaning through Waldo's voluminous writings provide us with an overview of the discipline, offers a series of penetrating insights and criticisms, comments on more recent developments and his speculations about the future of the 'enterprise of public administration'. He reveals the implicit assumptions and the hidden premises that underlie the various approaches to public administration. Although Waldo may not provide definitive answers, he raises right questions and provides some insights that better equip us to make more informed choices between difficult alternatives.

Waldo was actively associated with the American Society for Public Administration and its Comparative Administration Group and served on the Society's Council (1963-1966). He served on the Council and the Executive Committee of the American Political Science Association (1957-60), became its vice-president in 1961 and was president of the National Association of Schools of Public Affairs and Administration (1977-78). He served on the editorial boards of the *American Political Science Review* (1959-1963) and *Public Administration Review* (1958-66) and as its Editor-in-Chief (1966-77). During his long association as editor Waldo 'redefined public administration as an autonomous field that merged academics and practice.' Several of the symposium issues published during his tenure 'retain their value as classic contributions to the field'. He was also a member of the editorial board of the *International Review of Administrative Sciences*. In recognition of his lifetime achievements and contributions to public administration the American Society for Public Administration in 1979 named its highest award as Dwight Waldo Award in his honour. In 1987, he received John Gaus Lecture Award.

The Administrative State

Waldo represents a perspective on public administration - the administration as politics approach - that emerged in the 1940s. His position was initially based on his response to the classical approach, but his later writings extend elements of that critique to the behavioural approach. Waldo denies that politics and policy considerations can be excluded from the administration. Moreover, facts cannot be separated from values. Consequently, administration is inevitably both an art and a science and perhaps more art than a science. Since administration cannot be separated from politics, Waldo argues that public administration is different from private administration; distinguished by the political environment in which the public administrator operates. To him the objective should not be to keep administrators out of policy and political matters, but to encourage cooperation between the political and administrative domains and to discover ways in which we can benefit from the creative potential as well as substantive contributions of administrative officials.

Waldo viewed public administration as a 'lower' field of endeavour preoccupied with such relatively mundane things as counting the number of manhole covers.[6] Although he thought public administration and political theory to be at odds, his objective was to treat public administration as yet another aspect of political theory and thereby prove the usefulness and relevance of political theory itself. Waldo's dissertation was later published as *The Administrative State*.[7] In the eight years between the completion of the dissertation and its publication, his ideas and attitudes about public administration changed substantially. He incorporated the lessons of his bureaucratic experience and revised the dissertation before publication. Though Waldo considered himself a failure as a bureaucrat, his administrative experience started a process of re-socialisation that resulted in identification with public administration rather than political theory. He emerged from government service with respect for the difficulties of administration, empathy for administrators and a conviction that no one should be allowed to teach political science without experience in public administration.[8]

Waldo advanced four central ideas. Firstly, there is an intrinsic tension between democracy and bureaucracy that obliges career public servants to protect democratic principles. Secondly, the politics/administration dichotomy is false. Public servants hold political positions that require more than merely implementing policy set by elected officials. Thirdly, public servants must negotiate efficiencies demanded by the scientific management movement with due process and public access to government. Finally, government cannot be run like a business. Honouring the Constitution and other democratic imperatives make managing a unit of the government far more challenging than a comparable private sector organisation.[9] Waldo denied the possibility of constructing a science of public administration, doubted the existence of 'principles' of administration, questioned the plausibility of a unified theory of organisation, skeptical of those who would indiscriminately intermingle politics and administration and despairs of reaching a common agreement on a definition of the field of public administration. Nonetheless, he believed that the fate of civilisation well rest on our ability to master the functions of administration.[10] His interests run through sociology, business administration and organisation theory. He found these subjects more germane to the agenda of public administration than political science. He was a visionary and a great thinker determined to infuse public administration with democratic values.[11]

Public Administration - History

Public Administration, according to Waldo, [12] as a field and practice has its origin in the earliest times of human civilisation. Administration and civilisation have coexisted and each nourished the other. Both were internal parts of human progress. Civilisation promoted administration and administration made civilisational achievements possible. Both have contributed to the development of each other. If there is a single dominant theme in Waldo's work, it is probably the importance he attaches to history or as he puts it, a strong sense that "what is past in prologue." Waldo believes that there is much to be learned from history and he deplores the fact that much of the public administration literature has been anti-historical in nature. Waldo asserts that history does indeed repeat itself, though in different ways and with endless variations of its themes, and that ignoring the past denies an important source of insights, hypotheses and scientific conclusions. An important lesson of history, he argues, is that the techniques of administration are at the centre of political-governmental evolution. Indeed, he maintains that government and administration are substantially equivalent. In Waldo's phrase, administration 'frames civilization' by giving it a foundation or stage and by providing a base for growth. In effect, government, administration and civilisation are intimately joined.[13]

Waldo considers government and its administration to be more than merely an artificially created intruder in a state of nature that would otherwise be serene and prosperous. Government is no more a creation than markets or private enterprise and the sustaining, nurturing and creative role of government has largely been ignored. Waldo acknowledges that government is always marginally oppressive and sometimes massively so that there are things that government cannot do or can do only clumsily. However, the government and its administrative apparatus have performed their functions with at least moderate success despite increases in the scale and complexity of their activities.

With the 1940s came a series of challenges to the classical approach to public administration. In Waldo's words "heterodoxy replaced orthodoxy"[14]. Waldo says the field of public administration is characterised by a diversity of perspectives in which the classical approach has not been so much repudiated as absorbed, amended, extended and joined by new perspectives. In the process, some of the ideological and philosophical underpinnings of the classical approach have been rejected, and others have simply gone underground. The influence of the business mentality has diminished, the idea of "fundamental law" as a higher moral order has been largely abandoned, and there is increasing skepticism about the notion of "progress." Though pragmatism has declined as a fashionable philosophy, Waldo maintains that it continues to be the unarticulated working philosophy of public administration and is manifested in the effort to construct a new science of administration in a manner consistent with the tenets of behaviouralism[15].

A Classical Approach

Waldo emphasised that public administration did not begin in the 20th century. A stream of administrative technology has developed over the centuries to which, until recent times, the public sector has made the most important contributions. Waldo does credit the late 19th and early 20th centuries with the development of the self-conscious study of public administration on a scale new in human history and identifies the United States as a major focal point of administrative studies. Although a number of forces were important in shaping the overall contours of the field, Waldo asserts that the proximate determinants of the specific content of public administration were the reform movement and the progressive era. They emphasised executive leadership, civil service reform and education for citizenship and sought to expose inefficiency through scientific investigations.[16] All these characteristics were incorporated in what came to be known as the classical approach to public administration.

Waldo identified five basic characteristics of the classical approach to public administration, which dominated the field until roughly 1940. They were: acceptance of the politics-administration dichotomy, a generic management orientation, the search for principles of administration through scientific analysis, an emphasis on centralisation of executive bureaucracy, and a commitment to democracy[17]. A first and fundamental premise of politics-administration dichotomy was that politics should be separated from administration and that administration falls in the realm of expertise from which politics should be excluded. It calls for a strengthened chief executive to curb the centrifugal forces of the administrative branch.[18] A second characteristic - generic management orientation - assumed that the techniques of private management were applicable in the public sector. Waldo argues that public administration accepted both business procedures and a business ideology as the business model was used to deprecate the balance of powers and aggrandise the role of the chief executive as well as to justify hierarchical control mechanisms, merit appointment and the adoption of business-like budgetary procedures.

A third characteristic was the search for a science of administration. It was believed that the scientific study of administration could lead to the discovery of general 'principles' of administration on which efficient government could be based. [19] The fourth is the emphasis on centralisation of executive activities. The general prescription was centralisation, simplification, and unification. The objective was to centralise responsibility, to build the power of the chief executive by establishing stronger hierarchical controls within the executive branch, and to abolish the superfluous offices in the name of efficiency.[20] Finally, the classical approach contained a basic commitment to democracy. However, democracy was defined substantively rather than procedurally. Democracy was to be achieved by establishing a strong, responsive and responsible government designed to serve efficiently the needs of the people in an emergent 'Great Society'.[21]

Waldo was critical of the organisational paradigm of the classical approach. He criticises both the emphasis on supposed principles or commonalities among organisations and the rationalist bias of classical organisation theory. The search for commonalities, Waldo says "that classical organisation theory ignored the specificity that is the stuff of administration."[22] He maintains that organisations should be defined and structured to meet purposes, not general principles, and the organisation form and process actually adopted should be suited to the specific situation confronting the organisation. He also argues that classical organisation theory prescribed general operational forms and processes that were not readily adaptable to specific situations or changing circumstances. [23] Waldo claims that the classical approach ignores the irrational and informal aspects of organisations. A case in point is Weber's concept of bureaucracy. Waldo argues that Weber placed undue emphasis on the functional side of bureaucracy, ignored the informal and socio-emotional aspects of organisations, and elevated position over knowledge as the basis for hierarchical authority. [24] Waldo also chides the classical authors about their "scientific" pretensions. He says that the classical "science" of public administration relied primarily on a heaping up of facts and its principles were little more than an extension of common sense.

Waldo argues that public administration must deal with thinking and valuing human beings and that the techniques of science are inappropriate to such subjects. Values cannot be treated scientifically, and human free will means that the principles of mechanical cause and effect are inapplicable.[25] Though administrative science is not possible, Waldo believes that a scientific mind would at least make common sense more sensible and that some parts of administration may well be amenable to scientific investigation. Nevertheless, Waldo warns that we should not try to force on a subject matter a method that is not suitable to it.[26]

Finally, Waldo challenges the classicist's emphasis on efficiency intended to replace a moralistic approach to public administration. Waldo maintains that the idea of efficiency itself became imbued with a moral significance, however, as a pursuit of "technical efficiency" was transformed into a pursuit of "social efficiency." Although efficiency itself is not a value, it is a useful concept only within a framework of consciously held values. That is, one must consider the object of efficiency, since it is not reasonable to assume that it is desirable to accomplish *any* end efficiently.

Politics and Administration

Waldo unequivocally abandoned politics-administration dichotomy. He explains that politics/administration relate to democracy/bureaucracy.[27] He was known as a heterodox critic of the politics-administration dichotomy. This reputation seem to be based on his early publication *Administrative State* in which he conceptualised politics/administration narrowly as deciding and executing. But his later publications offer 'much broader conceptualisation and a more ambivalent and even a more positive appraisal of the dichotomy'. [28] Waldo contends that the separation is inadequate, either as a description of reality or as a prescription for administrative behaviour.[29] To him the dichotomy was intended to resolve the conflict between bureaucracy and democracy by making elected officials responsible for framing policy and restricting administrators to the execution of that policy. In actuality, public administration in the classical period was false to the ideal of democracy. Democracy was seen as desirable, but peripheral to the concerns of administration and hostile to the central principle of efficiency. [30] The classical movement indicted centrifugal democracy and sought to implement its own version of centripetal democracy by proposing a separation between politics and administration and relying on what Waldo calls the "dogmas of centralization" and the "canons of integration" as a solution to the problem of efficiency. The politics-administration dichotomy was also intended to solve the value problem. It was asserted that the political system would establish values and set goals for administration. Waldo regards this as disingenuous since it ignores the desire to extend the compass of the science of administration to an ever-larger complex of phenomena. As a result, public administration threatened to overrun the realm of policy – as the British conquered India – not by intent but by a continuous process of tidying up the border. Waldo contends that the real question raised by the classical authors was not whether politics and policy should be separated from administration, but how far the administrative function should extend in determining values and policies, question for which they failed to provide a suitable answer. Waldo's view is that we should move towards a philosophy that encourages cooperation among powers, be they administrative or political, not competition among separated powers.

Organisation Theory

Waldo divides the development of the organisation theory into three stages.[31] The first stage was the classical period, epitomised by the works of authors such as Taylor, Gulick, Fayol and Mooney. The classical stage of organisation theory was based on the machine model of the organisation and emphasised the rational aspects of human behaviour. This stage reached its zenith in the 1930s and culminated in the publication of the *Papers on the Science of Administration*.[32] Waldo labels the second stage of the development of organisation theory – the neoclassical approach. This stage began with the Hawthorne studies in the 1920s and retained major importance through the mid-century. In contrast to the classical, the neoclassical approach emphasised the emotive and socio-psychological dimensions of human behaviour in organisations. The final stage in the development of organisation theory is the modern organisation theory, which, according to Waldo, began with the publication of March and Simon's *Organisations* in 1958.[33] This theory is based on an organic or natural system model of the organisation and stresses organisational growth and survival. It endorses organisations that have less reliance on hierarchical controls, more recognised sources of authority, greater opportunity for personal mobility, and greater receptivity to organisational change. Modern organisation theory is decidedly behavioural in orientation, adopting the methods of the physical and biological sciences and seeking a value-free general theory of organisations true for all times and places.

Comparative Public Administration

The second major focus of the contemporary period has been comparative public administration. According to Waldo, comparative public administration (CPA) both resembles and differs from modern organisation theory. It shares with modern theory a concern for methodological problems; a reliance on models such as the systems framework and structural functionalism; an interdisciplinary orientation; a search for universal concepts, formulas and theories; and an emphasis on empirical description. However, CPA differs from modern theory in its explicit comparative perspective, its focus on cultural diversity and its fascination with Weberian bureaucracies.

Though it was at one time widely believed that CPA was the area of greatest promise in contemporary public administration, Waldo feels that that promise has yet to be fulfilled. CPA tells us about the relationship between administration and social ends, the critical dependence of civilisation on effective governmental administration and the difficulties in transferring the Western model of administration to other cultures. But the basic problem of the CPA movement was the distance between the theoretical models employed and the evidence of field research.[34] And even with its strong theoretical bent, Waldo asserts that the movement failed to produce anything in the way of rigorous theory.[35]

The pressure for practical results led to a switch from CPA to developmental administration, though such a switch did not produce encouraging results. Waldo charges that the developmental perspective has assumed that to be developed is to be "Western." The result, he asserts, is that developmental administration has become a powerful and subtle ideology with the characteristics of a "world-girdling religion," and the effort to achieve development has amounted to little more than an effort to reproduce the Weberian model of bureaucracy.

New Public Administration

A major development in contemporary public administration is the New Public Administration movement. This movement, spawned by the social and political ferment of the late 1960s and early 1970s, was, according to Waldo, part of the rebellion of youth and the counter culture of the non-Marxian left.[36] The conference was hosted by Waldo bringing together young and progressive scholars and practitioners who were under 35 and hell-bent in revolutionising the field of public administration. Minnowbrook - Syracuse University's Conference Centre - is considered as shorthand for an entirely new school of thought. The conference signaled the rise of the 'Waldovian perspective' keeping the future in mind.[37] Its goal was to establish new directions for the field and to reconcile public administrations' role in the context of social upheaval. The New Public Administration criticised the old public administration for its lack of an explicit ideological-philosophical framework and supported an activist role for the administrator in the pursuit of social equality. Waldo refers to the movement as a "New Romanticism," as it shares with the philosophical movement the assumption that man is inherently good but is corrupted by bad institutions, and it reacts to rationalism by emphasising the role of feeling over reason, senses over the mind, and spontaneity, creativity and self-fulfillment over convention and rules. [38]

The basic themes of the New Public Administration were participation, decentralisation and representative bureaucracy. Participation was supported both as a political process and as an organisational process. Political participation was seen as a means of dispersing power and increasing citizen involvement in government. The movement rejected both simple majoritarianism and pluralism in favour of alternatives described by Waldo as ranging from organic communitarianism to moral and political elitism. [39] Support for organisational participation was part of what Waldo sees as the movement's massive hostility to anything perceived as bureaucratic. It was to be a means for promoting change and dispersing power within the organisation. Decentralisation, like participation, was intended to disperse power and increase citizen involvement in governmental and organisational processes. Representative democracy was meant to promote client-centered administration and representation of clientele interests by administrators.

However, Waldo had certain misgivings on the concepts of New Public Administration movement.[40] On participation and representative bureaucracy, he asserts that the arguments are often *ad hoc* and inconsistent, if not dishonest. Supporters of participation, Waldo argues, seem to assume that some invisible hand will resolve the problems of coordination, order and survival in the new system of highly dispersed power. He finds the movement to be inconsistent in its desire to have democracy while rejecting majoritarianism and pluralism, and in effect, supporting rule by the minority. On decentralisation, Waldo points out that a cogent case can also be made for centralisation and that neither case is universally right or wrong.[41]

Waldo finds some validity in the anti-organisational stance of the New Public Administration, but he considers much of the indictment to be unfair, spurious and above all, unrealistic. He notes that most innovative techniques and technologies have been created in bureaucratic organisations and that the era of bureaucracy has been an era of rapid change. Even if the bureaucracy serves the *status quo*, the *status quo* itself is not a monolithic interest, but a diversity of interests, all of which must be served. In addressing the question of efficiency, Waldo charges that the critics attack a narrow conception of efficiency that had long been discarded. He says that there is no such thing called "public philosophy" and that the problem now is to find the boundaries of public administration.[42]

Public Administration as a Profession

Waldo was more sympathetic to a "professional" orientation in public administration. He acknowledges that public administration is not a profession in a strict sense, is not to become one, and perhaps should not even be done. However, he considers professionalism to be a good attitude or strategy and asserts that public administration should move from a disciplinary to a professional perspective with a separate professional school status in the university. [43] Waldo's favourite analogy in this regard is medicine, which, he says, is both science and art, both theory and practice, has a multidisciplinary focus rather than single theory, and is given direction by a broad social purpose. Thinking of public administration as a profession, Waldo maintains, frees public administration from its second-class status in colleges of liberal arts, frees it from a sense of guilt about not having a distinctive paradigm, and gives it license to seek whatever is needed, wherever it is located. Thus, Waldo suggests that public administration might act as a profession without being one, or even hoping to become one.[44]

Public Administration and the Future

Waldo, a self-described amateur futurist, sees the future as a world of turbulence and change. A major force for change is the current transition from an industrial to a postindustrial society. Although Waldo notes that many of the prophesies for the 1970s failed to come to pass, there is still validity to the notion that the postindustrial society will see the emergence of knowledge as a crucial factor in productivity, the creation of new technologies for processing information, the decline of the factory, the establishment of new power elites and power centres based on scientific-technological knowledge, and a shift in emphasis from production to distribution and service occupations. [45] All of this will result in an accelerated pace of economic-social-political change that will generate institutional and psychological social crises.

These forces raise an array of problems that must at least in part be addressed by public administration. A particular problem for public administration will be dealing with new forms of organisation and management and calls for the assumption of new responsibilities. Waldo predicts that organisations of the future will be less bureaucratic, increasingly of a mixed public-private nature, more chains, complexes or systems of organisations than unitary organisations, and more international and multinational in their operations. [46] These new organisational styles raise questions about how to develop less bureaucratic organisations without encouraging chaos, how to deal with increasing ethical complexity, and how to cope with the increasing likelihood of conflict and crisis. Moreover, public administration is apt to be called on to perform even more functions. This raises the danger of overload in a system that already has responsibility beyond the authority it can command or the virtue it can summon.

The implications of this future for public administration are manifold. Public administration is the government's primary mechanism for dealing with the forces noted above. It will thus be centrally involved in change and transformation. The decisions of public administrators will necessarily be a combination of policy judgments, instrumental judgments, legal judgments and moral judgments. The enterprise of public administration will be marked by philosophical, disciplinary and methodological pluralism as we attempt to survive, adapt and control change.

In looking to the future, Waldo observes that there are two major scenarios: the totalitarian and the anarchist.[47] The totalitarian scenario reconciles public and private morality by definition as government totally integrates and controls. The anarchist scenario, which Waldo sees as preferable, or at least less undesirable, sees the future as characterised by a multiplicity of diffuse and complex socio-economic-political institutions with considerable ambiguity in the concept of public morality. In reaction to the anarchist scenario, Waldo feels that it is akin to watching a movie in a reverse mode as the sovereign state is dissolved and its clear vertical structure of authority is replaced by complicated, contractual and informal horizontal relationships. This does not mean that he thinks history will repeat itself. Waldo believes that the future must be created, it cannot be copied, and he expresses the hope that reciprocal learning, mutual adjustment and institutional intervention may now be speeded; that a world unified, but not unitary, harmonious, but not homogenised, may develop.

An Evaluation

Waldo is more a critic and a commentator on the field of public administration than a creator. It is possible to quibble with the particulars of Waldo's approach to the history of public administration, but the larger problem with Waldo's work is his essential ambivalence. Waldo insists that public administration is necessarily involved in politics, but he sees some continuing value in the politics-administration dichotomy. He states that public administration is both art and science, but fails to specify an area in which each might be applicable.

He argues that public administration is both different from, and the same as, private administration without specifying in details the similarities and differences, or their consequences. He thinks we should have both democracy and bureaucracy, but he does not tell us either how the conflicts between those forces can be resolved or what the optimal balance between them is. He says that public administration is not, and perhaps should not be, a profession, but he urges that it act like one. Waldo believes that administration and civilisation are intimately linked and that administration is the government's central mechanism for dealing with change.

In Brief

Waldo's contributions to the discipline of public administration can be summarised as:

- Dwight Waldo (1913 - 2000), public administrations' leading philosopher, historian-theoretician, is a 'defining figure' in the teaching and study of public administration. The publication of *The Administrative State*, a revised version of his doctoral dissertation, made him a 'pariah' in the public administration discipline.

- Waldo unequivocally abandoned political-administration dichotomy and contends that the separation is inadequate, either as a description of reality or as a prescription for administrative behaviour. Waldo represents 'the administration as politics' approach in public administration.

- Waldo believes that there is much to learn from history and is critical of anti-historical nature of public administration literature. An important lesson of history, he argues, is that the techniques of administration are at the centre of political-governmental evolution.

- He was critical of organisational paradigm of classical theory and identified three different stages of development of organisation theory viz., classical period, neoclassical approach and modern organisation theory. Discussing the trends in modern organisation theories, Waldo examined critically the nature of comparative and development administration.

- Waldo played an important role in New Public Administration Movement, also known as 'Minnowbrook perspective" and 'Waldovian perspective'. Its goal was to establish new directions for the field and to reconcile public administrations' role in the context of social and political ferment of the late 1960's and early 1970's. Waldo referred the movement as 'New Romanticism'.

- Waldo was more sympathetic to a 'professional' orientation in public administration. Aware of the limitations of public administration becoming a profession, Waldo prefers it as a desirable strategy and suggests that public administration might act as a profession without being one or hoping to become one. Waldo's favourite analogy in this regard is medicine.

- Foreseeing the future world as turbulent and characterised by change, he examines the role of public administration in such turbulent times. He predicts that organisations of future will be less bureaucratic and more complex. The enterprise of public administration, according to him, will be marked by philosophical, disciplinary and methodological pluralism as we attempt to survive, adopt and control change.

- Waldo's works are criticised for its essential ambivalence. Some of the areas where his ambivalence is reflected are: views on politics-administration relations, public and private administration differences and professional nature of public administration.

- Waldo may not have provided definitive answers to problems in public administration, but raised right questions and provided insights that better equip us to more informed choices between different alternatives.

References

[1] Carroll, James D. and Frederickson, H. George, "Dwight Waldo 1913-2000", *Public Administration Review*, Vol, 61, No. 1, January-February, 2001, p.8.

[2] See, Ibid., p.7.

[3] Information on Waldo's early life is taken from information provided by Professor Waldo and from *Who's Who in America*, 42nd ed., vol. 2, 1982; See also Carroll, James D. and Frederickson, H. George, op.cit., pp. 2-8.

[4] Introduction to the 2nd edition of *The Administrative State: A Study of the Political Theory of American Public Administration*, New York, Ronald Press, 1984, p.1.

[5] Waldo, Dwight, *The Enterprise of Public Administration*, Novato, California: Chandler and Sharp, 1980, p.119.

[6] Waldo, Dwight, "The Administrative State Revisited," *Public Administration Review*, Vol. 25, No.1 (March 1965), p.6.

[7] Stivers, Camilla, "The Significance of The Administrative State", *Public Administrative Review*, Vol.68, No. 1.January-February, 2008, pp.53-56.

[8] Waldo, Dwight, "The Administrative State Revisited," op.cit. 6-7.

[9] Ibid.

[10] Fry, Brain R., *Mastering Public Administration: From Max Weber to Dwight Waldo*, Chatham, NJ, Chatham House Publishers, 1989. p.218.

[11] George Lowery, http://www1.maxwell.syr.edu/news.aspx . For a detailed account of Waldo's views on policy, research, training, agenda for future, etc., see Brown, Brack, and Stillman II, Richard J., "A Conversation with Dwight Waldo: An Agenda for Future Reflections", *Public Administration Review*, Vol.45.No.4.,1985, pp.459-467.

[12] Waldo, Dwight, *The Enterprise of Public Administration*, op.cit. p.1.

[13] Ibid., p.18.

[14] Fry, Brain R., op.cit. p.228.

[15] Waldo, Dwight, The Administrative State Revisited, op.cit., p.11.

[16] Waldo, Dwight, "Public Administration," *Journal of Politics*, Vol. 30, No. 2, May 1968, pp. 447-48.

[17] Fry, Brain R., op.cit. p.223.

[18] Waldo, Dwight, *The Administrative State: A Study of the Political Theory of American Public Administration*, op.cit.

[19] Waldo, Dwight, *The Study of Public Administration*, New York, Random House, 1955; and "Public Administration," in Sills, David, (Ed.), *International Encyclopedia of the Social Sciences*, New York, Macmillan and Free Press, 1968, p.148.

[20] Waldo, Dwight, *The Administrative State*, op.cit., pp. 133-34.

[21] Waldo, Dwight, "Public Administration," in Uveges, Jr. Joseph A., (Ed), *The Dimensions of Public Administration: Introductory Readings*, Boston, Holbrook Press, 1971, p. 26.

[22] Waldo, Dwight, *The Administrative State*, op.cit. p.175.

[23] Waldo, Dwight, "The Future of Management", *The Bureaucrat*, Fall 1977, pp. 106-109.

[24] Waldo, Dwight, *The Novelist on Organization and Administration: An Inquiry into the Relationship between Two Worlds*, Berkeley, Institute of Government Studies, 1968.

[25] Waldo, Dwight, *Administrative State*, op.cit. pp. 181-82.

[26] Ibid.

[27] Overeem, Patrick ,"Beyond Heterodoxy: Dwight Waldo and the Politics-Administration Dichotomy", *Public Administration Review*,Vol.68.No.1, January-February, 2008, p.40.

28. Ibid., pp.36-45
29. Waldo, Dwight, *Democracy, Bureaucracy and Hypocrisy*, Berkeley, Institute of Governmental Studies, 1977.
30. Waldo, Dwight, "Development of the Theory of Democratic Administration," *American Political Science Review*, Vol. 46, March 1952, p. 87.
31. Waldo, Dwight, "Organization Theory: Revisiting the Elephant," *Public Administration Review*, Vol. 38, No. 6, November-December, 1978, pp. 589-90.
32. Gulick, Luther, and Urwick, Lyndall, (Eds.), *The Papers on the Science of Administration*, New York, Institute of Public Administration, 1937.
33. March, James G., and Simon, Herbert A. *Organizations*, New York, Wiley Publications, 1958.
34. Waldo, Dwight, *Comparative Public Administration: Prologue, Performance and Problems in Preston LeBreton* (Ed.) Comparative Administrative Theory, Seattle, University of Washington Press, 1968, p. 7.
35. Waldo, Dwight, *Enterprise of Public Administration*, op.cit., p. 127.
36. Waldo, Dwight, "Developments in Public Administration," in *Current Issues in Public Administration*, (Ed.), New York, Frederick S. Lane, St. Martin's Press, 1978, p 554.
37. See Frank Marini (Ed.), *Toward A New Public Administration: The Minnowbrook Perspective,* Scranton, Pa., Chandler Publishing Company, 1971. See also George Lowery, op.cit.
38. Waldo, Dwight, *Some Issues in Preparing Science Administration Leadership for Tomorrow*, Program of Policy Studies in Science and Technology, Occasional Paper No. 6, Washington D.C., George Washington University, 1969, pp. 6-7.
39. Waldo, Dwight, "Some Thoughts on Alternatives, Dilemmas, and Paradoxes in a Time of Turbulence," in Waldo, Dwight, (Ed.), *Public Administration in a Time of Turbulence*, Scranton, Chandler Press, 1971, p. 271.
40. Ibid., p.263.
41. Ibid., p.259-60.
42. Ibid., p.280-81.
43. Waldo, Dwight, "Administrative State Revisited," op.cit., p. 28.
44. Waldo, Dwight,, "Foreword", In Frank Marini (ed.) Toward a New Public Administration, Scranton, PA, Chandler Publishing Company, 1971, pp. xiii-xv.
45. Waldo, Dwight, *Enterprise of Public Administration*, op.cit., pp. 158-60.
46. Waldo, Dwight, "Developments in Public Administration", op.cit., pp 538-42; Waldo, Dwight, *Enterprise of Public Administration*, op.cit., pp. 167-68.
47. Waldo, Dwight, "Reflections on Public Morality," *Administration & Society*, 1974; Vol. 6: p.277.

20

PETER DRUCKER

D. Ravindra Prasad

Introduction

Peter Drucker, management guru, consultant, professor, economist, writer and 'social ecologist'[1] through his writings over seven decades explained how humans are organised across business, government and non-profit sectors of society. He created foundations of modern management and is considered as one of the greatest management thinkers of the last century. He took a humanistic approach to management, emphasised that it is people who create organisations and they have a crucial role in modern society. He is a writer of uncommon verve, practicality and incisiveness and dealt with management matters in the context of larger society. He considered managers as a leadership group and felt that if the managers of major institutions do not take responsibility for the common good; no one else can or will.[2] His vision can be uncovered from his voluminous writings over the last several

(1909-2005)

decades and extrapolated to governmental administration. Drucker concentrated mostly on business sector and as a result his views on public sector were passed over and unpublicised.[3] Drucker, as a management theorist, wrote on non-profit organisations and federal government reforms in the US. But public administration scholars have not yet explored the implications of his thought for government and public administration - particularly the future of public management.[4]

Life and Works

Peter Ferdinand Drucker (1909-2005)[5] was born in Vienna, Austria and had schooling at the Doubling Gymnasium. In 1927, he went to Hamburg, Germany to undergo a one-year apprenticeship in a trading company. Alongside he enrolled in Hamburg University Law School and obtained the law degree. In 1929, he moved to Frankfurt where he worked as a financial journalist with a local newspaper as well as worked for an American bank. He obtained Ph.D in International Law and Public Law in 1931 from the University of Frankfurt. For some time he taught in the University of Frankfurt, history and international law. In 1933, during the Nazi regime, he migrated to London where he worked as a securities analyst for an insurance company and as an economist for a bank. He also worked as an American correspondent to the British newspapers. After four years in London, he migrated to the United States in 1937. He was influenced by economists like Joseph Schumpeter of Austria and John Keynes of Britain.

In the United States Drucker started his career as a freelance journalist chiefly to Harper's and Washington Post. He taught economics at Sarah Lawrence College in Bronxville, New York and later at Bennington College in Vermont (1942-49). He was Professor of Management at the New York University (1950-71), and Clark Professor of Social Sciences and Management at the Claremont Graduate School at California University from 1971 until his death. At the School he developed the country's first Executive MBA Programme. In his honour, the University Management School was named as Peter F. Drucker Graduate School of Management in 1987 (and later renamed as Peter F. Drucker and Masatoshai Ito Graduate School of Management). He took his last class at the School in 2002 at the age of 92.

Drucker, considered as the doyen of business consultants, had a long consultancy career beginning from 1943 with major corporations like General Motors, General Electric, Citicorp, Coca-Cola, Intel and IBM and many government and non-government organisations in the US, Canada, Japan and other countries. He was consultant to Alfred Sloan (General Motors), Jack Welch (General Electric), Andrew Grove (Intel) AgLafley (Proctor and Gamble), Shoichiro Toyoda (Toyota Motors), etc. He worked with several non-profit originations and social sector groups including universities and hospitals.

A polymath and prolific writer, Drucker published 39 influential books and contributed several articles in reputed professional journals like *Harvard Business Review*, *The Economist*, *Harpers*, and *The Atlantic Monthly*. He wrote a regular column in *Wall Street Journal* for two decades. His books include *The Concept of the Corporation* (1946), *The Practice of Management* (1954), *The Effective Executive (1966), Management - Tasks, Responsibilities, Practices (1974), The Discipline of Innovation (1985), Managing for the Future (1992), Management Challenge for the 21st Century (1999).*[6] In his writings he treated economics and management in a broad context of humanities. Some of his books were translated into more than 30 languages. Interdisciplinary thinking, avoidance of academic jargon and conspicuous absence of footnotes characterise his authorship. He also wrote novels, co-authored a book on painting, made educational films on management, developed professional programmes and on-line courses on management apart from a personal memoir *Adventures of a Bystander*. His books are bestsellers and some have got dozens of editions selling millions of copies. He also dedicated time to the service sector and founded the New York-based Peter F. Drucker Foundation for Non-profit Management, which since 2003 is known as the Leader to Leader Institute.

Drucker was awarded the Presidential Medal of Freedom (2002), the U.S.'s highest civilian honour, Orders from the governments of Japan and Austria, New York University's Presidential Citation (1969), Seventh McKinsey Award (2005) for his article in HBR "What Makes an Effective Executive?", Junior Achievement US Business Hall of Fame (1996), etc. He was awarded 25 honorary doctorates from American, Belgium, Czechs, English, Spanish, and Swiss universities. He received countless awards in recognition of his contributions to the study of management.

Drucker anticipated privatisation, decentralisation, emergence of information society with necessity for life-long learning, role of knowledge workers, etc. For over seven decades his writings on management focused on relationships among human beings and they provide lessons on how organisations can bring out the best in people and how workers can find a sense community and dignity in modern society organised around large institutions.[7] As a consultant he specialised in strategy and policy for governments, business and non-profit organisations. His focus was on the organisation and work of the top management. He considered management as a liberal art and infused his management advice with inter-disciplinary lessons from history, sociology, psychology, culture and religion. As a practical man of management, his influence was worldwide and his ideas and practices are valued by politicians as well as mangers in many countries across the globe. He evinced keen interest in Japanese management, and based on his writings on Japanese system, new insights were brought into organisational analysis. He is considered to be a 'bridge' between academics and the business to the benefit of both.

Generic Management

Drucker believed that the term 'management' is generic and not related to business or any other profession. It pertains to every human effort that brings together in one organisation people of diverse knowledge and skills. Management is part of the organisation - public or private - and there is no difference between private enterprise, the nationalised industries of the UK, or government monopolies and ministries of Russia.[8] To Drucker, management is the specific and distinguishing organ of any and all organisations and concern with the management and its study began with the emergence of large organisations - business, governmental, civil services, army, etc.[9] To him, linking management with the business is of recent origin.[10] Thinkers like F.W. Taylor and Chester Barnard assumed that business management is just a sub-species of general management and basically no more different from management of any other organisation.[11] He felt that the term 'manager' did not originate in business but originated in city administration from the city manager system of city administration. He says that the first conscious and systematic application of management principles was not in business but in the US Army in 1901 by Elihu Root, Theodore Roosevelt's Secretary of War; the first Management Congress held at Prague in 1922 was not organised by business people but by Herbert Hoover, US Secretary of Commerce and Thomas Masaryk, founding President of the Czechoslovak Republic, and Mary Parker Follett never differentiated between business and non-business management and when she talked of the management of organisations, the same principles applied to all.[12]

The Great Depression, with its hostility to business and contempt for business executives, led to the identification of management with business management. Drucker says that 'in order not to be tarred with business brush, management in the public sector was re-christened as *Public Administration* and proclaimed as a separate discipline with its own university departments, terminology and its own career ladder'.[13] In the same vein, study of management of hospitals was christened as Hospital Administration and so on. At the same time, many 'business schools' in the United States were re-named as 'management schools' and they began to offer programmes to non-profit organisations and government. He laments that despite these developments a feeling that management is business management still persists and asserts that management is NOT business management - any more than Medicine is Obstetrics.[14]

Drucker saw differences in management - mission, strategy and structures - of different organisations; though differences are mainly in application rather than in principles. There are no major differences in tasks and challenges. Ninety per cent of what each organisation is concerned with is generic. The differences in respect to the remaining ten per cent are no greater between business and non-business than they are between different industries. In every organisation - business and non-business alike - only the last ten per cent of management has to be fitted to the organisation's specific mission, 'it's specific culture, it's specific history and it's specific vocabulary'.[15] It is in this context Drucker's contributions are applicable to public administration. According to Drucker, management is spreading to government for two reasons. Firstly, the governments need to regulate economy and non-profit organisations to expand social service responsibilities. Secondly, seeping of knowledge and skills to non-corporate organisations and corporate executives joining public service. This is in tune with Woodrow Wilson's assertion that administration should be run on business lines. [16] The other considerations for Drucker's belief that management is generic include enhancing quality of life; pressure for the dissemination of management experience and knowledge to government and non-profit organisations; spread of management after World War II to the newly independent countries to build their economies.[17] Drucker predicted the growth of non-profit social sector in the 21st century in the developed countries, and that is also the sector where management is most needed and where systematic, principled, and theory-based management can yield the greatest results the fastest.

Drucker observed that the emergence of generic management as a field of knowledge is based on the premise that there are valid tenets of administration, regardless of the organisational setting. He believed that the application of such knowledge to the government, among other institutions, would increase its effectiveness, but would not be pivotal. The decisive force, in his view, would be recognition of the limits of government responsibility and the need for a diminished role. [18]

Drucker was the first to see management as a profession – a body of theoretical and practical knowledge about organisations, tasks and people. To him management is a function, a discipline, a task to be done, and managers are professionals who practice this discipline, carry out functions and discharge these tasks. To Drucker management - public and corporate - is a repository of theories, practices, and skills transferable through generic approaches through education and training - that is, adoption of business administration instructions to public sector.[19] Drucker aptly noted that the schools of business are rapidly changing their names to schools of management to emphasise that the business concepts and skills are applicable to any organised activity.[20]

Drucker emphasised on the need for right organisation and its principles like hierarchy and unity of command. He brushes aside the talk of the 'end of hierarchy' as 'blatant nonsense'. The other principles of organisation, Drucker talks about, include transparency, authority be commensurate with responsibility, one master, etc. What Drucker says is that these principles should not tell us what to do, but only tell us what not to do. They do not tell us what will work. They tell us what is unlikely to work. These principles are not too different from the ones that inform an architect's work; they do not tell him what kind of a building to build. They tell him what the restraints are. And this is pretty much what the various principles of organisations do.[21]

Management in Government – A Critique

Drucker mostly wrote on corporate administration and very little directly on government and public administration. He was a serious critic of administration in government.[22] His observations on government and administration are mainly focused on the United States; though they have a general application. Drucker characterised government administration as 'fat, flabby, expensive, and unproductive. It is entangled in a web of vested interests, and pressure groups. It is fragmented, uninspiring, and ungovernable...It cannot abandon any activities, even if they are disasters. It is very sick and in desperate need of treatment. Impotence rather than omnipotence may well appear the most remarkable feature of government in the closing decades of the twentieth century.'[23] He felt that many bureaus and agencies of the federal government in the US undertake functions that are no longer required and regulate that no longer need regulation. He laments that the bureaucracy is out of control and the agencies have become ends in themselves, driven by their own desire for power, their own rationale, their own narrow vision, rather than by national policy and by the national government.[24] Policy is fragmented, policy direction is divorced from execution and the entire process is governed by bureaucratic inertia. As politicians cannot pay adequate attention to programmes, bureaucrats are left to their own devices. But they are protected from political processes and also demands of performance.[25] He felt that benchmarking and continuous improvement would be resisted by bureaucracy, interest groups, and even the Congress. He suggests that every Act, every agency, and every programme of government should be conceived for a fixed time period and should automatically be abandoned based on a study of its need. [26]

A major element in effective management is the ability of the organisation to rid itself of yesterday's functions and free the resources for new and more productive ones and for the future. But Drucker says that government is the worst offender because of its inability to stop doing anything that it should not do and calls this a central degenerative disease. His greatest disenchantment 'is that government has not performed'.[27] He argued that the government is a poor manager and is concerned with procedures and in the process becomes bureaucratic. [28] He says that the government is not a doer but a decision-maker and focuses its energies on dramatising issues.

Non-performance of Public Agencies

Drucker was critical about non-performance of public agencies. He identified six features which he called as 'sins' which contribute to non-performance. They are:[29]

Firstly, having lofty objectives like 'best medical care for the sick'. Such objectives are vague, and not operationable. He suggests that objectives should be specific, measurable and attainable and can be converted into work and performance. It requires clear targets for appraisal and judgments;

Secondly, attempting to do several things at the same time without prioritising them;

Thirdly, belief in 'fat is beautiful'. But Drucker believed that over-staffing is a sure way for non-performance and focuses on 'administration' than on 'results';

Fourthly, 'dogmatism' on work being undertaken and reluctance to experiment and innovate;

Fifthly, failure to learn from 'experience'; and

Finally, belief in immortality and inability to abandon and continue the policies, programmes and institutions long after they are unnecessary and their need disappeared.

Drucker was clear that these factors, if avoided, may not guarantee best results and contribute to performance, but avoiding them is a prerequisite for performance and results. But "most administrators", Drucker believed, "commit most of these 'sins' all the time and indeed all of them most of the time. Administrators feel it 'risky' to spell out attainable, concrete and measurable goals".[30]

Drucker, influenced by nazism and fascism, became skeptical and doubted the ability and effectiveness of governments.[31] He was a critique of western bureaucratic society, believed in 'debureaucratisation' of government and has strong attachment to managerialism. He strongly believed that the corporate executives are best qualified and are most competent to administer even the government, and to overcome its deficiencies by setting or recasting its functions. Similarly, he believed that business management is applicable to others including government.

Deficiencies of Government

Drucker argued that the government needs to be decentralised and debureaucratised. This is mainly because that no individual or group knows enough to manage effectively and humanely the complex governmental functions and economy. He believed that ineffective government would result in totalitarianism. Unfortunately despite limited ability, the governments always assume far more responsibilities than they can effectively handle. Such excessive responsibilities deprive the governments the ability to set priorities, strategies, targets, timetables, measurement standards, etc.[32] He was also critical that the national governments are reluctant to abandon any structure and activity as they develop strong constituencies around agencies and programmes.[33]

The principal deficiencies of the national government, according to Drucker are: inability to manage macro-economies effectively, tendency to assume an excessive number of tasks and to eschew priorities and reluctance to abandon dysfunctional structures and regulations. The other deficiencies he identifies include chronic cost overruns, proliferation of agencies, programmes and paper work, inter-agency rivalry, fragmentation in policy formulation, separation of policy direction from execution, bureaucratic inertia, focus on rules over results, poor management, premium on *status quo* over initiative and innovation and inability to fulfill promises. [34]

Drucker felt that the national governments should undertake defense, justice, internal order, etc. He desired that national government should undertake limited tasks but regulate most others. He strongly believed that functions like transportation, garbage collection and fire protection should be in private hands and should be contracted out. [35] Drucker expounded a vision involving extensive decentralisation and debureaucratisation to make the administration effective. As Gazell noted that 'One implication of his outlook for public administration is its reduced salience at the federal level .....growing prominence at the state and local levels and by its extension to the third and fourth sectors' [36] Federal government should formulate broad goals and policies while entrusting their execution to non-governmental and non-profit organisations. To Drucker improved effectiveness of governments is imperative to avoid totalitarianism.[37]

Drucker believed that managers are made and not born. This underlines the significance he attached to education and training of the executives. He developed and influenced the curriculum of the executive programmes at the Claremont Graduate School and the courses offered include 'Managing Public Service Institutions', 'Management of Change', etc. His class 'Management in Society' explores 'the issues of politics and public policy, managerial roles and conduct, economics, morality and ethics, which result from modern society's evolution into a society of organisations'.[38] This course, as Gazell notes, applies to the field of public administration readily, thereby reflecting the growing convergence between management and public administration instruction and the implicit need for incorporating it in all education and training programmes for public managers.[39] This also facilitates exchange of executives between business, government and non-profit sectors. Talking about ethics, Drucker says that there should be no business ethics, no public rules of conduct, no moral code, etc., and desired that there should be only universal ethics.[40]

Restructuring Government

The government is characterised by 'non-results' and the reason for this is resistance by the bureaucracy with its redtape and inane rules that prevent performance. Drucker finds the basic approach of even 'dedicated' people in government is wrong and hence non-performance or poor results. He notes that any attempt to 'patch-and-spot weld' here and there can never yield results and it requires 'radical change' in government and the way they are managed. Drucker suggests that concept of continuous improvement should be built into the functioning of government and that only contributes to sustainability. The second aspect is 'benchmarking' - a concept which compares performance with all others and making the best the standard.[41] Drucker favours continuous improvement and benchmarking which are absent in government. They require radical changes in 'policies and practices' which the bureaucracy and unions fiercely resist. This also requires that public organisations to define objectives of performance, quality and costs. Drucker proposes negative incentives or penalties like budgetary cuts for non-performance. Individual officials who perform below benchmarks need to be penalised - may be in terms of salary and wages, promotions and demotions or retirement. Organisations need to change their structure if there are changes in their 'size'. All organisations, government or others which are old and growing need to be restructured as they outlive the policies and rules of behaviour. Unless they are restructured, they become ungovernable, unmanageable and uncontrollable.[42] He gives the examples of American public administration in support of his propositions. He says that the American government has outgrown the structures, the policies and the rules designed for it are still in use.

Management exists to achieve institutional results; it has to start with the intended results and has to organise the resources of the institution to attain these results. It is the organ to make the institution, whether business, church, university, hospital or a battered women's shelter, capable of producing results outside it.[43] The management's concern and responsibility are everything that affects the performance of the institution and its results - whether inside or outside, whether under the institution's control or totally beyond it.[44] Drucker suggests that programmes and activities initiated at a particular point of time are unlikely to be productive later. They may become unproductive and even counter-productive. Drucker suggests that the organisations that malfunction should be abolished rather than reforming.

Rethinking and Abandonment

The governments resort to patching and down-sizing whenever they face problems as most business organisations do. According to Drucker, in the past fifteen years (before 1995) one big American company after another laid off a large number of employees in anticipation of turn around, but without any results in many, if not most cases. He says that downsizing has turned out to be something the surgeons for centuries have warned against 'amputation before diagnoses' and the result is always a 'casualty'. A better approach to Drucker is to 'rethink',[45] which organisations like GE and several hospitals have adopted and achieved turn around. To 'rethink' is to identify activities that are productive and need to be strengthened, promoted and expanded; not downsizing and expenditure reduction. Agencies should review the policies, programmes, activities and 'rethink' about the mission and question was it the right mission? Is it still worth continuing? Whether the mission is viable any longer? etc. Such exercises are undertaken both by government, business and even religious organisations. Drucker explains that we would not establish the Department of Agriculture now as farmers are just three per cent and productive farmers are less than half of that as a Bureau of Commerce or Labour can undertake these limited functions. [46]

Drucker also suggests that there is a need for a 'rethink' on the organisational set-up based on activities and questions the need for a scientific agency like Geographical Survey to run a retail business of selling maps. He proposes that they should be entrusted to book stores. To him continuing such activities is 'wasteful' and should be 'abandoned'. According to him two-fifths of the activities of civilian agencies and programmes in the US Administration are unproductive, counter-productive, and unviable and should be 'abandoned' and their functions entrusted to other appropriate agencies. Drucker was conscious that 'rethinking' is not easy, often impossible, and there will be opposition from the bureaucracy, and special interests. But 'rethink' is inevitable and needs to be carried out to perform effectively. He suggests that there is a need for "a theory of what government can do", but he laments that the political and administrative theory has not addressed this aspect. Drucker was conscious that rethinking about government, its programmes, its agencies, its activities would not by itself give a new theory or answers. But it gives factual information to help to raise right questions on performance and restructuring. Based on his experience he says that where 'rethinking' was undertaken, it gave substantial improvements.

Another question is that organisations that worked well at a point of time may not work later and needs to be reviewed periodically with the same questions discussed earlier and abolished based on 'functionality'. Drucker, giving examples from American experience, says that in all such cases the general prescription is to 'reform'. But to him, "reform something that malfunctions - let alone something that does harm - without knowing why it does not work can only make things worse. The best thing to do with such programmes is to abolish them". Drucker suggests that there is a need to undertake controlled experiments on 'different approaches' before 'abolishing', 'down-sizing' and choosing alternatives. He says that 'rethinking' helps to understand as to the activities that need to be strengthened, abolished or refocused. Rethinking, to him, is not about cutting costs. It contributes to increase in performance, quality, service and helps to change in work approaches and rethinking rank activities, policies, and programmes according to results than conventional 'intentions' approach. [47]

Management by Objectives

The concept of Management by Objectives (MBO) was first conceptualised as it is understood today by Drucker in his book *The Practice of Management*. Though there were many precursors like James O. McKinsey, Barnard, Fayol, Follett, etc., who wrote on the subject, they did not use the term MBO but each underpinned its philosophy in their writings. It was Drucker who coined the term during 1948-51 and made numerous contributions to its philosophy.[48] The idea generated considerable interest both in business organisations as well as in public administration. MBO refers to collective setting of organisational goals, targets, and measurements.

Peter Drucker conceptualised Harold Smiddy's Manager's Letter, introduced in General Electrics incorporating goals, activities and standards for each month and reported the results against previous month objectives as MBO.[49] He argued that management by drive characterised by ineffectiveness and mis-direction should be replaced by MBO. He wrote that 'an effective management must direct the vision and efforts of all the managers towards a common goal. It must ensure that the individual manager understands what results are demanded of him. It must ensure that the superior understands what to expect of each of its subordinate managers. It must motivate each manager to maximum efforts in the right direction. And while encouraging high standards of workmanship, it must make them the means to the end of business performance, rather than ends in themselves.'[50] He adds that each manager from senior executive to production foremen needs clearly to spell out objectives, layout what performance each manager's unit is supposed to produce and what contributions the unit is expected to make to other units to obtain their objectives and emphasis is on team work and team results. For the MBO to work each manager should measure performance against a goal. He suggested that the objectives should reflect the functions of the organisation and should be derived from the goals of the organisation.[51] The MBO substitutes management by domination with management by self-control.

Drucker says that each manager should develop and set the objectives of the unit and for himself though the higher management has powers to approve or disapprove them. But development of objectives is a part of the manager's responsibility; indeed his first responsibility.[52] Every manager should responsibly participate in the development of objectives in the higher unit of which he is a part. The greatest advantage of MBO is that it makes possible for a manager to control his own performance. Self-control means stronger motivation, desire to do best, higher performance goals and broader vision. To Drucker, MBO gives individual strength and responsibility and at the same time, gives common direction of vision and effort, establish team work and harmonise the goals of the individual with the common weal.[53]

Knowledge-based Organisations

Drucker predicted that information would bring major changes in the society and knowledge workers, his name for the new professional managers and specialists, would constitute the largest group in organisations. He introduced the concept of knowledge worker early in 1959 and his later writings reflect on knowledge work, knowledge worker and their productivity. He believed that 21st century organisations and management - business or non-business – would be characterised by knowledge workers and their productivity. [54] The new worker would be based on knowledge, not physical labour or management. Drucker believed that business succeeds because of their ability to generate and use knowledge. He, therefore, suggests that knowledge worker productivity is the most important challenge of the 21st century. He says that if we apply knowledge to tasks we already know how to do, it is 'productivity' and if we apply knowledge to tasks that are new and different it is 'innovation'.[55] Every executive in modern organisations is a knowledge worker and is responsible for contributions that materially affect the capacity of the organisation to perform and to achieve results. To Drucker information is data endowed with relevance and purpose. Converting the data into information requires knowledge and knowledge by definition is specialised. To him the defining characteristic of the knowledge worker is the level of his education and training to some degree will be the central concerns of the knowledge society. Drucker identifies six factors that determine the knowledge worker's productivity.[56] They include the tasks to be performed, responsibility and autonomy, continuous innovation, continuous learning and quality of output. He adds that the knowledge worker should be seen as an asset than as a cost.

Drucker explains that the knowledge workers have to attend to many activities beyond their core tasks which demand their time and attention which impact their productivity. He recommends that the knowledge workers' other tasks and activities should be minimised or delegated to others to enable them to concentrate their efforts on the core tasks. He insists that the knowledge workers should learn to manage themselves. This enables them to be creative and be continuous learners. They need to keep the knowledge up to date and use it as required.

This should be independent of their employers. Drucker argues that making the knowledge workers productive requires changes in the attitudes of individual workers as well as the entire organisation.[57] Despite organisations pronouncing and acknowledging that the employees are their greatest asset, few practice what they preach,[58] Drucker laments.

An Evaluation

There are several criticisms on Drucker's contributions to the field of management in government.[59] The most serious criticism came from Joseph Coates who says that 'I don't think of Drucker in terms of intellectual leadership'. He further says that "what he's always done is to listen to ideas already being discussed within business and been the first to write about and anoint the already clear trends. It's key function, the journalist kind of work. But he's not a seminal thinker". Warren Bennis, a student of Drucker, agrees with Joseph Coates and says that 'Peter's gift is that of a journalist'.[60]

The Wall Street Journal researched several of his lectures in 1987 and reported that Drucker was sometimes loose on facts, and was not always correct in his forecasts.[61] Drucker often 'used government and bureaucracy as negative examples of what happens when a business fails to act like a business'. But as Guy and Hitchock have noted that excellence exists - has always existed - in government, although it does not always take the same form as in business. According to them, Drucker attempted to compare government (apples) from business (oranges) perspective and it does not make sense because the differences override the similarities. Public administration is set for failure, they argue, on a test designed and normed for business. Drucker's thought lacks comprehensive applicability to public management that it offers to business.[62] To rely too heavily on Drucker's formulations for good management, however, will blind administrators to the unique context and constraints that publicness involves. They agree, however, that the public administrators should heed Drucker's advice on the importance of objectives, mission-focused management and the knowledge worker, etc. [63]

The concept of MBO articulated by Drucker, was criticised by several on different grounds. Firstly, despite Drucker's claim that the essence of the MBO is employee collaboration and inputs into setting the work objectives, Halpern and Osofsky argue that he failed to give specific protection to the subordinate in the MBO process against superior manipulation or arbitrariness nor recourse to any appeals procedure.[64] Secondly, Jackson and Mathis argued that the MBO practice has failed to link performance to the evaluation and reward process based on studies.[65] Thirdly, the MBO is just a technique and has no theoretical foundations. [66] Finally, the MBO has never proved its effectiveness, difficult to implement and often companies wind up over-emphasisng control as opposed to fostering creativity, to meet their goals[67].

Drucker's position on government 'is highly critical but unsubstantiated or anecdotal, it might be considered merely anti-statist bureaucrat bashing'. His 'diagnosis of government as too large and intrusive, ineffective, inefficient, and unresponsive, captured by numerous constituencies or vested interests, for example represents the simplistic and superficial criticism which, too often, passes for analysis and understanding. His prescription - apply market approaches to all manner of problems, privatise, and even ignore some problems - is equally inadequate, on both theoretical and practical level.'[68] Drucker's position on privatisation was criticised as 'unsatisfying'. His argument that privatisation or, more precisely, contracting out of public services will yield a competent and functioning government overlooks the myriad issues identified by many privatisation analysts.[69]

Critics argue that Drucker was unable 'to discern' the actual tenor and texture of public management, its variety and subtleties and resorts to gross generalisations and therefore,

'Drucker's work as a benchmark for the evaluation of public management is marginal at best'. Drucker's treatment of public management falls short, failing to appreciate the dynamics of cultural and constitutionally imposed restraints. Though it provides useful insights, it lacks comprehensive applicability to public management.[70] Though Drucker's writings helped public administrators, to rely heavily on Drucker's formulation for good management, 'will blind administrators to the unique context and constraints that publicness brings to the table.'[71]

Public administration scholars may deemphasise Drucker's criticism of government administration and, his over-simplification of obstacles to effective public management. But it is difficult to summarily reject his criticism of the working of the government and its performance. His contribution to the discipline of public administration lies in the promotion of the concepts like mission orientation, MBO, privatisation, decentralisation, etc., and they have a profound influence in public administration theory and practice across the globe. [72]

Notwithstanding the criticisms, the contributions of Drucker to the study and practice of public administration and management are substantial. He delineated the facets of leadership, emphasised the need for mission orientation in organisations, analysed the nature of decision- making, conceptualised MBO, forecasted the advent of knowledge worker, saw management as a profession, recognised the emergence of non-profit sector, and expanded the non-governmental and non-business realm, all of which have substantial bearings on public administration. Drucker escorted the organisational theory and thinking from its ivory tower and put it to work on line.

In Brief

Peter Drucker's contributions to the art and science of public management and administration can be summarised as:

- Peter Ferdinand Drucker (1909-2005), the management guru and consultant, is a writer of uncommon verve and practicality and dealt with management matters in the context of larger society. His vision can be uncovered from his voluminous writings over the last several decades and extrapolated to governmental administration.

- Drucker believed that the term 'management' is generic and not related to business or any other profession. He laments that management is business management, still persists. To him management is the specific tool, specific function and specific instrument to make institutions capable of producing results and ninety per cent of it is generic to all types of organisations.

- Drucker described management as liberal art. It is liberal because it deals with fundamentals of knowledge, wisdom and leadership. It is art because it is practice and application. Drucker was the first to see management as a profession – a body of theoretical and practical knowledge about organisations, tasks and people. He believed that managers are made and not born and emphasised the importance of management education and training.

- He was very critical about the non-performance of public agencies and identified several 'sins' which contributed to non-performance. He argues that the government is a poor manager and is concerned with procedures and in the process becomes bureaucratic.

- Drucker advocated restructuring of government based on 'rethinking' and suggested continuous improvement based on benchmarking. Aware of difficulties in 'rethinking' in government system, he pleads for 'a theory of what government can do'.

- The concept of Management by Objectives was first conceptualised as is understood today by Drucker. It refers to collective setting of organisation goals, targets and measurement. MBO is an important tool for performance assessment and management by self-control.

- Drucker developed the concept of knowledge worker in organisations. He identified several factors that determine knowledge worker's productivity and argues that making them productive requires changes in the attitudes of individual workers as well as the entire organisation.

- The criticisms of Drucker's contributions includes the journalistic nature of work, failure to appreciate the different contexts of public administration, failure to recognise the limitations in application of market approaches in government, and failure to discern the actual tenor and texture of public management.

- Drucker through his writings on management focused on relationships among human beings and they provide lessons on how organisations can bring out the best in people and how workers can find a sense of community and dignity in modern society. Many of his ideas formed the basis for New Public Management.

Notes and References

[1] Drucker, Peter F., "Reflections of a Social Ecologist", *Society*, May-June, 1992. See http://en.wikipedia.org/wiki/Peter_Drucker

[2] Drucker, Peter F., *Management – Tasks, Responsibilities, Practices*, New York, Harper &Row, 1973, p.325

[3] Gazell, James A., "Drucker on Effective Public Management" in Wood, John D. and Wood, Michael D., (Eds.), *Peter Drucker: Critical Evaluations in Business and Management*, New York, Rutledge, 2005, p.325.

[4] Gazell, James A., "Peter F. Drucker's Vision in Public Management, 2000", *International Journal of Public Administration*, Vol.17, Nos.3&4, 1994, p. 675.

[5] For details of Drucker's life and career See http://en.wikipedia.org/wiki/Peter_Drucker; http://www.woopidoo.com/biography/peter-drucker/index.htm; http://www.peterdrucker.at/en/bio/bio_start.html; http://www.businessweek.com/magazine/content/05_48/b3961001.htm.

[6] For details of Drucker's writings and publications see Cowan, Roberta A., "An Abbreviated Annotated Bibliography: Peter F(erdinand) Drucker 1909 -", in Wood, John D. and Wood, Michael D., (Eds.), op.cit., pp.11-71. The articles included in the volume discuss various aspects of Drucker's philosophy, ideas and influence in the realms of management and government. See also Edershien, Elizabeth Haas, *The Definitive Drucker*, New York, McGraw-Hill, 2007, pp.271-73. One of his books *The Effective Executive* (1966) was made a required reading by the then Speaker of the House Newt Gingrich for every newly sworn-in Representatives.

[7] Drucker Institute - The Drucker Legacy, Quoted in http://en.wikipedia.org/wiki/Peter_Drucker

[8] In 1954, however, Drucker maintained that though the other institutions such as the government and the military have management, 'management as such is the management of a business enterprise' and its essence is economic performance which distinguishes management from business and other institutions. He also argued that the business skills and experiences cannot be transferred and applied to other institutions. Success in business management is not a promise or a guarantee for success in government. A career in management is by itself not a preparation for a political office. What are transferable are administrative and analytical skills. Quoted in Garofalo, Charles, "Can Elephants Fly? Drucker and Governmental Reform", in Wood, John D. and Wood, Michael D., (Eds.), op.cit., p.294

[9] Drucker, Peter F., *Management Challenges for the 21st Century*, New York, HarperBusiness, 2001, p.9.

[10] Ibid., p.6

[11] Ibid.

[12] Ibid., pp.6-7.

[13] Ibid.p.7

[14] Ibid., p.8

[15] Ibid.

[16] Woodrow Wilson, "The Study of Administration", *Political Science Quarterly*, 1887, pp.216-219. For details see the companion article on Woodrow Wilson in this volume.

[17] Gazell, James A., "Peter F. Drucker's Vision in Public Management, 2000", op.cit., pp: 682-683.

18 Gazell, James A., "Peter F. Drucker and Decentralised Administration of the Federal Government", *Administration & Society*, Vol.24. No.2, August, 1992, p. 203.

19 Gazell, James A., "Peter F. Drucker's Vision in Public Management, 2000", op.cit., p.687.

20 Drucker, Peter F., *The New Realities*, Oxford, Butterworth-Heinemann, Classic Edition, 2000, p.170.

21 Peter F. Drucker., *Management Challenges for the 21st Century*, op.cit., pp.11-13.

22 See Peter F. Drucker, *The Age of Discontinuity: Guidelines to Our Changing Society*, London, Heinemann, 1969, pp.198-226.

23 See Garofalo, Charles, op.cit., p. 295.

24 Drucker, Peter F., *The Age of Discontinuity: Guidelines to Our Changing Society*, op.cit.,205.

25 Garofalo, Charles, op.cit., 296

26 Ibid., 294,

27 See Ibid.296

28 Ibid.

29 Peter F. Drucker, "The Deadly Sins in Public Administration", *Public Administration Review*, Vol. 40. No. 2, March-April, 1980, pp.103-106.

30 Ibid., p. 105.

31 Gazell, James A., "Peter F. Drucker and Decentralised Administration of the Federal Government", op.cit., p.185.

32 Drucker, Peter, F., "What Results should you Expect? A User's Guide to MBO," *Public Administration Review*, Vol.36, No.1. p.16.

33 Drucker, Peter F., The Frontiers of Management, New York, Truman Talley, 1986, p.335.

34 See James A. Gazell, "Peter F. Drucker and Decentralised Administration of the Federal Government", op.cit., pp.187-192.

35 Ibid., pp.193-200.

36 Ibid., p.201

37 Ibid.

38 Gazell, James A., "Peter F. Drucker's Vision in Public Management, 2000", op.cit., p.689.

39 Drucker, Peter, F., *Managing the Non-Profit Organisation*, Oxford, Butterworth-Heinemann, 1990, p.xv.

40 Gazell, James A., "Peter F. Drucker's Vision in Public Management, 2000", op.cit., pp.690-91.

41 Peter F. Drucker, "Really Reinventing Government", *The Atlantic Online*, See http://www.theatlantic.com/politics/polibig/reallyre.htm Retrieved on 20th October , 2009

42 Ibid.

43 Drucker, Peter, F., *Management Challenges for the 21st Century*, op.cit., p.39.

44 Ibid., p.40.

45 Drucker, Peter, F., "Really Reinventing Government", op.cit.

46 Ibid.

47 Ibid.

48 For details see Greenwood, Ronald G., "Management by Objectives: As Developed by Peter Drucker, Assisted by Harold Smiddy", in Wood, John D. and Wood, Michael D., (Eds.), op.cit., pp.153-174.

49 Ibid.

50 Drucker, Peter, F., *The Practice of Management*, London, Heinemann, 1955, p. 108.

51 Ibid., pp.108-109.

52 Ibid.,111.

53 Ibid.,117.

54 Drucker, Peter, F., *Management Challenges for the 21st Century*, op.cit., p. 135.

55 Drucker, Peter, F., *Managing for the Future*, Oxford, Butterworth- Heinemann, Classic Edition, 2000, p. 23.

56 Drucker, Peter, F., *Management Challenges for the 21st Century*, op.cit., p. 142.

57 Ibid., p. 156

58 Drucker, Peter, F., *Managing in a Time of Great Change*, Oxford, Butterworth- Heinemann, 1995, p. 77.

59 For a detailed critique see Garofalo, Charles, op.cit.; Guy , Mary E,.and Hitchcock, Janice R., op.cit.

60 Quoted in Stuller, Jay, "The Guru Game", in Wood, John D. and Wood, Michael D., (Eds.), op.cit. p.188.

61 Drucker, Peter F., *Leading Management Guru, Dies at 95*, Bloomberg, Nov 11, 2005, Quoted in http://en.wikipedia.org/wiki/Peter_Drucker

62 Guy, Mary E., and Hitchock, Tanice R., "If Apples are Oranges: The Public/Non-profit/Business Nexus in Peter Drucker's Work" in Wood, John D. and Wood, Michael D., (Eds.), op.cit., pp. 328 and 344.

63 Ibid., p.344.

64 Halpern, David, and Osofsky, Stephen, " A Dissenting View of Drucker's Classical Formulation of MBO", in Wood, John D. and Wood, Michael D., (Eds.), op.cit., p. 175.

65 Quoted in Ibid., p. 182

66 Ibid., p.180.

67 Krueger, Dale, "Strategic Management and Management by Objectives", Small Business Advancement National Center, 1994, Quoted in http://en.wikipedia.org/wiki/Peter Drucker

68 Garofalo, Charles , op.cit., pp.300-301.

69 Ibid., p.302

70 Ibid., p.304

71 Guy, Mary E., and Hitchock, Janice R., op.cit., p.

72 Hays, Steven W., Russ-Sellers, Rebecca , "On the Margins of Public Administration?: A quasi-empirical analysis of Peter Drucker's Impact", *Journal of Management History*, Vol.6,No.2, 2000, pp.65-76.

21

KARL MARX

Prabhat Kumar Datta

Introduction

Marxism, based on the writings of Karl Marx and Friedrich Engels, has profound influence on all social science disciplines. Marx, along with Emile Durkheim and Max Weber, is considered as the principal architect of modern social sciences. Karl Marx, a philosopher, economist, historian, political theorist, sociologist, and revolutionary unraveled the working of economic and political system within which modern organisations function. His ideas are the foundation of modern communism. No other thinker has as much influence as Karl Marx on the twentieth century mind. His works inspired the foundations of many regimes of the world. No debate on state, society and administration in social sciences, therefore, is complete without a discussion on Marx and his impact. Outside his economic theories, Marx's main contribution to the social sciences has been his theory of historical materialism, which is

(1818 – 1883)

considered as an attempt at unifying all social sciences into a single science of society. Human beings cannot survive without social organization.[1] In each mode of production, a given set of relations of production constitutes the basis (infrastructure) on which is erected a complex superstructure, encompassing the state and the law, ideology, religion, philosophy, arts, morality, etc. His philosophy provides deeper insights into the working of modern organisations.

Life and Works

Karl Heinrich Marx was born on May 5, 1818 in the City of Trier in the erstwhile Prussian State. He studied at the University of Berlin where he was introduced to Hegelian philosophy. He was politically a rebellious student. In April 1841, he received his doctorate from the University of Jena. His thesis analysed the difference between natural philosophies of Democritus and Epicurus. In 1843, he went to Paris to continue his revolutionary activities, which at that time served as head quarters of revolutionaries. In 1849 he was charged with instigating armed rebellion and was forced out of Paris. He went to London in August 1849, where he sought refugee and stayed till his death on March 14, 1883. Marx authored several books including *Critique of Hegel's Philosophy of Right* (1844), *The Holy Family* (1844) (with Fredrick Engels), *Theses of Feuerbach* (1845), *The German Ideology* (with Engels), *The Poverty of Philosophy* (1847), *The Communist Manifesto* (1848), *Wage, Labour and Capital* (1849), *The Class Struggles in France* (1850), *The Eighteenth Brunaire of Louis Bonaparte* (1850), *A Contribution to the Critique of Political Economy* (1859). First Volume of *Capital*, his most important work, which remained incomplete due to ill health, was published in 1867. The second and third volumes of *Capital* were revised and published by Engels in 1885 and 1894.

Origins of Bureaucracy: Marxist Perspective

In Karl Marx's and Friedrich Engel's theory of historical materialism, the historical origin of bureaucracy is to be found in *four* sources: religion, the formation of the state, commerce, and technology.[2] The earliest bureaucracies consisted of castes of *religious* clergy, officials and scribes operating various rituals, and armed functionaries specifically delegated to keep order. In the historical transition from primitive egalitarian communities to a civil society divided into social classes and estates, beginning from about 10,000 years ago, authority is increasingly centralized in, and enforced by a state apparatus existing separately from society. The state formulates and enforce laws and levy taxes, giving rise to an officialdom undertaking these functions. Thus, the state mediates in conflicts among the people and keeps those conflicts within acceptable bounds; it also organizes the defense of territory. Most importantly, the right of ordinary people to carry and use weapons of force becomes increasingly restricted and forcing other people to do things becomes increasingly the legal right of the state authorities only.

But, the growth of trade and commerce adds a new, distinctive dimension to bureaucracy, insofar as it requires the keeping of accounts and the processing/recording of transactions, as well as the enforcement of rules governing trade. If resources are increasingly distributed by prices in markets, this requires extensive and complex systems of record-keeping, management and calculation, conforming to legal standards. Eventually, this means that the total amount of work involved in commercial administration outgrows the total amount of work involved in government administration. In modern capitalist society, private sector bureaucracy is *larger* than government bureaucracy, if measured by the number of administrative workers in the division of labour as a whole. Some corporations nowadays have a turnover larger than the national income of whole countries, with large administration supervising operations.

A fourth source of bureaucracy, Marxists have commented on, inheres on the technologies of mass production, which require many standardized routines and procedures to be performed. Even if mechanization replaces people with machinery, people are still necessary to design, control, supervise and operate the machinery. The technologies chosen may not be the ones that are best for everybody, but which create *incomes* for a particular class of people or maintain their power. This type of bureaucracy is nowadays often called a technocracy, which owes its power to control over specialized technical knowledge or control over critical information.

Bureaucracy as an Exploitative Instrument

Karl Marx looks upon bureaucracy as an integral part of the exploitative social system. Marx formed his theory of bureaucracy on the basis of his personal experience of the malfunctioning of state administration at the time of the Moselle district famine. He deduces the notion of bureaucracy from the bureaucratic relationships existing between the power-holding institutions and social groups subordinated to them. In an exploitative society like the capitalist one, bureaucracy gets ingrained in the society and acts as a mechanism for perpetuation of exploitation. For Marx, abolition of the state will be achieved institutionally by the destruction of the bureaucratic apparatus and the bureaucratic dimension of political reality provides a yardstick for the assessment of different political structures. Marx emphasises the importance of understanding bureaucracy both functionally and historically. For him, bureaucracy is central to the understanding of the modern state. It is generally held that bureaucracy is subsumed in Marx's macro theorization of the capitalist state. And since it is the political expression of the division of labour it has to be explained not only in functional but also in structural terms. He uses allusions to Feuerbach's transformative criticism stating that under bureaucracy the human subject becomes a mere object of manipulation. What 'fetishism of commodities' is to economics, bureaucracy is to politics.

It may be necessary to bear it in mind that Marx never wrote extensively on bureaucracy, as did Weber, although Marx did not overlook the significance of bureaucracy in modern society. Incidentally, after taking over as Chief Editor of *Die Rheinische Zeitung* Marx wrote articles in the newspapers on free press and state censorship and on the law of the thefts of woods. He spoke of the repressive character of the bureaucracy's censorship of press. He regarded censorship as a bureaucratic instrument for maintaining politics as a reserved domain of a particular class. Marx's reflections on bureaucracy were first found in his *Critique of Hegel's Philosophy of Right* in which he viewed bureaucracy as the institutional incarnation of political alienation. Since it institutionalizes the inverted nature of the modern state, where everything, according to Marx, looks different from its true character, bureaucracy can be abolished only when the general interest becomes *real*. As Marx developed his concept of bureaucracy through his *Critique of Hegel's Philosophy of Right*, it seems useful to briefly recall Hegel's views on bureaucracy as a backdrop for the study of Karl Marx's thought.

Hegel's Universalistic Emphasis

Hegel viewed bureaucracy as the principal governing organization[3]. The state, for Hegel, is the last development in a series of rational social orders, the other two being the family and the civil society. Once the state is established, it is supposed to provide the grounds where the unconscious and particularly oriented activities become gradually self-conscious and public spirited.[4] For Hegel, the prince, the bureaucrats and the deputies of the estates are political actors' par excellence.

Hegel finds in the society the existence of three classes, namely, the agricultural class, the business class, and the universal class, each of which reflects three modes of consciousness viz., conservatism, individualism and universalism respectively. He distinguishes between civil society and the state on the ground that the former represents the particular interest and the latter, the general interest. Bureaucracy plays the role of a link between the civil society and the state. It is what Avineri, while explaining Hegel's views, has called "the paradigm of mediation"[5] between the particular and the general, between the civil society and the state. Hegel says that "the universal class (bureaucracy) has, for its task, the universal interest of the community".[6] Bureaucracy is a 'universal estate' which sees to "the maintenance of the general state interest and of legality". It is to be mentioned that bureaucracy represents the universal interest not because of the negative universality of their wants, but because of the positive universality of what they already have, the state itself. Hegel says that the universal class should not be misunderstood as the 'unhappy consciousness' suffering from a sense of estrangement from its own product. They are, on the contrary, a 'self-satisfied consciousness' which understands and accepts the world as world.

Hegel on Regulatory Mechanism

Hegel believes that the universal insight and will are not the property of the bureaucrats as individuals but of bureaucracy which is a system of relations defined by hierarchy and specialization plus a certain position in a large ensemble. The self-seeking orientation and instability of the middle class from which the bureaucrats are recruited, do not stand in the way of bureaucracy because on their recruitment they become a part of the bureaucratic system. They also submit themselves to a series of internal and external pressures which educate them to the will and knowledge of the universal interest. The internal control refers to the bureaucratic ethos which is the result of bureaucratic habits plus the motivation that accompany the fulfillment of the bureaucratic duties.[7] The external mechanisms of control include control from above by the prince as well as from below in the form of grievances, and petitions by corporations, free press and public opinion. Thus Hegel has given us an outline of regulatory mechanism which has a good effect on the bureaucrats.

Hegel was looking for a sphere which transcends private interests. Avineri says that Hegel's attempt is 'similar to the Platonic endeavour but while Plato tried to neutralize Guardians totally from civil society by depriving them of family and private property, Hegel's solution is less radical....'[8] It is necessary to mention that Hegel's attempt to provide for checks and balances indicate his awareness that bureaucracy may view itself as owning the state and encroach upon the rights of the people. Hegel regards bureaucracy as "the embodiment of the ideas". Bureaucracy, by virtue of its autonomy and independence, will act as a brake on the civil society itself and ensure that public policy does not become a reflection of society. Evidently, Hegel does not regard bureaucracy as a social category with distinct characteristics. Hagedus says that Hegal refers to "the officials and functionaries as those who acted on behalf of the enlightened ruler, or, later, on behalf of the constitutional monarchy and the modern state".[9] It seems also clear that Hegel explains bureaucracy from what may be called the Weberian perspective because he, like Weber, associates such qualities as dispassionateness, uprightness and politeness with bureaucracy.

Hegel's Impact on Marx

The Hegelian concept of bureaucracy representing the general interest of the community has not been accepted by Marx although he agrees with Hegel that the rational state should represent the general interests of the community. But he feels that the existing state does not represent the general interest and for Marx, the prominence of bureaucracy may be attributed to it. It is significant to note that Hegel's notion of the universal class influenced many early writings of Marx in which he uses the term 'proletariat' possessing the qualities of the universal class.

Early Formulations

When Marx was making a critical appraisal of Hegel's theory of bureaucracy in 1843, the term itself did not figure prominently in serious political writings. Marx must be credited with attempting an analysis of bureaucracy in substantive terms, in the sense of a social category. Bureaucracy, in the sense of a ruling formation of some kind, first appeared in a *German* book by C. J. Krans (1808). By the term bureaucratic he meant a stratum which ruled Prussia. It had earlier been put to use in a German periodical with regard to the French Revolutionary Development after 1879. The *Brochans Encyclopedia* (1819) had recognized it, and the German publicist, J. J. Corres, had popularized the term in the 1820s. Young Marx is reported to have been acquainted with these writings.

Marx came out with his first explicit attack on bureaucracy in 1843. He complained of the 'presumptious officiousness' of government officials and 'the contradiction' between the real nature of the world and that ascribed to it in *Biuros*. Marx was interested in explaining how bureaucracy emerged and drew its sustenance from the society and how it reflected the production relations at a time when it worked. It was not the structure of bureaucracy but its content that merited his attention. For Marx, bureaucracy is "a particular closed society within the state". There are three basic elements in Marx's perception of state. First, state is an organ of class domination. Secondly, its aim is to create an order which legalizes and perpetuates the oppression of one class by moderating conflicts. Thirdly, state is a temporary phenomenon; it will wither away with the abolition of classes. Bureaucracy refers to all the elements in the hierarchical system as outlined by Hegel including the collegial advisory boards. In Marx's usage it embraces both the system of administration and the persons who are charged with the implementation of that system.

Parasitic Role of Bureaucracy

Marx considers the objective political system as the product of the producing activities of the totality of men in society. In the Preface to *A Contribution to the Critique of Political Economy*, Marx wrote that he was convinced from his early work on the critique of Hegel that law and state were neither autonomous nor were they the products of human mind. It is "the material conditions of life" from which law and state originate. It is applicable to the prince whose position is to be seen as a product, not of nature, but of social consent, and to the bureaucracy and the state. It is the productive activity which is of pivotal significance for human affairs. According to Marx, the mode of production should not be viewed "simply as reproduction of the physical existence of individuals". He further stated that ' it is definite form of their activity, a definite way of expressing their life. As individuals express their life, so they are. What they are, therefore, coincides with what they produce and how they produce. The nature of individuals thus depends on the material conditions which determine their production'.[10]

Marx believes that "the social structure and the state continually evolve out of the life process of definite individuals, but individuals not as they appear in their own or other people's imagination, but rather, as they really are...."[11] The bearers of the relations of production are social classes. Within each mode of production there are two social classes, one which owns the means of production, and the other which does not. In class-society, Marx denies bureaucracy an organic position because it is not directly connected with the production processes. He calls bureaucracy 'parasites' designed to maintain *status quo* and the privileges of the dominant section of the society.

Bureaucrat's Private Ends

State power plays the same role for the bureaucracy as the private property does for property-owning class. To quote Marx, "bureaucracy holds in its essence of the state, the spiritual essence of the society, it is its private property."[12] It "constitutes the imaginary state besides the real state, and is the spiritualism of the state". Further, "In the case of individual bureaucrat, the state objective turns into his private objective, into chasing after higher posts, the making of a career".[13] It may be remembered here for Marx, the state is not, as with Hegel, logically prior to, and ethically superior to its constituent elements, the family and civil society. It is an illusion to suppose that the state has a universal character capable of harmonising the discordant elements of civil society and uniting them on a higher level. In his *The German Ideology*, Marx traces the origin of the state together with social institutions to the division of labour. In the course of history each method of production gives rise to a typical political organization furthering the interests of the dominant class. Thus the state, as Marx writes, "is the form in which the individuals of a ruling class assert their common interests". Marx considers bureaucracy, as an instrument of exploitation in the state, to be the main function which consists in exploiting the affairs of the community in such a manner as to promote and sustain its private ends. It does not instill public spirit in the social body through its influence on and dialogue with the corporations. It attempts to 'privatise' the civil society as a whole.

The Deliberate Mysteriousness

In order to achieve its objective of "privatising" the civil society, bureaucracy presents the affairs of the state to the outsiders in the garb of secrecy. As Marx says, "The general spirit of the bureaucracy is the secret, the mystery...."[14] It is afraid of conducting the affairs of the state in public, and considers political consciousness "as treason against its mystery". "Authority is the principle of its knowledge, and the deification of authoritarianism is its credo".[15] A majority of people look at bureaucracy with awe and veneration and as a mysterious and distant entity. The spirit of mystery is safeguarded within itself by hierarchy and outside by its nature as a closed corporation. Thus the masses get alienated. The bureaucrats also develop in them a sense of alienation because they fail to understand the parasitic and oppressive nature of the job.

A Critique on Characteristics of Bureaucracy

Marx provided a critique on some of the characteristics of bureaucracy, viz., division of labour, hierarchy, recruitment and rules, which reflect his approach to bureaucracy:

Division of Labour

Marx agrees that the division of labour makes the organization of capitalist society highly productive. However, he points out that the basic division of labour which we intend to overlook is between 'intellectual and material activity'. While the workers perform the productive activity, the capitalists and bureaucrats perform only intellectual activity. Hence all the hard work falls on the workers in the name of division of labour. Further, the gains of higher productivity go mostly to the capitalists who share these to some extent with the bureaucracy, as indicated by the bureaucracy's higher salaries. So far the workers are concerned, higher productivity tends to lead to higher unemployment among them, as it happens when high technology is introduced. Increased unemployment tends to tower wages also. Hence, increased productivity due to heightened division of labour may lead to little gain for the workers.

Hierarchy

The safeguards referred to by Hegel in the form of external and internal control do not, according to Marx, prevent bureaucracy from furthering private ambitions of individual careerism. The hierarchy of bureaucracy is a hierarchy of knowledge. The apex entrusts the lower circles with insights into the individual while the lower circles have insights into the universal to the apex. To Marx:' the bureaucracy is a circle from which no one can escape. Its hierarchy is a hierarchy of knowledge—the top entrusts the understanding of the lower levels, whilst the lower levels credit the top with understanding of the general, and so, all area mutually deceived'.[16]

The hierarchical structure of bureaucracy is no safeguard because "the oppositionist is itself tied hand and feet....where is the protection against the bureaucracy?" Further, to be sure that lesser evil (bureaucratic abuse) is abolished by greater (hierarchy) in so far as it disappears to make way for it,[17] Marx rejects the view that any safeguard can be made to depend on the human qualities of the officials themselves. He observes: "The human being as the official against himself. What a unity that is!"[18]

Recruitment

Hegel argues that liberal education humanizes civil servants. However, Marx maintains that the mechanical character of a civil servant's work and the compulsions of office lead to his dehumanization. Marx is also critical of the recruitment of members of the bureaucracy through competitive examinations. He says that members of a bureaucracy need statesmanship which cannot be tested through an examination: "One does not hear that the Greek or Roman statesmen passed examinations." Marx's class analysis would indicate that the main function of examination is to ensure that only persons of the upper class who can afford the costly higher education are able to enter the bureaucracy. Apart from being costly, higher education inculcates values and attitudes which are supportive of capitalism. Higher education tends to create social distance between the rich and the poor; highly educated people generally think they are a class apart. Hence if a highly educated person is appointed as a manager, the exploitation of workers does not hurt him.

Rules

Marx points out those bureaucratic minds are so bound in subordination and passive obedience that they come to think that adherence to rules is an end in itself, and not merely a means to an end. They attach more importance to rules than to human beings.

Theory of Alienation

Marx's Theory of Alienation[19] is the contention that in modern industrial production under capitalist conditions workers will inevitably lose control of their lives by losing control over their work. Workers thus cease to be autonomous beings in any significant sense. Under pre-capitalist conditions a blacksmith, or a shoemaker would own his own shop, set his own hours, determine his own working conditions, shape his own product, and have some say in how his product is bartered or sold. His relationships with the people with whom he worked and dealt had a more or less personal character. Under the conditions of modern factory production, by contrast, the average worker is not much more than a replaceable cog in a gigantic and impersonal production apparatus. Where armies of hired operatives perform monotonous and closely supervised tasks, workers essentially lost control over the process of production, over the products which they produce, and over the relationships they have with each other. As a consequence they have become estranged from their very human nature, which Marx understood to be free and productive activity. Human beings cannot be human under these conditions, and for this reason the implication was obvious for Marx: Capitalism has to be abolished as much as any political oppression if a society's emancipation is to be complete. As absolute monarchy limits people's autonomy by controlling them in the sphere of politics, capitalism does so by controlling their workplaces and their economic life. A society of truly free citizens, according to Marx, must therefore not only be a political, but also an economic and social democracy.

The most basic form of workers' alienation is their estrangement from the process of their work. An artist, unlike an industrial worker, typically works under his or her own direction; artists are in total control of their work. (That is why artists usually do not mind working long hours and even under adverse conditions, because their creative work is inherently meaningful, and an expression of their most personal desires and intuitions.) Even the typical medieval artisan, although more closely motivated by economic needs, usually worked as a relatively independent person – controlling his own shop and up to a point choosing his own projects. Marxist concept of alienation applies equally to the proletariat and the bureaucracy. According to Marx, alienation has four main aspects viz., loss of freedom, loss of creativity, loss of humanity and loss of morality.

Loss of Freedom

Wherever there is exploitation, the exploiters as well as the exploited suffer from alienation. Therefore, all the members of the organization suffer from alienation. Thus workers are under compulsion to take up jobs; they can no longer function as independent artisans. Once they have accepted the jobs, they are under the authoritarian command of the management. They are coerced, controlled and threatened with punishment. The managers also suffer from alienation since they are themselves employees. The capitalist also loses his freedom. Marx says that the capitalist is not free to eat, drink, buy books or go to the theatre, or even to think, love, theorise, sing, paint, etc., as he wishes. He is constrained by the nature of his business.

Loss of Creativity

The nature of bureaucracy interferes with the creativity of its members. Such interference is sometimes called a dysfunction. Thus division of labour interferes with creativity and no worker produces the whole product. He will have no job satisfaction. Hierarchy also has the result that no worker can say that he independently produced anything. The worker himself becomes a mere tool. Rules ensure that workers are all the time under detailed control. The administrator also loses his creativity. For this reason alone, the administrator is anonymous. Even policy making has to be done jointly. Even if an administrator is responsible for drawing up a certain policy, he cannot take credit for it.

Loss of Humanity

In modern large scale organizations, workers tend to function like machines, thereby losing their humanity. Due to division of labour most of them have no part in deciding the objectives of the organization. The office is also structured like a big machine and suffers from lack of humanity. The managers are in a similar situation, for, they are also part of a machine-like structure. Human values do not play any role in the functioning of bureaucracy.

Loss of Morality

According to Marx, loss of freedom and humanity necessarily leads to loss of morality. Thus, it is immoral to take away the freedom of workers and convert them into mere animals. Loss of creativity also leads to immorality. If engineers or doctors are more interested in making money than in building safe bridges or in curing patients they become immoral. Loss of humanity, in the sense of being insensitive to the suffering of others, is certainly unethical.

Proletariat's Alienation from Bureaucracy

To Marx, bureaucracy symbolizes alienation for the toiling masses. This alienation has two implications. In the first place, it implies that the abolition of the state precedes the destruction of the bureaucratic apparatus. In *The Eighteenth Brumaire*, Marx suggests that unlike the previous revolutions that had wrestled against the control of bureaucracy, the proletariat must smash the institution itself. In the *Manifesto*, Marx and Engels observe that it is the teaching of the commune that "the working class cannot simply lay hold of the ready–made state machinery and wield it for its own purposes".[20] Secondly, it implies that it is the extent of bureaucratization which determines the amount of violence required to overthrow the political system of a given society. In the bureaucratic countries of Europe, Marx writes, "the task of the proletarian revolution will be, no longer, as before, to transfer the bureaucratic machine from one hand to another, but to smash it".[21] Perez-Diaj sums up Marx's views thus: "Hierarchical and functional differentiation results in a mere juxtaposition and mutual enforcement of incompetence, of the superior who does not know the specifics of the case, of the inferior who does not know the general principles of everyone, who does not get a lack of the ensemble of the situation".[22] The external relations of bureaucracy are often intrinsic and conflictual in nature. It has a corporate particular interest to defend against other particular corporations and classes of society besides other political forces of similar character. In order to prove his thesis that bureaucracy lacks both the spirit and will of the universal, Marx argued that inside bureaucracy the manipulation of information and other resources are done in such manner that they can be used for the realisation of private ambitions and promote individual careerism.

Eventual Withering Away of Bureaucracy

Marx is of the opinion that the society born out of the proletarian revolution will do without bureaucracy. For him, "the abolition of bureaucracy is only possible by the general interest actually become real."[23] With the end of the state, the nature of the state functions undergoes a complete change. Marx wrote: "As soon as the goal of the proletarian movement, the abolition of classes, shall have reached, the power of the state, whose functions is to keep the great majority of producers beneath the yoke of a small minority of exploiters, will disappear, and governmental functions will be transformed into simple administrative functions."[24]

It should be made clear that the demolition of state does not conflict with the need for centralization in a proletarian state. Centralisation is the chief feature of the new state. Elaborating the idea, Marx wrote: "The proletariat will use its political supremacy to wrest, by degrees, all capital from the bourgeoisie, to centralise all instruments of production in the hands of the state...."[25] That there is no contradiction between centralization and state destruction has been made clear by Marx in *The Eighteenth Brumaire*. He observed: 'The demolition of the state machine will not endanger centralization. Bureaucracy is only the low and brutal form of a centralization that is still afflicted with its opposite, with feudalism.[26]

Bureaucracy in a Transitional State

In a transitional state, the character and role of the public functionaries will undergo a radical change. They would first be brought under the control of proletariat, and thereafter, of the whole people. In his *The Civil War in France* which Marx wrote immediately following the bloody supersession of the rising in Paris against the provisional government known as Paris Commune, he tried to paint the picture of the transitional state. The Commune was to be the form of local government, from the great industrial centres down to the smallest village hamlet. Marx says, "The few and the important functions which would still remain for a central government were not to be suppressed...but were to be discharged by communal and, therefore, strictly responsible agents."[27] The officials in the transitional state would consist of workers and their representatives. Marx opined that these measures would give a death blow to "the delusion as if administration and political governing were mysteries, transcendent functions only to be entrusted to the hands of a trained caste of parasites, richly paid sycophants and sinecurists...doing away with the state hierarchy altogether, and replacing the haughteous masters of the people with removable servants, a mock responsibility by a real responsibility as they act continuously under public supervision."[28] The administrative functionaries will survive the transition to socialism. But "from the member of the Commune downwards the public service had to be done at workman's wages. The vested interests and the representation allowances of the high dignitaries of state disappeared along with high dignitaries themselves."[29]

Weber's Rational and Marx's Class Approach to Bureaucracy

Weber concluded that all new large-scale organizations were similar and each was a bureaucracy of its own. Weber's purpose was to define the essential features of new organizations and to indicate why these organizations worked so much better than traditional ones. Weber emphasized that bureaucratic organizations were an attempt to subdue human affairs to the rule of reason, to make it possible to conduct the business of the organization "according to calculable rules". For people who developed modern organizations, the purpose was to find rational solutions to the new problems of **size**. Weber saw bureaucracy as the rational product of social engineering, just as the machines of the Industrial Revolution were the rational products of mechanical engineering. He wrote that[30]"the decisive reason for the advance of bureaucratic organization has always been its purely technical superiority over any former organization. The fully developed bureaucratic mechanism compares with other organizations exactly as does the machine with non-mechanical modes of production."

For Weber the term *bureaucracy* was inseparable from the term *rationality*. And we may speak of his concept as a "rational bureaucracy" But what were the features developed to make bureaucracies rational? We have already met them: (1) functional specialization (2) clear lines of hierarchical authority, (3) expert training of managers, and (4) decision making based on rules and tactics developed to guarantee consistent and effective pursuit of organizational goals. Weber noted additional features of rational bureaucracies that are simple extensions of the four just outlined. To ensure expert management, appointment and promotion are based on merit rather than favoritism, and those appointed treat their positions as full-time, primary careers. To ensure order in decision making, business is conducted primarily through written rules records, and communications.

Furthermore, hierarchical authority is required in bureaucracies so that highly trained experts can he properly used as managers. It does little good to train someone to operate a stockyard, for example, and then have that manager receive orders from someone whose training is in advertising. Rational bureaucracies can be operated, Weber argued, only by deploying managers at all levels that have been selected and trained for their specific jobs. Persons ticketed for top positions in bureaucracies are often rotated through many divisions of an organization to gain firsthand experience of the many problems that their future subordinates must face.

In contrast, Karl Marx adopted the "class" approach towards bureaucracy and found its origins in the social divisions of the society. He said: "The bureaucracy is a circle from which one cannot escape. Its hierarchy is a hierarchy of knowledge. The top entrusts the understanding of detail to the lower levels, whilst the lower levels credit the top with understanding of the general, and so all are mutually deceived. "To Marx, bureaucracy is not an independent social category. It depends directly on the separation between civil society and the state and it rests on the existence of division within civil society, of corporations, each concerned with its particular interest. The examination by which the bureaucrats are recruited does not represent 'mediation' between civil society and state, but the separation from civil society of men and their activities for the common good and their transfer to another sphere, that of the state.[31] Marx says that "the examination is nothing but the bureaucratic baptism of knowledge". This second relationship is a complicated one. Marx has adduced two grounds in order to explain the complicated, intricate nature of the second relationship. In the first place, bureaucracy looks upon the other corporations as rivals and fights against them. Secondly, it presupposes the existence of corporations, or at least, "the spirit of corporations",[32] for, like them it seeks simply to serve its particular interests.

An Evaluation

Marx's theory of bureaucracy has tremendous sociological, political and economic significance. Avineri points out that "the bureaucratic structures do not automatically reflect prevailing social power but pervert and disfigure them. Bureaucracy is the image of the prevailing social power distorted by its claim to universality."[33] Marx does not look upon bureaucracy as an apparatus of the modern state detached from, and independent of, the state. For Marx, as Hal Draper explains, bureaucracy "is not a mere accretion...not simply an unfortunate tumor on the otherwise sound body of the state, but rather inherent in and inseparable from the very existence of the state."[34] The political significance of Marx's concept of bureaucracy lies in its message for the proletariat. Marx was not interested in interpreting the world, but in changing it. He believes in violent overthrow of the state machinery. The amount of violence required to bring about a revolution should be determined by the strength of the military and bureaucratic apparatus of the state. Thus it is a prime task on the part of the proletariat to undertake a serious appraisal of the nature and strength of bureaucracy in an oppressive state.

In Brief

Karl Marx's analysis of state, administration and bureaucracy can be summarized as:

- Karl Marx (1818-1883), a radical philosopher, has had and continues to have tremendous influence on revolutionary movements across the world. The body of thought and beliefs, known as Marxism, are based on the writings of Marx and Engels. Marx's class analysis of state and bureaucracy provides an alternative view of nature and role of bureaucracy.

- Marx examined bureaucracy in the overall analysis of nature of state and considered bureaucracy as 'a particular closed society within the state'. There are three basic elements in Marx's perception of state. Firstly, state is an organ of class domination. Secondly, its aim is to create an order which legalizes and perpetuates the oppression of one class by moderating conflicts. Thirdly, state is a temporary phenomenon; it will wither away with the abolition of classes. The role of bureaucracy has to be understood in the context of these formulations on state and his materialistic interpretation of history.

- Marx looked at bureaucracy, as an integral part of the exploitative social system. He traced its origins to social divisions unlike like Hegel who considered bureaucracy as a functional imperative.

- Marx elaborated the partisan role of bureaucracy in a class society. He calls bureaucrats 'parasites' designed to maintain *status quo* and the privileges of the dominant sections of the society. To Marx state power plays the same role for the bureaucracy as the private property does for property owning class.

- To Marx bureaucracy symbolizes the alienation of the masses and says that what fetishism of commodities is to masses, bureaucracy is to politics. Marx was critical of hierarchy and secrecy in administration and considers them as tools of incompetence and exploitation.

- Marx explained the social base of bureaucracy in France. He considered that the small holding property owners have provided the stable basis of all powerful and innumerable bureaucracy under Napoleon.

- Marx discussed the nature of bureaucracy in a transitional state, particularly in the context of Paris commune. Recognising the need for administrative functionaries in the transition to socialism, Marx visualized that they will function under workers' control with workers' wages.

- Marx's views on bureaucracy are criticized for failure to recognize the relative autonomy of bureaucracy in democratic societies. His views on materialistic interpretation of history and nature of state, which are the basis for his propositions on bureaucracy, were also criticized.

- Marx provides deeper insights into the dysfunctions of bureaucracy. His macro analysis of social formations and transformations is of immense help in the study of administrative systems in a broader canvas.

References

1 Mandel, Ernest, *An Introduction to Marxist Economic Theory*, (2nd edition), New York, Pathfinder Press, 1974, p.9.

2 Hal Draper, *Karl Marx's Theory of Revolution, Vol.1: State and Bureaucracy*, New York, Monthly Review Press, 1979.

3 Shaw, Carl. K.Y., Hegel's Theory of Modern Bureaucracy, *American Political Science Review*, Vol.86, No.2, June 1992, p.381.

4 For details see, G. W. F. Hegel, *Philosophy of Right*, tr. Knox, London: Oxford University Press, 1967, paras 256 and 159.

5 S. Avineri, *The Social and Political Thought of Karl Marx*, London: Cambridge University Press, 1968, p. 23.

6 For details see, G. W. F. Hegel, op. cit., Para 205.

7 Ibid., p. 301.

8 S. Avineri, *Hegel's Theory of Modern State*, Oxford: Oxford University Press, 1972, p. 161.

9 A. Hagedus, *Socialism and Bureaucracy*, London: Allison and Busby, 1976, p. 11.

10 D. McLellan, *Karl Marx: Selected Writings* (hereinafter cited as KMSW), Oxford: Oxford University Press, 1967, p. 160.

11 Marx, Karl & Engels, Frederich, German Ideology, Electric Book Company, 2001, p. 111

12 McLellan, *Karl Marx: Selected Writings*, op.cit., p. 31.

13 Sayer, Derek, Capitalism & Modernity: An Excursus on Marx and Weber, Routledge, New York, 1991, p. 87-101

14 Ibid., p. 46.

15 Quoted by Avineri op. cit., p. 24.

16 McLellan, *Karl Marx: Selected Writings*, op.cit.,, p. 31.

17 Marx, Karl, Critique of Hegel's Philosophy of Right, 1843 (Source: www.marxists.org/archive/marx/ works/1843/critique-hpr/ch03.html)

18 Ibid.

19 It was not until the 20th century that scholars found an unpublished study by Marx, the so-called *Economic and Philosophical Manuscripts of 1844*. This study consists of somewhat unorganized, difficult to read, but highly insightful notes which Marx jotted down while giving a first reading to the classical economists as a young man. The study has since gained prominence because in it Marx formulated more or less explicitly his Theory of Alienation—his analysis of how people are bound to become estranged from themselves and each other under the conditions of capitalist industrial production. This Theory of Alienation is often considered the philosophical underpinning for his later more technical critique of capitalism as an economic system.

20 Marx and Engels, *Selected Works*, Moscow: Progress Publishers, 1970, p. 30.

21 Marx and Engels, *Selected Correspondence*, Moscow: Progress Publishers, 1955, p. 262.

22 V. Perez-Diaj, *State Bureaucracy and Civil Society: A Critical Discussion of the Political Theory of Karl Marx*, London: Macmillan, 1978, p. 30.

23 Marx and Engels, *Collected Works*, p. 175.

24 Quoted by M. Krygier in his "Saint Simon, Marx and the Non-governed Society", in E. Kamenka, ed., *Bureaucracy: The Career of a Concept* (London: Arnold Heinemann, 1979), p. vi.

25 McLellan, op. cit. p.237.

26 Marx, Karl, The Eighteenth Brumaire of Louis Bonaparte, *Die Revolution*, Vol.1. No.1, New York, 1852, source: www.marxists.org/archive/marx/works/1852/18th-brumaire/notes.htm#n64

27 Ibid., p. 228.

28 www.marx.org/archive/marx/works/1871/civil-war-france/drafts/ch01.htm

29 McLellan, op. cit. p.541.

30 . Rodney Stark, "The Organizational Age," in *Sociology*, 3rd Edition, Cengage Learning, 1996.

31 Karl Marx, *Critique of Hegel's Philosophy of Right*, ed. J. O'Malley (London: Cambridge University Press, 1970), p. 51.

32 Karl Marx and F. Engels, *Collected Works*, Vol. 3 (Moscow: Progress Publishers, 1975), p. 45.

33 Avineri, *The Social and Political Thought of Karl Marx*, p. 51.

34 Draper, op. cit., p. 184.

Select Bibliography

Books

Albrow, Martin, *Bureaucracy*, London, Macmillan, 1970.

Argyris, Chris, *The Applicability of Organizational Sociology*, Cambridge, England, Cambridge University Press, 1972 .

............*Management and Organizational Development: The Path from XA to YB*, New York, McGraw-Hill, 1971.

...........*Organization and Innovation*, Homeword, III: Irwin, 1965.

............*Integrating the Individual and the Organisation*; New York Wiley, 1964.

.............*Interpersonal Competence and Organizational Effectiveness*, Homewood, III, Dorsey Press and Richard D. Irwin, Inc., 1962.

.............*Interpersonal Competence and Organization* Behaviour, London, Tavistock Publication, Dorsey Press, 1962.

............*Understanding Organisational Behaviour*, Homewood, III, Dorsey, 1960.

.... *Personality and Organization*, New York, Harper and Row, 1957.

.... and Donald, A. Schon., *Organizational Learning: A Theory of Action Perspectiveness*, Reading, Mass: Addison-Wesley, 1978.

.............*Theory in Practice: Increasing Professional Effectiveness*; London, Jossey Bass Publishers, 1974.

Arora, Ramesh K.(Ed.), *Administrative Theory*, New Delhi, Indian Institute of Public Administration, 1984.

............(Ed.). *Perspectives in Administration Theory* New Delhi, Associated Publishing House, 1979.

............*Comparative Public Administration: An Ecological Approach*, New Delhi, Associated Publishing House, 1972.

Augier, Mie and March, James G., *Models of Man : Essays in Memory of Herbert A. Simon*, MIT Press, 2004

Avineri, S., *The Social and Political Thought of Karl Marx*, London: Cambridge University Press, 1968.

........., *Hegel's Theory of Modern State*, Oxford: Oxford University Press, 1972

Baker, R.J.S., *Administrative Theory and Public Administration*, London, Hutchinson University Library, 1972.

Barnard, Chester I., *The Functions of the Executive*, Cambridge, Mass, Harvard University Press, 1938.

............*Organisation and Management*, Cambridge, Massachusetts, Harvard University Press, 1948.

Bedeian, Arthur G., *The Administrative Writings of Henri Fayol: A Bibliographic Investigation*, MonticeIllo, III: Vane Bibliographies, 1979.

Bendix, Reinhard, *Max Weber - An Intellectual Portrait*, Garden City, New York, Doubleday, 1960.

Bennis, Warren G., *Changing Organizations: Essays on the Development and Evolution of the Human Organizations*, New York, McGraw-Hill Book Company, 1966.

..............*Organization Development: Its Nature, Origins and Prospects*, Reading, Mass, Addison-Wesley Publishing Company, 1969.

..............*Beyond Bureaucracy: Essays on the Development and Evolution of Human Organizations*, New York, McGraw-Hill Book Company, 1973.

Blau, Peter, M., *Bureaucracy in Modern Society*, New York, Random House, 1962.

.........*The Dynamics of Bureaucracy*, Chicago, University of Chicago Press, 1955.

Bragden, Henry W., *Woodrow Wilson: The Academic Years*, Cambridge, Massachusetts, Harvard University Press, 1967.

Brodie, M.B., *Fayol on Administration*, London, Lyon, Grant and Green, 1967.

Brown, Douglas, J., *The Human Nature of Organization*, New York, Amacom, 135 W. 50th St., 1973.

Caiden, Gerald E., *The Dynamics of Public Administration: Guidelines to Current Transformations in Theory and Practice*, New York, Holt. Rinehart and Winston, Inc., 1971.

Charlesworth, James C., (Ed.), *Theory and Practice of Public Administration : Scope, Objectives, and Methods*, Philadelphia, American Academy of Political and Social Sciences, 1968.

Crainer, Stuart, *Key Management Ideas: Thinkers that Changed the Management World,*, London, Financial Times, 1998.

Dale, Ermest, *Management: Theory and Practice*, New York, McGraw- Hlll Book Company, 1965.

Downs, Anthony, *Inside Bureaucracy*, Boston, Little Brown, 1967.

Dror, Yehezkel, *Policy-making Under Adversity*, New Brunswick, Transaction Books, 1985.

..............*Public Policy-making Re-examined*, (New Ed.) New Brunswick, NJ, Transactions Books, 1983.

..............*Ventures in Policy Sciences: Concepts and Applications*, New York, American Elsevier Publishing Company Inc., 1971.

..............*Design for Policy Sciences*, New York, American Elsevier Publishing Company, Inc., 1971.

Drucker, Peter, F., *Management Challenges for the 21ˢᵗ Century*, New York, HarperBusiness, 2001.

..............*Management: Tasks, Responsibilities, Practices*, Bombay, Allied Publishers,]975.

..............*Age of Discontinuity*, New York, Harper and Brothers, 1968.

..............*The Practice of Management*, .London, Mercury Books, 1965.

Dubin, Robert, *Human Relations in Administration*, Englewood Cliffs Prentice-Hall, 1951.

Etizioni, Amitai., (Ed), *Readings on Modern Organizations*, Englewood Cliffs, Prentice-Hall, 1969.

..............*Modern Organizations*, Englewood Cliffs, Prentice-Hall, 1964.

..............*Complex Organizations*, New York, Ho]t, Rinehart and Winston, 1962.

Fayol, Henri., *General and Industrial Management*, London, Isaac Pitman, 1957.

Follett, Mary P., *Creative Experience*, London, Longmans Green, 1924.

...........*The New State*, London: Langmans Green, 1918.

Freund, Jolien, *The Sociology of Max Weber*, Hammondsworth: Penguin, 1968.

Fry, Brain R., *Mastering Public Administration: From Max Weber to Dwight Waldo*, Chatham,NJ, Chatham House Publishers, 1989.

George Jr., Claude S., *The History of Management Thought,* 2nd ed., Prentice-Hall of India Private Limited, 1974.

Gerth, H.H., and Mills, C. Wright, (Ed.), *From Max Weber: Essays in Sociology,* New York, Oxford University Press, 1946.

Golembiewski, Robert T., *Public Administration as a Developing Discipline,* 2 Parts, New York, Marcel Dekker, Inc., 1977.

Gross, Bertram M., *Organisations and Their Managing,* New York, The Free Press, 1968

. ...*The Managing of Organisations: The Administrative Struggle,* 2 VoL, New York, The Free Press, 1964.

Griffiths, Daniel E., *Administrative Theory,* Bombay, D.B. Taraporevala Sons & Co. Pvt. Ltd., 1978.

Gvishiani, D., *Organisation and Management: A Sociological Analysis of Western Theories,* Moscow, Progress Publishers, 1972.

Haire, Manson, (Ed.), *Modern Organization Theory.* New York: Wiley, 1959.

Hal Draper, *Karl Marx's Theory of Revolution, Vol.1: State and Bureaucracy,* New York, Monthly Review Press, 1979.

Haynes, Warren W., and Massie, Joseph. L. *Management: Analysis: Concepts and Cases,* Englewood Cliffs, N.J., Prentice-Hall, Inc.,1961.

Heady, Ferrel, *Public Administration: A Comparative Perspective,* 2nd Ed., New York, Marcel Dekker, Inc., 1984.

Henderson, Keith M., *Emerging Synthesis in American Public Administration,* Bombay, Asia Publishing House, 1970.

Hersey, Pau and Blanchard, Kenneth, H., *Management of Organisational Behaviour: Utilising Human Resources,* New Delhi, Prentice-Hall of India Pvt. Ltd., 1974.

Henry, Nicholas, *Public Administration and Public Affairs,* Englewood Cliffs, New Jersey; Prentice- Hall, Inc., 1975.

Huczynski A., *Management Gurus - What makes them and How to become one,* London, Thomson Business Place, 1996.

Huneryager, S.G. and Heckmann, L.L. (Eds.), *Human Relations in Management,* Bombay, D.B. Taraporevala Sons & Co., 1972.

Hunter , Crowther-Heyek, *Herbert A. Simon: The Bounds of Reason in Modern America,* Baltimore, The Johns Hopkins University Press, 2005.

Jong S. Jun (Ed.), *Rethinking Administrative Theory - The Challenge of the New Century,* Praeger Publishers, 2001.

Kangle R.P., *The Kautilya Arthashastra* , New Delhi, Motilal Banarsidas, 1972.

Koontz, Harold (Eds.), *Toward a Unified Theory of Management,* New York, McGraw- Hill Book Co., 1964.

Likert, R., *Profile of Organisational Characteristics: Forms,* Ann Arbor, Michigan, Rensis Likert Associates, 1977.

.............*Past and Future Perspectives on System-4,* Ann Arbor, Michigan, Rensis Likert Associates, 1977.

............*The Human Organization,* New York, McGraw-Hill Book Co., 1967.

............*New Patterns of Management,* New York, McGraw-Hill Book Co 1961.

.... and Likert, J.G., *New Ways of Managing Conflict,* New York, McGraw-Hill Book Co., 1976.

Gulick, Luther, and Urwick, L., (Eds.), *The Papers on the Science of Administration*, New York, Institute of Public Administration, 1937.

McGregor, Douglas., *The Humanside of Enterprise : Annotated Edition*, Tata-McGraw Hill, 2006.

............*The Professional Manager*, McGregor Caroline and Bennis, Warren G., (Eds.), New York, McGraw-Hill Book Co., 1967.

.... *Leadership and Motivation*. Boston, MIT Press, 1966.

............*The Humanside of Enterprise*, New York, McGraw-Hill Book Co .. 1960.

Malick, Sidney and Vanness, Edward H., (Eds.), *Concepts and Issue in Administrative Behaviour*, Englewood Cliffs, N.J., Prentice-Hall, Inc., 1962.

Malterson, Michael T. and Ivaneenich, John M., *Management Classics*, Santa Monica, Good Year Publishing Co., 1977.

March, James G., and Simon, Herbert A., *Organisations*, New York, Wiley, 1958.

Marini, Frank (Ed.), *Toward a New Public Administration: The Minnowbrook Perspective*, Scranton, Pa. Chandler Publishing Co., 1971.

Maslow, A., *Motivation and Personality*, New York, Harper & Row, 1954.

Mayo, George Elton, *The Human Problems of Industrial Civilization*, Boston, Harvard Business School, 1946, 2nd Ed.

...........*The Social Problems of Industrial Civilization*, London, Routledge & Kegan Paul, 1945.

Merril, Harwood F., (Ed.), *Classics in Management*, New York, American Management Association, 1960.

Merton, Robert K., et. al., (Ed.), *Reader in Bureaucracy*, Glencoe, Free Press, 1952.

Metcalf, Henry C., and Urwick, Lyndall F., (Eds.), *Dynamic Administration: The Collected Papers of Mary Parker Follett*, New York, Harper & Row, 1940.

Miner, John B., *Theories of Organisational Structure and Process*, Chicago, The Dryden Press, 1982.

Mooney, James D. and Reiley, Alan C. *The Principles of Organization*, New York, Harper & Brothers, 1939.

Mosher, Frederick C., (Ed.), *American Public Administration: Past, Present, Future*, Alabama, The University of Alabama Press, 1975.

Ostrom, Vincent, *The Intellectual Crisis in American Public Administration*, Alabama, The University of Alabama Press, 1973.

Pauline Graham (Ed.) *Mary Parker Follett: Prophet of Management - A Celebration of Writings from the 1920s*, Cambridge, MA: Harvard Business School Press, 1995

Pfiffner, John M., and Sherwood, Frank P., *Administrative Organization*, Englewood Cliffs, N.J., Prentice-Hall, 1960.

Presthus, Robert, *Behaviour Approaches to Public Administration*. Alabama, University of Alabama Press, 1965.

Pugh, D.S., (Eds.), *Organisation Theory: Selected Readings*, London, Penguin Books, 1971.

............and Hickson, D.J., and Hinings, C.R. *Writers on Organisations*, Ontario, Penguin, 1976.

Purcell, Ralph, *Woodrow Wilson: The Study of Public Administration*, Washington, D.C. Annals of American Government, 1955.

Rabin, Jack, and Bowman, James S., *Politics and Administration: Woodrow Wilson and American Public Administration*, New York, Marcel Dekker Inc., 1984

Rangarajan, L N., *Kautilya: The Arthashastra*, Penguin Books, New Delhi, 1992.

Riggs, Fred, W., (Eds.), *Prismatic Society Revisited*, Morristown, N.J., General Learning Press, 1973.

...........*Frontiers of Development Administration,* Durham, N.C., Duke University Press, 1971.

............*Administration in Development Countries: The Theory of Prismatic Society,* Boston, Houghton Mifflin, 1964.

............*The Ecology of Public Administration,* New Delhi, Asia Publishing House, 1961.

..........and Daya Krishna, *Development Debate,* Jaipur, Printwell Publishers, 1987.

Rorthlesberger, J. and Dickson, William J., *Management and Worker,* Cambridge, Mass, Harvard University Press, 1939.

Sapre, S.A, F.W., *Taylor: His Philosophy of Scientific Management,* Bombay, Government Central Press, 1970.

.... *Mary Parker, Follett: Her Dynamic Philosophy of Management,* Bombay, Government Central Press, 1965.

Self, Peter, *Administrative Theories and Politics,* London, George Allen & Unwin Ltd., 1972.

Selznick, P., *Leadership in Administration,* Evanston, III, Row, Peterburt Company, 1957.

Shafritz, Jay M ., and Hyde. Albert C., (Eds.), *Classics of Public Administration.* Oak Park, Illinois, Moore Publishing Company, 1978.

Shamasastry, R., *Arthashastra of Kautilya,* University of Mysore, Oriental Library Publications, 1908.

Sheldrake, John., *Management Theory,* London, Thomson Learning, 2003.

Simon, Herbert A., *The Science of the Artificial.* Mass. Mit Press. 1969.

..........*The Shape of Automation.* New York, Harper and Row. 1965.

...........*The New Science of Management Decision,* New York. Harper. andRow. 1960.

...........*Models of Man.* New York. Wiley,1957.

..........*Administrative Behaviour: A Siudy of Decision-Making Processes in Administrative Organization,* New York. The Free Press, 1957.

.... Smithsburg, Donald W. and Thompson., Victor A., *Public Administration,* New York. Knopf. 1950.

Singh. R.N, *Management Thought and Thinkers,* Delhi, Sultan Chand & Sons. 1977.

Taylor, Fredrick W, *Principles of Scientific Management.* New York, Harper, 1947.

Urwick, Lyndall F ., *The Life and Work of Elton Mayo,* London, Urwick, 1960.

............*The Golden Book of Administration.* London. Newsman Neame Ltd . 1956.

.............*The Elements of Administration.* New York. Harper,1943.

.... and Brech. E.F.L., *The Making of Scientific Management,* 3 Vols ., London. Management Publications Trust, 1949.

Waldo, Dwight, (Eds.), *Public Administration in a Time of Turbulence.* Scranton-, Chandler. 1971.

............*The Study of ·Public Administration.* Garden City, New York, Doubleday, 1955.

............*The Administrative State.* New York. The Ronald Press Company. 1948.

Warner, M. (Ed.) *Management Thinking,* London, Thomson Learning, 2001

Weber, Marianne, *Max Weber: A Biography,* Translated and edited by Harry Zohn. New York: Wiley. 1975.

Weber, Max . *Economy and Society,* Vols., I-III, Translated and edited by Guenther Roth and Claus Wittich, New York: Bedminster Press ,1968.

.........*The Theory of Social and Economic Organization,* Trans., A.H. Henderson. and Ed. Talcott Parsons, New York. Oxford University Press, 1946.

Wolf, William B ., *The Basic Barnard: An Introduction to Chester 1.Barnard and his Theories of Organisation and Management,* Ithaca, New York, Cornell University Press, 1974.

.... *Conversations with Chester I. Barnard,* School of Industrial Labour Relations: Cornell University, ILR Paperback Number 12, Ithaca, NY, 1973

............*How to Understand Management: An Introduction to Chester l. Barnard,* Los Angeles. Lukas Publishers, 1968.

Wood, John D. and Wood, Michael D., (Eds.), *Chris Argyris : Critical Evaluations in Business and Management,* London, Rutledge, 2009.

...........*Herbert Simon: Critical Evaluations in Business and Management,* 3 Vols., London, Rutledge, 2007.

.........., *Peter Drucker: Critical Evaluations in Business and Management,* New York, Rutledge, 2005

.........., *George Elton Mayo : Critical Evaluations in Business and Management,* London, Rutledge, 2004.

.........., *F.W.Taylor : Critical Evaluations in Business and Management,* New York, Rutledge, 2002

............*Henri Fayol: Critical Evaluations in Business and Management,* 2 Vols, London, Rutledge, 2001.

Wren, Daniel A ., *The Evolution of Management Thought, (4th Edition),* Chichster, Wiley & Sons, 1994.

Articles

Aiyar. S.P. and Marina Pinto, "Humanistic ethics in the writings of Chester Barnard", *Administrative Change,* Vol. 12, Jan. 1985, No. 2. pp. 182-93.

Al-Koubaisy. Amer. "The Classical vs. Modern Organization Theories in Developing Countries," *Development Policy and Administration Review,* 4(1) Jan.- June, 78,pp. 50-64.

Argyris, Chris, "Making the Undiscussable and its Undiscussability Discussable," *Public Administration Review.* Vol. No. 40, May-June, 1980,pp.205.

.... "Double Loop Learning in Organizations", *Harvard Business Review,* Vol. 55, No.5, 1977, pp. 115-25.

.........."Personality vs. Organization", *Organizational Dynamics,* Vol. 3, No.2, 1974, pp. 3-17.

.... "Some Limits to Rational Man 'Organization Theory", *Public Administration Review,* Vol. 33, No.3, (May-June,1973), pp. 253--67.

.... "Organizational Effectiveness under Stress," *Harvard Business Review.* Vol. 38, No.3. 1960, pp. 137-46.

.........."The Organization: What Makes it Healthy". *Harvard Business Review.* Vol. 36, No.6. 1958.pp. 107-16.

.........."The Individual and Organization: Some Problems of Mutual Adjustment", *Administrative Science Quarterly,* Vol.2, No. I, June, 1957, pp. 1-22.

.........."The Fusion of an Individual with the Organization", *American Sociological Review,* Vol. 19, No.3, June-July, 1954, pp. 267-72.

Bagozzi, Richard P., and Lynn W. Phillips., "Representing and testing organizational theories: A holistic construal", *Administrative Science Quarterly,* Vol. 27, No.3, Sept.,1982, pp. 459-89.

Banfield, Edward C., "The Decision-Making Scheme," *Public Administrative Review,* Vol. XVII, No.4, Autumn 1957, pp. 278- 285.

Bendix, Reinhard and Fisher, Lloyd H., "The Perspectives of Elton Mayo", *The Review of Economics and Statistics,* Vol. 31, No.4, Nov., 1949, pp. 312-19.

Bennis, Warren G., "Leadership Theory and Administrative Behaviour: The Problem of Authority", *Administrative Science Quarterly,* Vol. IV, No.3, Dcc., 1959, pp. 259-301.

Bhargava, B.S., "Riggs' Concept of Formalism", *Prashasnika,* Vol. VI, No.4, Oct. - Dec., 1977, pp. 4-11.

Blau, Peter M., "Critical Remarks on Weber's Theory of Authority", *American Political Science Review,* Vol. LVII, No.2, 1963, pp. 305-16.

Boulding, Kenneth E., "Evidences for an Administrative Science", *Administrative Science Quarterly,* Vol. 3, No. I, June, 1958, pp. 1-22.

Bourgeois, V. Warren and Craig C. Pinder, "Contrasting Philosophical Perspectives in Administrative Science: A Reply to Morgan", *Administrative Science Quarterly,* Vol. 28. No.4, Dec., 1983, pp. 608-13.

Bowman, James S., "Managerial Theory and Practice: The transfer of knowledge in Public Administration", *Public Administration Review,* Vol. 38, No.6, Nov. - Dec., 1978, pp. 563-70.

Breeze, John D., and Frederick C. Miner, "Henri Fayol: A New Definition of Administration", *Academy of Management Proceedings,* 1980, pp. 110-13.

Brodie, M.B., "Henri Fayol: Administration Industrielle et Generale: A re-interpretation", *Public Administration,* 40, Autumn, 1962, pp. 311-317.

Brooks, Stephelt, "The Western Marxist Critique of Organisation Theory: Towards a Rebuttal", *The Indian Journal of Public Administration,* Vol. 28 (4), Oct. - Dec., pp. 767-82.

Buchrig, Edward H., "Woodrow Wilson to 1902: A Review Essay", *The American Political Science Review,* Vol. 67, No.2, June, 1973, pp. 589-591.

Carey, Alex, "The Hawthorne Studies: A Radical Criticism", *American Sociological Review,* Vol. 32, No.3, June, 1967, pp. 403-416.

Carroll, James D. and Frederickson, George H. "Dwight Waldo 1913-2000", *Public Administration Review,* Vol, 61, No. 1, January-February, 2001.

Chapman. Richard, A., "Prismatic Theory in Public Administration: A Review of Theories of Fred W. Riggs", *Public Administration,* Vol, 44, Winter, 1966, pp. 415-433.

Chi-Yuen Wu, "Public Administrators and Public Policy-Making", *International Review of Administrative Sciences,* Vol.44. No. 4, 1978, pp.333-46.

Chitlangi, B.M., "A Study of Administration 1987: Centenary of Woodrow Wilson's Essay", *Indian Journal of Public Administration,* Vol. 33, No.4, Oct-DcC1987, pp. 913-917.

Chowdhury, Mustafa, "Weber's ideal type of bureaucracy", *The Indian Journal of Public Administration,* 30(1) Jan. - Mar., 1984, pp. 177- 83.

Cleveland, Harin, "The Future of Public Administration", *Bureaucrat,* 11(3), Fall, 1982, pp. 3-8.

Dahl, Robert, A., "The Science of Public Administration: Three Problems", *Public Administration Review,* Vol. VII, No.1, 1947, pp.3-11.

Dallenbach, Karl M., "The Place of Theory in Science", *Psychological Review,* Vol. 60, No.1, Jan., 1953, pp. 38-39. .

Daya Krishna, "Towards a Saner View of 'Development': A Comment on Fred W. Riggs' Comment", *Administrative Change,* Vol. 3, Jan. - June, 1976, pp. 19-26.

.........."Shall We Be Diffracted? A Critical Comment on Riggs' Prismatic Society and Public Administration," *Administrative Change,* Vol. 2, June, 1974, pp. 48-55.

De Leon, Peter, "Policy Sciences: The Discipline and the Profession," *Policy Sciences,* 13 (13), Feb., 1981, pp. 1-7.

Denhardt, Robbert B. and Kathryn G. Denhardt, "Public Administration and the Critique of Domination," *Administration and Society,* 11 (1), May, 1979, pp. 107-20.

Dimock, Marshall E., "The Study of Administration," *American Political Science Review*, 31, Feb., 1937, 28-40.

Doig, James W., "If I see a Murderous Fellow Sharpening a Knife Cleverly: The Wilsonian Dichotomy and the Public Authority Tradition;" *Public Administration Review;* Vol. 43 (4), July-August 1983, pp. 292-304.

Dror, Yehezkel, "On becoming more of a Policy Scientist," *Policy Studies Review*, Vol. 4, No.1, August, 1984, pp. 13-21.

..........."Policy Sciences: Some Global Perspectives", *Policy Sciences*, Vol. 5, No. I, March, 1974, pp. 83-85. .

..........."Policy Analysts: A New Professional Role in Government Service," *Public Administration Review*, Vol. XXVII, No.3, 1967, pp. 197-203.

..........."Muddling Through - Science or Inertia," *Public Administration Review*, Vol. 24,1964, pp. 153-163.

Dwivedi, O.P. and J. Nef, "Crises and continuities in Development Theory and Administrative: First and third world Perspectives," *Public Administration and Development*, 2 (1) Jan. - Mar., 1982, pp.59-77.

Fayol, Henri, "The Importance of the Administrative Factor." In Ernest Dale (Eds.), *Readings in Management: Landmarks and New Frontiers*, New York: McGraw-Hill, 1970, pp. 148-49.

Finkle, Arthur L., "A Discipline in search of Legitimacy," *Bureaucrat*, 13 (2) Summer 1984, pp. 58-60.

Fox, Douglas, M., "What's Public Administration," *Administrative Science Quarterly*, Vol. 21, June, 1976, pp. 346-352.

Fox, Elliot M., "Mary Parker Follett: The Enduring Contribution," *Public Administration Review*, Vol. XXVIII, No.6, Nov. - Dec., 1968.

Franke, Richard H., and James D. Kaul, "The Hawthorne Experiments: First Statistical Interpretation," *American Sociological Review,*Vol. 43, 1978, pp. 623-43.

Gaus, John Merriman, "Trends in the Theory of Public Administration," *Public Administration Review*, 10, Summer, 1950, pp. 163-68.

Gazell, James A., "Peter F. Drucker's Vision in Public Management, 2000", *International Journal of Public Administration*, Vol.17, Nos.3&4, 1994.

..........."Peter F. Drucker and Decentralised Administration of the Federal Government", *Administration & Society*, Vol.24. No.2, August, 1992.

Gulick, Luther, "Time and Public Administration", *Public Administration Review*, 47(1),1987, pp. 115-119.

..........."The Dynamics of Public Administration today as guidelines for the future," *Public Administration Review*, 43 (3) May-June, 1983, pp. 193-8.

..........."Democracy and Administration face the future," *Public Administration Review*, Nov. - Dec., 1977, Vol. 37, No.6, pp. 706- 711.

Habennan, John, "Discipline Without Punishment," *Harvard Business Review*, Vol. XXXVI, May, 1967, pp. 62-68.

Hartwig, Richard, "Rationality and the Problems of Administrative Theory," *Public Administration*, 56 Summer 1978, pp. 159-79.

Hindy, Lauer Schachter, "Frederick Winslow Taylor and the idea of Worker Participation: A Brief Against Easy Administrative Dichotomies", *Administration and Society*, Vol.21, NO. 1, May, 1989, pp.20-30.

Jam, Tej K., "Utility of Max Weber's Concept of Ideal-Type Bureaucracy," *Prashasnika*. Vol. VI. No.4, Oct. - Dec. 1977 pp 125-130. ' ,.

Kaufman, Herbert, 'Fear. of Bureaucracy: A Ranging Pandemic", *Public Administration Review*, 41 (1), Jan. – Feb., 1981, pp. 1-9.'

.... "Emerging Conflicts in the Doctrines of Public Administration" *American Political Science Review*, 50, Dec., 1956, pp. 1057-73.

Khanna, Kishan, "Contemporary Models of Public Administration: An Assessment of their Utility and Exposition of Inherent Fallacies" *Philippine Journal of Public Administration*, Vol. XVIII, No.2, April. 1974, pp. 103-126.

Koubaisy, Amer A., "The Classical vs. Modem Organisation Theories in Developing Countries," *Development Policy and Administrative Review*, Vol. IV, No. I, Jan. - June, 1978, pp. 50-64.

Kramer, Fred A., "Using classics to expand Public Administration Thought", *The American Review of Public Administration*, 1992, (22(4). pp. 301-306.

Likert, Rensis., "System A: A Resource for Improving Public Administration," *Public Administration Review*, Vol. 46, No.6, Nov. - Dec., 1981, pp. 674-678.

..........."Measuring Organizational Performance," *Harvard Business Review*, Vol, 36, No.2, 1958, pp. 41-52.

Likert, Rensis, and William F. Dowling, "Conversation with Rensis Likert," *Organizational Dynamics*, Vol. 2, No: I, 1973, pp. 33-49.

..........."Measuring Organizational Performance," *Harvard Business Review*, XXXVI, No.2, 1958, pp. 41-50.

Litchfield, Edward H., "Notes on a General Theory of Administration," *Administrative Science Quarterly*, Vol. I, No. I, June, 1956, pp.3-29.

Locke, Edwin A. "The Ideas of Fredrick W. Taylor: An Evaluation", *Academy of Management Review, Vol. 7*, No.1, 1982, pp 14-24.

Lyle C. Fitch, "Luther Gulick", *Public Administration Review*, Vol. 50. No.6, 1990, pp.604-08.

Mahoney, Joseph T., "The Relevance of Chester I. Barnard's Teachings to Contemporary Management Education: Communicating the Aesthetics of Management", *International Journal of Organisation Theory & Behaviour*, Vol. 5, No. 1 & 2, 2002.

Mc Daniel, Thomas R., "The Search for the Administrative Novel," *Public Administrative Review*, 38 (6), Nov. - Dec., 1978, pp. 55-9.

Michael, J. Wriston, "In Defense of Bureaucracy," *Public Administration Review*, Vol. 40, No.2, March-April, 1980.

Millet, John D., "A Critical Appraisal of the Study of Public Administration," *Administrative Science Quarterly*, Vol. I, Sept., 1956, pp. 177-188.

Pearson, Norman M., "Fayolism as a Necessary Complement to Taylorism," *American Political Science Review*, Vol. 39, No. I, Feb., 1945, pp. 68-85.

Pinto, Marina R., "Human Nature in Administration - The Contribution of Douglas McGregor," *Administrative Change*, 10 (1-2) July, 1982 - June, 1983, pp. 76-90.

Purushottam Nagar, "Administrative Thought of Chester Barnard," *Prashasnika*, Vol. VI, No. I, Jan. -March, 1977, pp. 79-84.

Ramos, Alberto, Guerreiro, "Misplacement of Concepts and Administrative Theory," *Public Administration Review*, 38 (6) Nov. - Dec., 1978, pp. 550-7.

Riggs, F.W. "The Ecology and Context of Public Administration: A Comparative Perspective," *Public Administration Review*, March--April, 1980, pp. 107-115.

.........."Introduction: Shifting meaning of the term Bureaucracy," *International Social Science Journal*, 21 (4), 1979, pp. 563-84.

………."Further Considerations on Development: A Comment on Daya Krishna's Comment," *Administrative Change*, Vol. 4, July-Dec., 1976, pp. 1-20.

………."The Prismatic Society and Development," *Administrative Change*, Vol. 2, Jan. - June, 1975, pp. 127-135.

………."Prismatic Societies and Public Administration," *Administrative Change*, Vol. 1, Dec., 1973, pp. 12-24.

………."Administration and a Changing World Environment," *Public Administration Review*, Vol. XXVIII, No.4, July-Aug., 1968, pp. 348-61.

………."Administrative Development: An Elusive Concept," in John D. Montgomery and William, J. Siffin, *Approaches to Development Politics Administration and Change*, New York, McGraw- Hill 1966, pp. 225-255.

……….Relearning an Old Lesson: The Political Context of Development Administration," *Public Administration Review*, Vol. XXV, No.1, March, 1965, pp. 70-79.

………."Trends in the Comparative Study of Public Administration", *International Review of Administrative Science*, 1962, pp. 9-15.

………."Prismatic Society and Financial Administration," *Administrative Science Quarterly*, 1960, pp. 1-46.

………."The Use of Models for Administrative Analysis: Confusion or Clarity?", *The Indian Journal of Public Administration*, Vol. VI, No.3, 1960, pp. 225-242.

………."Agraria and Industria: Toward a Typology of Comparative Administration," in Siffin, William, J., (Eds.), *Toward the Comparative Study of Public Administration*, Bloomington, Indian University Press, 1957, pp. 23-116.

………."Public Administration: A Neglected Factor in Economic Development," *Annals of the American Academy of Political and Social Science*, Vol. 305, May, 1956, pp. 70-80.

………."Notes on Literature Available for the Study of Comparative Public Administration", *The American Political Science Review*, Vol. XLVIII, No.2, June, 1954, pp. 515-37

Rosenbloom, David H., "Public Administrative Theory and the Separation of Powers," *Public Administrative Review*, 43 (3) May--June, 1983,pp. 219-27.

Satya Deva, "State and Bureaucracy in Kautilya's Arthashastra" *The Economic and Political Weekly*, 19 (19) 12, May, 1984, pp. 811-15

……….."Theory of Administration," *Economic and Political Weekly*, Vol.XVII, No. 48, November 27, 1982, pp.M115-M122.

………."Western Conceptualisation of Administrative Development: A Critique and an Alternative," *International Review of Administrative Sciences*, 45 (1) 79, pp. 59-63.

………."The Contribution of Karl Marx to Administrative Theory," *Journal of the Institute of Public Administration*, Vol. 1, No, 2, July-September 1980, pp. 31-41.

Scott, William, G., "Barnard on the nature of Elitist-Responsibility", *Public Administration Review*, Vol. 42, May-June, 1982.

Simon, Herbert , A., "Organizational Man: Rational or Self-Actualizing," *Public Administration Review*, Vol. 33, No.4 (July-Aug., 1973), pp. 346- 353.

………."A Comment on 'The Science of Public Administration,'", *Public Administration Review*, 7, Summer, 1947, pp. 200-203.

………."The Proverbs of Administration," *Public Administration Review*, Vol. VI, No.1, Winter, 1946, pp. 53-61.

Stupak, Ronald, J., "Organizational Behaviour in the 1970's: The Missing Links," *The Bureaucrat*, Vol. 5, No.3, Oct., 1976, pp. 335- 340.

Subramaniam, V., "The Fact-Value Distinction as an Analytical Tool," *The Indian Journal of Public Administration*, Vol. XVII, No.1, Jan; - March, 1971.

............"Dror on Policy-making," *The Indian Journal of Public Administration*, Vol. 16, No.1, Jan. - March, 1970, pp. 86-87.

............"The Classical Organisation Theory and its Critics" *Public Administration*, Vol. 44, Winter, 1966, pp. 435-46.

Thompson, James D., and Frederick L. Bates, "Technology, Organization, and Administration," *Administrative Science Quarterly*, 2, Dec., 1957, pp. 325-42

Udy, Starnley H .. "Bureaucracy and Rationality in Weber's Organization Theory: An Empirical Study," *American Sociological Review*, Vol. 24,1959, pp. 791-95.

Urwick, Lyndall F., "V.A. Graicunas and the Span of Control," *Academy of Management Journal*, Vol. 17, 1974, pp. 349-54.

............, "The Manager's Span of Control," *Harvard Business Review*, Vol. 34, No.3, May-June, 1956, pp. 39-47.

Van Riper, Paul P., "The Literary Gulick: A Bibliographical Appreciation", *Public Administration Review*, Vol. 50.No.6, 1990, pp.609-14.

............"The American Administrative State: Wilson and the Founders-An Unorthodox View," *Public Administration Review*, 43 (6), Nov. - Dec., 1983, pp. 477-90.

Vohra, Neharika, Mukul, Kumar, "Relevance of Peter Drucker's Work: Celebrating Drucker's 100th Birthday," Vikalpa, Vol.34. No.4, Oct.-Dec., 2009, pp1-7.

Waldo, Dwight, "Administrative Theory in the United States: A Survey and a Prospect," *Political Studies*, Vol. 2, No.1, Feb., 1954, pp. 70-86.

............"Development of Theory of Democratic Administration," *American Political Science Review*, 46, March, 1952, pp. 81-103.

White, William F., "Human Relations Theory - A Progress Report," *Harvard Business Review*, Vol. XXXIV, No.5, 1965, 125-134.

Wilson, Woodrow, "The Study of Administration," *Political Science Quarterly*, Vol. 2, June, 1887, pp. 197-222.

.........."The New Meaning of Government," *Public Administration Review*, Vol. 44, No.3, May-June, 1984, pp. 193--195.

Index

About the Contributors

1. *A. Amruta Rao*, Ph.D formerly Professor of Public Administration, Kakatiya University, Warangal, Andhra Pradesh.
2. *V. Bhaskara Rao,* Ph.D formerly Professor of Public Administration, Kakatiya University, Warangal, Andhra Pradesh. He also taught Public Administration at Osmania University.
3. *B.P.C. Bose*, Ph.D Professor of Public Administration, Nagarjuna University, Guntur, Andhra Pradesh.
4. *G. Haragopal*, Ph.D, Professor of Political Science, Hyderabad Central University, Hyderabad. Earlier worked at the Centre for Economic and Social Studies, Hyderabad and taught Public Administration at Osmania and Kakatiya Universities.
5. *N.R. Inamdar*, Ph.D, formerly Professor of Political Science, University of Poona, Pune, Maharashtra. He worked as Professor of Public Administration, Indira Gandhi, National Open University, New Delhi.
6. *PA. James,* Ph.D formerly Professor of Public Administration, Kakatiya University, Warangal, Andhra Pradesh. He also taught Public Administration at Osmania University.
7. *M. Kistaiah,* formerly Professor of Public Administration, Kakatiya University, Warangal, Andhra Pradesh. He also taught Public Administration at Osmania University.
8. *C. Lakshmanna*, Ph.D, formerly Professor of Sociology, Osmania University. He was a Member of Parliament (Rajya Sabha) and Indian Ambassador to Trinidad and Tobago.
9. *V. Lakshmipathy*, Ph.D. formerly Professor and Director, Regional Centre for Urban and Environmental Studies, Osmania University. He also worked as Professor of Management, Jawaharlal Nehru Technological University, Hyderabad.
10. *K. Murali Manohar*, Ph.D formerly Professor of Public Administration, Kakatiya University, Warangal, Andhra Pradesh. He also worked as Professor of Public Administration, Dr.B.R Ambedkar Open University.
11. *Y. Pardhasaradhi*, Ph.D Professor of Public Administration, Osmania University, Hyderabad. He was the founder Head, Department of Public Administration, University of Asmara, Eritrea, Africa.
12. *Prabhat Kumar Datta*, Ph.D Centenary Professor of Public Administration, Calcutta University, Kolkata, West Bengal.
13. *V.S. Prasad*, Ph.D, formerly Project Director, Open University, Mauritius. He worked as Director, National Assessment and Accreditation Council, India; Vice-chancellor, Dr. B.R. Ambedkar Open University, Hyderabad and Pro-Vice-chancellor, Indira Gandhi National Open University, New Delhi. He worked as Professor of Public

Administration, Dr. B.R Ambedkar Open University and taught Public Administration at Osmania and Kakatiya universities.

14. *C.V Raghavulu*, Ph.D. formerly Professor of Political Science and Public Administration, Nagarjuna University, Guntur, Andhra Pradesh. He worked as Vice-chancellor, Nagarjuna University. He also taught Public Administration at Andhra University.

15. *S.P. Ranga Rao*, Ph.D, formerly Professor of Public Administration, Osmania University, Hyderabad.

16. *D. Ravindra Prasad*, Ph.D, Advisor, Administrative Staff College of India, Hyderabad. He was Professor of Public Administration, and Director, Regional Centre for Urban and Environmental Studies, Osmania University, Hyderabad. He also worked at the Indira Gandhi National Open University, New Delhi.

17. *A.V. Satyanarayana Rao*, Ph.D former Professor of Business Management, Osmania University, Hyderabad. He also taught Public Administration in the University.

18. *P. Satyanarayana*, Ph.D, formerly Director, Regional Centre, Indira Gandhi National Open University, New Delhi. He worked as Dy. Director, Southern Regional Centre, Indian Council for Social Science Research and taught public administration at AV College, Hyderabad.

19. *P. Seshachalam*, Ph.D formerly Senior Faculty, Administrative Staff College of India, Hyderabad.

20. *P.D. Sharma*, Ph.D, formerly Professor of Political Science, University of Rajasthan, Jaipur, Rajasthan.

21. *N. Umapathy*, Ph.D, formerly Professor of Public Administration, Osmania University, Hyderabad. He worked as Professor of Public Administration, University of Asmara, Eritrea.